THE APOCALYPSE OF ADAM

SOCIETY OF BIBLICAL LITERATURE

DISSERTATION SERIES

edited by
Howard C. Kee

Number 46
THE APOCALYPSE OF ADAM
A LITERARY AND SOURCE ANALYSIS
by
Charles W. Hedrick

Charles W. Hedrick

THE APOCALYPSE
OF ADAM
A LITERARY

AND SOURCE ANALYSIS

Scholars Press

Distributed by
Scholars Press
101 Salem Street
Chico, California 92659

THE APOCALYPSE OF ADAM
A LITERARY AND SOURCE ANALYSIS
Charles W. Hedrick

Ph.D., 1977
Claremont Graduate School

Supervisor:
James M. Robinson

Library of Congress Cataloging in Publication Data

Hedrick, Charles W.
  The apocalypse of Adam.

  (Dissertation series — Society of Biblical Literature ;
no. 46 ISSN 0145-2770)
   Bibliography; p.
   1. Apocalypse of Adam. 2. Gnosticism. I. Title. II.
Series: Society of Biblical Literature. Dissertation series
; no. 46.
BT1390.H36   1980   229'.913   79-26013
ISBN 0-89130-369-3
ISBN 0-89130-370-7 pbk.

Printed in the United States of America
1 2 3 4 5
Edwards Brothers, Inc.
Ann Arbor, Michigan 48106

To Peggy
and our offspring,
Charlie, Cindi and Kay:
Small payment for their considerable expense

TABLE OF CONTENTS

PART II
TEXT, TRANSLATION AND NOTES

ABBREVIATIONS

Abbreviations of biblical and apocryphal books, Nag Hammadi tractates and contemporary publications are taken from the Instructions for Contributors to the *Journal of Biblical Literature* (95 [1976] 330-46). For classical and patristic references, I have used the abbreviations appearing in *The Oxford Classical Dictionary* ([2nd ed.; ed. N. G. L. Hammond and H. H. Scullard; Oxford: Clarendon, 1970] ix-xxii) and *A Patristic Greek Lexicon* ([ed. G. W. H. Lampe; Oxford: Clarendon, 1961] xi-xlix).

The following list of abbreviations are those that have been used when abbreviations were not found in the above-mentioned sources, or when a different abbreviation was selected.

A	Source A to the *Apocalypse of Adam*
ADAIK	Abhandlung des Deutschen Archäologischen Instituts Kairo
ApocPaul	Apocalypse of Paul (Latin text published by M. R. James)
APet	Acts of Peter
AscenIsa	Ascension of Isaiah
B	Source B to the *Apocalypse of Adam*
CH	Corpus Hermeticum
De haer.	Augustine: *De haeresibus ad Quodvultdeum*
ET	English translation
GL	Left *Ginza*
Keph.	Kephalaia
Pan.	Epiphanius: *Panarion seu adversus LXXX haereses*
R	The redactor of the *Apocalypse of Adam*
Ref.	Hippolytus: *Refutatio omnium haeresium*
WZMLU	*Wissenschaftliche Zeitschrift der Martin-Luther-Universität*

References to the following authors are to the works cited below unless otherwise indicated.

Beltz — Walter Beltz. "Die Adam-Apokalypse aus Codex V von Nag Hammadi: Jüdische Bausteine in gnostischen Systemen." Dr. Theol. dissertation; Berlin: Humboldt-Universität, 1970.

Böhlig — Alexander Böhlig and Pahor Labib. *Koptischgnostische Apokalypsen aus Codex V von Nag Hammadi im Koptischen Museum zu Alt-Kairo.* Halle-Wittenberg: Wissenschaftliche Zeitschrift der Martin-Luther-Universität, 1963.

Crum — Walter Crum. *A Coptic Dictionary.* Oxford: Clarendon, 1939.

Hennecke-Schneemelcher — Edgar Hennecke and Wilhelm Schneemelcher, eds. *New Testament Apocrypha.* ET and ed. R. McL. Wilson et al. Vol. 1: *Gospels and Related Writings,* Vol. 2: *Writings Relating to the Apostles; Apocalypses and Related Subjects.* Philadelphia: Westminster, 1959, 1964.

Kasser — Rodolphe Kasser. "Bibliothèque gnostique V: Apocalypse d'Adam." *Revue de Théologie et de Philosophie* 17 (1967) 316-33.

Krause — Martin Krause. "The Apocalypse of Adam." Pp. 13-23 in *Gnosis.* 2 vols. Ed. Werner Foerster, trans. and ed. R. McL. Wilson. Oxford: Clarendon, 1972-74.

MacRae — George MacRae. "The Apocalypse of Adam." Pp. 151-95 in *Nag Hammadi Codices V, 2-5 and VI with Papyrus Berolinensis 8502, 1 and 4.* Ed. Douglas M. Parrott. Leiden: E. J. Brill, 1978.

Schenke — Hans-Martin Schenke. "Alexander Böhlig und Pahor Labib, Koptisch-gnostische Apokalypsen aus Codex V von Nag Hammadi im Koptischen Museum zu Alt-Kairo." *OLZ* 61 (1966) cols. 23-34.

Till — Walter Till. *Koptische Grammatik: Sahidic Dialect.* Leipzig: VEB Verlag, 1966.

SYMBOLS

[ ]   Square brackets indicate lacunae in the text.

< >   Pointed brackets indicate the author's corrections of a scribal error.

{ }   Braces indicate Coptic material that has been included in the text through scribal error, such as a dittography or letters deleted by the scribe.

( )   Parentheses in the translation enclose Greek loan words used in the Coptic text and interpretative material added by the author to clarify the meaning of the Coptic text.

...   Sublinear dots appearing alone in the transcription indicate illegible Coptic letters. Each dot represents one letter. Sublinear dots beneath letters in the transcription indicate that the letters are not visually certain.

\ /   High diagonal strokes enclose letters that are written above the line by the Coptic scribe.

*   Asterisks in the transcription and translation indicate lines in lacunae. Each asterisk represents one line.

/   The solidus in the transcription and translation indicates the beginning of every fifth line of Coptic text. The line number to which it corresponds is shown in the left margin.

//   A double solidus in the transcription and translation indicates a change in Coptic page number. The new page number and beginning line number are indicated in the left margin.

‡   This sign alerts the reader to the fact that additional text follows this point in the redacted version of the text as it appears in Codex V. The critical notes may be consulted for the location and extent of such text.

| Long vertical lines in the transcription and translation indicate Coptic line division.

The idea for this approach to the *Apocalypse of Adam* grew out of a seminar on the Nag Hammadi texts with Professor James M. Robinson in 1970. The argument for sources underlying the present text of the *Apocalypse of Adam* was originally developed in a seminar paper, then later revised and published in the book of seminar papers for the 1972 annual meeting of the Society of Biblical Literature ("The Apocalypse of Adam: A Literary and Source Analysis," *The Society of Biblical Literature One Hundred Eighth Annual Meeting Book of Seminar Papers, Friday-Tuesday, 1-5 September 1972, Century Plaza Hotel, Los Angeles, Ca.* [2 vols.; ed. Lane C. McGaughy; Missoula: Society of Biblical Literature, 1972] 2.581-90).

The transcription in part two was originally collated against photographs taken by the Center of Documentation of the Arab Republic of Egypt and supplied to UNESCO in 1963 and loaned to me by Professor Robinson, Permanent Secretary of the International Committee for the Nag Hammadi Codices, from the Archives of the Institute for Antiquity and Christianity, Claremont, California. Later I had the opportunity of collating the transcription against the papyrus manuscripts in the Coptic Museum in Old Cairo during several work sessions at the museum in connection with the American project to conserve the manuscripts, the international project to publish them in facsimile edition, and the project to publish an English language edition of the Nag Hammadi Codices sponsored by the Institute for Antiquity and Christianity. From 1971-1973, several work sessions at the Coptic Museum in Cairo from two weeks to one month in length were made possible for me through grants by the American Philosophical Society, The Mills Foundation, Claremont Graduate School and the Institute for Antiquity and Christianity. A seven-month period of research, 1974-1975, was made possible through a federal grant by the Smithsonian Institution. Part of the expense of typing the manuscript for publication was defrayed by Wagner College, Staten Island, New York.

The present transcription represents an improvement over the *editio princeps* published by Alexander Böhlig in 1963.

Since his publication, new readings in the text have been made possible by the placement of fragments on pp. [65]/[66] and [79]/[80] and by the acquisition of early photographs taken by Jean Doresse prior to 1949. The Doresse photographs reveal more text on pp. [65]/[66] than was extant on the papyrus at the time Böhlig's transcription was made. The greatest improvement has been the restoration of text at many points through the use of ultraviolet light. In many instances, the text is illegible under natural light but is clearly visible when the papyrus is read with magnification under ultraviolet light.

I have been cautious in the conjectural emendations of lacunae and have only restored text where such restorations seemed virtually certain. All restorations have been carefully measured to insure that the restoration was possible when compared to the average size of letters elsewhere in the text. The translation and transcription are presented in paragraph form on the basis of thought units, while retaining Coptic line numeration.

The study is divided into two parts. Part One presents the argument for sources underlying the edited form of the *Apocalypse of Adam* as it appears in Codex V and an analysis of the text on the basis of that source division. It also includes a chapter on the history of research on the *Apocalypse of Adam*. Part Two presents transcription and translation with critical notes. The translation is broken down into the two underlying sources and the redactor's comments.

Coptic page and line numbers are indicated in the left margin of both translation and transcription. The beginning of every fifth line of Coptic text is signalled in the translation and transcription by a single solidus. Long vertical lines indicate Coptic line division. A double solidus indicates a change in Coptic page number.

ACKNOWLEDGMENTS

All quotations from *Ginza: Der Schatz, oder das grosse Buch der Mandäer* by Mark Lidzbarski reprinted by permission of Vandenhoeck & Ruprecht.

All quotations from *The Apocrypha and Pseudepigrapha of the Old Testament* edited by R. H. Charles, vol. II and from *Gnosis* by Werner Foerster, translated and edited by R. McL. Wilson, vols. I and II reprinted by permission of Oxford University Press.

All quotations from *The Nag Hammadi Library in English* edited by James M. Robinson, copyright 1977 by E. J. Brill, The Netherlands, reprinted by permission of Harper and Row Publishers, Inc.

INTRODUCTION

Discussions of the *Apocalypse of Adam* have generally proceeded on the assumption that the document was written by a
single author. Although many have recognized that the collection of narratives on the origin of the illuminator ([77],27-
[83],4) is traditional material and as such has a history in
the tradition prior to its incorporation into the *Apocalypse of
Adam*, few have considered this as an indication that the document as a whole may have been composed using earlier collections of material. Or, put another way: few have considered
the possibility that the *Apocalypse of Adam* is an edited document compiled from earlier source material. In fact, few have
speculated on the possibility of sources underlying the present form of the text, and no one has yet examined the text in
an attempt systematically to isolate such sources.[1] Even
Walter Beltz, who made the text the subject of a *Habilitationsschrift* and who thinks the document is a composite work, has
not attempted to work out an identification of the sources.

If indeed the *Apocalypse of Adam* is a composite text, it
is essential that its history of redaction be clarified. Not
to do so places the interpretation of the text in question
since one would be unable to distinguish between the various
stages in the transmission of the text, and therefore could not
identify the theology of a later redactor from the theology of
his sources. The usual approach to the text, i.e., regarding
it as written by a single author, is much like trying to identify the theology of Mark or John without using literary or
source analysis and form criticism.

The search for sources or prior collections of material
underlying a given text is a recognized and established part
of the total hermeneutical enterprise. In fact, modern biblical criticism may be said to trace its beginning to the recognition of sources in Genesis in the eighteenth century. At the
close of the nineteenth century, one of the assured results of
biblical criticism was that certain biblical texts were derived
from earlier collections of material. While there was no consensus as to the exact limits of the sources, there was general

1

agreement that these texts did incorporate earlier collections
of material.

In the twentieth century, in an attempt to get behind
these early collections of material, the focus of interest
shifted to the smaller literary units, i.e., stories and sayings, and to the history of their transmission. The new form
critical research was never intended to replace source analysis, but it enabled the scholar to break through the impasse
at which critical research had arrived and to identify still
earlier layers of tradition. Each method is important in itself as a hermeneutical tool for understanding a text. This is
demonstrated by the fact that the search for possible sources
underlying the Gospel of John plays a significant role in
today's discussion along with the continuing form critical
analysis.

More recently, in research on the Synoptic Gospels, the
focus has again shifted back to the gospel as a whole. While
the form critic stressed the composite nature of the gospels
and regarded the evangelists simply as collectors or editors
of the tradition, the new approach regards them as theologians
or authors in their own right, and seeks an understanding of
their theology in the way each evangelist arranged or redacted
his material. In this enterprise, the identification of material *received* by the evangelist, the smaller literary units as
well as longer collections of material, is essential since the
redaktionsgeschichtliche Methode proceeds by studying the evangelist's redaction of the material he received. All three ap-
proaches to the text (literary or source analysis, form criticism and redaction criticism) are not exclusive disciplines;
they are complementary parts of one hermeneutical process. A
biblical scholar will allow all three methods to guide his research, since all can contribute to his understanding of the
text. In a sense, literary criticism and form criticism are
incorporated into redaction criticism since these two methods
are basic tools for the redaction critic.

This study utilizes that kind of methodology. I am concerned with the *Apocalypse of Adam* as a literary whole. However, in order to understand the whole I must also be concerned

with earlier collections of material underlying the composite whole of the text as well as the tradition history of the smaller units. The discussion proceeds on the assumption that an understanding of the whole is achieved only through a clear understanding of its parts.

INTRODUCTION

[1]There has been one preliminary attempt to analyze the
literary development of the *Apoc. Adam*: Rodolphe Kasser,
"Textes gnostiques: Remarques à propos des éditions récentes du
Livre secret de Jean et des Apocalypses de Paul, Jacques et
Adam," *Le Muséon* 78 (1965) 91-98 and "Bibliothèque gnostique V:
Apocalypse d'Adam," *RTP* 17 (1967) 316-33. Kasser identifies
two primary divisions to the tractate which, he says, can be
easily identified by their style and "probably" also by their
content. The larger section (64,1-[77],27a; [83],8b-[85],31)
is principally a gnostic reinterpretation of certain events in
Genesis and can be called "the Revelation of Adam to Seth."
This section Kasser believes to be an ancient Semitic poem
whose metrical characteristics are still distinguishable in
spite of having been blurred through an initial translation
into Greek and then from Greek into Coptic. Into this poem of
sixty-three four-line strophes an ancient editor has inserted
an equally archaic shorter section ([77],27b-[83],8a). Kasser
identifies this unit as an ancient Semitic (or Iranian) hymn
whose original literary structure was modified before being incorporated into the *Apoc. Adam*. In its original form, the hymn
had fourteen strophes of six units each. Originally the hymn
alluded to fourteen now unidentifiable mythical figures that
came to be associated with biblical and pagan heroes. Even-
tually both of these divisions were united and edited to form
the present apocalypse.

PART ONE

ANALYZING THE DOCUMENT ON THE BASIS OF SOURCES

CHAPTER I

HISTORY OF RESEARCH

A. Text and Translations

In 1963, the *editio princeps* of the *Apoc. Adam* appeared in the publication of the four apocalypses in Codex V by Alexander Böhlig and Pahor Labib (*Koptisch-gnostische Apokalypsen aus Codex V von Nag Hammadi im Koptischen Museum zu Alt-Kairo* [Halle-Wittenberg: Wissenschaftliche Zeitschrift der Martin-Luther-Universität, 1963] 86-117). Their transcription was the only published transcription of the text available to scholarship until 1979. In light of the fact that critical editions of a large percentage of the Nag Hammadi tractates have yet to appear, their early publication of these texts is to be commended. The editors of the text were justifiably cautious in the restoration of lacunae; consequently, much of the text was unrestored in their edition.

In 1965, Rodolphe Kasser, working primarily with photographs supplied by Martin Krause (although he did at least see the papyrus manuscripts), suggested new readings for the vestiges of ink around the lacunae (in particular the missing tops and bottoms of pages) and restorations based upon those readings ("Textes gnostiques: Remarques à propos des éditions récentes du Livre secret de Jean et des Apocalypses de Paul, Jacques et Adam," *Le Muséon* 78 [1965] 91-96 and "Textes gnostiques: Nouvelles remarques à propos de Apocalypses de Paul, Jacques et Adam," *Le Muséon* 78 [1965] 304-306). While Kasser did correct some incorrect readings in the Böhlig-Labib edition, many of his extensive restorations are based upon incorrect readings of ink traces around lacunae.

In 1966, Hans-Martin Schenke published a review of the Böhlig-Labib edition suggesting new parallels and restorations as well as translation and transcription corrections ("Alexander Böhlig und Pahor Labib, Koptisch-gnostische Apokalypsen aus Codex V von Nag Hammadi im Koptischen Museum zu Alt-Kairo," *OLZ* 61 [1966] cols. 32-34). There is no indication that Schenke had access to a set of photographs of the text, and at that time

9

he had not yet been to Cairo to consult the originals. Other
reviews of the Böhlig-Labib edition did not deal with specific
problems of transcription and translation, but were concerned
only with a description of the text, and the interpretation of
the text by Böhlig-Labib (Kurt Rudolph, *TLZ* 90 [1965] cols.
361-62; A. Orbe, *Gregorianum* 46 [1965] 170-72; R. Kasser,
BO 22 [1965] 163-64; Jean Daniélou, *RSR* 54 [1966] 291-92;
R. Haardt, *WZKM* 61 [1967] 155-59).

Other translations of the text have been published in
French and German. In 1967, Rodolphe Kasser published a French
translation based upon his own (unpublished) transcription of
the text that employed his own suggestions for lacunae restorations published earlier (see above) ("Bibliothèque gnostique V:
Apocalypse d'Adam," *RTP* 17 [1967] 316-33). In 1971, Martin
Krause published a new German translation of the text. Krause
had access to the original manuscripts and in addition possessed a complete set of photographs of the text. He adopted
suggestions for lacunae restorations made by H.-M. Schenke, R.
Kasser and W. Beltz insofar as their restorations to him seemed
assured ("Die Apokalypse Adams," *Gnosis* [2 vols.; ed. Werner
Foerster; Zürich: Artemis Verlags-AG, 1969-1971] 2.17-31; ET
Werner Foerster [ed.], *Gnosis* [2 vols.; trans. and ed. R. McL.
Wilson; Oxford: Clarendon, 1972-1974] 2.13-23).

In 1970, Walter Beltz completed his as yet unpublished
Habilitationsschrift on the *Apoc. Adam*. Using photographs
loaned to him by Martin Krause, Beltz sought to improve on the
transcription of the Böhlig-Labib edition. Unfortunately, because of numerous incorrect readings and extensive unwarranted
lacunae restorations, the text does not represent an improvement over Böhlig-Labib. The real value of Beltz's work is his
collection of numerous parallel passages from the Jewish rabbinic tradition, and his recognition of the heavy dependence of
the text upon the Jewish traditions ("Die Adam-Apokalypse aus
Codex V von Nag Hammadi: Jüdische Bausteine in gnostischen Systemen," Dr. Theol. dissertation, Berlin: Humboldt-Universität,
1970).

In 1977, Stephen E. Robinson published an English language translation of *Apoc. Adam* apparently based on the critical text published by Böhlig-Labib ("The Apocalypse of Adam," *Brigham Young University Studies* 17 [1977] 131-53).

Early in 1977, George W. MacRae published an English language translation reflecting an improved transcription of the Coptic text in connection with the Coptic-Gnostic Library Project of the Institute for Antiquity and Christianity, Claremont, California ("The Apocalypse of Adam," *The Nag Hammadi Library in English* [ed. James M. Robinson; San Francisco: Harper and Row, 1977] 256-64). It was followed in 1979 by a new critical edition of the Coptic text with an improved English language translation along with critical introduction and notes. This publication was part of the English language edition of the Nag Hammadi Codices sponsored by the Institute for Antiquity and Christianity. The publication represents a vast improvement over the edition of Böhlig-Labib, as it reflects considerable work with the original manuscripts under ultraviolet light over several work sessions in the Coptic Museum ("The Apocalypse of Adam," *Nag Hammadi Codices V, 2-5 and VI with Papyrus Berolinensis 8502, 1 and 4* [ed. Douglas M. Parrott; Leiden: E. J. Brill, 1978] 193-95).

B. Secondary Literature

In 1969, Kurt Rudolph published a brief *Forschungsbericht* on *Apoc. Adam* that summarized the state of the discussion to that time ("Gnosis und Gnostizismus, ein Forschungsbericht," *TRu* 34 [1969] 160-69). The discussion in the early period evolved around two central issues. Stimulated by the claim of Böhlig (later revised) that the text reflected a kind of "pre-Christian" Gnosticism, the discussion centered on the character of the text, i.e., was it a Christian text or a non-Christian text? Since there were motifs that seemed to reflect a Christian provenance, Böhlig's characterization was challenged. Closely related to this issue was a second issue about the character and purpose of the list of statements by the personified kingdoms and the kingless generation ([77],27-[83],4),

since some of the motifs suggesting a Christian provenance fell
within this section. In the early period there was no real
consensus with respect to these two issues. Instead, the discussion seemed to have reached a methodological impasse with
parallels accumulated on both sides of the issue.

Since 1969, the pace of publication has slowed and the
direction taken by the discussion has changed. The earlier
discussion seemed to be primarily concerned with the relationship of the *Apoc. Adam* to the Christian tradition, and the
discussion proceeded in an attempt to clarify that relationship. More recently, there has been an interest in the theology
of the text. In 1969, Luise Schottroff published an article in
which she examined the anthropology of *Apoc. Adam* ("Animae naturalitur salvandae. Zum Problem der himmlischen Herkunft des
Gnostikers," *Christentum und Gnosis* [ed. Walther Eltester;
BZNW 37; Berlin: Alfred Töpelmann, 1969] 68-83). (The article
was apparently unavailable to Rudolph at the time he published
his work.) Schottroff's approach represents a first attempt to
come to grips with the theology of the text itself. She understands the *Apoc. Adam* as a mythological description of gnostic
anthropology. The anthropological thesis of the text according
to her is that the gnostic has a heavenly origin. Thus, he
originates undefiled and remains undefiled. Not all men have
such an origin; only the gnostic has a heavenly origin. This
group the text describes as the men of gnosis. They are the
saved. All other men are lost. They are described as creatures
of the dead earth, men defiled by desire who serve the demiurge.

All men are threatened in the world. These threats are
reflected in the text in mythological categories as flood, fire
and darkness. Only the gnostic will be saved, i.e., taken above
to a heavenly dwelling place. The emphasis in the text is on
the gnostic community. There is no concept of individual
salvation.

The section on the statements of the kingdoms ([77],27-
[83],4) appears to be a gnostic polemic against an argument for
a mixed nature for the illuminator, and therefore also for the
gnostic (see below). In this respect, the first thirteen
statements are slanders against the illuminator. They assert

that he has a mixed and defiled origin, i.e., that his origin is partially from heaven and partially from the defiled chaos. This slanderous attitude is rejected by the author of the statement of the kingless generation who for Schottroff is the author of *Apoc. Adam*.

There are only two possible origins that one can have: one's origin is defiled and earthly, or one's origin is undefiled and heavenly. The gnostics have a heavenly origin in that they come from Seth and eternal gnosis. Therefore they can receive revelation. This is not true of those who have a defiled origin.

Schottroff identifies the illuminator as Seth, who is also the *Urmensch*, and as the savior. She notes that the situation of the gnostic community and that of the illuminator are identical: both have a heavenly origin, neither is defiled and both are threatened by the demiurge without falling under his control. In this respect, the formula *salvator-salvandus* does not apply since the illuminator in the *Apoc. Adam* can in no sense be said to be in need of salvation.

In his *Habilitationsschrift*, completed in 1970, Walter Beltz (see above) argued that, while the text drew heavily upon Jewish traditions, it nevertheless has a Manichaean provenance ca. A.D. 297.[1] The list of thirteen explanations by the kingdoms and the final explanation by the kingless generation were all explanations for the birth of Jesus. Thus the document came out of Christian Gnosticism and was written as a *Lehrschrift* for beginning gnostics. This latter character of the text, he argues, explains its simple concepts in comparison to other texts with complicated cosmological descriptions such as *Ap. John* and *Gos. Eg.*

Although Beltz recognized that the document is a composite text, he does not attempt to define the extent of redaction or to write the history of redaction. The *Habilitationsschrift* belongs to the early period of research on the text in the sense that Beltz studied *Apoc. Adam* against the backdrop of the Christian tradition. Since completing the *Habilitationsschrift*, Beltz has published three times on the *Apoc. Adam* reaffirming his original position ("NHC V, 5/p.64,1-85,32: Die Apokalypse

des Adams (ApocAd)," *Gnosis und Neues Testament* [ed. Karl-
Wolfgang Tröger; Berlin: Evangelische Verlagsanstalt, 1973]
46-47; with P. L. Márton, "A gnósiz-Kutatás jelenlegi állása.
Az Adám-Apokalipszis a Nag Hamadiban talált V. Codexben,"
Theologiai Szemle 12 [1969] 266-70; and "Bemerkungen zur Adam-
apokalypse aus Nag-Hammadi-Codex V," *Studia Coptica* [ed. Peter
Nagel; Berlin: Akademie-Verlag, 1974] 159-63).

In 1971 in an article on the Gospel of the Egyptians, Jean
Doresse included a brief section on the relationship between
Gos. Eg. and *Apoc. Adam* ("'Le Livre sacré de grand Espirit
invisible' ou 'L'Evangile des Egyptiens': Texte copte édité,
traduit et commenté d'après la Codex I de Nag'a-Hammadi/
Khénoboskion: II. Commentaire," *JA* 256 [1968 (1971)] 289-386).
On pages 370-376, Doresse briefly describes his theory that
Apoc. Adam was a source for *Gos. Eg.* He does not systematically
work out his argument proving such exclusive dependence, but
simply cites points where both texts have common material; in
effect, he illustrates their close relationship by their common
tradition. For Doresse, their relationship is not a literary
one; that is, the present form of *Gos. Eg.* did not draw its
material from the present form of *Apoc. Adam*. Rather, both
texts, as we now possess them, go back to an earlier common
abbreviated *Vorlage*. After reading his discussion, the reader
is keenly aware that Doresse has not solved the problem of relationship as much as he has emphasized it. By not eliminating
the possibility that *Apoc. Adam* drew upon *Gos. Eg.* as a source,
Doresse leaves that option open as an explanation for the relationship of the two texts.

In 1972, three articles on the *Apoc. Adam* appeared together in *The Society of Biblical Literature One Hundred Eighth
Annual Meeting Book of Seminar Papers, Friday-Tuesday, 1-5 September 1972, Century Plaza Hotel, Los Angeles, Ca.* ([2 vols.;
ed. Lane C. McGaughy; Missoula: Society of Biblical Literature,
1972] 2.573-99). That year, the *Apoc. Adam* was one of two
texts considered by the Nag Hammadi Seminar. A short article
by the chairman of the seminar, George MacRae, introduced the
primary topic for discussion in the three-hour seminar ("The
Apocalypse of Adam Reconsidered," 573-77). MacRae proposes

that the motifs in the tractate that are usually regarded as
indicating Christian influence are not specifically Christian.
Thus, he regards the *Apoc. Adam* as a non-Christian gnostic
tractate.

He notes that continuing study of *Apoc. Adam* suggests that
it is the result of one or more redactional processes. In his
opinion, this approach may be the key to "discovering the process of transition from apocalyptic Jewish thought...to properly
gnostic thought without passing through the Christian Kerygma."
He also stresses the importance of investigating thoroughly the
suggestion of Böhlig that the document comes from a Syrian-
Palestinian baptismal sect. This will require a careful examination of the conclusion of the tractate where the baptism motif
is most evident.

In a historical sense, his article reflects the shift from
an earlier stage of the discussion, where the concern was to
gather *religionsgeschichtlich* parallels and to interpret *Apoc.
Adam* in relationship to the Christian tradition, to a later
phase where the concern is to understand the theology of the
text on the basis of its tradition history. The later approach
does not argue over the provenance of individual motifs, but
attempts to identify the traditions out of which the text
evolved and the trajectory of those traditions. The earlier
approach focuses on individual motifs and argues provenance.
The later approach tries to determine provenance from the text
as a whole.

In a second article, Pheme Perkins investigated *Apoc. Adam*
from the standpoint of its close relationship to the Jewish
tradition. She regards the text as a gnostic work with no
motifs that are unambiguously Christian. It reflects apocalyptic schematization of individual traditions (i.e., in the
periodization of the history of revelation of gnosis) and in
the overall composition of the work. The major patterns in
Apoc. Adam are derived from the apocryphal Jewish Adam literature. In fact, the overall structure of the apocalypse she
describes as a testament. This is particularly clear with
respect to the preamble to the text (64,1-6).

There are also other patterns that have Jewish roots. The most important of these is the schematization of gnostic history that forms the structure of the apocalypse proper, i.e., flood, Sodom/Gomorrah and the end of the world. This periodization of cosmic destruction occurs only in *Adam and Eve*, Josephus, *Apoc. Adam*, *Gos. Eg.* and *Paraph. Shem*. It is reasonable, she thinks, to conclude that the exegesis reflected in the use of schematization by *Apoc. Adam* reflects an early gnostic reworking of Genesis traditions ("Apocalyptic Schematization in the Apocalypse of Adam and the Gospel of the Egyptians," 591-99). In a later paper ("Apocalypse of Adam: The Genre and Function of a Gnostic Apocalypse," *CBQ* 39 [1977] 382-95), Perkins describes the text as "an ironic work whose effect depends on the reader's ability to perceive the incongruity between... what is implied by the genre in which the whole is cast and what is actually going on." What is "going on," according to Perkins, is a satire of a final testament by Adam in which Adam, a well-known figure in Israelite religious traditions, actually "reveals the futility of serving the god of Israel." The purpose of the text in Perkins' judgment, is to reinforce the group identity of the community that possesses the key to the real meaning of the text.

The third paper in the SBL volume was my own initial argument setting out the redaction history of the document as I understood it then ("The Apocalypse of Adam: A Literary and Source Analysis," 581-90). Minor points have since been modified.

In September 1975, Françoise Morard delivered a paper at the Oxford International Congress of Patristics entitled "L'*Apocalypse d'Adam* de Nag-Hammadi: un essai d'interpretation." It was later published in an abbreviated form in *Gnosis and Gnosticism* ([ed. Martin Krause; Leiden: E. J. Brill, 1977] 35-42), and in a revised expanded form as "L'*Apocalypse d'Adam* du Codex V de Nag Hammadi et sa polémique anti-baptismale" (*RevScRel* 51 [1977] 214-33). Morard's paper represented an attempt to understand the provenance of *Apoc. Adam* on the basis of the redactor's conclusion to the *Apoc. Adam* ([84],4-[85],3 less [84],19-22). From this block of material, Morard concludes that the author recognized two baptisms, one superior to the other. The lower form of baptism, i.e., by water, was condemned because through it one submitted oneself to the powers of the demiurge. The author of *Apoc. Adam* opted for a higher more spiritual understanding of baptism, i.e., a baptism of gnosis, that was transmitted by the mythological figures Yesseus, Mazareus, Yessedekeus.

Morard recognizes that the opposition to water baptism by the text might suggest a Manichaean provenance, but excludes that possibility because the text also prohibits the writing of the words of revelation in a book ([85],5-6). While Manichaeism rejected water baptism, it was also characterized as being a religion of the book. A Manichaean would scarcely have insisted that revelation was *not* to be written in a book. The few motifs in the text that could be considered as Christian allusions, the lack of importance the text gives to a redeemer figure and the rejection of water baptism lead Morard to the conclusion that *Apoc. Adam* is in an ideological continuity with the (Sethian) gnostic sect described by Epiphanius as Archontics. The text as we possess it today in Codex V is presented as a gnostic utilization at several levels of a legend inherited through apocalyptic Judaism. A redactor later attempted to harmonize several writings already gnostic and added certain statements of his own faith, in particular the conclusion containing the statement about baptism.

NOTE

CHAPTER I

[1]The only other published date for the text (Hans Goedicke, "An Unexpected Allusion to the Vesuvius Eruption in 79 A.D.," *American Journal of Philology* 90 [1969] 340-41) sets it not later than the first decade of the second century A.D. MacRae (152) speculates that its date may be as early as the first or second century A.D.

CHAPTER II

IDENTIFICATION OF SOURCES IN THE *APOC. ADAM*

A. Two Introductory Sections to the *Apoc. Adam*

One indication that the *Apoc. Adam* is the result of a
complicated literary development is initially suggested by the
fact that one can identify what appear to be two introductory
sections to the body of the tractate.

Section A: 64,6 (ΟΤΑΝ) - [65],23
             [66],12 (ΤΟΤΕ) - [67],12 (ΠΕΝϢΝϨ)[1]
Section B: [65],24-[66],12 (ΝΝΑϨΡΑΪ)
             [67],12 (ΑΪΕΙΜΕ) - [67],21 (ΕΒΟΛ)[2]

One is instantly struck by the difference between these
two units. Section A takes the form of a gnostic midrash on
Gen 2:7, 21-22 and 4:1 (LXX).[3] It describes the primordial
origins of humanity and explains why mankind in general does
not now possess the knowledge of God, the Eternal.[4] An androgynous aeon, Adam-Eve, has been created by god (= the demiurge). Initially, after creation, Adam-Eve continued in the
glory and knowledge of the aeon from which (s)he had come.
(S)he resembled the eternal angels (i.e., in his/her androgynous state) and was therefore greater than the god who created
him/her (64,6-19). Adam-Eve was divided into two distinct
aeons by the creator god. As a result of this devolution, the
two (divided) aeons no longer resembled the great (androgynous)
eternal angels (64,14-19). Consequently, they lost the
"glory" and the "first knowledge" that they had brought with
them from the (eternal) aeon (64,6-14, 24-28). Adam and Eve
were then enslaved by the creator god ([65],16-21) and their
heart was "darkened" ([65],21-23). In this depressing and
hopeless situation, Adam and Eve uttered a deep sigh that was
heard by the creator god. He stood before them and asked why
they were sighing. Had he not "blessed" them by their creation
and had not he, the creator, made them a "living soul" ([66],
12-23)? Then Adam experienced desire for Eve. In this instant,
their devolution into two aeons became complete, the knowledge

of the eternal God was lost to them, and they were subject to
the vicissitudes characteristic of mortality ([67],2-12).[5]

The section is characterized by an interesting use of
plurals that appears no place else in the tractate. Adam always speaks in the plural (viz. "we" or "I and Eve your
mother").[6] This unusual feature can be seen most clearly at
[66],12-[67],12. Both Adam and Eve utter a deep sigh ([66],
12-14) yet god addresses only Adam ([66],17) but unexpectedly
addresses him in the second person plural rather than the
second person singular ([66],17-23)! It is true that the *Apoc.
Adam* is not always precise in the use of singular and plural,[7]
but the use of plurals in this section is too consistent to be
considered as an accident or an oversight on the part of the
translator, particularly when one compares the consistent use
of the singular actor expression in section B. The singular
use of Adam or Eve as an independent actor expression in section A is the exception rather than the rule.[8] By the use of
the plural actor expression, section A is set apart from
section B in a graphic way.

This cohesive narrative (section A) forms a self-contained
literary unit that is broken up by another self-contained unit
(section B) of quite a different order. In section B, Adam
appears to be in a state of unenlightenment when three unidentified men appear to him ([65],24-33).[9] The men call on Adam
to "arise from the sleep of death," and listen to their words
"about the aeon and the seed" ([66],1-8). When Adam heard
these words, he became aware of his servitude to the "authority
of death" ([67],12-14). He then proposes to reveal to Seth
what had been revealed only to him ([67],14-21). This second
narrative (section B) is characterized by a change in setting
and actors. From the primordial "garden of Eden" in section A,
the scene now shifts to a different setting in which Adam alone
receives three men whose revelatory words bring about Adam's
enlightenment.[10] In this second scene, there is no suggestion
of the previous "garden of Eden" setting.

The awkward way that the narratives are joined clearly
exposes literary seams ([65],23-24; [66],12; [67],12). The
first seam between [65],23 and [65],24 is distinguishable by an

abrupt change of scene[11] and a shift from the plural "we" or
"I and Eve your mother" to the singular "I." By associating
the motif of ignorance in [65],21-23 ("darkened in heart") with
the motif of ignorance in [65],24-25 ("heart sleeping") and
adding the conjunction ⲇⲉ in [65],24 as a connective device,
the redactor links the two narratives together.

At the second seam, the editor has rather awkwardly
divided a sentence that at one time ran from [66],9-12
(ⲚⲚⲀ2ⲣⲀⲓ̈), picks up with [67],12 (Ⲁⲓ̈ⲉⲓⲙⲉ), and continues
through [67],14 (ⲡⲙⲟⲩ).[12] The new sentence created by the
editor in [66],9-14 when he brings the two narratives together
is confusing. In the protasis, it is Adam only who hears the
words of the three men, but in the apodosis, suddenly Eve appears and it is "we" (i.e., Adam and Eve) who react to the
revelation of the three men, a revelation that ostensibly only
Adam heard. Further, this sentence created by the redactor has
the words of the three men producing just the opposite of the
desired and expected result. Adam and Eve become depressed and
go on to complete ignorance and mortality ([67],1-11) after
hearing words that are intended to produce enlightenment and
happiness. The result that one would expect does not occur
until [67],12. In the sentence created by the redactor, there
is a shift from one setting reflected in the protasis to a
different setting reflected in the apodosis. Several questions
immediately arise: What happened to the three men? Where was
the creator while they were talking to Adam? If the revelation
was made to Adam alone, why does Eve also sigh?

At the third seam in [67],12, the redactor has made a
partial attempt to smooth out the contradiction between [67],
2-11 and [67],12-14[13] by inserting the conjunction ⲅⲁⲣ and by
using an adverb (ⲚϢⲟⲣⲡ̄) in [67],20. The adverb is intended
to recall the revelation that took place in [65],24-[66],12 and
to give a certain consistency to the passage by acknowledging
that something had transpired between the revelation and Adam's
decision to make it known to Seth, that is, to account for
[66],9-[67],11. However, if one were to acknowledge that the
text has been redacted and then were to arrange the material in
the order as I have suggested, the transition from [65],23 to

[66],12b (TOTϵ) is perfectly natural and makes a coherent sentence: As a result of their loss of knowledge of the eternal God and their resultant servitude to the creator god, Adam and Eve, "darkened in their heart," utter a deep sigh over their hopeless situation. Both segments A and B appear to form independent narratives. When one reads each segment as an independent unit, there is no abrupt change of setting or subject and one plot is maintained throughout each segment.[14]

Böhlig attempts to explain the narrative about the revelation of the three men in section B as a vision of Adam that comes to him in sleep.[15] If this were indeed the case, it could explain some of the problems we have noted in the text. For example, one might argue that dreams have a "world" of their own. Therefore one should not be surprised if the garden scene, the creator god and Eve disappear during Adam's dream. Further, since it is Adam's dream, it is not unusual that only he should appear in it as actor.[16] In other words, that part of the argument offered above for detecting the hand of the redactor on the basis of abrupt shift of scene, change of character and plurality of subject is called into question.

To support his interpretation, Böhlig cites Gen 18:1-15 as a parallel to the scene in the *Apoc. Adam*. It is to be admitted there is a certain affinity between the parallel cited by Böhlig and the *Apoc. Adam*, but it is not very extensive. There appear to be only three analogues between the two narratives: three men bring the revelation (Gen 18:2 and [65],24-29), they were not recognized (Gen 18:13-14 [not until later in the narrative is one of the guests identified as "the Lord"] and [65],24-29), and the revelation concerned a son to be born to Adam and Abraham (Gen 18:10-15 and [65],33-[66],8). It is immediately noticeable that Abraham is not asleep and dreaming, but evidently wide awake. There is simply no indication in the text to suggest that Abraham was asleep.[17] Böhlig apparently assumed that Adam was asleep, and having a dream on the basis of *Apoc. Adam* ([65],24-25 -- "Now I was sleeping in the thought of my heart"), and because of the general similarity between the two narratives, simply read the sleep motif into the Abraham story.

The statements that led Böhlig to think that Adam was
asleep or dreaming ([65],24-25) are better understood as gnostic *topoi* describing Adam's spiritual condition in the world
rather than as statements about physical sleep, or a visionary
experience. This understanding of the language seems evident
from the text itself, for Adam describes himself as "sleeping
in his heart" ([65],24-25) and as being called upon to arise
"from the sleep of death" ([66],1-3), statements more correctly
describing being-in-the-world than a state of physical alert-
ness, although the physical implications of the word "sleep"
cannot be denied. He is called upon to change his being-in-
the-world by heeding the words of revelation ([66],3-8), and
when he does, he is enlightened ([66],9-12; [67],12-14). The
situation is clearly the familiar gnostic *topos* of spiritual
sleep, the call from without and the response, described in
detail by Hans Jonas.[18]

To explain the revelation of the three men in section B as
a vision of Adam which comes to him during sleep does not seem
to be a suitable description of the content of the narrative,
nor would it explain all the problems noted in the preceding
argument. A simpler and more satisfying explanation is that
we are dealing with two independent narratives that have been
inadequately harmonized by an early redactor.

Both narratives reflect general gnostic *topoi* and have
different subject matter. For these two reasons one is forced
to look closely at them if one would recognize any material
differences. Section B, the narrative about the revelation of
the three men, does not satisfactorily accomplish what the redactor intended it to do, but is in tension with its context at
two points. The redactor intended the segment to show how Adam
had regained his lost knowledge of the eternal God.[19] Initially, the androgyne Adam-Eve possessed this knowledge (64,
12-13), but lost it when (s)he became two aeons (64,2-29;
[65],9-13). The problem that confronted the redactor was that
the Adam of section A now had no special knowledge to communi-
cate! He was ignorant, and subject to desire and death. How
could he, then, pass on to Seth what he did not possess? Ob-
viously he could not, and it was necessary for the redactor to

provide some way for him to regain his lost knowledge.   To this
end he employed the narrative about the three men.[20]

However, notice that the three men have nothing at all to
say about the eternal God ([65],33-[66],8)!   Adam is called on
to arise from sleep (= awake),[21] and challenged to hear about
the "aeon and the seed."   One would have expected something
more general.   For example:

> Hearken, ye folk, men born of earth, who have given
> yourselves up to drunkenness and sleep in your ignor-
> ance of god; awake to soberness, cease to be sodden
> with strong drink and lulled in sleep devoid of
> reason.[22]

Or one would have expected something that related more specifically to the situation in section A.   But certainly one would
not expect such a specific kind of revelation that has no foundation in section A, and apparently little to do with section
A.[23]

The revelation is also in tension with what immediately
follows section B.   Since the men challenged Adam to hear about
the "aeon and the seed," this is what we are expecting Adam to
relate to Seth when he says, "So now my Son, Seth, I shall reveal to you these (things) that those men...revealed to me"
([67],14-21).   Instead, we are launched into a gnostic midrash
on the Genesis account of the great flood.   In effect, the
revelation made by the three men to Adam is in tension not only
with section A, but also with the revelation that Adam communicates to Seth, ostensibly on the basis of what the men had told
him.   What he was supposedly told by the men and what he told
Seth that they revealed to him are not the same thing.

As pointed out above, section A intends to explain how man
came to lose the knowledge of the eternal God and to be enslaved by his ignorance.   Thus, the motif of knowledge 64,
12-14; 64,23-28; [65],9b-13; [67],4-8), and the devolution of
Adam into ignorance are the cohesive ideas in the narrative.
For these reasons, the passage explaining why Seth received his
name ([65],3-9) strikes a discord in the narrative and has the
marks of a redactional insertion.   Lines [65],3-9 interject
theological ideas and motifs that do not arise naturally out of

the subject matter of section A.[24]   The statement presupposes
mythologomena and a conceptual world for which section A has
not prepared the reader.

It is possible that the redactor left a visible seam when
he prematurely explains what happened to Adam's knowledge. In
64,24-25, we are told that the glory in the heart of Adam and
Eve left them, and (in 64,29-31) it entered into another
great aeon and generation (if the lacuna restoration is correct). Likewise, their knowledge left them (64,27), withdrew
far from them ([65],10-13), and finally was totally destroyed
([67],4-9) when Adam's devolution into ignorance was complete.
The narrative intends to show the stages of the devolution of
Adam and Eve from primordial bliss to earthly ignorance by the
loss of both of these qualities of immortality (i.e., glory and
knowledge). Glory was lost instantly and knowledge in varying
degrees. In short, Adam's devolution into ignorance provides
the structure for the section.

Apparently, the redactor was not sensitive to this loss of
knowledge by degrees and noticed in his *Vorlage* that both glory
and knowledge were lost by Adam and Eve (64,24-28), but only
glory entered into another great aeon and another great generation (64,28-[65],1). What he understood to be an oversight
in his *Vorlage*, i.e., its failure to describe where knowledge
had gone, provided him with the opportunity to include his
statement about the origin of Seth's name ([65],3-9), failing
to realize that it was in tension with the intent of his
Vorlage. If knowledge was completely gone at [65],3-4, there
is no need for the statements at [65],9-13 and [67],4-9.

B. Two Conclusions to the *Apoc. Adam*

The *Apoc. Adam* has two different concluding statements:[25]

Conclusion A: [85],19-22a (Є ρ ο ο ϒ)[26]
Conclusion B: [85],22b-31[27]

While the two conclusions are similar in form and function, in
content and intent they are quite different. Conclusion A is a
simple concluding statement. It states that Adam made known
revelations (ἀποκάλυψις) to Seth, and Seth taught his seed

about them.[28] It introduces no new ideas, but concludes the
tractate in a very general way. By contrast, conclusion B, the
redactor's conclusion,[29] is theologically more sophisticated.
It presupposes a mythological world only hinted at in the tractate. In effect, it is comparable to an iceberg. We are allowed to see that part of the mythological structure protruding
above the waterline of the text's surface, but beneath the surface in the self-understanding of the redactor lies a mythological structure and thought-world for which the text has not
prepared the reader. In conclusion B, Adam has not simply made
an indefinite "revelation" or "revelations," but he communicates a particular secret (ἀπόκρυφον) knowledge specifically
identified in the conclusion as the "holy baptism of those who
know eternal gnosis." This gnosis is transmitted by a select
group: "those born of the word and the imperishable illuminators, who came from the holy seed." This specificity of the
content of revelation and insistence on a special group to
transmit the revelation suggest a Sitz im Leben of rival baptismal sects.[30]

The document as a whole does not reflect this concern for
baptism. If one excludes the explanation of the kingless generation[31] in section B, there are only two other evident references in the document to baptism: [84],4-23; [83],4-6 (and only
one of these unquestionably refers to baptism, [84],4-23), and
both of them have been identified elsewhere as redactional
statements.[32] Therefore the baptism motif appears to be a special concern of the redactor. By presenting it in the conclusion of the tractate, the redactor intends that the whole document be read under its influence. He is not simply adding to
the document another conclusion like conclusion A, but rather
he is establishing a basis for understanding the document by
interpreting conclusion A in the light of his own self-
understanding. The revelations that Adam told Seth and that
Seth taught his seed were in reality the hidden gnosis of the
redactor's community.[33]

C. The Body of the Tractate

An initial casual reading of the main body of the tractate leaves one with a sense of confusion. The storyline is not consistent; a certain kind of action appears, is dropped and reappears; subject matter changes and actors appear, disappear and reappear.[34] For these reasons, it will be helpful to make an initial division of the tractate on the basis of its main thought units.

In the main body of the document, there appear to be three phases to the narrative that initially can be identified by a change in subject matter: [67],22-[76],7; [76],8-[83],7 (ΤΗρογ); [83],7-[85],18.[35] The first phase ([67],22-[76],7) describes a special race of men who have come "from the knowledge of the great eons and the angels" ([71],10-13 and [73], 15-20) and their conflict with god, the Pantocrator (also called "Sakla," [74],3-4, and "god of the eons," [74],26-28). It recounts his attempts to destroy them and their eventual preservation through divine intervention. The narrative takes the form of a midrash on the traditional biblical account of the great flood.

Phase two ([76],8-[83],7) describes a conflict between the illuminator (φωϲΤΗρ) and the archon of the powers (also called the god of the powers). The illuminator performs "signs" and "wonders." This totally confuses the archon of the powers and in bewilderment he asks about the power of the man who is loftier than he and his powers ([77],4-7).[36] The archon and his powers then abuse the illuminator physically and in perplexity ask after the source of the confusion, i.e., the error and the lying words that had so disrupted their (apparently) well-established order ([77],18-27). Response to the question is made in a series of fourteen stories apparently referring to the origin of the illuminator ([77],27-[83],7). With one exception, each story has a similar structure and most are clearly marked out in the manuscript.[37]

Phase three ([83],7-[85],18) is more difficult to describe briefly since it contains divergent motifs. It is treated here as a separate "phase" as a matter of convenience because it

contains material different from the two preceding "phases."[38]
It describes the recognition of the righteous character of the
special race by an indefinite group of people ([83],7-23) and a
confession by the indefinite group of their own unrighteousness
([83],23-[84],3). It also describes a condemnation of those
who have defiled the "water of life" ([84],4-26). The end of
the section describes the faithfulness of those men who know
the eternal God ([85],1-18).

On the basis of having identified redactional activity at
the beginning and ending of the tractate, it seems legitimate
to assume that there may be other redacted elements in the
tractate, and to ask further questions on this basis. The
question arises naturally as to whether phase one and phase
two were originally separate and independent units brought together by an ancient redactor.[39] This possibility directs our
attention to the place where the first two "phases" come together ([76],7-8). The second phase begins: "Once again for
the third time the illuminator of knowledge will pass through
in great glory (ΠΑλΙΝ ΟΝ ΥΝΑϹΙΝЄ ΜΠΜЄΖ ϢΟΜЄͲ ΝϹΟΠ
[76],8-9). The statement is difficult to understand since this
is the first time that the illuminator of knowledge has been
mentioned in this tractate.[40]

The problem is not evident in Böhlig's translation. He
translates ΜΠΜЄΖ ϢΟΜЄͲ ΝϹΟΠ as "thirdly,"[41] and understands it to be the third epoch of salvation in the history of
the special race of men.[42] Although they are unnumbered, he
regards the deliverance from the flood and the rescue from the
fire as the unnumbered first and second epochs in this redemptive history. The third numbered epoch is the appearance of
the illuminator who comes to assist in the redemption of the
sons of Noah and especially Ham and Japheth.

This explanation of the problem has the merit of support
from the *Gospel of the Egyptians* (III,*2*)62,24-63,12; (IV,*2*)
74,9-27 which specifically speaks of the great Seth passing
through three "parousiai": flood, conflagration and judgment of
the archons, powers and authorities.[43] Thus there is some
reason to understand these events in the *Apoc. Adam* as succes-
sive stages in the redemption of the special race of men. At

least one must acknowledge that these three events in *Apoc.*
Adam were connected in gnostic mythology, although their connection in *Apoc. Adam* may have been a contrivance of the
redactor.

If, however, as I would argue, the phrase in [76],8 refers
to an action which is being repeated for the third time, i.e.,
to the third passing of the illuminator, then one is able to
see the difficulty with clarity since there is no mention in
the *Apoc. Adam* of two prior "passings" of the illuminator of
knowledge.[44] The first two occurrences of redemption noted by
Böhlig are not, narrowly speaking, manifestations of the
illuminator of knowledge.[45]

The lack of connection between phase one and phase two
becomes even more apparent when one notes that, prior to the
descent of the illuminator of knowledge, there have already
been three events of deliverance in which the special race of
men are preserved ([69],19-25ff.; [71],bottom-[72],9;[46] [75],
17-[76],6), and that the descent of the illuminator does not
signal a "redemption," or at least not a redemption in the
sense of the "flood" and the "fire." Rather, the illuminator
comes for the purpose of leaving in the "world" a witness for
himself, since the special race of men had already been taken
out of the world ([75],17-[76],6). There will be an act of
redemption at a future time ([76],15-23), but that event is
something different and should not be associated with this
"pass" of the illuminator.[47] It seems that one is justified
in recognizing a redactional seam between phase one and phase
two and asking further questions on the basis of it.

There is also a noticeable lack of consistency in setting
between phase two and phase three. Phase two (described above)
seems to be an otherworldly scene depicting the standard gnostic
motif of the divine beings (archons and powers) that hold mankind in slavery. The problem is that, after the "response" of
the kingdoms to the question of the angels and the powers
([77],27-[83],7),[48] this scene and subject matter radically
change. The otherworldly scene with its angels, powers,
archon, and descent of the illuminator so strongly prominent in
phase two, vanishes when we enter phase three.

Phase three (described above) is set in the "historical"
world and idealized. An indefinite group of people (all the
races of the world?) acknowledge their own wickedness ([83],8-
[84],3) and confess the righteousness of those men "who have
known God through a knowledge of the truth" ([83],11-23). One
is compelled to ask: What happened to the archon, powers,
angels and kingdoms? Where is the illuminator? Whence came
the indefinite group of people in [83],9-10, and who are they
exactly? If one insists that the *Apoc. Adam* is a literary
unit, the questions admit of no solution, for the second scene
has simply been replaced by a completely different third scene
that has no connection with the preceding scene in storyline or
actors. Therefore, for these two reasons--a complete break in
the theme or storyline for no apparent reason and the radical
transition in dramatis personae--there appears to be a literary
seam at [83],7 after ΤΗρΟΥ.[49]

As indicated above, phase three was divided as a matter of
convenience. One difficulty with recognizing it as a separate
unit was that it did not maintain a consistent theme or storyline. The scene shifts from the blessing pronounced on the
special race of men ([83],7-[84],3) to a condemnation of those
who have defiled the water of life ([84],4-[85],18). The shift
in scene in itself does not disqualify the phase as a literary
unit. The blessing and judgment motif would actually make a
good concluding unit to the tractate.

The unity of the two sections in phase three becomes more
difficult to maintain when one realizes that each section in
phase three has its own blessing-judgment motif! In section
one (cf. [83],7-[84],3), the indefinite group of people acknowledge that "those men" will live forever, but admit that, because
of their own opposition to the God of truth, they themselves
will die. In section two of phase three ([84],4-[85],18), the
actions of "those over the holy baptism and living water" are
condemned, while the actions of "those men they have persecuted" are approved. Within phase three, the motif of blessing-
judgment occurs two separate times involving at least three and
probably four different groups.

The shift in dramatis personae between section one and two of phase three occurs at [84],3 and [84],4 in a rather dramatic way. The first of the two sections ([83],7-[84],3) is a confession made by the indefinite group of people (ΝΙλλος) in [83],10. In [84],4 a (heavenly) voice suddenly breaks into the narrative and addresses an indefinite "them" (ψαροοΥ).[50] The problem is, to whom does "them" refer? If it fits into the context that follows [84],4 ([84],5-[85],18), the ones addressed by the voice would appear to be the guardians of the holy baptism and the living water, Micheu, Michar and Mnesinous. If it goes with the context that precedes [84],4 ([83],7-[84],3), its antecedent is without doubt the indefinite "people" in [83],10. But if the latter is true, why does the "voice" completely ignore the "people" and abruptly address Micheu, Michar, and Mnesinous? And if ψαροοΥ refers to the three guardians, as it appears to do, how does one explain their sudden appearance and the equally sudden disappearance of the "people"?

One solution is simply to ignore the problem and translate the text as it appears without trying to clarify the identity of the indefinite "them."[51] This solution implies an identification between the three guardians and the "people" of [83],10, and is undoubtedly the effect that was intended by the redactor (see below, pp. 192-94). However, the desired effect is not achieved satisfactorily as the guardians are not an indefinite group of "people" but specific mythological beings with a definite title surely known to the redactor.

I suggest that there is a redactional break following [84],3 which accounts for the sudden change in the actors of the drama. The relative clause ([84],6-8) immediately following the direct address to the three guardians may be a redactional comment intended to clarify the identity of the guardians, Micheu, Michar and Mnesinous, because of their abrupt appearance in the tractate.[52]

In the above discussion on the redactional seams in the body of the tractate, the contents of phases two and three have been discussed. There remains only the necessity of making a

closer examination of the details in phase one. We begin by
observing that phase one ([67],22-[76],7) has the character of
a midrash on the flood narrative. There are four units in this
section ([67],22-[69],10; [70],3-[71],4; [72],15-17; [73],25-27)
that reduce the traditional Genesis flood narrative to bare es-
sentials. Each of these traditional sections is followed by a
gnostic "narrative" interpretation that explains the heretofore
unknown story of the special race in relationship to the
flood.[53] The literary method followed is to narrate briefly
salient motifs from the traditional biblical material and to
incorporate the interpretation of these motifs as a part of the
narrative.[54] Each of the gnostic interpretations ([69],19-
[70],2; [71],8-[72],15; [72],15-[73],24;[55] [73],27-[76],7)
understands its "exegeted" passage as an attempt of the Pantocrator to destroy the special race of men.[56]

In summary, we may say that there appear to be three redactional seams in the main body of the tractate: following
[76],7; in [83],7 (after ⲦⲎⲢⲞⲨ) and following [84],3.[57]
These seams are initially identified by both linguistic and
stylistic problems in the Coptic text. As one examines the
literary units isolated by the redactional seams, it is discovered that the setting, plot and dramatis personae of each
unit are also different.

D. The Redaction History of the *Apoc. Adam*

The recognition of redactional seams in the tractate has
only begun our task. We must now inquire about the relationship of these seams to one another. More specifically, we must
put two questions to the smaller units of material isolated by
those seams: What is their relationship, if any, to one
another? How and why have they taken on their present form and
relationship in the *Apoc. Adam*? That is to say, we must inquire into the redaction history of the *Apoc. Adam*.[58] The
method of reconstructing the original sources that lie behind
the present version of the *Apoc. Adam* and of explaining their
redaction begins by identifying contradictory motifs in the
various divisions of the tractate and separating the divisions

on that basis. It then proceeds to match motifs that correspond closely to motifs in other divisions of the tractate and
concludes by requiring that the finished product have coherence
and verisimilitude.

The attempt to reconstruct the redaction history of the
tractate is hampered to a large extent because the document is
a translation into Coptic of what was originally a Greek *Vorlage*.[59] Since the document was redacted before being translated into Coptic, one would expect that the primary "indicators" normally used to separate sources--i.e., the similarity
and dissimilarity of vocabulary and stylistic peculiarities--
would for the most part be obscured by the process of translation into Coptic. While certain vestiges of the original
vocabulary distinctions between sources might remain after
translation, one could not expect to find a consistent pattern
of vocabulary differences and similarities,[60] and stylistic
peculiarities, if observable at all, would be but a faint echo
of the original Greek *Vorlage*.

However, these indicators are actually part of the broader
concept of "world" that operates in a given unit of literature.
For example, on the basis of the tendencies and the "givens" of
any literary unit, one can project forward or backward to the
broader conceptual framework that supports the unit. In other
words, the "tendencies" and "givens" of the unit evoke in the
reader's mind a certain kind of "world" without which the unit
makes no sense.

One is justified then in comparing the broader projected
framework of one unit to the broader projected framework of
another unit to see if there is harmony or clash. If one unit
does not suit well the "world" of another unit, then the probability is increased that one is dealing with different
traditions.

At its most obvious point, such a clash evidences itself
at the surface level of given texts by differences in vocabulary and style. At its most subtle point, such a clash would
evidence itself in the "projected" unstated "world" from which
the text takes its frame of reference, its meaning. By considering the "world" which provides a frame of reference for

the text, one is merely pushing this same principle (i.e.,
similarity or dissimilarity in vocabulary and style) a step
further into an unverbalized area but an area necessarily as
definite as the surface level of the text, since it is the un-
spoken "world" that gives the text meaning. In fact, no text
is fully understandable until one is able successfully to reconstruct that unverbalized world. Thus, by using the givens
of a text, one is able to roll back the curtain of the concealed world that supports the text. It is on this basis that
we approach the *Apoc. Adam*.

I begin by recognizing some of the dominant motifs in the
first phase of the body of the tractate ([67],22-[76],7). The
special race of men are those who have rejected a dead knowledge ([73],30-[74],2). They are the ones who have come forth
from the knowledge of the great eons and the angels ([71],10-
14; [73],18-20). Once safe from the flood, they shall dwell
six hundred years in a knowledge of imperishability ([72],9).
The sign of their purity is the fact that only the knowledge of
God shall dwell in their hearts ([72],12-15). The shadow of
their power (i.e., the power that comes from their knowledge)
shall protect those who sojourn with them ([73],20-24) from
every unclean desire. They will not be defiled by desire
([73],24; [75],2-4), but will be protected from every evil
thing ([73],23).

These same motifs play an important role in the first half
of phase three ([83],7-[84],3): The people bless "those men"
because they have known God through a knowledge of the truth
([83],10-14). They have stood before the creator in knowledge
of the eternal God ([83],19-21), and because they have not been
corrupted by desire they will live forever ([83],14-16). It
will also be recalled that the motif of knowledge (of the
eternal God) being lost by Adam and Eve was the cohesive thread
in introduction A (64,6-[65],23); [66],12-[67],12), and it was
Adam's desire for Eve that constituted the ultimate act that
resulted in the complete loss of all knowledge of the eternal
God and subjected Adam and Eve to the vicissitudes of mortality
([67],4-12).[61]

If, on the basis of these motifs, introduction A (64,6-
[65],23; [66],12-[67],12), the narrative midrash on Genesis
6-10 (phase one of the main body of the tractate--[67],22-
[76],7) and section one of phase three of the main body of the
tractate ([83],7-[84],3) along with the incipit (64,1-6) and
conclusion A ([85],19-22) are read as one continuous narrative,
it will be discovered that there is a consistent plot and a
connected theme that opens, develops and concludes.[62] In this
narrative, the knowledge of the eternal God that Adam and Eve
lost through desire is preserved in the special race of men who
came from the great eternal knowledge. These men are saved
from perishing in the flood, protected from another threat of
the creator god, rescued from the fire, sulphur, and asphalt
and finally taken from the world to a heavenly dwelling place.
As a result, a great cloud of darkness will descend upon the
descendants of Ham and Japheth. When the special race has been
removed from the world ([75],21-[76],6), those people who remain will acknowledge their wickedness ([83],23-[84],3), confess the righteousness and purity of the special race ([83],8-
23), and accept their fate ([84],2-3).[63]

A similar connection is possible with introduction B
([65],24-[66],12; [67],12-[67],21), and phase two of the main
body of the tractate ([76],8-[83],7). These two units cohere
rather well, and seem to reflect a common theme, suggesting a
single, although incomplete, literary unit.[64] Indeed, [76],8-
[83],7 to a certain extent seems to have been already antici-
pated in the statement made to Adam by the three men ([66],
3-8): "Hear about the aeon and the seed of that man to whom
life has come, he who came from you and Eve." In [76],8-[83],7
we are told about a certain apparently semi-divine being (cf.
[77],16-18), described as the illuminator of knowledge. He
comes to leave fruitbearing trees for himself and to save their
souls (i.e., the group described as fruitbearing trees) from
the day of death. He is opposed by powers, but succeeds in
thwarting them and sharing his glory with those whom he chose.
The generation of those men he has chosen for himself will
shine over the whole aeon. The difference in plot and theme

between source B and source A is evident. In source A, the
spotlight is directed on a special group of people, but in
source B the center of attention is a single person.[65]

Finally, we must consider the redactor's method through
which he attempted to harmonize these two major units, and to
ask what relationship the final section ([84],4-[85],18) has to
the whole. I begin by noting that throughout the *Apoc. Adam*
there are three words used for seed: ⲤⲠⲈⲢⲘⲀ , ⲤⲦⲞⲢⲀ and
ⲋⲣⲟⳓ. With one exception, both ⲋⲣⲟⳓ, used only twice in
the *Apoc. Adam* ([73],2,6), and ⲤⲠⲈⲢⲘⲀ , used seven times in
the *Apoc. Adam* ([72],24; [73],13,25,28; [74],11,17; [76],12),
appear only in what has been identified as the gnostic interpretation to the flood narrative.[66] ⲤⲠⲈⲢⲘⲀ is used once
apart from the midrashic interpretation sections and that is in
source B immediately following the redactional seam in [76],7
where source B is joined with source A. The purpose of ⲤⲠⲈⲢⲘⲀ
here seems to be as a connecting device to smooth over the seam
between the two sections.

For three reasons it has the character of an editorial
device. In the first place, [76],11-13 (Ⲍ̄ⲒⲚⲀ ⲬⲈ . . . ⲒⲀⲫⲈⲐ)
is the only reference in source B to Noah and his sons, and for
that reason the statement clashes with the plot of source B.
Once one has recognized the distinction between source A and
source B, this reference to Noah and his sons is an unexpected
intrusion into the storyline of source B and evokes a mythological structure that is not present at the textual level of
source B, nor discernible in the projected world that makes
source B understandable.[67]

In the second place, in this context there are two object
clauses: [76],11-13 and [76],14-15 (ⲬⲈ... ⲞⲨⲦⲀⲌ). While a
double object clause in Coptic is certainly possible, as used
here it is awkward. One would have expected the two clauses to
have been linked by the conjunctive,[68] or perhaps ⲀⲨⲱ ⲬⲈ,
rather than simply ⲬⲈ . In the third place, the only other use
of Ⲍ̄ⲒⲚⲀ ⲬⲈ in the codex is also identifiable as a redactional
device.[69] It appears in *Apoc. Adam* in source B near the conclusion of the section of the stories about the illuminator
([82],18-19). For two reasons the second Ⲍ̄ⲒⲚⲀ ⲬⲈ clause

appears to be a redactional comment. In the first place, it
deviates from what is recognizable as a highly stylized structure in the statements of the first twelve kingdoms,[70] and, in
the second place, it adds a pejorative character to the concluding line in the first twelve kingdoms. The purpose clause
disposes one to read as a negative motif the statement about
"coming to the water." In the first twelve kingdoms, this expression was understood simply as a neutral part of the answer
describing the appearance of the illuminator.[71]

The simple redactional attachment of the purpose clause
([82],18-19) to the conclusion of what was for the redactor the
final incorrect answer of the powers[72] effectively negated the
expression about the water-appearance not only in the thirteenth kingdom but in all the preceding kingdom statements.[73]
In other words, the redactor prepares for what he considers to
be the true explanation of the illuminator's appearance (i.e.,
the explanation of the "kingless generation") by identifying
all explanations describing his appearance as "coming to the
water" as a misunderstanding.[74]

The last word for seed that is used, СΠΟΡΔ, occurs ten
times in all parts of the tractate. It is found in both introductions ([65],4,8; [66],4). In the midrash on Genesis, it
occurs between the paraphrase of the biblical material and its
interpretation ([69],12; [71],5). It occurs at the end of the
section of the threat of fire, sulphur and asphalt just before
the redactional seam ([76],7). It is also found in the appearance stories ([79],16-17), between the end of source B and the
beginning of the last part of source A ([83],4), and in both
conclusions ([85],22,29).

I notice a very subtle difference in the use of these
words for seed. СΠΕΡΜΔ and бροб are always used in a
natural sense (that is, with respect to human reproduction),[75]
and always with reference to Noah, Ham, Japheth and Shem.[76]
СΠΟΡΔ, on the other hand, with one possible exception
([79],16-17), is used with theological overtones in the sense
of a special kind of seed, that is, of the seed of a special
race of men.[77] This phenomenon does not seem to be accidental.
With few exceptions, the references to СΠΟΡΔ have both a

polemical and explanatory character that give them the appearance of redactional comments. Compare the following passages—
as a part of a redactional comment: [65],3-9, [69],11-18,
[71],4-8, [76],6-7, [83],4-7; as an integral part of a larger
context: [66],4, [79],16-17, [85],22,29.[78]

I would argue that sources A and B were brought together
by a gnostic redactor who added section [84],4-[85],18, conclusion B ([85],22b-31), and the polemical passages containing
ⲤⲠⲞⲣⲁ, cited above as redactional. The redactor's purpose is
to identify the special race (ⲤⲠⲞⲣⲁ), i.e., his own community,
as the holy seed ([85],29) that preserved a special knowledge
([85],26). This eternal knowledge, lost through the "fall" of
Adam and Eve (64,24-28),[79] was regained by Adam through the
special revelation of "three men" (introduction B), and passed
on by Adam to Seth ([67],14-21), and then by Seth to his descendants ([85],20-22). The redactor describes the divine
source of the knowledge ([65],3-9) and indicates that it had
been preserved, and continued through the special race of men
descended from the ⲤⲠⲞⲣⲁ ([69],11-15). These men were
threatened with destruction through the flood ([69],11-15)
because they dared to oppose the creator god ([71],4-8), and
they will continue to struggle against those who have surren-
dered to the power of the evil god and have taken his name
"upon the water" ([83],4-7).

In his final statement ([84],4-[85],18), the redactor
argues that his community has the true understanding of baptism.
In fact, receiving the secret knowledge, termed the words of
imperishability and truth ([85],10-18), that has been preserved
and passed on *is* the holy baptism ([85],22-29). This holy baptism of eternal knowledge is only available through the redactor's community. It has not been written in books, but has
been passed on through divine means to the holy seed ([85],
1-9), and preserved through their faithfulness ([85],3-4).
Since this proper understanding of baptism has been preserved
only in the redactor's community, those practicing water baptism practice it in ignorance, and thereby defile true gnosis
baptism ([84],5-23). They have even persecuted those who have
the true knowledge ([84],23-24).

This redactional analysis of the text takes its many
anomalies seriously and attempts to make some sense of them.
In some cases it clears up ambiguities in the tractate. For
example, it explains the contradictory use of the title "god
of the aeons." Most students of the *Apoc. Adam* have, no doubt,
already recognized and pondered this particular problem: How
can the tractate apply this same title to both the demiurge
([74],26-27) and the eternal God ([85],4-5) with no sense of
discontinuity? The solution is made possible by the source
analysis. Apparently the rather unsophisticated redactor simply
failed to adjust his *Vorlage* (source A, [74],26-27) to his own
theology ([85],4-5) at this point.[80]

It will perhaps be objected that we can't expect gnostic
texts to be "logical" or "consistent" as a twentieth-century
product of a basically nonmythological, technological culture
might judge logicality or consistency. Any attempt to super-
impose contemporary western standards of logic on ancient gnostic texts is an incorrect procedure. The *Thunder, Perfect Mind*
([VI,2]13-21) is an example in the extreme. This text certainly
breaks with what one would judge to be accustomed patterns of
logicality. For example:

> For I am knowledge and ignorance.
> I am shame and boldness.
> I am shameless; I am ashamed.
> I am strength and I am fear.
> I am war and peace.
> Give heed to me.
> I am the one who is disgraced, and the great one.[81]

When one applies contemporary standards of logic to *Thund.*,
one is tempted to discount it as nonsensical gibberish. On
closer examination, however, one observes that there is a logic
or rationale to the text. For example, it is consistent in its
use of antithetical or paradoxical statements and in this sense,
even by contemporary standards, can be called "logical."

The problem, then, is not logic versus lack of logic in
ancient texts, but a lack of an understanding of the inherent
logic of the text. The exegete's task is not to judge the text
on the basis of his own understanding of logic and reality, but
to discover the key that admits him to the inner logic of the

text, that is, to discover its meaning.   I have tried to show
that the key that admits one to the inner logic of the *Apoc.*
Adam is the recognition that it is the result of a redactional
process, and not a very polished one at that.   What follows is
an attempt to understand the several layers of meaning in the
text on that basis.

[1]See below, pp. 231-33.

[2]See below, p. 261.

[3]That only these verses from the LXX are reflected by the text is evident from the omission of any reference to the cosmic creation (Gen 1:1-19, 2:1-6), animal creation (Gen 1:20-25, 2:18-20) and the events surrounding the tree of the knowledge of good and evil (Gen 2:16-17, 3:2-25). The latter motif commonly appears in gnostic texts in reverse form; that is, the enlightenment of Adam and Eve (Gen 3:8) is a good thing. See Birger A. Pearson, "Jewish Haggadic Traditions in *The Testimony of Truth* from Nag Hammadi (CG IX,*3*)," *Ex Orbe Religionum: Studia Geo Widengren* (*Numen* Supplement 21; Leiden: E. J. Brill, 1972) 457-70. The author would scarcely have omitted this favorite gnostic *topos* unless it were far removed from his literary purpose. This appears to be the situation. His primary objective is to describe the separation of the primordial androgyne by the demiurge (cf. *Gos. Phil* [II,*3*]68, 22-24; 70,9-11), and only Gen 2:7, 21-22 and 4:1 allude to that event. The biblical order of these verses is presupposed by the text in the *Apoc. Adam*. The creation of Adam as a living soul (Gen 2:7) is already presupposed by the midrash. [66],12-23 indicates that Adam's creation as a living soul had already occurred and is assumed at 64,6-11. 64,6-19 describes the "happy days" of the unified androgyne Adam-Eve prior to the separation, that is, prior to Gen 2:21-22. 64,20-[65],3; [65],9-23; [66],12-30 describe the separation of Gen 2:21-22 and the resultant devolution of Adam-Eve. [66],31-[67],12 describes the sexual reunification of the separated aeons, Adam and Eve, on the basis of desire as described in Gen 4:1.

[4]The author's purpose in the section is to show that the "glory" and "knowledge" lost by Adam at creation have been preserved in the "great generation" (64,20-[65],3).

[5]See CH 1.18-19. The parallel is striking. Originally man was bisexual and was later divided into male and female entities. The cause of death is carnal desire. On the motif of bisexuality, see Clem. *exc. Thdot*. 1.21.1-3; Hipp. *Ref*. 5.6.5, 7.14-15, 8.4; *Eugnostos* (III,*5*)76,21-77,4; *Gos. Phil*. (II,*3*)70,24-26; and Mircea Eliade, *Patterns in Comparative Religion* (New York: Sheed and Ward, 1958) 420-25. *Orig. World* (II,*5*)113,24-25 also refers to the creation of the first man as an androgynous being.

[6]In only two places in the entire section is Adam or Eve mentioned as actor without the other: 64,6-11: "That she had seen in the aeon..." and [66],31-[67],4: "Then I was defiled in thought through my madness and I knew a sweet desire for your mother."

[7]For example, in five instances, the text has used a singular where one would have expected a plural: "our heart" instead of the expected "our hearts" (64,24; [65],23; [66],14, 18) and "our life" instead of "our lives" ([67],11). These do appear to be slips on the part of the translator; cf. [66],24-25: "our eyes." Compare Beltz for an explanation of the shift in actors.

[8]See n. 6 above. [66],31-[67],4 can be explained on the basis of the theology of the segment. At this point in the narrative, the androgyne Adam-Eve had been separated into two separate aeons. In order for the author to express the idea of sexual desire, he had to treat them as independent units. The other occurrence is not so easily explained (64,6-11). One would have expected the text to read ЄTѦTNNѦY , "that we had seen." It is possible that the use of the singular feminine actor expression suggesting Eve as the one who preserved primal revelation is an echo of that tradition found elsewhere; see *Orig. World* (II,5)115,31-116,8; *Hyp. Arch.* (II,4)89,10-17.

[9]Schenke identifies the three men as Jesseus, Mazareus and Jessedekeus ("Zum Gegenwärtigen Stand der Erforschung der Nag-Hammadi-Handschriften," *Koptologische Studien in der DDR* [Halle-Wittenberg: Martin-Luther-Universität, 1965] 127). This identification may be correct. In the theology of the redactor, these three figures were conceived as revelation bringers ([85],22-31); see below, pp. 202-203.

[10]The appearance of Adam as an individual actor is significant. It has been shown that section A, with one unexplained exception, always included Eve with Adam in the actor expression. On the other hand, in section B, Adam is the only actor and is addressed in the singular. The only mention of Eve describes her and Adam as the parents of "the seed" ([66],1-8).

[11]The shift is abrupt because no foundation has been laid for the new scene. Suddenly, the garden setting, Eve, and the use of the plural actor expression vanish and Adam is receiving three "guests." For the argument that the text reads like a vision that comes in a dream, see pp. 24-25.

[12]See Coptic text below, p. 261.

[13][67],2-11 is the statement describing the final result of Adam's devolution from original androgynous unity into two separate aeons. They had lost the knowledge of the eternal God and were subject to human desires and frailties. In this unenlightened condition, how could Adam "know" that he was under the authority of death and then pass on to Seth a secret revelation that he had supposedly lost? Further, if it was necessary for Adam to receive new revelation after his admitted ignorance in [65],16-23 (this is apparently why the three men appear to him at [65],24-[67],21), why should not there also be a necessity for further revelation after Adam's admitted ignorance in [67],1-11?

[14]The redactor intended to use section B, the narrative of the revelation of the three men, to show how Adam had regained his knowledge of the eternal God. Since section A recounts the story of Adam's devolution, eventual servitude and loss of knowledge, it afforded the redactor no basis for Adam's revelation to Seth. In it Adam ends up ignorant and subject to fleshly vicissitudes. Thus, the redactor needed some way for Adam to regain his lost knowledge, and therefore was compelled to provide the narrative about the revelation of the three men. Fortunately, he inserted the segment in a careless "wooden" way, i.e., on the basis of catchwords. Had he added it after [67],11, it would have blended much better. The seam would have then been less obvious, and far more difficult to detect.

[15]Böhlig, 88. See also Alexander Böhlig, "Die Adam-apokalypse aus Codex V von Nag Hammadi als Zeugnis jüdisch-iranischer Gnosis," *OrChr* 48 (1964) 44-49.

[16]However, this would not explain why Eve is apparently aware of what takes place in Adam's dream ([66],9-14). If Adam is dreaming, it is his dream and Eve should not react on the basis of what Adam dreamed. If Eve sees the three men and reacts on the basis of what she saw and heard, then Adam must not be dreaming. But it is nonsense to have Adam dream and to have Eve in the real world respond to his dream with no prior knowledge of it.

[17]Cf. Beltz, 57.

[18]See the examples gathered by Hans Jonas, *Gnosis und spätantiker Geist* (2nd ed.; Göttingen: Vandenhoeck & Ruprecht, 1955) 113-39; idem, *The Gnostic Religion* (2nd ed. rev.; Boston: Beacon Hill, 1963) 68-91. See below, pp. 97-109.

[19]See above, n. 14.

[20]For two reasons I suspect that the section is traditional material that the redactor used for his purposes without much adaptation. (1) It does not exactly suit the situation for which he had employed it. If he had written it himself, he could have easily eliminated the problems that set it in tension with section A. (2) Section B has certain affinities with another part of the text. See below, pp. 97-115.

[21]As Jonas has indicated, it is not necessary that the gnostic "call" to the man in ignorance cite the content of revelation. The "call" may itself be the whole message (*Gnostic Religion*, 80). Here the content is specified but not elaborated upon.

[22]CH 1.27. English translation by Walter Scott, *Hermetica* (4 vols.; London: Dawsons, 1924-1936) 1.133 (reprint, 1968). For the text, see A. D. Nock and A.-J. Festugière, *Corpus Hermeticum* (4 vols.; Paris: Société d'édition, Les Belles Lettres, 1945) 1.16.

[23]With respect to [65],3-9, see below, pp. 185-86.

[24]For example: "seed of great aeons" ([65],3-5); "the seed of the great generation" ([65],8); the "name of that man" ([65],7).

[25]Beltz (195) has also independently recognized that the tractate has two different conclusions. What is here referred to as conclusion A, he calls the original conclusion to the tractate.

[26]See below, p. 241.

[27]See below, p. 287.

[28]Conclusion A corresponds to the incipit (64,2-6a) which promised revelation (ἀποκάλυψις), and to the title (64,1) and subscript title ([85],32), both of which use the term "revelation" (ἀποκάλυψις). All three--conclusion A, incipit and subscript title--are similar in their simplicity. By contrast, conclusion B refers to the secret (ἀπόκρυφον) knowledge and is theologically more sophisticated.

[29]Cf. Beltz, 197. Beltz is quite right that this conclusion provides the basis for an understanding of the text, but it is important that one recognize that the conclusion is appropriate only for understanding the text in its final redacted state. There are several levels at which the material must be examined.

[30]See below, pp. 192-201.

[31]The concluding line to twelve of the explanations, "in this way he came to the water," could possibly make reference to baptism in the understanding of the redactor. No one has yet understood it in this way (Beltz, 144), but then the questions being put to the kingdoms section ask after its original Sitz im Leben rather than its setting in the understanding of the redactor. See below, pp. 192-201.

[32]See pp. 39-40.

[33]One cannot help wondering why the redactor retained conclusion A at all. It is apparently nonessential. He actually accomplished the same thing with his own special conclusion. All conclusion A does is provide a summary ending to the tractate, and his interpretative conclusion also does this. Also in his arrangement of the material it is necessary for him to insert the A conclusion inside his own concluding statement in a "scissors and paste" way. It would have been simpler to have dropped it. However, see below, p. 217 n. 12.

[34]If for no other reason, this calls into question Beltz's understanding of the document as a textbook (*Lehrschrift*) for beginning gnostics (cf. Beltz, 178, 200).

[35]Böhlig (87) divides the main body of the tractate into three sections roughly paralleling the present division. In addition, his two major sections to the tractate with slight differences correspond closely to my division between the introductory section and main body of the tractate. Kasser's division is similar to the present division in its broad outlines ("Textes gnostiques: Remarques," 91).

Böhlig:	*Kasser:*	*Present Division:*
I. 64,5-[67],14	I. 64,1-[77],27	I. Introductions:
II. [67],14-[85],18	[83],8-[85],31	64,6-[67],21
A. [67],22-[73],24	II. [77],27-[83],8	II. Main Body:
B. [73],25-[76],7		[67],22-[85],18
C. [76],8-[77],27		A. [67],22-[76],7
Excursus: [77],27-[83],4		B. [76],8-[83],7
D. [83],4-[85],18		C. [83],7-[85],18
III. [85],19-31		III. Conclusions:
		[85],19-31

[36]Behind the question of the archon lies the classical boast of the demiurge. See *Gos. Eg.* (III,*2*)58,23-59,1; *Treat*. *Seth* (VII,*2*)53,30-31; 64,18-31; *Ap. John* (II,*1*)11,19-22; 13,8-9; *Trim. Prot.* (XIII,*1**)43,33-44,2; *Hyp. Arch.* (II,*4*)86,27-32; 94,19-26; *Orig. World* (II,*5*)103,9-15.

[37]The stories are generally clearly marked out by a decorative device in the margin at the beginning of each story and by a blank space between the end of one story and the beginning of the next. These phenomena occur with regularity through the section. The pattern is as follows.

	Space	*Decoration*
Between 1 and 2	none	none
2 and 3	none	none
3 and 4	yes	(lacuna)
4 and 5	yes	yes
5 and 6	none	(lacuna)
6 and 7	yes	yes
7 and 8	yes	yes
8 and 9	(lacuna)	yes
9 and 10	yes	yes
10 and 11	yes	yes
11 and 12	yes	yes
12 and 13	yes	yes
13 and the kingless generation	none	none

[38]I do not mean to imply that the material forms a cohesive unit but only wish to note that it is not immediately recognizable as belonging to either phase one or phase two.

[39]Phase three is a different problem; see below, pp. 32-33.

[40]The tractate does use the word "illuminator" in the plural (ΝΙϕⲰⳞⲦⲎⲣ) at [75],14-15 (see the note at [75],11-16).

[41]Kasser (325) translates ⲙ̄ⲡⲙⲉϩ ϣⲟⲙⲉⲧ ⲛ̄ⲥⲟⲡ correctly as "for the third time," but incorrectly regards the appearance of the three men ([65],26-[66],12), and the transformation of the great men ([71],8-15) as the first two appearances of the illuminator. Beltz (122) translates correctly, but does not speculate on the first two appearances of the illuminator.

[42]But if we may exempt the statement of the kingless generation from consideration for the moment (since it may also be redactional), the special race does not appear at all in phase two!

[43]This parallel in the *Gos. Eg.* is quite significant. The statement reflects the kind of understanding of the events in the *Apoc. Adam* to which a correct translation of ⲙ̄ⲡⲙⲉϩ ϣⲟⲙⲉⲧ ⲛ̄ⲥⲟⲡ would lead one. Understanding this appearance of the illuminator as his third time to "pass through" naturally inclines one to look for his two previous appearances. Thus the redemption from the flood and the preservation through the fire could have been understood by an ancient exegete as appearance one and appearance two or, conversely, by indicating that the illuminator was making his third appearance, an ancient redactor could have intended that the first two events be understood as appearance one and appearance two. The first situation would assume the priority of the *Apoc. Adam* in the tradition history and the latter situation would assume the priority of the *Gos. Eg.*

[44]The parallel from the *Gos. Eg.* quite specifically speaks of the one figure, Seth, passing through three separate trials on three separate occasions, and this is what one would expect in the *Apoc. Adam* on the basis of [76],8.

[45]What I am arguing is that all three events must be viewed narrowly as specific acts of the illuminator, since this is the way [76],8-11 predisposes one to see them. At [76],8-11, the text implies that the first two acts of redemption are acts of the illuminator when it says that the illuminator passes through "for the third time." However, in the text, the first two redemptive acts have nothing to do with the "passing through" of an illuminator. They are only related generally to the third event as two preceding acts of redemption. Therefore, if the text at [76],8-11 specifically requires the first two events of redemption to be acts of the illuminator and they are not, then the essential unity between phase one and phase two is seriously in doubt.

[46]Cf. Schottroff, "Animae naturaliter salvandae," 71 n. 17; Beltz, 93. At this point (bottom of Coptic p. [71]), the text is fragmentary so it is difficult to say anything about the threat against the special race with certainty (however, see my conjectural reconstruction of [71],27-30), but it certainly appears on the top of Coptic p. [72] ([72],1-15) that a redemptive act has previously taken place. The special race is released, taken to a special land, and supplied with a holy dwelling place

where they remain for 600 years. In the first event of redemption, the special race is taken to the place where the spirit
of life dwells ([69],18-24); in the third, it is taken above
the aeons where they will be with the holy angels. One might
make a case for a difference among the three events on the basis that in what I have here called the second event the special
race is not "taken out of the world" as in the first and third.
But at this point we are debating the *character* of the redemption and not whether it actually is an act of redemption. If
the character is different, it could account for the fact that
the redactor failed to recognize it as an event of redemption,
or did not count it so because of its difference. Therefore,
since he recognized only two events (flood and fire), he was
compelled by his theology to add the third--the judgment of the
archons. Cf. the three periods of world destruction of the
Mandaeans: sword, fire and flood; Mark Lidzbarski, *Das Johannesbuch der Mandäer* (Giessen: Töpelmann, 1915) 93.

[47]This redemptive act takes on characteristics of the
Eschaton (cf. with [76],17-20). However, cf. Beltz, 125. He
has made a good argument for understanding "day of death" as
the day of the individual's death. In either case, however, it
is a future event.

[48]The identity of the "kingdoms" is a problem. It is
reasonable to assume that they were also a part of the "heavenly" structure ruled over by the archon of the powers, i.e.,
archon, powers, angels and then kingdoms (cf. CH Asclepius
3.19b,27c). Each of these subordinated deities tried to answer
the questions; see below, pp. 137-41.

[49][83],7-8 can be easily understood with what follows as
the basis for the cry and confession that follow ([83],8ff.).
Darkness is a sign of the *Eschaton* (see parallels at [83],8).

[50]Note that the unexplained intrusion of a "heavenly"
voice is a common feature in apocalyptic texts. See, for example, Rev 1:10; 11:12; 12:10; 14:2,13; *2 Apoc. Bar.* 8:1.

[51]All other translators follow this procedure. Beltz (187)
has recognized the problem but is unable to offer a satisfactory
solution. In a footnote, he suggests an emendation of the text,
but does not follow it himself.

[52]The relative clause ([84],6-8) is a problem. It functions as an explanatory clause in the third person where one
expects direct address in the second person. In its present
context, the clause appears to have vocative force; that is, the
heavenly voice addresses by name the ones to whom the clause is
directed. However, if this were the case, one would have expected the clause ([84],6-8) to read: ⲚⲦⲰⲦⲚ ⲈⲦϨIϪⲚ ⲠIϪⲰKⲘ
rather than ⲚⲎ ⲈⲦϨIϪⲚ ⲠIϪⲰKⲘ as it appears in the text.
Böhlig (116) notes the problem, but offers no solution, and
Kasser (331) emends the text. Schenke (cols. 33-34) suggests
that it should be read as a nominal sentence: "Micheu, Michar
and Mnesinous are those who are over the holy baptism and the

living water." However, he regards "the sentence" as presently
displaced from its original position which he thinks to be after
line [84],18 (Beltz translates as a nominal sentence--see p.
25,1). Actually, the clause seems to be a literal Coptic translation of the Greek *Vorlage*. The use of a modifying relative
clause in apposition to a vocative is a common Greek construction; cf. Mark 15:29 and Matt 6:9. The *Vorlage* must have read
as follows: οἱ ἐπὶ τῷ βαπτίσματι τῷ ἁγίῳ καὶ τῷ ὕδατι τῷ ζῶντι.
The use of a second (unnecessary) ϪⲈ ([84],8) is unexpected
and suggests that the clause is actually a scribal insertion.
If we understand the relative clause ([84],6-8) as a marginal
note which some scribe introduced into the body of the tractate
along with the second ϪⲈ ([84],8) in order to pick up again
the direct address that had begun in [84],5, only to be broken
up by the relative clause in [84],6-8, the problem is resolved.
Micheu, Michar and Mnesinous are addressed by the heavenly
voice in [84],5-6, a later scribe--because he sensed the dis-
sonance of their abrupt appearance--clarifies the identity of
the three guardians in [84],6-8, and in [84],8 (ϪⲈ ⲈⲦⲂⲈ) the
direct address is again picked up.

[53]Cf. A. G. Wright (*The Literary Genre: Midrash* [New York:
Alba House, 1967] 58-59) describes rabbinic midrashim as having
three literary structures that he termed exegetical midrashim,
homiletic midrashim and narrative midrashim. The form of the
midrash in the *Apoc. Adam* is identical to that which Wright
describes as "narrative midrashim."

> These works exemplify what Geza Vermes has called "the
> rewritten Bible" type of midrash: a completely re-
> written biblical narrative embellished with legends
> and non-biblical traditions....In this type the
> interpretative material is not given at the side of
> the Scripture text, as it were, but is worked right
> into the biblical text to form a continuous narrative.

Cf. Geza Vermes, *Scripture and Tradition in Judaism* (Leiden:
E. J. Brill, 1961) 67-95.

[54]For the biblical passages corresponding to these traditional sections, see the following:

[67],22-[69],11	- Gen 6:6-18	(LXX)
[70],3-6	- Gen 7:22-24	(LXX)
[70],6-[71],4	- Gen 8:1-19	(LXX)
[72],15-17	- Gen 9:1-2, 18-19	(LXX)
[73],25-27	- Gen 10:2-6	(LXX)

[55]In this gnostic interpretation, the traditional material
and interpretation have become so closely intertwined that the
traditional material is an essential literary part of the interpretation rendering impossible a convenient separation between
traditional material and interpretation as we have it in the
first two segments of the midrash. The first two sentences
([72],15-17) are modelled on Gen 9:1-2,18-19), and to this extent are recognizable as paraphrase. However, they are also
essential to the passage that follows and to this extent they
must be included with the interpretation.

[56]The pattern is as follows:

Narration	Interpretation
[67],22-[69],11	[69],19-[70],2
[70],3-[71],4	[71],8-[72],15
[72],15-17	[72],15-[73],24 (Gen 9:25-27)
[73],25-27	[73],25-[76],7

At one point, Beltz has recognized both the logical continuity of the paraphrase and the essentially different character of the narrative interpretation. He calls [71],9-[72],14 (corresponding to my gnostic interpretation, [71],8-[72],15) a *Zwischentext* that separates two sections that logically belong together, i.e., [71],4-8 and [72],15-20. See Beltz, 87 and 89.

[57]This division of the text does not include the section of stories on the origin of the illuminator. This section in itself is a difficult problem. On the basis of form alone, it appears to be separable from its context (cf. Kasser's observations [317]). There also seems to be some evidence of redactional development in certain of the stories. For example, on the basis of a comparison with Kasser's "ideal form," the last two narratives may have been subjected to editorial activity. The collection of narratives is understandable in its context as a response to the questions of the powers, but as a response it exceeds the limits of the question by answering far more than the questions ask. One can only conclude that the setting is artificial and not original. See below for further discussion, pp. 115-19.

[58]The term "redaction history" (*Redaktionsgeschichte*) was coined by Willi Marxsen in 1954 in connection with a discussion of Conzelmann's *Theology of St. Luke*. Whereas the emphasis of NT research had been on the small isolated units that made up the Synoptic Gospels (*Formgeschichte*), Conzelmann's work emphasized the Gospel of Luke as a whole unit. See Joachim Rohde, *Rediscovering the Teaching of the Evangelists* (trans. D. M. Barton; Philadelphia: Westminster, 1968) 9-11. Rohde states (14):

> The most important discovery of redaction criticism which goes beyond form criticism is that it is not the gospels as a whole which must be claimed as composite material but only their content, whilst the redaction of it, that is to say, its grouping, its composition and arrangement into a definite geographical and chronological framework with quite different theological viewpoints, must be regarded as the work of the evangelist.

[59]There are a number of indications of this in the text. First, there are several passages in the Coptic text that can be explained only on the basis of a Greek *Vorlage*. See the notes to the following passages in the translation: [65],22-23; [83],14-15; [84],3; [65],9; [71],4-8. In several cases, the biblical text used by the *Apoc. Adam* can best be explained as being the LXX: 64,2-4; [72],17; [73],26-27. And in two instances, Greek case endings, rare in Coptic, have been

preserved: [80],6 and [81],3. However, see Beltz (181),
following Schenke (col. 33), who incorrectly believes that the
fourteen stories about the illuminator were originally composed
in Coptic and cites as support the fact that there are few
Greek conjunctions in the section.

[60]Vocabulary differences and similarities should be preserved in the Greek words used by the translator to the extent
that they had become loan words in Coptic. However, even here
one should be prepared for inconsistency. See below, n. 66.

[61]See the discussion above on introductory segment A.

[62]See source A in Part Two.

[63]It is to be admitted that the motifs of "knowledge" and
"desire" are common gnostic motifs, and are to be found in most
gnostic texts. Further, these general *topoi* are also found in
all the other sections of the *Apoc. Adam*. However, I am not
arguing here that these units are from a single source on the
basis of the common motifs of knowledge and desire. I am arguing that these segments that I have brought together employ the
motifs within a distinctive framework that is not operative in
what will be described as source B. In other words, source B
material does not suit well the framework that gives source A
meaning. This should become evident in the discussion that
follows.

[64]See source B in Part Two.

[65]The abbreviated character of source B is interesting and
will be discussed below, pp. 119-22.

[66]Why the text shifts from ⲥⲡⲉⲣⲙⲁ to ϭⲣⲟϭ is perplexing
since the text regularly uses ⲥⲡⲉⲣⲙⲁ in these interpretative
sections. It seems to me that there are only four possible
explanations: (1) There was a different Greek word in the *Vorlage* and the Coptic translator simply translated it with a word
different from ⲥⲡⲉⲣⲙⲁ. This is an appealing possibility, but
I can detect no compelling reason for a different Greek word at
this point. It is true that ϭⲣⲟϭ is only used in the speech of
Shem. It could be that the text wishes to distinguish between
the seed of Shem (ϭⲣⲟϭ), and that of Ham and Japheth (ⲥⲡⲉⲣⲙⲁ).
However, note that in Noah's challenge to his progeny he uses
the word ⲥⲡⲉⲣⲙⲁ in referring to all three of his children,
Ham, Japheth and Shem. (2) The editorial change from ⲥⲡⲉⲣⲙⲁ
to ϭⲣⲟϭ was made by the Coptic redactor-translator for some
particular reason not immediately evident. Although that possibility cannot be excluded, I think it to be unlikely since
all indications are that the text was redacted before translation into Coptic. (3) The change from ⲥⲡⲉⲣⲙⲁ to ϭⲣⲟϭ was
made by the Coptic translator for no particular reason--an
accidental emending of the text. Since ϭⲣⲟϭ and ⲥⲡⲉⲣⲙⲁ were
synonyms in his Coptic, he simply decided to use ϭⲣⲟϭ. Because
of the absence of any detectable theological motive for the
change and the regularity of ⲥⲡⲉⲣⲙⲁ throughout the remainder

of the interpretations to the flood narrative, this seems to be
the most probable explanation. (4) Of course, there is always
the possibility that what seems to be a regular and systematic
use of ⲤⲠⲈⲢⲘⲀ throughout the interpretation sections is actually illusionary and accidental. In other words, the Greek
Vorlage did not regularly use any particular word. The Coptic
translator simply selected the word ⲤⲠⲈⲢⲘⲀ (being a loan-
word in Coptic from Greek; thus it was actually a Coptic word)
to translate whatever Greek words were used. If this were the
case, then one would also have to attribute the regular use of
ⲤⲠⲞⲢⲀ (see below) to the Coptic translator. This I feel to
be highly unlikely since several of the passages that can be
explained only on the basis of projecting a Greek *Vorlage* occur
precisely in these redactional sections. This argues that
these sections reflect a literal rendering of the Greek *Vorlage*
and suggests that the term ⲤⲠⲞⲢⲀ belongs to a level of the
tradition earlier than the Coptic translator. The most plau-
sible explanation for the change from ⲤⲠⲈⲢⲘⲀ to ϨⲢⲞϬ seems
to be number three discussed above.

[67]However, on the basis of *Gos. Eg.* (III,2)63,4ff., one
could argue that the flood *motif*, at least, is part of the textual level of source B, assuming that before its redaction
source B narrated in expanded form the three "passings" of the
illuminator, a tradition that appears in *Gos. Eg.* only as a
brief reference.

[68]Till, §322.

[69]However, note that it is reconstructed by Bohlig (20)
at [18],12.

[70]The following formal analysis covers only the statements
of the thirteen kingdoms. The kingless generation has little
formal similarity to the thirteen kingdoms and for that reason
is excluded from consideration here. Each of the thirteen
kingdom statements has an identical introductory formula: "The
--- kingdom says about him." The statements of the kingdoms
are highly stylized into a four-unit structure. Although there
are some variations and differences, all statements appear to
be basically the same. The structure is as follows.

    1. A statement of birth:
       "He came from...", (kingdoms 1-5,7-8,12).
       Kingdom 6: "She...gave birth to him."
       Kingdom 9: "He was born."
       Kingdom 10: "He was born."
       Kingdom 13: "Every birth of their ruler is a word."
       The statement is lacking in Kingdom 11.

    2. A statement about nourishing:
       "He was nourished..." (kingdoms 1-3,12).
       Kingdom 4: "When he had been nourished."
       Kingdom 6: "The angels of the flower garden nourished
                 him."
       Kingdom 8: "The angels who were above the cloud
                 nourished him."

Kingdom 9: "The angels who were over the desire nour-
          ished him."
Kingdom 11: "The angel nourished him in that place."
The statement is lacking in kingdoms 5,7,10,13.

3. A statement about receiving glory and power:
"He received glory and power..." (kingdoms 1,3-10,12,13).
Kingdom 2: "He received glory and strength."
The statement is lacking in kingdom 11.

4. A statement about "coming to the water":
"In this way he came to the water" (kingdoms 1-13).

Cf. Kasser's five-unit structure ("Textes gnostiques: Remarques,"
92). What Kasser understands as the third unit in the structure should actually be included as part of what he calls the
second unit. It will be observed that, while there are slight
variations elsewhere, in the fourth unit of the structure there
is no variation. Therefore, the introduction of the purpose
clause following the thirteenth kingdom is quite unusual (see
below, n. 74). Note also the formal similarity to *Zost.* (VIII,
1)129,12-17; see p. 197 below.

[71]In its original Sitz im Leben, the concluding line to
the stories about the illuminator could have had a meaning
different than "birth" or "appearance." However, in its present setting there can be little doubt that the intention of the
redactor is that it be understood as an explanation of the
appearance of the illuminator. See Schenke (col. 33) and
Beltz (179-80).

[72]While the kingless generation is different in form from
the thirteen kingdoms, it is by no means certain that it is a
composition of the redactor; but see below, pp. 118-19, 200-201.

[73]The redactor intends to reject the first thirteen explanations given by the "kingdoms" as inadequate since they
reflect the faulty misunderstanding of the deceived powers (cf.
George MacRae, "The Coptic Gnostic Apocalypse of Adam," *HeyJ* 6
[January, 1965] 30-31).

[74]One might object that, since the purpose clause appears
only in the thirteenth kingdom, it is intended to negate only
the statement of the thirteenth kingdom. This is possible, but
for several reasons unlikely. In the first place, if the
clause negated the statement of this kingdom only and was an
essential part of the statement, it should have appeared in the
first unit of the structure as follows: "Every birth of their
ruler is a word. And this word received a mandate in that
place in order that the desire of these powers might be satisfied." All the other statements do it this way. If the purpose clause is an essential part of the thirteenth kingdom, it
would be the only qualifying statement in all thirteen kingdoms
that follows unit four in the structure (see above).
In the second place, this clause is the only indication in
the text that a statement of the kingless generation is intended
as a contrast. If we limit that contrast to a juxtaposing of
kingdom thirteen and the kingless generation, what are we to do

with the first twelve. Should they not also be included in the
contrast? Because of the close similarity in verbal expression
and form, all thirteen of the kingdoms must be linked together
and therefore must be included in the contrast to the kingless
generation. One indication that this interpretation of the intention of the redactor is correct is that the statement about
the "coming to the water" does not appear in the statement of
the kingless generation. If it were simply a neutral expression for "birth" or "appearance," it could have easily been
used in the kingless generation, making it conform more closely
to the form of the first thirteen kingdoms. The fact that it
is not used in the kingless generation, and the fact that
"coming to the water" is defined as "fulfilling the desire of
the powers" in the thirteenth kingdom, de-neutralize the expression and make it a bad concept. And if it is a negative
expression in the thirteenth kingdom, it must also be so in the
remaining twelve kingdoms, and if it is negative in the first
twelve kingdoms, why would they not also be included in the
contrast?

In the third place, the clause states that "he came to the
water in order that the desire of *these* powers might be satisfied." Who are *these* powers? There are *no* powers mentioned in
the thirteenth kingdom! In fact, there are no powers mentioned
in any of the kingdoms! There are powers mentioned at the beginning of source B in the framework into which these stylized
statements have been inserted. "These" powers are those whose
god was disturbed at the appearance of the illuminator ([77],
4-7); those who were blinded ([77],12-15), and who asked the
questions to which the kingdom statements are a response
([77],18-26). The absence of "powers" as a motif in the kingdom statements and their essential position in the storyline of
source B argue that the purpose clause is a redactional device
used by the redactor to effect a contrast between the wrong
answers of kingdoms one through thirteen, to de-neutralize the
concept of water-appearance, and to make the kingdom statements
more clearly understandable as a response to the questions of
the powers.

[75]In [73],28, CΠЄΡΜΔ is used from the perspective of Ham
and Japheth of that part of their seed that had gone into
another land to sojourn with the special race of men (cf.
[73],13-29).

[76]The shift from CΠЄΡΜΔ to бροб in the speech of Shem
([73],1-12) is interesting (see above, n. 66), but бροб is
still used in the sense of natural reproduction.

[77]The use of CΠΟΡΔ in the statement of the fourth kingdom ([79],16-17) creates a problem. If, as we have argued
above (pp. 38-39), the redactor has rejected all of the first
thirteen kingdoms as incorrect answers to the origin of the
illuminator, and if he uses CΠΟΡΔ in a special positive way,
why has he allowed the use of CΠΟΡΔ here in the fourth kingdom, since its appearance in this context apparently gives the
word a negative thrust? There are two possibilities that could
account for its inclusion in the fourth kingdom that would be

in keeping with the interpretation that has been offered above. In the first place, the redactor may simply have overlooked this reference to ⲥⲡⲟⲣⲁ. His redactional methodology elsewhere suggests that he does not handle his material skillfully, but in a rather wooden, unimaginative way. Thus, one is not surprised to see another instance of his carelessness. The one time that he did change ⲥⲡⲉⲣⲙⲁ to ⲥⲡⲟⲣⲁ ([85],22), it could scarcely have been overlooked or ignored (see above) because of its proximity to his own conclusion. In the second place, it is possible that he was aware of the ⲥⲡⲟⲣⲁ reference in the fourth kingdom, but it did not create for him the problem that it does for the modern reader since he was able to read the fourth kingdom in such a way that the ⲥⲡⲟⲣⲁ reference was not understood as a negative motif. Since the precise significance of the stores is unclear, this possibility cannot be excluded. For example, for Böhlig they are different explanations on an ascending scale from lower to higher concepts of the origin of an unidentified illuminator, whom Böhlig describes as a "suffering savior" ("Jüdisches und iranisches in der Adamapokalypse des Codex V von Nag Hammadi," *Mysterion und Wahrheit: Gesammelte Beiträge zur spätantiken Religionsgeschichte* [Leiden: E. J. Brill, 1968] 155, 158). For Kasser, the stories concern different people or perhaps one person in different incarnations ("Textes gnostiques: Remarques," 92). For Beltz, the stories contain thirteen incorrect gnostic myths about the birth of Jesus. Only the fourteenth has the correct myth (157). For Schottroff, they are thirteen slanderous statements made against the illuminator. The kingless generation reflects the correct opinion ("Animae naturalitur salvandae," 74).

[78]We have already argued above that [85],29 is the redactor's conclusion. Here it should be stated that the appearance of ⲥⲡⲟⲣⲁ in conclusion A ([85],22) can also be explained on the basis of redactional activity. Since the terms ⲥⲡⲉⲣⲙⲁ and ⲥⲡⲟⲣⲁ were "loaded" expressions, the redactor just could not have the teaching of Seth passed on to a progeny referred to as ⲥⲡⲉⲣⲙⲁ. In the redactor's vocabulary, the descendants of Seth were ⲥⲡⲟⲣⲁ. The ⲥⲡⲉⲣⲙⲁ was an unenlightened generation; the ⲥⲡⲟⲣⲁ was an enlightened generation. Since Seth could hardly have handed down his secret tradition to the unenlightened, it was necessary that the text be corrected to read ⲥⲡⲟⲣⲁ. So by virtue of this theological rationale, and the fact that conclusion A immediately preceded conclusion B, i.e., because of its proximity to conclusion B, the redactor changed the ⲥⲡⲉⲣⲙⲁ in conclusion A to ⲥⲡⲟⲣⲁ.
The redactor would have felt no necessity for altering ⲥⲡⲟⲣⲁ in [66],4 since "the seed" (ⲥⲡⲟⲣⲁ) referred to here was none other than Seth, the father of the special race. In fact, its inclusion in B was undoubtedly one of the reasons that the redactor pulled these two units of traditional material together. [79],16-17 is admittedly a problem (see above, n. 77).

[79]The redactor is careful to note that it was not hopelessly "lost," but really preserved in the seed of great eons ([65], 3-5). Thus it could be returned to Adam by the "three men."

[80]A more detailed analysis of the theological position of sources A and B and the redactor follows in Chapters III through V.

[81](VI,*2*)14,27-34. Translation by George MacRae in *The Nag Hammadi Library*, 272-73.

THE CHARACTER OF THE A SOURCE

A. Form

By title and incipit, source A identifies itself as an
ἀποκάλυψις, a "revelation," or, if the word were transliterated
into English, as is often done, an "apocalypse." The literal
meaning of the word is "an uncovering" (of that which is
covered), "a disclosing" (of that which is closed), "a making
known" (of that which is unknown) from the verbal root ἀποκα-
λύπτειν, "to uncover, to disclose."[1] The nature of the contents
of source A corresponds to the title. Adam "makes known" to
Seth the unknown truth about the creation and his fall from
paradise. He projects into the future to tell about the flood
of Noah, the destruction of Sodom and Gomorrah[2] and the end of
the world. In the latter instances, Adam "uncovers" the concealed future to describe those events that will come to pass.
However, since from the perspective of the reader (and the
author) the events have in fact already occurred, it is not
enough simply to predict their occurrence, he must also disclose their hidden meaning.

Adam's disclosure is made to Seth "in the 700th year,"
that is, just prior to Adam's death.[3] The time that the disclosure is made gives it the character of a last testament, and
associates the document with other testamentary discourses in
antiquity.[4] In effect, it increases the significance of the
discourse. It is not just any discourse that Adam made at
sometime during his lifetime to Seth, but it is his final
discourse.

However, title and even incipit do not necessarily determine the literary structure or form of a document.[5] One must
look beyond the literary type suggested by title and incipit--
regarded in isolation they can be misleading--to the actual
structure of the document.[6] For example, the Gospel of Mark,
the Gospel of John, and the *Gospel of Thomas* all bear the ancient title "gospel," suggesting that all these documents belong
to the same literary genre. However, in each instance the

incipit and structure are different. Mark bears the incipit
"Beginning of the *Gospel* of Jesus Christ" (Mark 1:1),[7] and
takes the form of a collection of narratives about the deeds
and sayings of Jesus; it has several parables and one collection of sayings arranged as a discourse. *Gos. Thom.* bears the
incipit "These are the *secret words* which the living Jesus
spoke" ([II,*2*]32,10-11), and takes the form of a collection of
the *logia* of Jesus loosely connected by brief introductory for-
mulae including several parables. John bears the incipit "In
the beginning was the *word* and the word was with god and the
word was god" (1:1), and takes the form of a collection of
miracles and discourses by Jesus with no parables. They were
all called "gospel" by the church, but formally and structurally
each is different. Therefore, while the title and incipit of
source A may dispose one to read it as a revelation discourse,
a speech made by Adam in which he discloses unknown truths, it
is still necessary to examine the formal literary structure of
the text.

Source A in the main is an example of gnostic haggadic
exegesis. It is a midrashic commentary on Genesis in narrative
style that concludes with a judgment scene.[8] The ancient exegete attempted to work his exegesis into the traditional biblical material in order to form a continuous narrative. In the
story of Adam's fall, he has done an excellent job of blending
text and exegesis,[9] but in the flood narrative he has not been
as careful, and the transition from text to exegesis is clearly
discernible in all but one point.[10] In fact, his "text" and
exegesis read like two independent narratives that have little
relationship to one another.[11] Because of his poor blending of
exegesis and text, the storyline of his composite narrative is
difficult to follow.

The saga-like narrative describes the origin of a special
race of men and their struggle with, and eventual victory over,
the creator god and his servants. The plot needs clarification
in some detail in order to be understood.

1. 64,6-19

    After creation, the androgynous aeon Adam-Eve continued
walking in the glory and knowledge of the aeon from which (s)he
had come. (S)he resembled the great eternal angels in his/her
androgynous state, and was higher than the god who had created
him/her.[12]

2. 64,20-[65],3; [65],9-23; [66],12-[67],12

    The creator then divided the androgyne Adam-Eve into two
distinct aeons and as a result they no longer resembled the
great eternal (androgynous) angels and consequently lost the
glory and the first knowledge they had brought into the lower
aeon. Their glory left them returning to the great aeon, and
to the great generation that had come from the higher aeon from
which Adam-Eve had come. Presumably this generation also possessed both the knowledge and glory that Adam-Eve had lost
since they (i.e., the generation) were from the same aeon.
Adam and Eve learn about "dead things," recognize the authority
of the creator god and serve him in fear and servility. Darkness falls over their eyes, and Adam "desires" Eve. In that
moment their devolution into a mortal state is complete and
their knowledge of the eternal aeon is gone.[13]

3. [67],22-[69],10; [69],19-[71],4

    Apparently the creator recognized that these men possessed
a unique glory and knowledge and he attempted to destroy them
by a flood along with all mankind because they were strangers
to him; that is, he did not know their origin. However, he
failed in this attempt when great angels from the higher aeon
preserved the special race. The creator god was apparently
unaware of their redemption and preserved Noah and his sons to
repopulate the earth and to rule it in obedience to him.[14]

4. [71],8-[72],14

    However, the race of men from the higher aeon returned and
presented themselves before Noah and the aeons of the creator

god. As a result, Noah is accused of producing another race of
men to scorn the power of the creator. At this point, the text
is fragmentary, but it appears that the great men from the
higher aeon are again preserved from a threat of the creator
and taken into "a land worthy of them" where they dwell in
safety and holiness for 600 years.[15]

5. [72],15-[76],6

    After the second altercation between the creator and the
special race, Noah cautioned his sons to ensure that their
progeny will serve the creator. However, 400,000 of the seed
of Ham and Japheth entered into the land where the men from
the great eternal knowledge dwelled. There they were protected
from "every evil thing and every unclean desire." The archons
of the creator god who control the seed of Ham and Japheth
plotted against this group and the special race. They went to
Sakla and accused the great men and those who dwelled with them
of opposing the creator's power. In response, Sakla sent fire,
sulphur, and asphalt upon the inhabitants of the holy dwelling
place in an attempt to destroy them. Yet for the third time
they were saved. Abrasax, Sablo and Gamaliel descended from
the clouds to return them to the higher aeon where they will
dwell in safety, resembling the holy angels.

6. [83],7-[84],3

    When the great men are removed to safety for the third
time, a cloud of darkness will descend upon the aeon of the
creator god. The people who accused the great race before the
creator god will utter a loud cry of repentance and lament.
They will recognize the holiness of the great race. The great
race has not been corrupted by desire nor have they performed
the will of the powers. Rather, they have stood "like light"
before the creator in the knowledge of the eternal God. The
"people" will confess their sin and lament their fate. The
narrative ends with the translation of the great race into a
blessed state and the defeat and condemnation of their opposition. The secret knowledge that Adam communicates to Seth and
Seth passes on to his progeny is this narrative.

The text evokes the image of a community about to lose
faith while undergoing severe persecution. The author's purpose seems to be to reassure the community by appealing to the
example of the pioneers of the faith. The illustration of
their persecution, their perseverance and ultimate redemption
through divine intervention is designed to encourage the community in their own current distress. The apocalyptic conclusion to the text assures the community that at the end they
will be vindicated while their persecutors are condemned.

A striking feature of the narrative is the time frame in
which these events take place. The creation and fall are narrated in past tense (64,6-[65],3; [65],9-23; [66],12-[67],12),
but the flood sequence and the judgment scene are narrated in
future tense ([69],1-10; [69],19-[71],4; [71],8-[76],6; [83],7-
[84],3). Thus, the narrative is related from the perspective
of Adam. For Adam the creation and the fall were naturally
past time, while the flood and the *Eschaton* for him would have
been future events.

In summary, the literary structure of source A bears a
striking resemblance to the structure of the "testament" identified by Klaus Baltzer in the *Testaments of the Twelve
Patriarchs*.[16]

Baltzer's Analysis	*Apoc. Adam*
A. PREAMBLE "A copy of the words of ____ which he recited to his sons before his death in the ____ year of his life ....Hearken my children to your father and hear his speech."	"The revelation which Adam taught to his son, Seth, in the 700th year: Listen to my words, my son Seth." (64,2-6)
B. NARRATIVE "Each of the patriarchs recounts stories from his life. They usually begin with an explanation of their name illustrating a particular characteristic or unique experience. The biblical tradition is borrowed...but then expanded by...haggadic details."	The *Apoc. Adam* begins with an account of Adam's fall in the garden (64,6-[65], 3; [65],9-23; [66],12-[67], 12). Then Adam recites the biblical flood tradition and the account of Sodom and Gomorrah expanded and interpreted with haggadic detail. ([67],22-[69],11; [69],18-[71],4; [71],8-[76],6)

Baltzer's Analysis	Apoc. Adam
C. ETHICAL SECTION A section of ethical instructions introduced by a distinctive formula followed by a series of imperatives commanding general types of ethical conduct.	
D. BLESSINGS AND CURSES An eschatological section frequently concludes the *T. 12 Patr.* in blessing-curse format.	"Blessed is the soul of those men for they have known God through a knowledge of the truth....But we have done every work of the powers senselessly....Now we know that our souls will surely die."[17] ([83],7-[84],3)
E. CONCLUSION "When he said this he died. And his sons laid him in a coffin. After ____ they brought his bones to ____ and laid him with his fathers."	"These are the revelations that Adam made known to Seth, his son, and his son taught his seed about them." ([85],19-22)

The blessing-curse format that appears in the *Apoc. Adam* is structurally the eschatological conclusion to the midrashic commentary that comprises most of Adam's revelation to Seth, rather than part of a concluding personal admonition by Adam to Seth and his posterity, as the blessing-curse form generally appears in the *T. 12 Patr.* In the context of the midrashic commentary, the blessing-curse is not spoken by Adam, but rather is spoken by the enemies of Seth's descendants as a confession of their own personal failure. Nor does it have the distinctive form of the blessing-curse sections that Baltzer identified in a majority of the testaments of the patriarchs. Therefore, in a narrow sense, i.e., in the sense of Baltzer's analysis, the blessing-curse motif that appears in *Apoc. Adam* may not be called "testamentary."

However, in a general sense, it does seem to qualify as a "testamentary" blessing-curse. It does not seem to be accidental that the blessing-curse section in the structure of source A occupies a position identical to that held by the

blessing-curse format in the structure of the testament, that
is, immediately before its conclusion. By its position in the
structure of source A, it would tend to displace a separate
blessing-curse section identified by Baltzer as a frequently
appearing fourth part of the structure of the testament. It is
after all part of Adam's final revelation to Seth. The blessing in the statement does apply to Seth's spiritual descendants
as the curse applies to their "wicked" and "sinful" enemies.
Further, it does have a form similar to the Testament of
Naphtali. According to Baltzer, the majority of the testaments
reflect a later stage in the development of the blessing-curse
form and assume a temporal sequence: sin, curse, repentance and
blessing. Naphtali, however, resembles more closely an earlier
stage of the form as is reflected in the OT (for example,
Leviticus 26 and Deuteronomy 28). The blessing-curse form in
source A is modelled on the blessing-curse form as it appears
in the OT tradition.

There is, of course, another possibility. Source A may
have had a separate "testamentary" blessing-curse section that
was removed by the redactor in light of the fact that it was
preceded already in the redacted form of the Apoc. Adam by two
separate blessing-curse sections. One of these was the conclusion to the midrash ([83],7-[84],4). This section would have
resisted exclusion because it concluded the commentary. To have
omitted it would have left the narrative without a sense of
closure. The other was the redactor's own conclusion ([84],4-
[85],18). To have left all three in the text may have seemed
excessive even to the redactor.

The overall resemblance in structure and literary form in
the testament as analyzed by Baltzer and source A is striking.
If it be granted that the blessing-curse format in source A may
be considered a testamentary blessing-curse, then there are
only two differences: source A is lacking a separate section of
ethical exhortation and does not have the stylized conclusion
that Baltzer identified in the T. 12 Patr. This similarity in
structure, form and content cannot be accidental and forces one
to the conclusion that the genre of source A is best identified
as a testament.

B. Periodizing in Source A

The narrative relates only six events told in very general
terms: the creation, the fall, the flood, a threat (uncertain
because of the lacuna), threat of fire, and the *Eschaton*. None
of these events are specific enough to be considered as particular occurrences in the actual history of a specific group
of people, but all appear to be idealized occurrences describing the history of the great race from the perspective of an
idealized world history, or more specifically an idealized
Jewish concept of world history, since the events are drawn
from the OT tradition. These idealized events are not everyday
occurrences happening within a narrow time frame, but they
periodize the history of the special race. The fact that the
story begins with the creation and ends with the *Eschaton* introduces a linear apocalyptic concept into the story, and
transforms the other generalized events from everyday occurrences into pivotal moments or periods in the forward movement
of an idealized history.[18]

The periodizing of history is a well-known motif in apocalyptic and gnostic texts. The periodized schemes that we encounter in these texts are similar in that they usually include
among their pivotal moments some reference to the Jewish biblical history, and they structure an idealized reality into a
series of periods. Beyond this, however, there is really only
little similarity among them. They employ different events as
pivotal moments to form their schemes, and there appears to be
no set number of periods required. Unfortunately, the parameters of the scheme are not always clear and frequently must
be inferred from the text. For example, the scheme might include the *Eschaton* and periods before the *Eschaton*, but would
assume the creation as an unstated pivotal moment. This is
largely due to the fact that the author has a different concern
at those points in the text where the periodizing surfaces.

In the following discussion of these texts, it is not
claimed that all occurrences of periodizing in apocalyptic and
gnostic texts have been collected,[19] but the sample seems extensive enough to provide a basis for comparison with the

narrative in *Apoc. Adam.* The discussion intends to provide a
background with which the form of the narrative in the *Apoc.*
Adam can be compared. For the most part, those periodizing
schemes have been selected that use all or some of the pivotal
moments appearing in *Apoc. Adam,* i.e., creation, flood, conflict, fire (Sodom and Gomorrah) and end-time.

In Dan 9:24-27, the periodizing scheme is discursively set
out. The angel Gabriel tells Daniel that there will be seventy
weeks of years (= 490 years) from the command to rebuild Jerusalem until the establishment of the Messianic era; that is, it
will be that long until "transgression is finished," sin is
ended, atonement for iniquity is made and everlasting righteousness is inaugurated and "prophecy and prophet are fulfilled"
(Dan 9:27; see also 7:13-14,27). The periods prior to the end
are set forth in cryptic language as follows: From the command
to restore Jerusalem to the coming of the anointed one is
seven weeks (= 49 years). For the next sixty-two weeks, the
holy city is restored (= 434 years). At the end of this second
period, the city and the sanctuary will be destroyed by flood
followed by war and desolations. For one week (= 7 years),
there shall be abominations and desolation, and then comes the
end. The scheme is as follows.

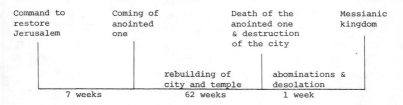

Command to restore Jerusalem	Coming of anointed one	Death of the anointed one & destruction of the city	Messianic kingdom
		rebuilding of city and temple	abominations & desolation
7 weeks		62 weeks	1 week

The history that is periodized is uniquely Jewish, for it
concerns the rebuilding of the holy city Jerusalem and the re-
institution of temple worship. The scheme, however, is not
complete. Because it has a narrow concern, i.e., the rebuilding of the holy city and the current tribulation that the Jewish
nation is experiencing, the scheme does not include the creation,
nor, for example, other tribulations that the people had faced.[20]

It starts with Daniel's current situation and projects to the
end. From the end, one may infer a beginning. It is highly
improbable that the Jewish prophet would not have conceived of
a beginning in terms of Genesis 1-3. Therefore, we should
assume that the prophet operated with an idealized concept of
history as follows.

[Creation]	Command to restore Jerusalem	Coming of anointed one	Death of anointed one & destruction of the city	Messianic kingdom
1	2	3	4	5

Between 1 and 2 there could have been any number of periods or
pivotal moments. The scheme could have been expanded or col-
lapsed. Its breadth hinged upon the prophet's concern at the
moment.

Another example from which the periodizing scheme must be
inferred is found in the Synoptic Gospels: Matt 24:37-39 = Luke
17:26-30. The passage is taken from Q by Matthew and Luke, but
arranged differently in the scheme of each evangelist. The
statement in Luke is more extensive, adding an additional
pivotal moment to the periodizing scheme that does not appear
in Matthew's structure. With very little divergence, Matthew
follows Mark's order in Mark 13, inserting the Q material between Matt 24:32 and 33. In Luke, the material parallel to
Mark 13 and Matthew 24 is broken up and appears in chapters 17
and 21. The Lucan periodizing statement appears in chapter 17.

The two statements differ in that Luke's account adds an
additional pivotal moment. Both cite Noah and the flood and
the coming of the Son of Man, but Luke's account adds the destruction of Sodom and Gomorrah. From the fact that the periodizing scheme in both accounts ends with the *Eschaton* (= the inauguration of the Messianic era), we can infer a beginning to
the world order, the creation. Although the creation is not
stated, it must be the *terminus a quo* that corresponds to the
coming of the Son of Man, the *terminus ad quem* of the scheme.
Thus, although the periodizing scheme is incomplete, we can
reconstruct its beginning.[21] The inferred schemes appear as
follows.

Matt: [Creation]---The flood---The coming of the Son of Man
Luke: [Creation]---The flood---Sodom & Gomorrah---The coming of the
                                                    Son of Man

But what are we to make of the fact that Luke has added an
extra pivotal moment, giving a total of four such moments and
three periods? There are two possibilities. The first is that
Luke was theologically motivated to add the extra pivotal moment. In other words, Luke's theology required that the forward sweep of idealized history include the destruction of
Sodom and Gomorrah so that there would be *only* three periods
set off by *only* four pivotal moments.

This seems unlikely for two reasons. We have already observed that both schemes are incomplete. If Luke was going to
be that precise in his statement, one would have expected him
to include the creation as a pivotal moment; that is, he would
have stated a complete system. Also in Luke 16:16 there is set
out a completely *different* periodizing scheme. This sharply
reduces the probability that the present scheme was regarded by
Luke as a definitive statement. It seems more probable that
the schemes in Matthew and Luke should be regarded as incomplete
and open-ended. In other words, the statements are not definitive descriptions of an idealized history, but they are ex-
cerpts from a broader scheme that stretches from creation to
end-time and could have included yet additional pivotal moments
and periods. Luke's addition of the destruction of Sodom and
Gomorrah was theologically motivated but not because he had to
have it to make up a certain number of periods or pivotal moments. He included it because it was already part of a broader
scheme of idealized history from which Q had already drawn the
flood incident, and because it made an admirable second illustration to describe the woes of the Messianic era.

Similarly, there is a disagreement in the periodizing
schemes found in Jude and 2 Peter.[22] However, here the disagreement does not lie in the number of pivotal moments or
periods in the scheme but in the disagreement in occurrences.
Again, the total historical scheme must be inferred from the
text. The difference is that Jude records the Exodus as one of
his pivotal moments where 2 Peter records the flood as a pivotal

moment. Again, the creation is omitted as a part of the scheme,
but can be inferred as the beginning of the scheme on the basis
of the *Eschaton* as the conclusion. The schemes appear as
follows.

```
2 Peter:   [Creation]----------------Sin of the---Flood---Sodom & ---Judgment
                                      Angels23              Gomorrah

Jude:      [Creation]---The Exodus---Sin of the----------Sodom & ---Judgment
                                     Angels              Gomorrah
```

What are we to make of the fact that 2 Peter reports a
different scheme than Jude? The consensus of contemporary
scholarship is that 2 Peter is dependent upon Jude,[24] and if
this is correct,[25] 2 Peter has altered the scheme he found in
Jude. The striking thing in the two different pivotal moments
is that Jude's example, the Exodus, is really more appropriate
to what he was trying to illustrate. He was trying to warn the
false teachers in the congregation of the judgment of God and
used the example of God destroying the unbelieving children of
Israel in the wilderness, although they were part of the people
of God. The example of 2 Peter, the flood, doesn't quite have
the same close parallel to the false teachers in the congregation. Here the people that were destroyed are not described as
part of the household of faith. They are simply the "unrigh-
teous," and their sin is immorality rather than unbelief.

The real issue, however, is not priority, but in which
text is the scheme a definitive statement of the author's concept of history, that is, which text requires just that scheme
as stated with no alterations? The answer is that neither one
is a definitive statement since the periodizing schemes are
not complete statements. The parameters of both schemes have
to be inferred, and Jude has even recorded his illustrations
out of "historical" order. It seems better to regard both
statements as incomplete and open-ended. They are part of the
author's idealized view of world history which includes a number of pivotal moments drawn from the OT tradition extending
from creation to the *Eschaton*.

In the *Gospel of the Egyptians* (III,2 and IV,2), there
appears a periodized scheme in which the Great Seth is said to

have passed through three "parousiai": the flood, the conflagration and the judgment of the archons, powers and authorities.[26] The scheme is different from those previously examined
because in addition to omitting the creation, it also omits the
Eschaton. The lack of reference to the beginning and end makes
the scheme suspect as a periodized scheme of an idealized history. However, the text does mention the consummation of the
aeon at (III,*2*)61,1ff. (= [IV,*2*]72,10ff.), and the conclusion
of the *Gospel of the Egyptians* says that the book was written
for the "ends of the times and the eras" ([III,*2*]68,10ff.).
The "ends of the times and the eras" and the "consummation of
the aeon" should be conceived as an event distinct from the
third parousia of the Great Seth ([III,*2*]63,4-8 = [IV,*2*]74,17-
22), i.e., the judgment of the archons, powers and authorities,
because the time frame of this latter event is past, while the
"consummation of the aeon" is yet a future event. Further,
these three events are related to the redemption of the special
race in the world rather than to the end of the age.[27]

The creation also appears elsewhere in the text, but not
in conjunction with the threefold parousia of the Great Seth.[28]
Thus, we do have both creation and *Eschaton* as a part of the
author's scheme of an idealized history, but not in connection
with the periodized scheme with which we began. A closer reading of the text reveals that these three appearances of the
Great Seth are not three separate pivotal moments in the author's scheme, but they represent only one pivotal moment in
the author's scheme of an idealized history of the immovable
race that stretches from creation to consummation, and includes
the origin of the immovable race ([III,*2*]60,9-61,1), the sending of 400 guards to protect the immovable race ([III,*2*]62,
13-24), a period of testing by the devil ([III,*2*]61,16-23) and
"the time and the moment of truth and justice,"[29] as well as
assorted plagues, famines, temptations, falsehoods and false
prophets ([III,*2*]61,1-15). In fact, the author has periodized
his idealized history at another point when he says that the
400 angels came forth "to guard the great incorruptible
race, its fruit and the great men of the Great Seth from

the time and the moment of truth and justice until the consummation of the aeon and its archons" ([III,2]62,16-22).

If we were to attempt a reconstruction of the author's
concept of idealized history, it would appear as follows.

	Origin of the	The	The		Testing by	
Creation---immovable	race---flood---conflagration---the devil --- (cont.)

Appearance		The moment	The three Parousiai	The
of the	and	of truth	---of the Great Seth	---consummation
400 guards		and justice	(flood, fire, judgment)	

However, it should be pointed out that this is a reconstructed
scheme, and does not reflect all the periods and pivotal moments that the author alluded to in (III,2)61,1-15 as famines,
temptations, falsehood and false prophets. One may assume that
these events, mentioned here in general terms, could refer to
events at least as specific as the flood and the conflagration.

The *Paraphrase of Shem* ([VII,1]1-49) also seems to have a
periodizing scheme, although it appears here less clearly
stated than in the other documents that have been discussed.
The author has a concept of creation (VII 20,20-24), or beginning (VII 1,21-25; 12,33-38; 36,1-3; 45,17-20). He also
looked for a final ultimate end to the world, conceived as
an inevitable catastrophic destruction of nature (VII 22,33-
23,1; 48,16-22; 44,2-45,20), and referred to as "the consummation" (VII 35,25-27; 48,16-22) and "the last day" (VII
39,17-21; 45,14-20). At no one point does the author
systematically set out his periodized scheme that takes place
within the time frame from creation to consummation. However,
he does provide sufficient hints stated in such a way that the
reader is aware of the author's periodizing proclivities. For
example, the flood is a pivotal moment in his scheme, for he
discusses events "before the flood" and "after the flood" (VII
28,5-22).[30] There are other indications of a periodizing
scheme, but the author provides no definitive statement, nor
does he clarify the relationship of the periods to one another.
Aside from the division suggested by the "before the flood" and
"after the flood" terminology, there are at least three other
periods that can be distinguished: "The appointed days of the

demon" (VII 31,14-22), "The appointed term of faith" that appears on the earth "for a short time" (VII 43,14-21), and a
time of "great evil error" that occurs in the world after
Derdekeas(?) withdraws from the world (VII 43,28-44,2). If we
may assume that the sequence of events in the revelation by
Derdekeas to Sēem correspond to the sequence of pivotal moments
and periods in the author's scheme of periodized history, that
scheme would appear as follows.

```
                    The        The
            The     appointed  appointed   Time of
Creation---Flood---days of  ---term of  ---great      ---Consummation
            the demon   Faith          evil error
```

Again, it should be pointed out that we have inferred this
scheme from the text as a whole. It represents a skeletal reconstruction of the author's concept of history. Allowance
must be made for other possible pivotal moments and/or periods
to the scheme.

In the Coptic *Asclepius* (VII,*8*)65-78, there appears a
periodizing scheme mentioned briefly in connection with a
statement about God's punishment of evil in the world (VII 73,
22-74,17).[31]

> Sometimes he submerged it in a great flood, at other
> times he burned it in a searing fire, and at still
> other times he crushed it in wars and pestilence....
> (VII 73,31-36)

The author's broader concept of history can be inferred
only from his statement about the punishment of evil since at
no other point in the tractate is there a clear reference to
the creation or consummation. There are only two brief allusions in the tractate and both in the present text. God is
referred to as the creator (δημιουργός) in a positive sense,
and in speaking of the restoration of nature, the author says
that "the restoration...will take place in a period of time
that has no beginning." This implies that prior to its restoration, nature has both beginning and end, but the restored
nature is timeless and eternal.

The problem is that the three events in the scheme are
general and not necessarily related in time sequence to either

the creation or the restoration. In other words, they are not
specific one-time-only sequential events in the forward movement of an idealized history that begins with creation and
rushes toward a restoration. Instead, they seem to be events
that can be repeated and not necessarily in their stated order.
When the text says "sometimes" (ZENCOTT) and "other times"
(ZENKECOTT), it implies more than one flood, more than one
fire and more than one occurrence of war and pestilence. Had
the author conceived of one particular fire or flood or pestilence, he would not have used a word implying several occurrences of a particular kind of event.

If this interpretation is correct, a mockup of the author's
scheme cannot be stated with any certainty. All that can be
said is that the events described as God's instrument of punishment bear a striking resemblance to some of the pivotal moments that have been discussed in the other texts above. For
example, the flood corresponds to the great flood in Genesis
and the fire recalls the destruction of Sodom and Gomorrah.

All the examples discussed above have been brief statements by an ancient author involving at the most several para-
graphs. A brief part of the periodizing scheme is simply
stated or alluded to in a few lines. It is not discussed in
detail, nor is reference made by the author to a broader schematized concept of time or history. The broader scheme can
only be inferred from the total document in which the brief
statement appears. The final three examples, however, are more
than brief statements, although they may be just as incomplete.
In the texts that follow, the author has adopted a periodized
scheme as a literary structure for his ideas.

In *The Book of the Secrets of Enoch* (*2 Enoch*), a periodized
scheme appears as the literary framework for God's revelation to
Enoch when he enters the tenth heaven (24:1-35:3), the sphere of
the Lord's presence.[32] He discusses two events that have appeared as pivotal moments in the schemes discussed above: the
creation (24:1-32:2) and the flood (33:3-35:3), and between
these two pivotal moments he alludes to the end of time (33:1-2).
It is clear that his concept of time and history is highly schematized since it is based upon the seven days of creation (33:1-2

Each day of the creation corresponds to a world day of 1000
years. As the world was created in seven days, so it has seven
world days, i.e., 7000 years, until its end. The beginning of
the eighth world day is simultaneously the end of time. The
creation is the beginning of his scheme and the beginning of
time.

The author describes only one pivotal moment in addition
to the creation and the end of time: the flood. That the flood
serves as a pivotal moment in the author's idealized and highly
schematized view is clear from the fact that he envisions a
pre-flood time and a post-flood time (34:3-35:1). That the
flood is not the only pivotal moment in his concept of time is
suggested by the division of time into seven 1000 year periods.
The flood must be one pivotal moment separating two 1000 year
periods, but we cannot be certain which moment. Thus we can
schematize the view of the text as:

```
          1000      1000      1000      1000      1000      1000      1000
          years     years     years     years     years     years     years
Creation-------1-------2-------3-------4-------5-------6-------End-Time
```

The numbers represent unidentified pivotal moments, one of
which is the flood.

A periodizing scheme is employed as the literary structure
for *The Assumption of Moses*, ostensibly Moses' final testament
to Joshua prior to the conquest of Palestine. The general outline of the book is as follows.

Introductory	1:1-18
The Testament	2:1-10:15
Response of Joshua	11:1-19
Conclusion	12:1-13

The testament proper is broadly structured into four periods as
follows.

The Exodus	2:1-19
1st visitation of divine wrath	3:1-7:10
2nd visitation of divine wrath	8:1-9:10
The Messianic kingdom	10:1-15

The author's periodizing proclivities are clearly evident
throughout the document. He "dates" the testament of Moses to
Joshua as taking place 2,500 years "from the creation of the

world" (1:1-3). This event falls between the Exodus and the
conquest of Palestine by Israel. One would have expected the
testament of Moses itself to have been a pivotal moment separating these two events into individual periods. However, the
author does not divide in this fashion. He incorporates the
Exodus into his first broad division and includes the conquest
of Palestine as a small part of the "62 year" span that separates his first broad division of 2,500 years from the first
visitation of divine wrath.[33]

According to Charles, who assigns the cryptic language of
the document specific values in terms of Israel's idealized
history, this first period of divine retribution stretches from
the deportation of Israel by Nebuchadnezzar (588-586 B.C.) to
Varus, Governor of Syria who subdued a Jewish rebellion in
4 B.C. The end of this period is the author's own time. In
the second period of divine retribution, the author "leaves
obvious historical allusions to obscure predictions and enig-
matical symbols."[34] The end of the second period comes rather
abruptly with a "hymnic" section describing apocalyptic woes
and the inauguration of the Messianic kingdom. The period from
the death of Moses to the advent of the Messianic kingdom is
"250 times" (11:12-13).[35] This second broad division corresponds rather nicely to his first broad division (from creation
to Moses) of 2,500 years. Thus, the author's scheme of history
would appear as follows.

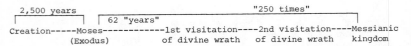

This scheme omits two of the most commonly used *topoi* previously noted in the periodizing schemes: the flood and the
destruction of Sodom and Gomorrah. The author instead concen-
trates on late Jewish history. This does not mean, however,
that the author could *not* have conceived of these events also
as pivotal moments in his first broad division. The very fact
that he also conceives of the period from Moses to the Messianic
kingdom as a single unit and yet can still cite individual

pivotal moments within the single broad division suggests that
the same could have been true for his first broad division. And
it is incredible that he would not have viewed the flood or
Sodom and Gomorrah as examples of divine retribution.[36] Thus,
one can only conclude that the author's scheme is incomplete.
His omission of the flood and Sodom and Gomorrah as pivotal
moments in his periodizing scheme should not be traced to theological necessity, that is, to the fact that he did not con-
ceive of them as distinct pivotal moments in the forward movement of history, but to the fact that the author was primarily
concerned with a later period of Israel's history.

The most striking parallel to the scheme in the *Apoc. Adam*
is found in *The Book of Jubilees*. R. H. Charles calls *Jub.*
"the most advanced pre-Christian representation of the midrashic
tendency."[37] Like the *Apoc. Adam*, *Jub.* presents the OT tradition rewritten from the perspective of the author's faith. He
begins with creation and proceeds through the giving of the law
at Sinai. There are six primary cycles of stories: Adam, Noah,
Abraham, Jacob, Joseph and Moses. Since both documents are
midrashim on the OT tradition, the events of the narrative in
the *Apoc. Adam* appear in *Jub.* in the same sequence: the creation (2:1-3:35), Noah and the flood (4:33-9:15), Noah and the
evil spirits (10:1-17), the destruction of Sodom (16:4-9), the
Eschaton (23:11-13).

Jub. also affords excellent examples of two ways of
periodizing. The author declares his intention to write a
"world history," that is, a history of the world from creation
to the judgment.[38] However, he does not achieve this goal, and
covers only the period from creation to the giving of the law
at Sinai. (His section on the Messianic kingdom [23:9-31] is
out of order and should have been recorded at least after the
Moses cycle.)[39] The predominant method of periodizing in the
document is the dividing of history from creation to Moses and
the law into Jubilee periods.[40] There are then forty-nine
Jubilees from the days of Adam until the giving of the law
(50:4). Within this broad timeframe, the author does not seem
to regard any of the events as moments of crisis or pivotal
moments as we observed to be the case in previous schemes. Here

all of the stories appear to be of equal weight. For example,
he does not break the forty-nine Jubilees from creation to the
giving of the law into subdivisions at particular events so
that these events serve in effect as major dividing points in
the scheme, unless one assumes that the giving of the law (the
end of the present document) should serve as the end of the
first broad period, and would be followed by another broad
division ending with the judgment and the Messianic kingdom, or
followed by other divisions, the last of which would end with
the judgment and the institution of the Messianic kingdom. The
Jubilee structure is not well balanced throughout the document.
The first half of the book (chaps. 1-23) incorporates Jubilees
1-44 and the last half of the book (chaps. 24-50) incorporates
Jubilees 44-49.

The other method of periodizing appears in what has been
described above as a parenthetical or explanatory section
(23:9-32). This scheme is more similar to what has been observed in the documents discussed above. Here the author
divides by indefinite periods rather than by Jubilees. For
example, from the creation to the flood,[41] men lived "19
Jubilees," but from the flood to the time of Moses, their age
was less than 19 Jubilees because of their wickedness, and from
the time of Moses until the judgment, men will grow old even
more quickly (23:9-11). The scheme can be mocked-up as follows.

```
                49 Jubilees                              (?)
┌────────────────────────────────────┐  ┌────────────────────────────┐
Creation--------Flood--------Moses and the law--------Judgment
```

If the author's stated intention (prologue) to write a complete
history from beginning to end may be taken seriously, then we
must conclude that his scheme is also incomplete.[42]

The narrative in the *Apoc. Adam* has a structure quite
similar to the last three texts discussed above.[43] It begins
with creation (64,6-[65],3; [65],9-23; [66],12-[67],12) and
concludes with the *Eschaton* ([83],7-[84],3). Between these two
terminal events, it traces the experiences of the men of gnosis
through three pivotal moments of divine judgment drawn from the
Jewish biblical, midrashic and apocalyptic traditions (cf. the

visitations of divine wrath in *The Assumption of Moses*): the flood ([69],1-[71],4; cf. *Jub.* 5:19-32), conflict ([71],8-[72],14; cf. *Jub.* 10:1-13) and fire ([74],26-[75],16; cf. *Jub.* 20:5). Like the last three texts discussed, source A of the *Apoc. Adam* has employed a periodized scheme as its literary structure.

C. Characteristic Religious Ideas

1. Theology

The text reflects the standard gnostic *topos* of the evil demiurge, who created the world and enslaved man in a mortal body. He is referred to as god (64,7; [67],29; [70],6,16; [71],16; [72],14), the god who created (64,17; [65],17-18; [66],14-15.25-26), god the ruler of aeons and powers (64,20-22), the lord ([66],14), god the Almighty ([69],3-4; [72],25; [73], 9-10), god of the aeons ([74],26-27) and Sakla ([74],3,7). From the fact that the author has drawn his material from the biblical creation and flood traditions,[44] it is clear that the demiurge is to be identified with Yahweh, the Jewish god of creation. He is characterized as an angry god (64,20-22; [70],6-8) who is full of power and might ([74],15-21). He demands fear and servility on the part of his subjects ([65],20-21) to whom he teaches "dead things" ([65],14-15) that produce ignorance ([65],21-23; [66],23-25), desire ([66],31-[67],4) and mortality ([67],10-12).

There is also the concept of the good God. He is called the eternal God (64,12-14), the God of truth ([65],9-13) or simply God, with a reference to knowledge ([83],13-14.19-21) that distinguishes him from the evil creator. He is described as eternal and as a God whose works will prevail ([83],25-30). His primary characteristic is that he is the God of gnosis (64,12-14; [65],9-13; [67],4-8; [71],8-14).

There is nothing irregular in these concepts. The motif of an evil demiurge who created the world and the God of knowledge whose revelation leads to enlightenment is common enough in gnostic texts. However, an interesting feature does appear in the way the demiurge is described. In the traditional account

of the flood, god the Almighty is described in neutral terms.
It is only in the gnostic exegetical section that it becomes
evident that he is to be identified with the evil demiurge.[45]
For example, in the traditional section, his destruction of the
world is not the whimsical act of an ignorant demiurge, but is
more understandable as the judgment of a righteous God upon
disobedient man as it is portrayed in Gen 6:5-8. Only in the
exegetical section is the deed placed in a true gnostic perspective.

   This suggests that the author was working with a text that
he expanded. The tension between the received traditional section and the gnostic exegetical section is subtle and would
scarcely have been sensed by anyone who believed that the creator was truly the demiurge. When he read "παντοκράτωρ" in the
traditional section, it would still equal "demiurge." However,
when one examines the traditional sections closely, it is only
this title for the creator that even faintly suggests a gnostic
tendency. In all other ways, the creator bears a striking resemblance to the righteous God of the OT. Far from being de-
meaned, he is described in positive terminology. And even the
title παντοκράτωρ is not exclusively gnostic, but would have
been known to pious Greek-speaking Jews as a title for Yahweh
in the LXX.[46]

2. The Heavenly World

   The text makes no overt attempt to organize or structure
its concept of the heavenly world. The language describing the
angels, aeons and powers that make up the hierarchy of heavenly
beings is imprecise and usually indefinite. The text seems to
assume that the reader knows their identity, and therefore no
explanation is required. In general, it may be observed that
it designates those beings of the heavenly world associated
with the God of knowledge by an adjective ascribing a positive
quality: the *great eternal* angels (64,12-16), *great* angels
([69],18-19), *great* aeons and angels ([71],13-14), angels of
the *great* light ([72],11-12), *great* aeons of *imperishability*
([74],1-2), *eternal* angel ([75],8), *great* aeons ([75],21) and

holy angels ([76],2-3). In one instance, angelic beings from
the God of gnosis are designated with specific names: Abrasax,
Sablo, and Gamaliel ([75],22-23), but no clarification is ever
made of their identity as is done by the *Gos. Eg*.[47] The title
"the great light" ([71],9-10; [72],11-12) is mentioned, but not
identified or clarified.[48]

The beings associated with the demiurge are mentioned with
no descriptive adjective as simply powers (64,18.22; [65],19;
[74],5; [75],27; [83],18-19.25), aeons (64,21; [75],26-31) and
rulers of the powers ([75],27). In three instances, it is
difficult to know whether the beings are to be associated with
the demiurge or the God of knowledge: aeons ([75],11-16), the
powers of the illuminators ([75],14-15) and angels ([83],17).
A further confusion is introduced by the use of "aeon" as both a
being inhabiting the heavenly world and as a place in the
structure of the heavenly world (64,10-12.[30-31]; [74],13).

The inhabitants of the heavenly world (aeons, powers, angels and rulers) are found in all sections of the narrative
except the traditional section on the flood. As noted above,
this section is free of all gnostic speculation.

3. Creation

The text has no interest in cosmogony, but assumes the
creation of the world. It briefly describes the creation of
man (64,6-10), but describes in detail Adam's "fall" from an
original androgynous state into separate male and female aeons
(64,6-[65],3; [65],9-23; [66],12-[67],12). The narrative takes
the form of a midrash upon Gen 2:7,21-22 and 4:1.[49] The striking thing about the account of Adam's "fall" is its view of
creation (64,6-10). It does not describe the creation of the
world as a mistake or as an evil act. In fact, there is some
basis for arguing that it views creation as a positive thing!
The description that it gives of the androgynous aeon Adam-Eve
after creation suggests this (64,6-19). After creation, Adam-
Eve "walked in glory" and still possessed knowledge of the
eternal God. In the created state, Adam-Eve resembled the
"great eternal angels" and exceeded the creator god and his

powers in greatness. It was not until the creator dissolved
the androgynous union that glory and knowledge were lost. Adam
and Eve then experienced carnal desire and were subjected to
servitude to the creator.

The separation of Adam into his male and female parts (Gen
2:21-23) was really the evil deed of the creator that pushed
man into carnal desire, but in the creation stage of androgynous union, Adam-Eve still possessed the perfection of that
aeon from which (s)he had come (Gen 2:1-17). Such a motif can
scarcely be considered gnostic, since gnostic texts almost
unanimously regard creation as an evil act.[50] In this respect,
Apoc. Adam is much closer to the Jewish traditions of creation
and the garden of Eden paradise, where Adam and Eve walked with
God until their fall (Gen 3:23-24).

4. Anthropology

The text recognizes only two classes of men in the world,[51]
the men of gnosis[52] and the seed of Noah.[53] The men of gnosis
apparently have a supernatural origin. Unlike Noah and his
sons, who are the natural descendants of Adam and are therefore
the "sons" of the creator, the gnostic community has been "cast
forth from knowledge" ([71],8-14; [73],15-20), and their soul
has come through a "great command of an eternal angel" ([75],
5-8). Possibly they have come from the same source as Adam
himself (64,6-12).[54] In fact, the creator himself is surprised
at their appearance in the world and accuses Noah of "creating
another generation" in order to discredit him ([71],16-27).

This group of men does not do the will of the creator, but
opposes his power ([74],21-26), converts some of the natural
seed of Ham and Japheth to their ways ([73],25-29; [74],21-26),
and in general is a disturbing element in a world supposedly
controlled by the demiurge. On the other hand, the descendants
of Noah obey the demiurge ([74],7-11.17-21) and oppose the men
of gnosis ([73],30-[74],4).

It is not until the end of the narrative that these two
groups assume an apocalyptic character in the sense of the
sheep and the goats in Matt 25:31-46 ([83],7-[84],3). Until

this concluding section, the two groups do not have this uni-
versalized dimension. In the conclusion, the opponents of the
men of gnosis represent all the peoples of the world who have
obeyed the demiurge and have not known God "through a knowledge
of the truth." The men of gnosis represent those who have
"known" God and have therefore not performed the works of the
powers, nor obeyed the demiurge, nor been corrupted by desire.
They shall enter a state of eternal blessedness while their
opponents will perish.

5. Soteriology

The text is not concerned with the salvation of the individual gnostic, but rather with the salvation of the gnostic
community. It describes the attempts of the demiurge to destroy the gnostic community by three great cosmic catastrophes.[55]
The first cosmic crisis is the great flood of Noah ([67],22-
[69],10), which the exegetical section of the midrash treats as
an attempt to destroy the gnostic community in particular. The
second attempt of the demiurge to destroy the gnostic community
is lost in lacuna ([71],27ff.), but from the statement of deliverance that follows ([72],1-12), it is clear that some kind
of threat statement was contained in the lacuna.[56] The third
cosmic crisis that threatens the gnostic community is destruction by fire, sulphur and asphalt ([75],9-16), paralleling the
destruction of Sodom and Gomorrah.[57]

All three attempts to destroy the gnostic community fail
and the community is preserved through divine intervention.[58]
On the first occasion, great angels come on high clouds and
remove the men of gnosis to "the place where the spirit of life
dwells" ([69],18-24). On the second occasion, the God of truth
causes their removal to a land worthy of them and builds for
them a holy dwelling place where they dwell for 600 years in
imperishable knowledge ([71],21-[72],15). On the third occasion, Abrasax, Sablo and Gamaliel, emissaries of the God of
knowledge, come in great clouds of light to remove the gnostic
community to the dwelling place of the great aeons where they
dwell with the holy angels ([75],17-[76],5).

In all three instances, the character of salvation is uncertain. The first two occurrences of redemption do not appear
to be a removal from the world since the community is still
threatened by the demiurge. On the other hand, the nature of
the third redemption does seem to be of an order different from
the first two. It makes claims not made in the first two occurrences of redemption; that is, the community is "with the
holy angels and aeons," and becomes "like them." This sounds
like the community has been translated into a higher state. On
the other hand, in the second redemption it is said that they
are in another land for only a temporary period: they will dwell
in the holy dwelling place prepared for them for 600 years. The
first redemption is too fragmentary to permit a description, but
the "place where the spirit of life dwells" does not have to be
a heavenly state. Indeed, if the demiurge could threaten them
a second time, it still must have been within his frame of reference and therefore is not a final heavenly dwelling place.

The basis of their salvation is simply the fact that they
possessed γνῶσις. The text does not specify the content of
their knowledge, but refers to it in a general and ambiguous
way, viz., they come from "the γνῶσις of the great aeons and
angels" ([71],10-14; [73],15-20), they dwell in a "knowledge of
imperishability" ([72],5-9), nothing dwells in their hearts
except "the knowledge of God" ([72],12-15; [83],19-23) whom
they know "in a knowledge of the truth" ([83],7-14).

6. Ethics

There is a marked ascetic bias to the text. The gnostic
community is described as being free of "desire" ([73],20-24;
[74],21-[75],4; [83],14-19). They are people of purity, for
nothing "loathsome" dwells in their hearts ([72],12-15). Precisely what is meant by "desire" and what is described as
"loathsome" is not clarified by the text. Schottroff has described "desire" as *more* than mere sexual attraction. In her
opinion, "desire" is the antithesis to γνῶσις and the equivalent of "doing the works of the powers."[59] Unfortunately, the
text never really discursively clarifies the meaning of these
terms, but is consistently ambiguous.

The account of Adam's fall, however, suggests a framework
in which the terms can be understood. Here it is precisely
sexual desire that Adam experienced for Eve that signals their
ultimate devolution into a mortal state ([66],25-[67],12).
Adam-Eve was created as an androgynous "aeon" (64,6-22). Creation did not affect his/her perfection in the slightest, but it
was separation into two distinct entities (i.e., loss of androgynous union) that brought about loss of knowledge and glory
(64,20-[65],3; [65],9-16), and it was not until the moment of
Adam's "sweet desire" for Eve that the devolution was complete
and total mortality realized.

"Sweet desire" can mean nothing other than the desire for
sexual union (Gen 4:1). It is in the light of Adam's sexual
desire for Eve that one must read the statements about desire
in the rest of the narrative. The gnostic community was pure
in heart because they had no desire for sexual union. The
creation state of androgynous union was not regained through
sexual intercourse (cf. Gen 2:24, Matt 19:5-6, Eph 5:31, 1 Cor
6:16); this was the act that brought ignorance, humiliation
(= loss of glory), and death. It was the "doing of the works
of the powers" and "the will of the creator" (cf. Gen 1:28)
from which the gnostic community had been freed ([74],17-26;
[83],14-19). The gnostic community possessed knowledge and
through knowledge they had overcome sexual desire and maintained
their purity, and through knowledge they would achieve eventual
androgynous reassimilation.

D. The Position of the Text in the History of Religions

The discussion of the characteristic religious ideas in
the text suggests a tentative positioning for the material with
regard to the history of religions, specifically in relation to
Jewish apocalypticism and Gnosticism. The tension between the
traditional sections and the exegetical sections in the narrative is quite striking, once it is recognized. The purpose of
the creator in sending the flood in the traditional sections is
"to destroy all flesh from the earth," as it appears in Gen 6:7,
Jub. 5:4-5 and *2 Enoch* 34:1-3 (cf. also 2 Pet 2:5), rather than

as a device of the demiurge to destroy the gnostic community, as it appears in the exegetical sections and the *Gos. Eg.* (III,2)61,1-15. Further, the charge given to Noah and his sons in the traditional section "to reign over the earth in regal fashion" ([71],1-4) sounds more like the command given to Noah and his sons in the biblical tradition (Gen 8:17) when contrasted to Noah's command to his sons in the exegetical section "to serve in fear and servility" ([72],18-26). The latter command sounds more like a requirement of the demiurge than the former. Finally, the fact that creation does not appear to be a negative deed puts the "creator" in a much better light, and is a remarkable concession for a gnostic text to make.

The situation that best explains these phenomena in the text is the assumption that the text stands near the border between Jewish apocalypticism and Gnosticism. The use of unaltered pro-Jewish midrashic material is a "slip" that would undoubtedly have been corrected by a more sophisticated gnostic exegete, unless he had a specific reason for leaving it unaltered so that it would purposely reflect characteristic non-gnostic ideas. While the author might have made use of characteristic pro-Jewish motifs to increase the effectiveness of his document as a missionary tract among Jewish groups, it seems improbable that he would purposely use material that conflicted in such a basic way with his own ideas. If we assume that the author had some esoteric reason for leaving the contradictions, we call the text into question as serious religious literature.

The imprecision in language, the superficial and general character of the Gnosticism reflected in the text, the lack of any evident structure to the religious system and the very strong Jewish influence indicate that the author was himself a beginning gnostic, or stood within a tradition that must be described as an emerging Gnosticism. Thus, the A source is not part of a catechism for beginning gnostics, as Beltz describes the *Apoc. Adam*,[60] but might better be described as a book by a beginner. As a catechism, the text could only serve to confuse the beginner.

Although the text draws heavily upon Jewish midrashic and apocalyptic traditions, there can be little question that it is gnostic. It does not stand on the border between Jewish apocalypticism and Gnosticism, but has already turned the corner into Gnosticism. Yet the emerging nature of that Gnosticism requires that it still use concepts and categories from Jewish traditions for expressing itself. The author (or his tradition) stood that close to his Jewish roots.[61] The text stands on the gnostic side of the shift, and the trajectory of the shift is quite clearly from Jewish apocalypticism into Gnosticism.

This positioning of the text is consistent with the history of ideas. One scarcely sees in a document the precise moment of shift when an individual radically alters his basic understanding of reality, but in the text one generally sees the individual either just before or immediately following the shift. For example, in Romans, Paul writes about his preconversion understanding of existence, but he writes from the perspective of Christian faith, that is, on the Christian side of the shift from Judaism to Christianity. While one may with confidence trace the trajectory of Paul's faith from Judaism into Christianity, one must do it from the Christian side of the shift looking backward into Paul's former faith. The A source in the *Apoc. Adam* is that kind of text. It is still near enough to the shift conceptually to reflect its roots quite clearly, but far enough from the shift that there can be little question of its basic orientation and thrust.

CHAPTER III

[1]G. Kittel and G. Friedrich, eds., *Theological Dictionary of the New Testament* (9 vols.; trans. and ed. G. W. Bromiley; Grand Rapids: Eerdmans, 1964-1974) 3.556-57, 570-71.

[2]I.e., the holy dwelling place of the gnostics; cf. [72],1-5 and n. 57 below.

[3]See below, p. 243, note to 64,1-2.

[4]See Klaus Baltzer, *The Covenant Formulary in Old Testament, Jewish and Early Christian Writings* (trans. David Green; Philadelphia: Fortress, 1971) 137-63.

[5]Compare, for example, the *Gospel of Truth* (I,2) in the Nag Hammadi Library. The document is formally a homily on the meaning of the gospel, but is described as a gospel in the incipit.

[6]See James M. Robinson, "Logoi Sophon," *Trajectories through Early Christianity* (Philadelphia: Fortress, 1971) 74-85.

[7]Cf. Matt 1:1 ("The *book of the genealogy* of Jesus Christ") and Luke 1:1-4 ("Inasmuch as many have undertaken to compile a *narrative* of the things which have been accomplished among us...it seemed good to me also...to write *an orderly account*....")

[8]See above, pp. 29 and 33-34. Cf. also Jean Daniélou, "Histoire des Origines Chretiennes," *RSR* 54 (1966) 292. Daniélou, so far as I can determine, was first to recognize this formal literary feature in the tractate. However, he regards the entire tractate as haggadic exegesis.

[9]See above, p. 43 n. 3.

[10]See above, p. 50 n. 55. In fact, there is a tension between the character of the creator in the paraphrased biblical passages and in the exegetical section. In the paraphrased passages god, the Almighty, does not appear evil, and his destruction of the world is not the act of a wicked demiurge. In the "textual" passages, his destruction of the world and all flesh still has the Genesis character of a righteous god punishing disobedient man but preserving righteous Noah, the one man who found favor in his eyes. It is only in the exegetical sections that god, the Almighty, clearly emerges as the evil demiurge who brought the flood as an attempt to destroy the special race of men who had preserved the knowledge of the eternal God lost by Adam and Eve.

[11]See above, pp. 33-34. The first narrative, the "text," is clearly a paraphrase of selections from Genesis 6-10. The second narrative, the "interpretation," taken apart from the rest of the document, describes Noah's failure to ensure that his progeny serve the creator god, and describes the origin of a new generation of men who don't serve the creator.

[12]Adam-Eve came from an aeon higher than that ruled by the creator god where they possessed the knowledge of the eternal God. Source A recognizes two deities that exist in a higher-lower relationship. The higher aeon from which Adam-Eve came is the dwelling of the great eternal angels where knowledge of the eternal God is still possessed. The lower aeon is under the control of the creator, the ruler of the aeons and the powers, and his lesser powers. Note that aeon is used in two different ways: Adam-Eve became two aeons (being) and Adam-Eve existed in a higher aeon (place).

[13]The knowledge and glory of the eternal aeon brought into the lower aeon by Adam-Eve is lost when their devolution into mortality is complete; the knowledge and glory is gone from the lower aeon except for the great generation.

[14]The first attempt to destroy the special race fails when they are taken to the place "where the spirit of life dwells."

[15]For the second time, the special race escapes from the attempt of the creator god to destroy them. See above, p. 48 n. 46 for a discussion of this episode as the second act of redemption.

[16]Baltzer, *Covenant Formulary*, 137-63. Compare Pheme Perkins, "Apocalyptic Schematization," 591-92. Perkins correctly recognized the similarity in introductions between the *Apoc. Adam* and Baltzer's standard testamentary preamble, but incorrectly on this basis alone regarded the "over-all literary structure" of the *Apoc. Adam* as a "testament" in Baltzer's technical literary sense. I would agree that the broad structure of *Apoc. Adam* as redacted does take the form of a testament. However, it should be understood that this is so only because source A provides that basic structure for the document; that is, source A is the framework into which have been redacted other source materials. The "over-all" formal structure of *Apoc. Adam* is actually more complicated. Into the testamentary structure of source A have been conflated several other clearly distinct literary forms (see above, pp. 33-34, 64-69, and below, pp. 97-109, 119-22, 130-32, 202-208). In this sense, the *Apoc. Adam* is not simply or even primarily a testament--although its broad framework may take that form. Rather, it is a highly complicated conflation of several literary forms.

[17]See above, p. 32, for a discussion of the blessing-curse motif. There is some question that this section should be called a testamentary blessing-curse. See the discussion below.

[18]Cf. Pheme Perkins, "Apocalyptic Schematization" (591-99) and her unpublished paper for the Nag Hammadi section of SBL, 1970, "Gnostic Periodization of Revelation and the Apocryphon of John." She treats the periodizing in the *Apoc. Adam* as a periodized scheme of revelation rather than an idealized history. The third period in her scheme, the appearance of the illuminator, clearly has the character of a revelation event, but this is not true of the preceding periods. They might be regarded as revelation events only in the broadest sense and then only under the influence of the illuminator's appearance. Perkins has probably correctly exegeted the redactor's theology, but is also misled by the redactor to attribute a character to the earlier periods that simply is not there. See Hans-Martin Schenke ("Das sethianische System nach Nag-Hammadi-Handschriften," *Studia Coptica* [ed. Peter Nagel; Berlin: Akademie-Verlag, 1974] 169-70) who, for different reasons, regards the scheme in *Apoc. Adam* as "world periods." The apocalyptic concept of an idealized world history occurring in periods or epochs may be due to the influence of Hesiod. See Martin Hengel, *Judaism and Hellenism* (2 vols.; trans. John Bowden; Philadelphia: Fortress, 1974) 1.181-96.

[19]For example, compare the vision of black and bright waters that symbolize the world's history from creation to the advent of the Messiah (*2 Apoc. Bar.* 56:1-69:5). Also, R. H. Charles, ed., *The Apocrypha and Pseudepigrapha of the Old Testament* (2 vols.; Oxford: Clarendon, 1913) 2.512-17.

[20]For example, the period of bondage in Egypt. Certainly it would have included the destruction of Jerusalem. These events, and others, would be considered part of the larger context that gave meaning to the prophet's present proclamation.

[21]Cf. the periodizing scheme in Matt 11:12-14 = Luke 16:16. The creation as a pivotal moment is also omitted but surely assumed in the scheme. It must have originally appeared as follows.

```
[Creation]---The advent of ---John---Now (the appearance---[The end]
             law & prophets          of Jesus)
```

Although both the beginning and ending of the scheme are absent, they are essential to give the rest of the scheme meaning.

[22]

2 Pet 2:1-3	= Jude 4	2 Pet 2:12	= Jude 10
2 Pet 2:4	= Jude 6	2 Pet 2:15	= Jude 11
2 Pet 2:6	= Jude 7	2 Pet 2:17	= Jude 12-13
2 Pet 2:10-11	= Jude 8-9	2 Pet 3:2-3	= Jude 17-18

[23]Cf. Gen 6:1-4; *2 Enoch* 29:4-5 (Charles, *APOT*, 2.447); *A Valentinian Exposition* (XI,2)38,34-39.

[24]See Werner Georg Kümmel, *Introduction to the New Testament* (trans. H. C. Kee; Nashville/New York: Abingdon, 1975) 429-34, and W. Marxsen, *Introduction to the New Testament* (trans. G. Buswell; Oxford: Basil Blackwell, 1968) 241.

[25]The arguments for the literary dependence of 2 Peter upon Jude do not rule out the use by both documents of a common *Vorlage*. In fact, those features that have been argued as proof for literary dependence seem better suited to the argument for a common *Vorlage*. For example, there is very little *exact* verbal agreement between Jude and 2 Peter, but there is *some* verbal agreement and considerable agreement in concepts expressed by synonyms. In my judgment, there is too little verbal agreement to argue on this basis alone for literary dependence, but the agreement is too close for there to have been no relationship between the two documents. In short, the documents reflect the kind of product one would expect if both authors had used a common *Vorlage*.

If one could argue for a common *Vorlage* to explain both similarities and differences in the two documents, then on literary grounds one must judge Jude to be closer to the *Vorlage* than 2 Peter. The construction of 2 Peter is more stylized than Jude and represents a slight refining of the material. For example, in the illustrations (angels that sinned, Exodus, Sodom and Gomorrah), Jude gives only the negative lesson (except for the Exodus). In each illustration, he emphasizes only God's judgment: God keeps the angels that sinned chained until the judgment, and he destroyed Sodom and Gomorrah for immoral acts. In the Exodus example, he does cite both God's saving action and judgment. On the other hand, 2 Peter draws out *both* the positive and negative lessons in the illustration except for the sin of the angels, where it was not possible. The sin of the angels, that appears in Jude after the Exodus, 2 Peter has properly placed first.

[26](III,*2*)63,4-8 = (IV,*2*)74,17-22. Cf. (III,*2*)60,25-61,15 = (IV,*2*)72,7-27.

[27](III,*2*)63,4ff.

[28]See for example (III,*2*)58,23-59,1 and the mythological section at the beginning of the tractate.

[29]Possibly the appearance of the 400 guards and the time of truth and justice are simultaneous events.

[30]He also mentions Sodom, but not in connection with a periodizing statement.

[31]Translation by James Brashler, Peter Dirkse and Douglas Parrott in *The Nag Hammadi Library* (304). The same statement with some modification appears in the Latin *Asclepius* 26 and in a Greek fragment of *Asclepius* appearing in Lactant. *Div. Inst.* 7.18.3-4.

[32]Citations are from Charles, *APOT*, 2, version A.

[33]The 62-year period is broken down as follows: Conquest, 5 years; Period of Judges, 18 years; Period of Apostasy, 19 years; Period of Faithfulness, 20 years. Cf. Charles (*APOT*, 2.416) for the significance of the "years" in terms of Israel's idealized history.

[34]Charles, *APOT*, 2.416-19.

[35]Charles (ibid., 423) regards this time period as 250 "year weeks," or 1,750 years, thus making a total time period from creation to consummation of 4,250 years.

[36]Cf., for example, *Jub.* 20:5 where the destruction of Sodom and Gomorrah appears as an example of God's judgment but was not used as a pivotal moment in the author's periodized scheme.

[37]Charles, *APOT*, 2.1.

[38]Prolog, 1:26. Cf. also 50:5 where the text implies that more Jubilees are to follow the giving of the law.

[39]The section 23:9-32 has a parenthetical and explanatory character, and may have been a later addition.

[40]A Jubilee period is 49 years or seven weeks of years; see Leviticus 25.

[41]At two other points in the document the flood appears as a turning point: 5:19 and 6:18.

[42]The destruction of Sodom (*Jub.* 20:5) is recognized by the author as an example of God's judgment, but he does not include it as a pivotal moment along with the flood as other texts previously discussed have done.

[43]Compare also the Sethian tradition about the world being destroyed once by flood and once by fire: Jos. *Ant.* 1.70; *Adam and Eve* 49:3.

[44]See above, pp. 21-22, 33-34. Also, one should compare the role of Sammaël in the *Ascension of Isaiah* (Eugène Tisserant, *Ascension d'Isaie* [Paris: Letouzey et Ané, 1909] 20-25).

[45]Cf. pp. 33-34 and n. 10 above.

[46]It is used frequently in the Septuagint. See Edwin Hatch and Henry A. Redpath, eds., *A Concordance to the Septuagint* (2 vols.; Graz: Akademischer Druck-V, 1954) 2.1053-54.

[47]See below, pp. 256-57.

[48]The title is known in the *Gos. Eg.* (III,*2*)51,14-22 and (IV,*2*)63,8-17 where the four great lights are mentioned: Harmozel, Oroiael, Davithe, Eleleth. The title is also used in the singular as the source of the four great lights (III,*2*)43, 2-3.13; 49,1-2; 50,12-13; 51,3.14-17; 63,21. Cf. 56,5-6; (IV,*2*)52,21; 62,[27-28]; 63,10-11; 75,10.

[49]See above, pp. 21-22.

[50]However, cf. Hipp. *Ref*. 7.21.1-27.12 where Basilides
apparently describes the creation in a neutral way.

[51]Schottroff, "Animae naturalitur salvandae," 69 n. 10.
The 400,000 men from the seed of Ham and Japheth who have come
under the protection of the gnostic community are full members
of the community, and do not represent a separate class
([73],13-20.25-29; [74],7-11.21-26).   Cf. Epiph. *Pan*. 39.1-5
where there are only two races of men: the descendants of Seth
and Cain.   Cf. Beltz (195) who sees three groups of men in the
text.

[52]The term is used by Schottroff ("Animae naturalitur
salvandae," 69) but is actually a modern convention.   In the
text, the gnostic community is designated by various ambiguous
titles: those men ([69],21-22; [71],10-11.24; [72],2; [74],
21-22; [75],11.23-24; [83],11-12), the men ([76],4), the great
men ([74],5-6; [75],2), another generation ([71],19), those
cast forth from knowledge ([71],11-13), and those men from the
great eternal knowledge ([73],18-20).

[53]The opponents of the men of knowledge are generally
Noah, his sons and their descendants ([70],8-12; [71],1-4.16-
27; [72],15-17; [73],25-29; [74],17-21), and in one instance,
the rulers of the aeons ([73],30-[74],4).

[54]The text that might have clarified their origin is in
lacuna.   Compare the suggested reconstruction at [71],20-[72],1.

[55]See above, p. 48 n. 46.

[56]There are only two other statements in the entire narrative parallel in intent to the statement ([72],1-12) following
the lacuna at [71],27ff.   Both are deliverance statements
([69],18-24; [75],17-27) that are immediately preceded by
threat statements.   This argues that the deliverance statement
at [72],1-12 was probably preceded by a threat statement.
Compare *Jub*. 10:1-13 where a second threat also comes upon Noah
after the flood.   This tradition is lacking in the biblical
material.

[57]In the biblical tradition, the destruction of Sodom and
Gomorrah is viewed as the judgment of God upon a wicked city
(cf. Gen 19:20,24-25), but in gnostic texts, the symbol has been
changed.   Sodom-Gomorrah is the home of the Great Seth (*Gos. Eg.*
[III,2]60,1-18 = [IV,2]71,18-30; cf. [III,2]56,4-13), and its
destruction is interpreted as an unjust act of the demiurge
(*Paraph. Shem* [VII,1]28,34-29,29).   It is probable that the
"land worthy of" the gnostics and their "holy dwelling place"
at [71],21-[72],15 should be identified as Sodom and Gomorrah.

[58]For a parallel, see the preservation of the Sethian community: Epiph. *Pan*. 39.2.6 (Foerster, *Gnosis*, 1.294).   See below, p. 225 n. 104.

[59]Schottroff, "Animae naturalitur salvandae," 69-70.

[60]Cf. Beltz, "Bemerkungen zur Adamapokalypse," 161-63.

[61]This is not a temporal nearness, but a conceptual nearness. The author or his tradition had not yet learned to conceptualize the new theology without heavy reliance on the older Jewish stratum.

CHAPTER IV

THE CHARACTER OF THE B SOURCE

Source B has been only partially preserved by the redactor.
That the text was once considerably longer is shown by the fact
that the first two appearances of the illuminator, required by
the stated third appearance, are not preserved by the text. The
threats against the men of gnosis in the A source and the episodes in which they are preserved are not, technically speaking,
appearances of the illuminator. Therefore, they do not qualify
in a narrow sense as appearance one and appearance two. Furthermore, there are already three separate episodes of redemption in
the text prior to the third appearance of the illuminator. Two
segments are all that remain of source B: the revelation of the
three men and the episode of the illuminator.[1] The literary
character and theology of these two segments will be discussed
separately.

A. The Revelation of the Three Men
([65],24-[66],12; [67],12-21)

1. Form

Böhlig has described this scene as a revelatory vision
that came to Adam while he was asleep. While this characterization of the narrative was rejected above as an inaccurate
description for the narrative, it must be admitted that there
is some basis for understanding it as a dream vision. It seems
clear that this is the way the redactor intended it to be understood. The metaphorical language about sleep does create an
illusion of physical sleep, and revelation through dreams is a
common *topos* in ancient literature. Faced with the problem of
Adam's loss of knowledge in source A, the redactor simply utilized the revelation story as a dream vision to have Adam regain
his lost knowledge. If one assumed that Adam was dreaming,
there would have been no loss of continuity between the two
sources, since dreams function independently of their literary
setting in the "real world." Understanding the passage as a

dream enables the reader to make the leap from the context of
the creator to the situation of the three men with no difficulty.

However, as was argued above, there is simply no indication
in the content of the narrative to suggest that Adam was actually
physically asleep and dreaming. The language in the text allud-
ing to sleep is more appropriately understood as metaphorical
language describing Adam's state of being-in-the-world. In
this connection, it was suggested that the closest parallels to
[65],24-[66],12 and [67],12-21 were to be found in the gnostic
narrative of the "call from without" or gnostic revelation
stories.[2]

The gnostic revelation story in the *Apoc. Adam* follows the
model of a dream vision, although without being totally incorporated into this genre; that is, it never clearly declares
Adam to be asleep, although it is certainly suggested by the
metaphorical language of the narrative. This is not unusual.
As will be seen below, it is possible for the revelation story
to take on the characteristics of another genre and in some
cases to be totally incorporated into another genre.[3]

The narrative in *Apoc. Adam* has a fourfold structure.

1. A statement of ignorance: [65],24-25

   Now I was sleeping in the thought of my heart

2. The appearance of the bearers of revelation:
   [65],25-33

   And I saw three men before me whose figure I was
   unable to recognize since they were not from the
   powers of the god who had created me. They were
   superior to the powers in their glory.

3. The revelation: [65],33-[66],8

   Those men spoke saying to me, "Arise, Adam, from
   the sleep of death, and hear about the eon and
   the seed of that man to whom life has come, he
   who came from you and Eve, your wife.

4. The enlightenment: [66],9-12; [67],12-14

   Then, after I had listened to these words from
   those great men who were standing before me, I
   knew that I was under the authority of death.[4]

The structure and content of this narrative in the *Apoc.
Adam* is related to a small group of what I have called gnostic
revelation stories. The genre seems to be endemic to gnostic

literature since it appears only in documents described as
gnostic. All the elements making up the structure of the revelation story in *Apoc. Adam* appear in these narratives although
not always in the same order, nor do all the stories have all
the units identified in the structure of the story in the *Apoc.
Adam*. In some cases, one of the units found in the *Apoc. Adam*
story is omitted, although implied elsewhere in the revelation
story.

Poimandres (CH 1,27-29)[5]

1. Appearance of the revealer:

    And I began to proclaim to men the beauty of
    piety and knowledge:

2. Statement of ignorance:

    You peoples, earth-born men, who have given
    yourselves up to drunkenness and sleep and to
    ignorance of god,

3. The revelation:

    sober up, stop being drunk, bewitched by un-
    reasoning sleep....Why, earth-born men, have
    you given yourselves up to death, when you have
    power to share in immortality?
    Repent, you who have travelled in company with
    error and have made common cause with ignorance.
    Separate yourselves from the dark light, for-
    sake corruption and partake of immortality.

4. The enlightenment:

    Some of them made fun (of me) and others went
    away...but the others threw themselves at my
    feet and begged to be instructed. But I made
    them stand up and become a guide of the (human)
    race, and taught them how and in what way they
    will be saved. I sowed in them the words of
    wisdom, and they were nourished by ambrosial
    water.

Two differences between the two narratives are immediately
obvious: in the structure and in the number of revealers. In
Apoc. Adam, three men bring the revelation, but in Poimandres
there is only one revealer. The structure of the Poimandres
segment is also slightly different, although all elements noted
in the *Apoc. Adam* are present. Poimandres begins with the appearance of the revealer rather than with the statement of ignorance. The earthly ignorant condition of the "earth-bound"

men in Poimandres is described as "drunkenness," "sleep" and
"death."[6] This parallels the *Apoc. Adam* where Adam is called
on to arise from the "sleep of death," and then once enlightened knew himself to be under the authority of death. The
desire of the earth-bound men to be instructed further by
Hermes can be attributed to the fact that they realized the
words of Hermes to be true in the same way Adam was enlightened
and knew himself to be under the authority of death. The revelation in Poimandres is a series of injunctions to the
audience.

The statement of ignorance appears as a separate unit, but
has also been incorporated into the statement of the revealer.
In fact, the statement of ignorance seems to be extraneous to
the story since what follows in the revelation makes the same
point with almost the same language.

Statement of ignorance   Revelation
᾽Ω λαοί, ἄνδρες γηγενεῖς   τί ἑαυτούς, ὦ ἄνδρες γηγενεῖς
οἱ μέθῃ καὶ ὕπνῳ ἑαυτούς   εἰς θάνατον ἐκδεδώκατε
ἐκδεδωκότες
                              ἔχοντες ἐξουσίαν τῆς ἀθανασίας
                              μεταλαβεῖν; μετανοήσατε,
                              οἱ συνοδεύσαντες τῇ πλάνῃ
                              καὶ συγκοινωνήσαντες
καὶ τῇ ἀγνωσίᾳ τοῦ θεοῦ   τῇ ἀγνοίᾳ

Had the statement of ignorance been omitted as a separate unit,
there would have been no loss to the revelation story. This is
apparently the reason for the absence of this unit in the *Trimorphic Protennoia*; *Zostrianos*; Left *Ginza* 1,2; Right *Ginza*
60,2 and the Mandaean *Book of John* (see below for a discussion
of these references). It was recognized as an unnecessary
duplication. The statement of ignorance is usually caught up
again in the statement of revelation as that from which the
audience is to arise, awaken, or sober up. Compare the statement of ignorance in *Apoc. Adam*, where Adam announces that he
was "asleep in the thought of his heart," to the statement of
revelation, where three men call on Adam to "arise from the
sleep of death." In the Hymn of the Pearl and Theodore bar
Konai (see below), the statement of ignorance is picked up
again in the revelation statement almost verbatim. In the

Apocryphon of John, the statement of ignorance is picked up
again in the revelation statement, but in modified and elaborated form.

The Hymn of the Pearl (Acts of Thomas 108-113)[7]

1. Statement of ignorance: (109,32-35)

   They (the Egyptians) dealt with me treacherously,
   and gave me their food to eat.
   I forgot that I was a son of kings, and I served
   their king; and I forgot the pearl, for which my
   parents had sent me and because of the burden of
   their oppressions I lay in a deep sleep.

2. Appearance of the revealer: (110,36-40; 111,49-52)

   But all these things that befell me my parents
   perceived, and were grieved for me; and a proclamation was made in our kingdom, that everyone should
   come to our gate, kings and princes of Parthia,
   and all the nobles of the East. And they wrote a
   plan on my behalf that I might not be left in
   Egypt; and they wrote me a letter and every noble
   signed his name to it....It flew in the likeness
   of an eagle, the king of all birds; it flew and
   alighted beside me, and became all speech.

3. The revelation: (110,41-48)

   From thy Father, the king of kings, and thy
   mother the mistress of the East, and from thy
   brother, our second (in authority), to thee our
   son, who art in Egypt, greetings! Up and arise
   from thy sleep, and listen to the words of our
   letter! Call to mind that thou art a son of
   kings! See the slavery, whom thou servest!
   Remember the pearl, for which thou wast sent to
   Egypt! Think of thy robe, and remember thy
   splendid toga, which thou shalt wear and (with
   which) thou shalt be adorned, when thy name hath
   been read out in the list of the valiant.

4. The enlightenment: (111,53-57)

   At its voice and the sound of its rustling, I
   started and arose from my sleep. I took it up
   and kissed it, and I began (and) read it; and
   according to what was traced on my heart were the
   words of my letter written. I remembered that I
   was a son of royal parents, and my noble birth
   asserted its nature. I remembered the pearl for
   which I had been sent to Egypt.

In the order that they appear in the text, units two and
three are reversed: the reciting of the letter comes before its
delivery. However, in the development of the action in the

revelation story and the effect of the letter on the recipient,
the revelation of the contents of the letter logically follows
the appearance of the letter. Hence, the above arrangement is
on the basis of the logical development of the story. Sleep is
again a description of being-in-the-world from which the king's
son must be "awakened." From the standpoint of the instrument
of revelation, there is only one revealer, the personified
letter, but from the standpoint of the initiators of revelation,
there are three revealers, the father, the mother and the
brother. The revelation consists of a series of injunctions to
the audience.[8]

Theodore bar Konai[9]

1. The appearance of the revealer:

    Jesus the Luminous approached Adam the innocent

2. The statement of ignorance:

    and woke him from the sleep of death in order that
    he might be delivered from the two great Spirits.
    And just as a man who is righteous and finds a man
    possessed of a mighty demon and quiets him by his
    act, like this was also Adam because that beloved
    One found him sunk in the great sleep.

3. The revelation:

    And he woke him and took hold of him and shook
    him; and he drove away from him the seductive
    demon, and bound away from him the great female
    Archon.

4. The enlightenment:

    Then Adam examined himself and recognized what he
    was.

The text has reversed the order of the first two units as it
appears in the *Apoc. Adam*. The description of Adam's being-in-
the-world is characterized as a "sleep of death," as we have it
in the *Apoc. Adam*. The revelation story is modelled on an
exorcism story where the demon is driven from Adam at the touch
of the miracle worker's hands.[10] No words of revelation are
spoken but at the driving out of the demons Adam "examines
himself." The sleep of death and ignorance are caused by Adam
being possessed by the seductive demon and the female archon.
At their exorcism, Adam recognized "what he was," i.e., where he
had come from, a standard gnostic *topos*.[11]

Trimorphic Protennoia ([XIII,*1**]41,20-36)[12]

1. Statement of ignorance: (lacking)

2. The appearance of the revealer: (41,20-24)

   I am the first one who descended on account of my
   portion which is left behind, that is, the Spirit
   that (now) dwells in the Soul, but which originated from the Water of Life.

3. The revelation: (41,24-28)

   And out of the immersion of the mysteries I spoke,
   I together with the Archons and Authorities. For
   I went down below their language and I spoke my
   mysteries to my own--a hidden mystery--

4. The enlightenment: (41,28-36)

   and the bonds and eternal oblivion were nullified.
   And I bore fruit in them, that is, the Thought of
   the unchanging Aeon, and my house, and their
   [Father]. And I went down [to those who were mine]
   from the first and I [reached them and broke] the
   first strand that [enslaved them. Then] everyone
   [within] me shone....

The statement of ignorance is missing from the story as an
individual part of the structure. However, it is implied in
the statements of revelation and enlightenment. That the revealer was required to "speak mysteries" implies an unenlightened
or uninformed state on the part of the audience. Further, that
from which he freed them is described as T̄Bⲱⲉ (sleep, forgetfulness), as in the *Apoc. Adam*, Adam is described as awakening from
the "sleep of death" and sleeping in the thought of his heart.
There is only one revealer.

Zostrianos ([VIII,*1*]130,4-132,5)

1. Statement of ignorance: (lacking)

2. Appearance of the revealer: (130,4-12)

   I came down to the perceptible world, and put on
   my temple. Because it was ignorant, I strengthened
   it and went about preaching the truth to all of
   them. Neither the angelic beings of the world,
   nor the rulers saw me,

3. The enlightenment: (130,12-15)

   for I destroyed a multitude of [disgraces] which
   brought me near death. But an erring multitude
   I awakened, saying,

4. The revelation: (130,16-132,5)

"Know those who are alive and the holy seed of
Seth...."[13]

The statement of ignorance although absent as a separate unit
is implied in the statement of enlightenment, i.e., the "awakening" of the erring multitude. Further, the ignorance of the
"temple" used by the revealer seems to be characteristic of the
perceptible world into which the revealer comes, and therefore
of the erring multitude. The order of the last two units is
reversed in comparison to the order in the *Apoc. Adam*. There
is only one revealer. The revelation consists of a series of
injunctions. The statement of enlightenment is only briefly
stated with no elaboration, just as it appears in Theodore bar
Konai.

Left *Ginza* 1,2[14]

1. Statement of ignorance: (lacking)

2. Appearance of the revealer:

Einmal sprach die Seele mit dem Geist und dem
stinkenden Körper doch der Geist und der stinkende
Körper gaben ihr keine Antwort. Während die Seele
dasteht und mit dem Geist und dem stinkenden
Körper spricht kam der Erlöser heran. Heran kam
der Erlöser, es langte an der Bote. Er kam heran,
trat an den Pfühl Adams, an dem Pfühl Adams trat er

3. The revelation:

und weckte ihn aus dem Schlafe. Er sprach zu ihm:
"Steh auf, steh auf Adam, leg ab deinen stinkenden
Körper, den Lehmrock, in dem du weiltest. Leg ab
den körperlichen Rock, den verwesenden Körper, in
dem du weiltest. Leg ab das körperliche Gewand, in
dem du weiltest, und schlag es den Sieben und den
Zwölf, den Männern, die es geschaffen, um den Kopf.
Lass den Körper sogleich in der Welt zurück, denn
deine Zeit ist gekommen, dein Mass ist voll, aus
dieser Welt zu scheiden. Das Leben hat mich zu
dir gesandt, denn es verlangt nach dir. Dein Gang
sei nach dem Orte des Lebens, nach dem Orte, an
dem du früher weiltest, nach der Wohnung, in der
dein Vater sitzet.

4. The enlightenment:

Als Adam dies hörte, jammerte er über sich und
weinte. Er jammerte und weinte, und in seinem Auge
löste sich eine Träne. Adam öffnete den Mund und
sprach zu dem Boten, der zu ihm gekommen war:

"Vater! Wenn ich mit dir komme, wer wird in dieser
so weiten Tibil Hüter sein? Wer wird diesem meinem
Weibe Hawwā Gesellschaft leisten? Wer wird diesen
Pflanzen, die ich gepflanzet, in den Zeitaltern
eine Stütze sein? Wer wird ihnen eine Stütze sein?
Wer wird in diesem Hause wohnen, in dem ich ge-
wohnet; wer soll darin...sein? Wenn die Palme
Früchte trägt, wenn der Christdorn Blüten trägt,
wer wird ihr Hüter sein? Wenn der Euphrat und der
Tigris herankommen, wer soll...mit der Hand er-
greifen und das Wasser zu den Pflanzen leiten?
Wenn die Gebärerin gebieret, wer soll ihnen bei-
stehen? Wer soll die Rinder vor den Pflug spannen
und wer den Samen in die Erde leiten? Wer soll die
Klapper in die Hand nehmen und den Schafen nach
ihrer Hürde und den Antilopen nach ihrer Herde zu-
klappern? Wer soll die Waisen zusammenhalten, wer
die Taschen der Witwe füllen? Wer soll den Nackten
kleiden und ihm ein Gewand um den Nacken legen?
Wer soll den Gefangenen auslösen, wer im Dorfe den
Streit schlichten?

The statement of ignorance is absent as a separate unit in the
structure of the story, but present in the motif of sleep from
which Adam must be awakened. See Jonas' discussion of the passage[15] where he points out that the message of awakening coin-
cides with the message of death. It is striking that the enlightenment segment parallels quite closely the enlightenment
segment in *Apoc. Adam*. In the *Ginza*, Adam is keenly aware of
his imminent death and clings desperately to the world as he
argues with the revealer. In *Apoc. Adam*, Adam realizes, when
he hears the words of revelation, that he has "come under the
authority of death" ([66],9-12; [67],12-14). Note that the
revelation is a series of injunctions, and there is only one
revealer.

Right *Ginza* 60,2[16]

1. Statement of ignorance: (lacking)

2. Appearance of the revealer:

   Ein Uthra ruft von aussen her
   und belehrt Adam, den Mann.

3. The revelation:

   Er spricht zu Adam:
   "Schlummere nicht und schlafe nicht
   und vergiss nicht, was dein Herr dir aufgetragen.
   Sei nicht ein Sohn des (irdischen) Hauses
   und werde nicht ein Frevler in der Tibil genannt.

Liebe nicht wohlreichende Kränze
    und finde kein Gefallen an einem lieblichen Weibe.
Liebe nicht Wohlgerüche
    und vernachlässige nicht das Gebet der Nacht.
Liebe nicht täuschende Schatten,
    nicht den Verkehr mit lieblichen Frauen.
Liebe nicht die Lust,
    noch lügnerische Schattenbilder.
Trinke nicht und sei nicht unmässig
    und vergiss nicht deinen Herrn aus dem Sinne.
Bei deinem Eintritt und deinem Austritt
    siehe zu, dass du deinen Herrn nicht vergessest.
Bei deinem Gehen und deinem Kommen
    siehe zu, dass du deinen Herrn nicht vergessest.
Bei deinem Sitzen und deinem Stehen
    siehe zu, dass du deinen Herrn nicht vergessest.
Bei deinem Ruhen und deinem Liegen
    siehe zu, dass du deinen Herrn nicht vergessest.
Sage nicht, ich bin ein erstgeborener Sohn,
    der ich, was ich auch tun mag, ohne Torheit bleibe.
Adam, siehe die Welt an,
    die ganz ein Ding ohne Wesen ist.
Ein Ding ohne Wesen ist sie,
    auf die du kein Vertrauen haben darfst.
Aufgerichtet sitzt die Wage da,
    und von tausend wählt sie einen aus.
Einen wählt sie von tausend aus,
    und zwei wählt sie aus zehntausend.
Die duftenden Kränze vergehen,
    und Frauenschönheit wird, als ob sie nie dagewesen.
Die Wohlgerüche vergehen,
    und die Lust der Nacht hört auf.
Alle Werke vergehen,
    nehmen ein Ende und werden, als ob sie nie dagewesen.

4.   The enlightenment:

Als Adam dies hörte,
    jammerte er und weinte über sich selbst.
Er sprach zum Uthra des Lebens
    folgendermassen:
"Wenn ihr wisset, dass dem so ist,
    warum habt ihr mich von meinem Orte weg in die
    Gefangenschaft gebracht und in den stinkenden
    Körper geworfen?
In den stinkenden Körper habt ihr mich geworfen,
    in das verzehrende Feuer mich geschleudert.
Ihr habt mich in das verzehrende Feuer geschleudert,
    dass täglich der Gestank in die Höhe steigt.

The statement of ignorance is missing as a separate unit in the
story, but is implied in the Uthra's call to Adam to awaken and
to remember his father's commission. It is also implied in
Adam's awakening where he becomes aware for the first time of
his condition in the world. Sleep is again a characteristic of

Adam's being-in-the-world.   There is only one revealer, and the
revelation is a series of injunctions.

The Mandaean *Book of John* 13[17]

1. Statement of ignorance: (lacking)

2. Appearance of the revealer:

    Aus Feuer und Wasser wurde der eine Himmel
    ausgespannt. Aus Feuer und Wasser haben sie die
    Erde auf dem Amboss gedichtet. Aus Feuer und
    Wasser sind Früchte, Trauben und Bäume entstanden.
    Aus Feuer und Wasser wurde der körperliche Adam
    gebildet. Sie schufen den Boten und schickten
    ihn zum Haupte der Generationen.

3. The revelation:

    Er rief mit himmlischer Stimme in die Unruhe der
    Welten hinein.

4. The enlightenment:

    Auf den Ruf des Boten erwachte Adam, der dalag.
    Adam, der dalag, erwachte und ging dem Boten ent-
    gegen: "Komm in Frieden, du Bote, Gesandter des
    Lebens, der vom Hause meines Vaters gekommen ist.
    Wie ist doch das teure, schöne Leben an seinem
    Orte fest gepflanzt! Wie ist mir aber (hier) ein
    Sessel aufgestellt und sitzt meine finstere Gestalt
    in Klage da!" Da erwiderte der Bote und sprach
    zum körperlichen Adam: "Schön hat man deinen Thron
    aufgerichtet, Adam, und deine Gestalt sitzt hier
    in Klage da? Alle gedachten deiner zum Guten und
    schufen mich und sandten mich zu dir. Ich bin
    gekommen und will dich belehren, Adam, und dich
    aus dieser Welt erlösen. Horche und höre und lass
    dich belehren und steig siegreich zum Lichtort
    empor.
       Adam hörte und wurde gläubig,--Heil dem, der
    nach dir hört und gläubig ist. Adam nahm Kuštā
    an,--Heil dem, der nach dir Kuštā annimmt. Adam
    schaute voller Hoffnung hin und stieg empor,--Heil
    dem, der nach dir emporsteigt.
       Horchet und höret und lasset euch belehren,
    ihr Vollkommenen, und steiget empor zum Orte des
    Lichtes.
       Und gepriesen sei das Leben.

The statement of ignorance is missing as a separate unit in the
structure of the story, but is implied in Adam's awakening, and
in the statement of the revealer that he will "instruct" Adam.
There is only one revealer. The call to awaken is briefly
stated in the third position and in this respect parallels

Apoc. Adam, *Ap. John* (II), Mandaean *Book of John*, *Trim. Prot.*
and Theodor bar Konai, but the statement of revelation is more
developed in the enlightenment segment in the fourth position
where the content of revelation is spelled out. Here the revelation contains a short series of injunctions. The conclusion
to the story seems to be a conclusion for the readers of the
material to make the same response to the revelation as Adam.

The *Apocryphon of John* ([II,*1*]30,33-31,26)[18]

   1. Statement of ignorance: (lacking)

   2. Appearance of the revealer: (30,33-31,4)

       Still for a third time I went--I am the light which
       exists in the light, I am the remembrance of the
       Pronoia--that I might enter into the middle of
       darkness and the inside of Hades. And I filled my
       face with the light of the completion of their aeon.
       And I entered into the middle of their prison which
       is the prison of the body.

   3. The revelation: (31,4-6)

       And I said, "He who hears, let him get up from the
       deep sleep."

   4. The enlightenment: (31,6-26)

       And he wept and shed tears. Bitter tears he wiped
       from himself and he said "Who is it that calls my
       name, and from where has this hope come to me,
       while I am in the chains of the prison?" And I
       said, "I am the Pronoia of the pure light; I am
       the thinking of the virginal Spirit, he who raised
       you up to the honored place. Arise and remember
       that it is you who hearkened, and follow your root,
       which is I, the merciful one, and guard yourself
       against the angels of poverty and the demons of
       chaos and all those who ensnare you, and beware of
       the deep sleep and the enclosure of the inside of
       Hades."
            And I raised him up and sealed him in the
       light of the water with five seals, in order that
       death might not have power over him from this time
       on.

As is the case in a majority of the examples of the revelation story cited above, the statement of ignorance is lacking
as a separate segment. However, the motif of ignorance is
present having been incorporated into the segment on the appearance of the revealer. This is clear from the allusions to the

"darkness" and the "prison of the body." The revelation segment is a bare call to awaken out of sleep, while the revelation proper is incorporated into the enlightenment segment.
This procedure is also observed in the *Johannesbuch*. Sleep is
again a description of man's being-in-the-world rather than
actual physical sleep. The revelation consists of a series of
injunctions.

In structure and content, the *Apoc. Adam* is closely related
to the structure of this collection of stories. Even the language and metaphors of the stories are similar. Sleep is a
common feature used to describe man's being-in-the-world as one
of delusion or ignorance. In order to dispel the delusion of
the world and awaken man from the sleep of death, a revealer
comes into the world.[19] He calls for man to arise, awaken and
hear. The actual revelation varies. Sometimes it is no more
than the simple call to awaken, at other times it is a quite
lengthy revelation that usually takes the form of a series of
commands. Man responds in various ways. He arises from sleep,
begs to be instructed further, cries and laments his fate, or
is shocked at the condemnation of death under which he stands.
The story in the *Apoc. Adam* is such a story and is best understood in this way.

2. Theology

On the basis of the preceding discussion, it can be seen
that the ideas in this revelation story are mostly quite general and resist any attempt to associate them with any particular gnostic group. Sleep is a common motif in gnostic texts
that describes man's being-in-the-world as one of ignorance or
delusion, and appears to be a common *topos* of the revelation
story. Likewise, in the *Apoc. Adam*, the qualifiers used to
describe the kind of sleep as "sleep of my heart" and "sleep of
death" add a different dimension to the word "sleep." It goes
beyond the normal physical act of sleep, and describes the unenlightened state of a man deluded by the concerns of the
world, as, for example, the Hymn of the Pearl (109,32-35).[20]
Adam had become so affected by the ignorance of the world and

the forgetfulness of his origin that he failed to recognize the
revealers from the God of knowledge because they did not belong
to his present world, i.e., to the world of the creator. The
calls "to arise" and "to hear" are also common *topoi* of the
revelation story, and an expected corollary of the motif of
sleep.

The expression "the authority of death" is more difficult
to define precisely. The motif of death is a regular feature
in gnostic texts, and a common *topos* of the revelation story.
It appears as a description of man's being-in-the-world, and as
such is a practical synonym for ignorance.[21] But it also appears once in these stories as a reference to physical death.[22]
The other references to death in source B do not really sharply
clarify this problem of whether by the "authority of death" is
meant Adam becoming aware that he had lived in ignorance
(= under the authority of death) or whether, like the Adam of
the Left *Ginza*, he suddenly becomes aware that he must physically die (cf. Gen 3:19).[23] Two of these instances ([76],17-
20 and [76],28-[77],1) are clearly pejorative metaphors describing the situation in which man finds himself (dead world =
ignorance = sleep). The phrase "power of death" occurs again
in a *parallelus membrorum* ([76],17-24).

> Every creature that has come from the dead earth will
> be under the power of death, but those who reflect
> on the knowledge of the eternal God in their heart
> will not perish.

On this basis, one could reason that if "being under the power
of death" is the equivalent of "perishing" then those who reflect on the knowledge of the eternal God have cast off the
power of death because they will not perish (= being under the
power of death); that is, they are not under the power of death
because they have been enlightened. Thus, one could argue that
the power of death (= perishing) does not refer to man's ultimate physical demise as does Gen 3:19, since one can scarcely
keep from physically dying by receiving knowledge, but it refers to man's being-in-the-world as a state of hopeless and
helpless ignorance, and describes his spiritual death.

However, the final reference ([76],15-17) in this same
context argues against this analysis: "and he will save their
souls from the day of death." Does the text refer to the inevitable day of the individual's death or to the *Eschaton* (cf.
[84],1-3)? There seems to be no way to understand the phrase
in a metaphorical sense. The expression regularly occurs elsewhere in a personal sense (i.e., "the day of *his* death") to the
moment of the individual's death: Gen 27:2, Judg 13:7, 1 Sam
15:35, 2 Sam 6:23, 20:3, 2 Kgs 15:5, Jer 52:11.34, Midrash
Tehillim 41,4, and in an impersonal construction (i.e., the day
of death) only where it is clear that it is referring to the
day of the individual's death: Eccl 7:2 (LXX), 8:8; Pirke Aboth
2:5.

Beltz's understanding of the passage ([76],15-24) as a
reference to the day of the individual's death is probably the
best solution.[24] On this day, knowledge of the eternal God in
one's heart will preserve one from the ultimate destruction
that awaits the dead earth and its unenlightened creatures.[25]
In this sense, the "power of death" is a reference to the total
effect of ignorance. In the dead world, death is the controlling power: unenlightened men are spiritually "dead," and physically they must also die. Eternal oblivion will be their
ultimate end. But those who are enlightened are spiritually
"alive." They have broken the power of "death" and have dis-
pelled ignorance. Thus, when the "day of their death" arrives,
they will also avoid eternal oblivion and enter into eternal
life. When Adam says, "I knew that I had come under the power
of death," he meant that he realized himself to be a creature
of the "dead" earth who had been "dead" in ignorance and delusion and who must yet physically die, for all creatures of the
dead earth face their "day of death" (Gen 3:19).

The revelation that the three men announce to Adam reflects the most distinctive and yet enigmatic ideas in the revelation story ([65],33-[66],8).

> Hear about the eon and the seed
> of that man to whom life has come,
> he who came from you and Eve, your wife.

The one who came from Adam and Eve is probably Seth. Although
Gen 5:4 reports that Adam had other sons and daughters, it is
quite clear that he had only three offspring whose names are
preserved by the tradition (Gen 4:25). Of these three, Abel
was killed and Cain was cursed for slaying him (Gen 4:11-14).
However, Adam had a third son "in his own likeness and after
his image" (Gen 5:3), that is, in the likeness and image of God
(cf. Gen 1:26). *Adam and Eve* 38:4 reports that Seth was born
"according to the appointment of God," and in some manuscripts
he alone is chosen to receive the revelation of Adam (*Adam and
Eve* 25:1ff.).[26] The same preference for Seth is reflected in
Epiphanius's account of the Sethians (*Pan.* 39.1-3).[27] Seth was
born through divine prerogative, chosen to purify mankind and
in him was vested divine purity and power (Epiph. *Pan.* 39.2.4,7).
All virtue and justice are ascribed to him (Epiph. *Pan.* 39.1.3).

   However, in spite of the probability that the man "who
came from Adam and Eve" is Seth, at no point in the tractate is
he *positively* identified as Seth! In fact, in *Apoc. Adam* there
are few references to Seth,[28] and the tractate seems deliberate-
ly to obscure such an identification.[29] This reluctance of the
text to identify more precisely the "man" as Seth and his "seed"
as descendants of Seth is puzzling, particularly when there is
no reluctance to talk about the seed of Noah ([74],17-21; [76],
11-13) or the seed of Ham and Japheth ([73],13-15.25-29; [74],
7-11; [76],11-13).

   The second distinctive characterization describes Seth as
the man "to whom life has come." There is nothing in the revelation story proper or the tractate as a whole that explains
the meaning of the phrase, nor is there an obvious referrant in
the tradition that would clarify it.[30] A similar expression is
used of the men of gnosis ([69],12-16); they are the men "to
whom passed the life of knowledge" that came from Adam and Eve.[31]
Perhaps the reference is to Seth's divine origin as is reflected
in Epiphanius (*Pan.* 39.2.4; cf. 40.7.1).[32]

> She [i.e., the Mother] took thought and caused Seth to
> be born and put into him her own power, implanting in
> him a seed of the power from on high and the spark
> that was sent from on high for the first foundation of
> the seed and of the institution (of the world).

Seth apparently imparted this "life" or divine power to his descendants (cf. *Ap. John* [II,*1*]26,7-19 for association of power and life) so that they are eternal (Epiph. *Pan.* 39.2.6) as he is eternal (39.3.5). The "life" in *Apoc. Adam* ([65],33-[66],8) would correspond to the divine "power" or "spark" in the Epiphanius tradition that Seth has passed on to his descendants ([69],10-16) and they, like him, would live forever ([75],17-[76],6). In this connection, see *Steles Seth* (VII,*5*) 118,12-13 where Seth is referred to as the father of the *living* and immovable race.

The reference to "the aeon and the seed of that man" is equally obscure.[33] There is little in the tradition that clarifies the mythological structures that give this statement meaning. One possibility is found in the *Gos. Eg.* (III,*2*) 51,5-14.[34]

> The incorruptible man Adamas asked for them a son out of himself, in order that he may become father of the immovable incorruptible race, so that through it (i.e., the race), the silence and the voice may appear, and through it, the dead aeon may raise itself so that it may dissolve.

Böhlig and Wisse understand this passage to refer to the introduction of the race of Seth (i.e., his seed) into the cosmos. The appearance of the seed serves as the judgment of the dead aeon.[35] With this as a background, one could understand the statement in source B ([65],33-[66],8) as a reference to the coming of the seed of Seth and the consequent judgment of the dead aeon.

The statement is actually most compatible with two comments made by the redactor of the *Apoc. Adam* and seems to reflect his theology.[36] For this reason, the possibility arises that the revelation story is really a creation of the redactor and not traditional material that he received and adapted for his purposes. In the preceding chapter I suggested that the two units comprising source B are related in only a general way, and did not exclude the possibility that the revelation story is actually the creation of the redactor; I have not yet discussed in detail how the two units are related.[37]

However, I think it highly unlikely that the revelation
story was composed by the redactor. It is more logical to explain it as traditional material received and secondarily
broken up by the redactor than to argue that the redactor acci-
dentally composed a classic revelation story in three separate
increments ([65],24-34; [66],1-12; [67],12-21)--separating them
by disparate and incompatible material--that fit together perfectly once that disparate material is removed.

There is another argument for the original unity of the
revelation story and for the fact that its present disarrange-
ment occurred *after* its initial composition. In the rationale
of the revelation story, the last sentence ([67],12-14) is a
positive assertion. It represents the desired objective of the
revealer, i.e., the statement of enlightenment. When Adam
heard the words of revelation for the first time, he realized
that his pre-revelation state was one of ignorance and death.[38]
However, in its present context, following [67],4-12, it takes
on a negative meaning. The passage preceding it reflects the
ultimate result of Adam's involvement in the physical world:
ignorance, carnal desire, and physical death. In its secondary
context in the *Apoc. Adam*, the last line is intended to clarify
and emphasize the sentence that precedes.

> A weakness overtook us; therefore the days of our life
> became few.

By this statement, the redactor of *Apoc. Adam* wants the reader
to understand the text to mean that Adam "had fallen under the
authority of death," a negative concept, and as it appears in
the redacted text of *Apoc. Adam*, negatively intended. Yet we
have previously seen that in its original context it was an
affirmative statement and had a meaning sharply opposed to the
meaning it is forced to assume in the present context, if one
is to make any sense of it at all.

If one assumes that the redactor originally composed the
revelation story, one must also assume that the redactor knew
what he was doing since it is so artfully and correctly done.
Therefore he knew that the statement at [67],12-14 was affirmative. Why then would he compose the story simply for the

purpose of breaking it up and use what he originally intended
as an affirmative statement as a summary line in a negative
assertion? The assumption is more difficult to maintain when
one realizes that if he could have composed the revelation
story he could also have composed a better conclusion for
[66],31-[67],12, and there would have been no necessity for
composing a revelation story and then adapting it for purposes
foreign to the genre.

     However, it is always possible that the redactor could
have reworked the revelation story, even if he didn't compose
it, by simply expanding the statement made by the bearers of the
revelation ([65],33-[66],8), or by substituting a completely
different statement of revelation. It is also possible that
the revelation story is traditional material so closely aligned
with the redactor's own theology that it required no editing.
If this is the case, it was unnecessary for him to redact the
revelation story; he merely had to incorporate it with no
change. There is really no way to be certain which of these
three possibilities is the correct option. In any case, as
will be seen below, the relationship of the statement of revelation to the redactor's theology is more than superficial;
it is substantial.[39]

          B. The Third Appearance of the Illuminator
          ([76],8-11; [76],14-[82],17; [82],19-[83],4)

1. Introduction

     The second unit of source B is a collection of explanations
about the origin of the illuminator of knowledge with a brief
narrative introduction.[40] The thirteen explanations by the
kingdoms have a similar form or structure, and seem to be in
contrast to the explanation of the kingless generation, which
appears to be the final and true explanation.[41] The explanations are stated ostensibly in response to a question of the
powers in the introduction regarding the source of error: "Where
did it (error) come from, or (rather) whence have come these
deceiving words that all the powers failed to discover?" ([77],
23-27).[42]

Although the question by the powers asks about the source
of error, and the explanations address themselves to an unposed
question about the origin of the illuminator, there is a sense
in which the collection of explanations can be related to the
question by the powers. One could reason that the thirteen
kingdoms represent the kingdoms or nations of the world. There
is some basis in the text to support this finding. In Genesis,
after the flood, the world is divided among the sons of Noah
(Gen 10:2-6). This same motif appears in the *Apoc. Adam* where
Ham and Japheth form twelve kingdoms (Gen 10:2-6 LXX) plus one
additional kingdom for a total of thirteen kingdoms ([73],
25-29). Therefore, the answers of the kingdoms--the nations
of the world--could represent the entire erroneous religious
history of mankind.

On the basis of this background, the answer to the question is that error, represented in the deception of the heavenly powers and by erroneous human traditions about the origin
of the illuminator, is characteristic of the cosmos. The oppo-
nent of error in the cosmos is gnosis, represented by the true
explanation for the illuminator's origin made by the kingless
generation. The theological intent of the collection of explanations as an answer to the question is to make clear this
contrast between error and gnosis. Error has been perpetuated
because generations of men have offered false explanations for
the source of enlightenment (as is indicated by the erroneous
explanations). The only solution to the problem is to discover
gnosis through the generation without a king: the gnostics
themselves. When one looks at the text from this perspective,
the collection of stories does seem well suited to the
question.[43]

However, in another sense there is a serious problem with
holding that there is an original compositional unity between
the narrative introduction ([76],8-[77],27) and the collection
of explanations ([77],27-[82],17; [82],19-[83],4). For one
reason, the stories in the collection taken individually do not
answer the question asked by the powers. The question of the
powers asks specifically about the source of the *error* (feminine
gender) that had deceived the powers, but the individual

explanations do not respond to this question. Instead, they
answer a question, not posed in the text, about the origin of
a certain supra-natural individual (masculine gender) who remains unidentified in the answers of the thirteen kingdoms. In
short, there is no substantial correlation between the question
and the answers; the answers do not arise naturally in response
to the question.

Further, there is a change in the actors of the drama between the narrative introduction and the collection of explanations. The powers (δου) pose the question, but the kingdoms
respond.[44] If one assumes that the kingdoms were evil powers
and part of the court of the archon of the powers ([77],1-3),[45]
and that their responses represent the attempt of this court
to come to grips with the disturbance that had invaded the
archon's realm, then one must ask why they are not mentioned
before, or after, this incident? If one assumes they represent
the kingdoms (= nations) of the world, then one must ask when
the shift from the archon's realm to the earth took place, and
how the nations heard the question? The abrupt shift from the
archon's sphere to an idealized earthly setting with no preparation for the shift maintains an illusion of continuity between
question and answer until one recognizes that, although they
are part of the same cosmos, they are essentially two different
realms and that one would not normally expect a rhetorical type
question asked in the sphere of the archon to be answered in
the earthly realm without some basis being given for the over-
hearing of the question on the part of the actors in the
earthly realm.

The lack of a specific identification for the subject of
the statement by the thirteen kingdoms is also a problem. With
the exception of kingdom thirteen where he is called an archon,
in the thirteen kingdoms the hero is not specifically identified. Only in the statement of the kingless generation is he
specifically identified as the illuminator. The kingdoms refer
to him generally as "he" or the "child." If there were a compositional unity between the two segments, the introduction and
the collection of answers, one would have expected additional
concrete allusions in the statements of the thirteen kingdoms

identifying the subject as the illuminator. At some point, the
text should have betrayed the fact that the illuminator, so
prominent in the introduction and specifically identified in
the statement of the kingless generation, is the subject of the
statements by the thirteen kingdoms. Coming as it does at the
end of the collection in the statement by the kingless generation, the identification has the character of a redactional
device included for the purpose of tying in the thirteen kingdom explanations to the preceding context, particularly because
the identification of the illuminator by the kingless generation is no more essential to that statement than it was to
those by the thirteen kingdoms.

     At what stage in the literary history of the *Apoc. Adam*
this redaction took place is difficult to tell.[46] It is probable that at the earliest stage the thirteen statements by the
kingdoms circulated as an independent literary unit without the
statement by the kingless generation. There are two reasons
for this: the fact that the kingless generation breaks with the
stylized form of the thirteen kingdoms, and the fact that there
is no indication within the explanations themselves to suggest
that they are false statements. The character of falsity is
only added with the statement of the kingless generation, and
the question of the powers in the narrative introduction. At
the next stage, the thirteen statements by the kingdoms, the
narrative introduction to the myth of the illuminator, and the
statement by the kingless generation were brought together as a
single composition. The final stage was the inclusion of this
new literary unit into the *Apoc. Adam* by the redactor of the
present received text. It seems unlikely that one can merge
stages two and three into a single stage and make the redactor
of the present text responsible for composing the statement of
the kingless generation to contrast with the thirteen kingdoms
and to agree with the narrative introduction. If this were the
case, the title "the kingless generation," a *terminus technicus*
for the gnostic community in several texts,[47] would have probably been the redactor's identification for his own community.
However, this title does not appear elsewhere in the tractate.
The redactor has, in fact, consistently utilized another title

(ⲤⲠⲞⲣⲀ) for his community,[48] or refers to them in a general
way.[49] The easiest explanation for this phenomenon is to assume that the title "kingless generation" came to the redactor
through his *Vorlage*.

Many students of the *Apoc. Adam* have regarded the collection of thirteen false explanations and one true explanation as
a unit of traditional material that had a life setting other
than its present literary setting in the *Apoc. Adam*.[50] This
evaluation has largely been based upon its systematic and highly
stylized form. To this argument should also be added the in-
appropriateness of its present literary setting. On this basis,
therefore, it seems justifiable initially to consider the material in the second segment of source B as two separate units for
the purpose of discussing form and theology.

2. The Narrative Framework: The Descent of the Illuminator
    ([76],8-[77],27)

a. Form

The narrative introduction to the collection of explanatory statements reflects the well-known gnostic myth of the
descent of the redeemer-revealer that has numerous parallels in
the Nag Hammadi library.[51] A majority of these parallels appear in various texts as brief isolated allusions that merely
hint at the broader myth.[52] There are three texts, however, in
which the myth is narrated in some detail.[53] These texts provide a convenient occasion for a consideration of the structure
of the myth as it appears in *Apoc. Adam*. In these three instances, the parallels are not limited to similarity in individual isolated motifs, but are extended to structural similarity; that is, motifs appear in these texts in a sequence
similar to that sequence in which they appear in the *Apoc. Adam*.
The following outline of the myth as it appears in the *Apoc.
Adam* reflects a highly schematic structure. The myth is narrated with minimal digression and no elaboration.[54] The sequence of events seems logical and there is no duplication of
motif. The author has used an economy of words in producing a
well-balanced story. The myth appears in six units; each unit
has three segments of varying lengths.

1. The illuminator of knowledge
    a. will pass by in great glory   [76],8-11
    b. to leave behind fruit-bearing trees;   [76],14-15
    c. he will redeem their souls.   [76],15-17

2. The illuminator of knowledge
    a. will come upon the dead creation   [76],28-30
    b. that will be destroyed through the   [76],30-[77],1
        sowing of Seth;
    c. he will perform signs and wonders to   [77],1-3
        scorn the powers.

3. Then the God of the powers
    a. will be disturbed: [77],4-5
    b. "What sort of power has this man?"   [77],5-7
    c. He will arouse great wrath against   [77],7-9
        that man.

4. And the glory
    a. will withdraw   [77],9-10
    b. to dwell in holy houses   [77],10-11
    c. chosen for it.   [77],11-12

5. And the powers
    a. will not see the glory,   [77],12-14
    b. nor will they see the illuminator;   [77],14-15
    c. they will punish the flesh of the man   [77],16-18
        on whom the holy spirit has come.

6. Then the angels and generations of powers
    a. will use the name in error: [77],18-22
    b. "Where did it come from?"   [77],22-23
    c. "Whence came the deceiving words,   [77],23-27
        that the powers failed to discover?"

The comparison of the texts in the table on the next page shows
the similarity in sequence of motifs among the four documents
using the sequence of motifs in the *Apoc. Adam* as a key. Parentheses indicate that the motif is present as a doublet or is
out of sequence.

There is a striking difference in structure between the
Apoc. Adam and the three parallel texts. In *Treat. Seth* and
Trim. Prot., the author seems to have made little attempt to
narrate the myth in an organized or ordered way. There is digression, duplication and expansion. Although the AscenIsa
seems better organized, and is therefore easier to follow, there
is still duplication and elaboration of motif. In all three of
these documents, the narration of the myth occupies considerably more text than that amount of text involved in the *Apoc.
Adam*. In contrast, the *Apoc. Adam* schematizes the myth by

Apoc. Adam [76],8-[77],27	Treat. Seth (VII,2) 50,23-56,32	Trim. Prot. (XIII,2*) 40,8-46,3	AscenIsa 10-11	New Testament[55]
1. a) [76],8-11	50,22-24	40,12 (40,29-30)	10,8 (10,14;11,24)	John 1:9
b) [76],14-15		(41,30)	(11,22)	Acts 1:8 John 1:14 Matt 28:18-20 John 15:16
c) [76],15-17		40,13-14 (41,15-35)		
2. a) [76],28-30			10,8 [not referred to as "dead" creation]	
b) [76],30-[77],1 [56]				
c) [77],1-3	52,14-17	(41,4-11)	11,18	John 7:31, 12:37, 9:16, 11:47
3. a) [77],4-5	54,23-27 (51,24-31) (52,8-14)	40,19-22 (43,4-17)	11,19a	
b) [77],5-7				Matt 9:8 Luke 4:36
c) [77],7-9	54,32-34		11,19b	
4. a) [77],9-10				
b) [77],10-11	(51,4-7) (51,20-21)			John 17:22
c) [77],11-12				
5. a) [77],12-14			(11,24)	
b) [77],14-15	55,36-56,2 (56,20-32)	(47,13-25) (49,6-21) (50,12-16)	11,19c (10,11,20-21) (11,14,16,26)	1 Cor 2:7,8 John 7:10 Mark 3:12 passim
c) [77],16-18	56,4-18 (52,25-30) (55,15-35)		11,19d-20	John 1:32 Mark 1:10
6. a) [77],18-22	65,9-13 (53,5-8) (55,10-15)			
b) [77],22-23		(43,17-44,10)	11,24 (10,12)	John 7:27, 8:14
c) [77],23-27	(52,30-36)		11,25-29	Matt 13:54

abridgement of the narration. It does not expand motifs, and in only one very noticeable instance does it digress from the development of the story.[57] In some cases it has even omitted material essential to understanding certain motifs in the myth.[58] It follows a logical and ordered sequence and uses an economy of narration.

There are no verbal parallels among the documents that would enable one to argue for a literary relationship. Yet the conceptual parallelism and the similarity in motif sequence seem too close to be accidental. The explanation that best

suits this set of circumstances is that the documents share a
common heritage in the tradition.[59] The myth in these texts
did not originate in a common literary *Vorlage* and evolve into
these parallel texts as recensions of an original archtype, but
the myth in each document represents a development out of a
common tradition. Therefore, none of the texts reflects an
"authoritative" tradition in the sense that it is nearer to an
archtype, but each text witnesses to a variation of the myth
that evolved in the tradition of a particular locale or
community.

b. Characteristic Religious Ideas[60]

(1) *The Third Appearance of the Illuminator*. I have argued above that the statement about the third "pass" of the
illuminator should be understood in a narrow sense as the third
appearance of a particular illuminator, rather than in a broad
sense as the third epoch in a three-staged episode of redemption in which the redeemer figures are different.[61] There are
two basic reasons for this: it is the simplest interpretation
of the language of the text, and what are generally taken to be
the first two epochs of redemption are not technically speaking
acts of the illuminator.[62] At its simplest language level, the
statement that the illuminator once again passes through for
the third time can only mean that he has already "passed through"
on two previous occasions. Unfortunately, these two previous
episodes are lacking in the text and there is no indication in
the text as to what they were. Thus, we have only a partially
preserved account of the episode of the illuminator. Fortunately, however, there are parallels in the Nag Hammadi texts
themselves that suggest what the other two appearances of the
illuminator-redeemer may have been.

The closest parallel to the third "pass" of the illumina-
tor in the *Apoc. Adam* is found in the parallel versions of the
Gospel of the Egyptians: Gos. Eg. (III,*2*)62,24-64,9 =
(IV,*2*)74,9-75,24. The pertinent statement is as follows:[63]

Codex III

Then the great Seth...
passed through
the three parousias
which I mentioned before:
the flood,
and the conflagration,
and the judgement
of the archons
and the powers
and the authorities
to save her...
who went astray.

Codex IV

Then the [great Seth]...
passes through
the three parousias
[which I] mentioned before,
through [the] flood,
and the conflagration,
and the judgement
of the archons
[and] the authorities
and the powers,
to save her...
who went astray.

The great Seth is sent forth into the world by the four lights, by the will of the self-begotten One. He passes through the same three visitations of wrath experienced by his seed: the flood, the conflagration, and the judgment of the archons, powers and authorities.[64] The experiencing of these visitations of wrath by the race of Seth seems to be an entirely different episode than Seth's experiencing of the visitations.[65] It appears that, independently of his seed, the great Seth also passes through the flood, the conflagration and the judgment of the archons. It is in this context that the illuminator episode in the *Apoc. Adam* should be understood. The text describes the third visitation of wrath through which the illuminator of knowledge passes in his saving work.

This same phenomenon of one illuminator-redeemer figure appearing three times is found also in two other Nag Hammadi tractates using motifs other than the flood-fire-endtime scheme: the longer ending to the *Ap. John* (II,1) and the *Trim. Prot.* (XIII,2*). In the *Ap. John*, the scheme of revelation involves three descents by the "perfect Pronnoia of the All" into the lower world. On the first occasion, the illuminator reached down to chaos and its foundations trembled. On the second occasion, the foundations of chaos were so severely shaken by the presence of the Pronnoia that they threatened to fall "before the (appointed) time." On the third occasion, the perfect Pronnoia of the All succeeded in awakening those who slept.[66]

Contrary to the analysis of Pheme Perkins, this threefold descent of the one illuminator-redeemer figure seems also to be true of the *Trim. Prot.*[67] Perkins was probably misled into

assuming three different revealers because the structure of the
tractate seems to imply it. The threefold pattern of revelation is utilized as the structure for the tractate:

1. The revelation through the voice: XIII 35,1-42,3.
2. The revelation through the sounds of the voice:
    XIII 42,4-46,4.
3. The revelation through the word: XIII 46,5-50,3.

Each of these sections is clearly set out in the text as a
separate unit by an appropriate title and each section employs
different designations for the redeemer figure suggesting that
in each unit the redeemer figure was different. However, it
seems clear from XIII 47,1-19 that all the units of revelation
are linked in a threefold scheme of revelation and that there
is only one illuminator-redeemer who communicates revelation in
three forms.[68] With reference to the second and third appearance, the speaker clearly says of himself:

2. The second time I came in the [Sound] of my Voice
    (XIII 47,11-12).

3. The third time I revealed myself to them [in]
    their tents as the Word (XIII 47,13-15).

The statement about the first appearance is mostly in lacuna,
but the editor restores the last few lines as: I taught [them
the mysteries] through the [Voice] (XIII 47,7-8). This threefold pattern of revelation corresponds to the scheme of the
tractate and suggests that the author of the text conceived of
the Trimorphic Protennoia as three revelatory appearances by
one illuminator-redeemer.

The *Gospel of the Egyptians* also provides a context for
understanding the threats against the men of gnosis in *Apoc.
Adam* source A. The attacks against the men of gnosis--the
flood, the unknown threat at [71],20-[72],15,[69] and the fire
correspond to the visitations of wrath through which the race
of Seth passed, and through which Seth himself later passed in
his redemptive activity (*Gos. Eg.* [IV,2]60,25-61,23).[70] Apparently the redactor of the *Apoc. Adam* intends to conflate into
one episode what appears in *Gos. Eg.* to be two different episodes, that is, the passage of the seed of Seth through persecution followed by the illuminator through the same acts of
persecution.[71]

(2) *The Saving Work of the Illuminator*. Unlike the
illuminator-redeemer figure in *Ap. John* and *Trim. Prot.*, the
illuminator in *Apoc. Adam* is not described as coming to reveal
a secret message, but he comes "to leave behind fruitbearing
trees for himself."[72] Presumably the term "fruitbearing trees"
describes the gnostics, those who remain in the world producing
converts to Gnosticism.[73] Exactly how the illuminator "leaves
behind" fruitbearing trees is not explicitly stated, but apparently he produces them through revelation, the imparting of
gnosis. This is implied both by his title: the illuminator of
knowledge (ⲠⲒⲫⲱⲤⲦⲎⲢ ⲚⲦⲈ ⲦⲄⲚⲰⲤⲒⲤ), and by the exegetical statement at [76],17-27 where it is stated that salvation comes
through a special kind of gnosis. The concept of revelation is
also basic to the work of the gnostic community. A close
parallel to this is found in the *Gos. Eg.* (III,*2*)62,14-24 =
(IV,*2*)73,27-29 where the incorruptible race is distinguished
from "its fruit," i.e., those who join with the community as
converts to Gnosticism. Apparently the children of Seth have a
missionary responsibility in the world that must be exercised
until "the consummation of the aeon." There is another parallel
in source A of the *Apoc. Adam* ([73],13-24 and [74],21-26) where
it is stated that the men of gnosis have produced converts to
Gnosticism.[74]

The illuminator is further described as redeeming the
souls of the "fruitbearing trees" ([76],15-17) and as performing "signs and wonders" ([77],1-3). The concept of redeeming
the individual soul at the time of death[75] is in contrast to
source A, where salvation was a group or community experience.[76]
The exegetical interpretation of the statement regarding salvation ([76],17-27) leaves little question about its meaning.[77]
The "fruitbearing trees" were formally "creatures of the dead
earth," who were therefore under the authority of death. However, because they now have gnosis in their heart (i.e., have
been illuminated), they will not perish, but will be redeemed.
Enlightenment brings with it a spirit different from the unenlightened inhabitants of a dead earth destined for death.

The exact nature of the "signs and wonders" that disturbed
the ruler of the powers is not specified in the text. Probably

the phrase is not really intended to refer to any specific act
as such, but is simply a traditional phrase serving to authenticate the work of the illuminator.[78] The text states that the
illuminator does these "signs and wonders in order to scorn the
powers and their ruler." They "scorn" the creator in the sense
that they call into question his authority and role as the only
true God. Thus, they are an insult and an embarrassment to him
precisely because they imply that there is an authority higher
than he, the creator, that has commissioned the illuminator.

The reactions to the appearance of the illuminator--the
confusion of the archon, the aroused wrath of the powers, the
physical suffering of the illuminator and his invisibility[79]--
are all consistent with the tradition, and appear in the
parallel accounts of the myth.[80] However, two of the events
that follow the illuminator's appearance are not reflected
elsewhere in the tradition: the loss of glory by the illuminator and the erroneous use of the "name" by the angels and
powers.

The glory that withdraws is probably the same glory in
which the illuminator appeared ([76],8-11). This glory the
illuminator passes on to his seed, i.e., the fruitbearing trees
that the illuminator selected and is to save. They are the
holy houses that the illuminator selected as repositories for
his glory. Why the powers fail to see the glory is not clear.
Nor is it clear why it is stated in this obtuse way ([77],9-12)
rather than simply saying: ⲁⲣⲱ ⲩϯ ⲉⲟⲟⲣ ⲙ̄ⲡⲉⲧⲁⲩⲥⲟⲧⲡⲟⲩ.
The implication seems to be that the illuminator, or his physical host, was completely drained of glory, and all glory came
to reside in his race (cf. John 17:22).

The combination of motifs at the beginning of this section
--Φωστήρ, glory, display of power, the disturbing of the heavens and redemption of the chosen ones--is similar to Mark 13:
25-27 and parallels:

> And the stars (ἀστέρες) will be falling from heaven,
> and the powers in the heavens will be shaken. And
> then they will see the Son of Man coming in clouds
> with great power and glory. And he will send out the
> angels, and gather his elect from the four winds, from
> the ends of the earth to the ends of heaven. (RSV)

In Mark, these events are a portent of the endtime. They
herald the end of the present age and the dawning of the messianic era. Because of the abbreviated character of the text,
i.e., the fact that source B is only a partially preserved account of the episode of the illuminator, and the fact that it
has been recorded in a highly schematized way,[81] it is impossible to know how they originally functioned in the source from
which source B was taken. However, if we may regard the explanation given for the third appearance of the illuminator as
valid,[82] there is some justification for regarding the circumstances surrounding this appearance of the illuminator as a
prelude to the endtime. It is, after all, the final appearance
by the illuminator in a threefold pattern of appearances. In
the *Gospel of the Egyptians*, the fact that the great Seth comes
the third time to save the race that went astray "through the
reconciliation of the world" (*Gos. Eg.* [III,*2*]62,24-63,11) suggests that the third time is the endtime. In the present redacted form of the text, the third appearance of the illuminator is definitely intended as a prelude to the endtime as is
indicated by the redactor's arrangement of this narrative immediately preceding the apocalyptic conclusion to source A
([83],7-[84],3).[83]

The identification of the "name" being misused by the
powers is not certain. Beltz understood it as a reference to
Seth.[84] And he is probably correct at the level of the redactor.[85] But it is not at all certain that in source B the "name"
originally referred to was that of Seth. There is evidence of
a similar use of the tetragrammaton "name" without any indication in the immediate text as to what it signifies in both the
Jewish and Christian traditions.[86] Both of these traditions
are unlikely possibilities as the background to explain the use
of the term in source B.

There is a parallel in the gnostic tradition (Naassenes)
that may provide a possible background for the use of the term:

> These men, according to their own doctrine, reverence
> beyond all others Man and the Son of Man. Now this
> Man is bisexual and is called by them Adamas. A great
> many hymns of various kinds have been composed for
> him; and the hymns, to put it briefly, are worded by

> them in some such fashion as this: "From thee, Father,
> and through thee Mother, the two immortal names,
> parents of the Aeons, thou citizen of heaven, Man of
> the mighty name."[87]

The Man of the mighty name, Adamas, is the androgynous *Urmensch*.[88] For the reasons stated above, it is not possible to
determine beyond question whether the illuminator was thought
of in this sense or not. He is referred to as "man" ([77],4-9),
a term reminiscent of the statement of the three men in the
first part of source B: "Hear about the aeon and the seed of
that man to whom life has come, he who came from you and Eve
your wife" ([65],33-[66],8). In this latter instance, the
reference is surely to Seth who is identified with the *Urmensch*.[89] But beyond these brief allusions, there is no suggestion in the immediate text that the illuminator is to be
identified as the *Urmensch*.

        (3) *Anthropology*. There are two classes of people recog-
nized by the text. One class is the saved, i.e., those who
reflect on the knowledge of the eternal God ([76],21-24). This
group is identical to those described as "fruitbearing trees"
([76],14-15) and as the holy houses chosen by the illuminator
as repositories of his glory ([77],9-12). The other class is
described as "creatures of the dead earth" who are subject to
the power of death ([76],17-20). The basis for the distinction
between the groups is the knowledge of the eternal God.[90]

        (4) *Cosmology and Dualism*. There is a suggestion of a
pronounced dualism between the cosmos and the eternal God, a
dualism that is maintained in both a spatial and qualitative
sense. The spatial motif is suggested by the disturbance of
the archon and his powers at the "passing through" of the illuminator. In the parallel texts (see above, p. 121), this
feature occurs at the passage of the redeemer figure *down*
through the aeons and into the inhabited world. It is also
suggested by the *upward* movement of the soul at death through
the aeons and powers who serve as penal guards to keep the unenlightened souls imprisoned in the flesh and the cosmos.[91]
If the same analogy holds, then the text reflects a common
gnostic perception of the cosmos as a structure in which the

cosmos is the lowest rung on an ascending ladder that concludes just short of the eternal God and passes through semi-divine and evil beings antagonistic to the soul of man. This description is not meant to imply that the eternal God is naturally accessible to the cosmos. On the contrary, he is accessible only through gnosis, a quality not possessed by the archon and his powers.

The distinction made between the inevitable death of the *earth* and of every *creature* (πλάσμα) originating from that earth on the one hand, and the salvation of the *souls* (ψυχή) of those who reflect on the knowledge of the eternal God ([76], 17-24) on the other, implies a negative view of materiality and also reflects a pronounced dualism; that is, because the earth and everything it produces is evil, it cannot be salvaged but must be destroyed. Only the soul of the enlightened, as opposed to the flesh ([76],15-17), will be preserved from destruction. Another suggestion of this dualism is found in the docetic motif at [77],16-18. As pointed out above,[92] the best explanation for the contradictory motifs of invisibility and punishment of the illuminator is a docetism that was not completely preserved in the present form of the text. However, a vestige of that docetism does remain in the fact that the text makes a conscious distinction between the illuminator on the one hand, and his host on the other, a figure identified as the "man on whom the holy spirit had come." The illuminator withdraws prior to punishment and the archon and his powers punish the "flesh" of the host.[93] This latter expression gives strong support to the idea of dualism that exists between "flesh" or materiality on the one hand and the "spirit" on the other. The men of this world (i.e., the dead earth, [76],17-20) are governed by its authority ([76],17-20.24-27). Thus they are characterized by their materiality ([76],17-20) or "flesh" ([77],16-18). The enlightened man, on the other hand, is characterized by "spirit" ([76],24-27).

3. The Thirteen Kingdoms and the Kingless Generation
    ([77],27-[82],17; [82],19-[83],4)

a. Form

    This section has been previously described as simply a
collection of stories or narratives, but it is more accurately
to be described formally as a catalog or list. Compare, for
example, the catalog of heroes in 2 Sam 23:8-39 and that in
Heb 11:4-31. An even closer and more pertinent parallel is to
be found in the catalog of beliefs on the origin of man assembled by Hippolytus (*Ref*. 5.7,2-6).[94]

> The basis of their system is the Man Adamas, and they
> say that he is the subject of the text, "His generation
> who shall declare it?"....
>
> The earth it was, according to the Greeks, that first
> produced man, bearing a noble gift; for she desired
> to be the mother, not of senseless plants nor of brute
> beasts but of a tractable and God-loving creature.
>
> But it is hard to discover, he says, whether the
> Boeotians beyond Lake Cephisis Alalcomeneus appeared
> as the first of mankind,
>
> or whether it was the Curetes of Mount Ida, that
> divine race,
>
> or the Phrygian Corybantes, whom first the sun beheld
> springing up like trees;
>
> or did Arcadia (see) Pelasgus, a man older than the
> moon,
>
> or Eleusis (see) Diaulus who dwelt in Raria;
>
> or did Lemnos engender the fair child Cabirus in an
> unspeakable ecstasy,
>
> or Pellene the Phlegraean Alcyoneus, the eldest of
> the giants?
>
> But the Libyans say that Garamas was the firstborn,
> who arose from the desert lands, and began upon the
> sweet acorn of Zeus.
>
> And in Egypt the Nile enriching her silt to this very
> day, he says, brings to life (creatures) clothed in
> flesh by her moist warmth and bears living beings.
>
> The Assyrians say that Oannes the fish-eater came from
> them,

> The Chaldaeans speak (likewise) of Adam. And they
> say that he was the man whom the earth produced by
> herself; and he lay without breath, without motion,
> without a tremor, like a statue, being an image of
> that celestial being praised in song, the Man
> Adamas....[95]

This parallel is pertinent in that the catalog describes different beliefs regarding the origin of the first man held by various races of people. In the catalog each explanation is posed in such a way as to exclude the rest. In other words, the author of the catalog assumes that only one of the various explanations can be correct, but he does not state which one. The catalog in *Apoc. Adam* contains thirteen erroneous explanations as opposed to one correct explanation.[96]

A close parallel in form is also found in a discussion of the Gospel of Matthew by Isho'dad of Merv in the ninth century A.D. In a discussion of Matthew 3:1, he lists four incorrect interpretations alongside the correct interpretation of the Interpreter.

> But how was John removed?

> Mar Ephraim and others say that
> Elizabeth withdrew him from before
> the sword of Herod; she had received in a revelation
> that she should make him flee to the wilderness; when
> by gracious dexterity she had made him a garment of
> hair of the wool of camels; Mar Ephraim alone calls it
> Ba'wa. Ba'wa is the hair which is on the belly of camels
> which is not very rough.... (Cf. kingdoms 3,4)

> Others say that an angel seized him from his mother's side,
> and neither she nor his father nor anyone else knew the
> place of his abode. (Cf. kingdoms 2,7)

> Others say that at one time, our Lord fled before the
> sword of Herod, and so did his messenger, the one to
> Egypt, but the other to the wilderness, and the one
> rode on an ass, but the other on the rush of the wind,
> like Habakkuk.

> But the Interpreter says that he retired after the
> reception of the word. (Cf. kingdom 13)

> Others say, that when Zecharia his father felt the sword
> of Herod, perhaps the boy was sought...and he took the
> child and put him on the altar of propitiation, where he
> received the conception by means of the angel; while he
> was blessing about this in prayer, the angel seized him
> and took him away to the inner wilderness.[97] (Cf. kingdoms 2,7)

The passage is interesting not only because of the similarity
in form, but also because of similarity in motif with the explanations of several of the kingdoms (as noted above).

The fact that we are dealing with an ancient catalog of
diverse explanations seems clear, and is hardly in need of
further argument. However, the arrangement of the explanations
in the catalog is a problem. Is the present order of the
statements systematic or indiscriminate, i.e., gathered at
random? If systematic, are they arranged on the basis of
catchword connections or motif associations, or on some other
basis? Böhlig has argued that there is a systematic order to
the explanations, and that they are ordered on the basis of an
ascending scale from a lower more natural explanation of the
birth of the illuminator to a higher more philosophical
explanation.[98]

His analysis of the explanations correctly recognizes that
some of them are similar, and can on the basis of those similarities be associated with one another. However, there are
problems with his analysis. For example, he describes the
catalog as an "ascending" scale (*aufsteigende Linie*), that is,
from a lower-type explanation to a higher-type explanation.
Presumably, on this basis, all explanations have some merit or
value and the kingless generation is the best explanation among
other possible explanations. As evidence for the "ascending"
sequence of the catalog, he offers the following analysis.

> Statements 1-4:   The illuminator originates through
>   human reproduction.
> Statements 5-8:   The illuminator originates through
>   physical-material celebrities.
> Statements 9-11:   The illuminator originates through
>   divine acts of desire.
> Statements 12-14: The illuminator originates through
>   scientific and philosophical
>   celebrities.

If his analysis and ordering of the statements were correct, there would be an ascending order to the explanations.
However, in some cases, the explanations do not always suit the
principle Böhlig has used to group them. In group one, he is
correct that explanations two to four are to be associated. In
these statements, the illuminator is the product of a natural

generation: 2--he is the son of a prophet; 3--he is the son of
a young woman (παρθένος); 4--he is the son of Solomon. Further,
in all of these explanations, the child is taken after birth to
a desolate area (2--mountain top; 3--desolate place; 4--border
of the desert).[99] There is also a strong catchword connection
between explanations three and four in παρθένος,[100] but no such
connection is evident between explanations two and three.[101]
It is difficult to say whether explanation one is to be associated with this group or not. Since it is mostly in lacunae,
we don't know whence in the view of this kingdom the illuminator originated. The extant text suggests, however, that after
birth perhaps he was taken to heaven ([78],1-- ЄTПЄ Ñ6I OYTTNⲀ).
If this is correct, it would align this explanation with explanations five and seven, found in Böhlig's second group where
it is stated that the illuminator returned to heaven (5), or to
the place from which the drop had come (7).

    Böhlig's descriptive phrase for his group two, "physical-
material celebrities," is drawn only from explanation six. In
none of the other explanations that he associates in this group
does the illuminator originate from a particular "being," or
celebrity: 5--he came from a drop of heaven; 7--he is a drop;
8--a cloud comes to earth and envelopes a rock; the illuminator
comes from that union. There is no reason to assume that either
the "drop" or the "cloud" is to be understood as a supra-natural
being as, for example, an archon or an aeon, nor is the source
from which the illuminator originates a physical or material
source! On the contrary, the organizing motif of explanations
five through eight seems to be that the illuminator has a *non*-
natural origin. He comes from heaven and in two of the explanations returns to heaven:[102] 5--he came from a drop of heaven...
brought him to heaven; 7--the drop came from heaven...was taken
above to the place where the drop came forth; 8--a cloud came
(from heaven) to earth; 6--a kingdom came down to this aeon below. Explanation eight does not have the ascent motif clearly
stated, but it does seem to be implied in the fact that the angels over the cloud nourished him. Explanation six is lacking
the ascent motif completely and, in fact, as will be seen below, actually has more in common with Böhlig's third group (9-11).

Explanation eight has some similarity with explanations
nine and ten. Explanations eight and ten are the only two in
which a cloud is mentioned: 8--a cloud came to earth; 10--his
god loved a cloud of desire. The association between eight and
nine is more formal than essential. The statements of nourishing in both eight and nine have the same form.

8-- ⲀⲨⲤⲀⲚⲞⲨⲰⲰ̄ Ⲛ̄ϬⲒ ⲚⲀⲅⲅⲈⲖⲞⲤ ⲚⲎ ⲈⲦⲌ̄ⲒⲬ̄Ⲛ̄ ⲦⲔⲖⲞⲞⲖⲈ

9-- ⲀⲨⲤⲀⲚⲞⲨⲰⲰ̄ Ⲛ̄ϬⲒ ⲚⲒⲀⲅⲅⲈⲖⲞⲤ ⲚⲎ ⲈⲦⲌ̄ⲒⲬ̄Ⲛ̄ ⲦⲈⲠⲒ̄ⲐⲨⲘⲒⲀ

When one considers that in only four of the explanations is
someone other than the mother of the child mentioned as nourishing him (2, 8, 9, 11), it is striking that only these two
explanations falling one after the other in the list have the
same form for the statement of nourishing.

According to Böhlig, the explanations in group three
(9-11) describe acts of desire by various divine personages.
The illuminator originates from those acts of desire. With
respect to explanations nine and ten, Böhlig's description is
accurate: 9--one of the muses conceives from her desire; 10--a
god loves a cloud of desire. However, explanation eleven makes
no mention of gods. Böhlig assumes that the father who desires
his own daughter is actually a divine figure, although the text
does not suggest it. It seems that an act of desire or, more
specifically, a sexual act stimulated by desire, is the basis
on which the explanations in group three are to be associated.

Explanation nine: One of the muses desires herself in
order to become androgynous. She fulfills her desire and conceives by herself through that desire. This explanation
closely parallels the myth of Sophia who desired to copy the
Father and to produce an offspring without a partner. She
achieved her desire and produced an abortion, an unformed and
incomplete substance.[103]

Explanation ten: The illuminator's god loved a cloud of
desire. The god begat it (i.e., the sperm) in his hands and
"seeded" the cloud; that is, the illuminator was produced as
the result of the masturbation of a god. Explanation eleven:
A father desired his own daughter, and through that desire the
father sired the illuminator by his own daughter; that is, the
illuminator was produced as the result of an act of incest.

Explanation six also has the motif of desire. An unidentified female conceives through desire for flowers presented to
her by a "kingdom." It is not clear who she was, or when the
conception takes place, but she conceives through her desire
and the illuminator is born. At first glance, the motif of
desire seems more evident than the principle on which group two
was associated and suggests that explanation six is more properly to be associated with group three, rather than group two.
However, as we have seen, it is not simply the motif of desire
around which group three is gathered. It is the motif of a
sexual act stimulated by desire. It is true that this motif is
also present in explanation six. In fact, in many ways it
seems to be a parallel tradition to explanation nine. In both
explanations six and nine, like Sophia, the female produces
androgynously, i.e., without impregnation by a male.

Before examining Böhlig's group four, the order of the
explanations within groups one through three ought to be considered. In none of these groups can I find a reason that
would explain the present order of the explanations as place-
ments of design. In a few instances, the order of some explanations can be explained on the basis of catchwords, but these
are the exception rather than the rule. In group one, explanations three and four have in common the catchword παρθένος.
No such catchword connection is evident for explanations two
and three. Nor can I find a reason to explain the present
order of the explanations within group two as a conscious redactional arrangement. In fact, in group two, the arrangement
suggests that the opposite is true and that the order of the
explanations in this group reflects a random and careless arrangement. It separates explanations five and seven, possible
doublets, with explanation six which has more in common with
group three (9-11). If explanation six were placed after eight,
the arrangement as far as catchword connections are concerned
would have been better. Explanation seven would then follow
immediately upon five, and six would immediately precede group
three and provide a better connection between groups two and
three than now exists. There seems to be no catchword connection between groups one and two, and the only connection between

groups two and three is the formulaic expression regarding the
nourishing of the illuminator.

Böhlig finds that the explanations in group four describe
the illuminator as arising from scientific or philosophical
celebrities. It is not too clear how his descriptive phrase
relates to all explanations in the group. It appears to be
simply a convenience for organizing the remainder of the explanations as a single group. Explanation twelve has little in
common with thirteen and the last explanation by the kingless
generation (Böhlig's fourteenth explanation). There is no evident catchword connection, nor a common motif that connects explanations eleven and twelve. In fact, except for form, there
seems to be little correlation between explanation twelve and
any of the other explanations. Twelve is in a category by itself in that it is the only explanation that describes the
illuminator's origin without some discussion as to how that
birth took place. However, it has in common with all the other
explanations the fact that the birth of the illuminator has a
mythological origin. This is true even of group one where the
origin of the illuminator comes as the result of a natural generation. As it stands in the text, explanation twelve can
hardly qualify as a "scientific" explanation even by ancient
standards. Nor do explanation thirteen and the explanation by
the kingless generation appear to be more philosophical in comparison to the first twelve explanations. In explanation thirteen, the subject of the statement is identified as an archon,
and the expression ϬΙΝⲖⲒⲤⲈ ΝΙⲖⲖ implies more than one birth.
The personification of λόγος implies a mythological background
without which the explanation is not understandable.[104]

When the kingless generation describes the origin of the
illuminator as being a selection "from all the aeons," it also
implies a particular mythological structure. Of course this
explanation differs from all the preceding thirteen in two re-
spects: it is not the statement of a kingdom, but of a generation over which there is no king, and it does not describe the
illuminator as being *born*, but as being *selected*. He is chosen
for his task and comes into the world as an alien (i.e., of a
foreign air). Therefore, in Böhlig's last group, I can find

no single integrating principle that would allow one to describe it as a unified group, nor is there an evident sequence
of catchwords pulling them together into their present order.
The positioning of the statement by the kingless generation at
the conclusion of the list does seem to be the only placement
made by design.   In form, content and source, it contrasts with
the statements made by the thirteen kingdoms.[105]   By virtue of
its position and the negative character attributed to the statements by the thirteen kingdoms,[106] the statement of the kingless
generation uses the thirteen explanations by the kingdoms as a
foil to enhance its own positive statement.   In summary, the
list of explanations does not seem to have the ascending character that Böhlig ascribed to it in his *editio princeps*.   With
the exception of those explanations that can be grouped for the
reasons indicated above, the first thirteen explanations seem
to be arranged in a random order, but are intended as a whole
to contrast with the statement of the kingless generation.

   Not everyone is agreed regarding the exact number of explanations for which a parallel is to be sought.   Some have
suggested that we are dealing with a total of fourteen mythological explanations and a parallel should therefore be sought
for the number fourteen.[107]   Some have suggested that perhaps
the original number of explanations in the list was only
twelve.[108]   Therefore, a parallel should be sought to twelve
explanations.   A third alternative, for which I have argued
above, is that we are dealing with a list of thirteen erroneous
explanations in contrast to one correct explanation.[109]   Therefore, a parallel should be sought to the number thirteen.

   The problem is compounded in that parallels have been
found to all three of these possibilities.   Three parallels
have been advanced with regard to the total number of fourteen
explanations.   Böhlig pointed out three parallels; two from the
Manichaean tradition: the fourteen aeons of light in the
Kephalia (Keph. 10, 42ff.), the fourteen vessels ascended by
Jesus (Keph. 8, 36ff.),[110] and also the fourteen aeons in the
Second Book of Jeû.[111]

   There are several possible parallels to the number twelve
that would be appropriate.   In source A there is a reference to

the sons of Noah forming twelve kingdoms ([73],25-29). This
would coincide with the tradition that the world is divided
into twelve regions ruled over by twelve angels.[112] Assuming
that the kingdoms are to be identified as ruled generations in
contrast to the kingless generation, these kingdoms could be
those twelve regions, and would represent the answer to the
question of the powers given by the whole of mankind, i.e., all
twelve kingdoms of the world. Assuming that the kingdoms are
to be identified as demonic powers, they could be the angels
who ruled over the twelve regions of the world. In this latter
case, the twelve points of the Zodiac would be an appropriate
parallel, assuming that they could be considered as the demonic
powers controlling the twelve regions of the heavens that re-
plied to the questions of the powers.[113] The major difficulty
with considering these parallels as the background that explains
the list is that we actually have thirteen explanations by the
kingdoms and a total number of fourteen explanations when the
explanation of the kingless generation is included. However,
Kasser has suggested that the list originally may have comprised
only twelve explanations.[114] On this basis one might argue that
originally the list contained a total number of twelve explanations that represented all the nations of the world, or the
twelve kingdoms formed by the sons of Noah, or the twelve angels
that ruled the world, or the twelve points of the Zodiac as
demonic powers.

     However, as far as the present form of the list is con-
cerned, there can be little doubt that we are dealing with a
total of thirteen explanations by the kingdoms and one (contrasting) explanation by the kingless generation, for the explanations by the kingdoms are *numbered* one through thirteen,
and for that reason alone, if for no other, we must conclude
that in the present context the fact that there are thirteen
kingdoms is not accidental but by design. Therefore, it seems
more appropriate to consider parallels to the number thirteen
in order to explain the list.[115]

     Two such parallels to the number thirteen have been iden-
tified in the Nag Hammadi gnostic texts. One of these, *Marsanes*,
refers to the loosening of the thirteenth seal (X,2,14-15). This

statement is followed by a numbered list of thirteen items
(X,2,14-4,23). Unfortunately, the text is highly fragmentary
and for that reason the significance of the list of the thirteen items is obscure. There is no indication that there is a
contrast of anything with these thirteen items. However, there
is an indication that they speak (X,4,13-14.20-21), but, as
mentioned above, except for its numerical sequence in the list
of items, the identification of the speaker is uncertain. There
is some grouping in the list, but it does not coincide with our
analysis above,[116] nor does the content of the items in the list
coincide with the list of explanations in the *Apoc. Adam*.[117]
The list does seem to ascend from a lower cosmic or material
level to a higher spiritual level.

   a) 1st, 2nd, 3rd: The cosmic and the material (X,2,18-28).
   b) 4th and 5th: Exist above the first three (X,2,28-3,17).
   c) 6th: Concerns the self-begotten ones, and those who
      exist in the truth of the All (X,3,18-25).
   d) 7th: Concerns the self-begotten power, and mentions
      the salvation of Sophia (X,3,25-4,2).
   e) 8th: Concerns the male Nous, incorporeal essence and
      the intelligible world (X,4,2-7).
   f) 9th: Too fragmentary (X,4,7-10).
   g) 10th: Mentions παθένος and αἰών (X,4,10-12).
   h) 11th and 12th: Speak of the highest, the one who
      possesses the three δύναμεις and the πνεῦμα that does
      not have essence, belonging to the first unbegotten
      (X,4,13-19).
   i) 13th: Speaks concerning the unknown silent one and
      the primacy of the one who was not distinguished
      (X,4,20-23).

The other Nag Hammadi parallel, mentioned briefly two different times in the same context in *Gos. Eg.*, seems more appropriate to the circumstances suggested by the *Apoc. Adam*: *Gos.
Eg.* (III,2)63,16-18 = (IV,2)75,4-6 and (III,2)64,3-4 = (IV,2)
75,18-20. The text describes a mythological figure, the god of
the thirteen aeons (= Sakla? [III,2]58,23-59,1) who, along with
the world, is renounced by the "saints." The thirteen aeons
appear to be evil powers who are antagonistic to the great Seth,
but who are "nailed down" (= defeated?) through "Jesus the living one, he whom the great Seth put on."[118] The text does not
clarify further the identity of the thirteen aeons or their
relationship to their god. The number of aeons in the *Gos. Eg.*
corresponds to the number of explanations in the *Apoc. Adam* as

does their negative character. If the god of the thirteen aeons
is Sakla, it would correspond to the redactor's identification
of the evil creator god in the *Apoc*. *Adam* (cf. [74],7). The
thirteen aeons in the *Gos*. *Eg*. also appear to be mythological
powers who are defeated in a struggle with the great Seth. A
similar struggle is suggested in the *Apoc*. *Adam*.

The most reasonable and simplest explanation for the number thirteen is that it represents a total of the seven kings
appointed over the seven heavens and the five kings appointed
over the abyss (*Ap*. *John* [II,*1*]11,4-7) plus the first archon,
Yaltabaoth (Sakla, Samael: *Ap*. *John* [II,*1*]10,19-25 and 11,11-
22). This makes a total of thirteen "kings." The same tradition is found in the *Gos*. *Eg*. where Sakla creates twelve aeons
each to rule over its own world (*Gos*. *Eg*. [III,*2*]57,1-58,22).
Apparently the redactor intends the reader to understand the
god of the powers ([77],4-7) as Sakla (cf. [74],3-4.7-11), and
those whom he ruled ([77],12-15) as the twelve "kings." These
together ([77],1-3) make a total of thirteen "kings." Twelve
rule over the seven heavens and the neatherworld and Sakla
rules everything below the Ogdoad.[119] The generations of the
powers ([77],18-22) should probably be understood as those
powers created by each "king" for his own kingdom (*Ap*. *John*
[II,*1*]11,22-25).

To a certain extent, this analysis is verified by parallels
in the Askew and Bruce Codices. In the Askew Codex, thirteen
aeons are mentioned and all appear to be dominions ruled over
by archons. The twelfth and the thirteenth are linked together
as part of the material world (Carl Schmidt, *Koptisch-gnostische
Schriften*, 40, lines 18-22), and the realm of darkness (ibid.,
121, lines 20-23).[120] All thirteen aeons lie between Chaos and
the "Midst" (ibid., 94, lines 5-7; 28, lines 6-12; 110, lines
29-31). While each aeon has a ruler, all thirteen seem to be
dominated by the "triple-powered self-willed one" (αὐθάδης)
(ibid., 27, lines 2-10; 66, lines 28-31; 88, lines 24-32; 90,
line 32 - 91, line 1; 93, lines 20-24). This agrees with at
least one reference in the Bruce Codex where thirteen aeons are
listed together as areas through which the soul must pass before
it reaches the world of light (ibid., 330-32). However, another

reference lists fourteen aeons (ibid., 327). The relationship
of the fourteenth aeon to the scheme for which I have argued,
on the basis of the *Gos. Eg.* and *Ap. John*, and to the scheme
elsewhere in the Bruce Codex, is not clear. In any case, the
fourteenth aeon was associated with the material world since it
too attempted to deter the soul from reaching the realm of
light.

b. Characteristic Religious Ideas

The formula ("and in this way he came to the water": ⲀⲨⲰ
Ⲛ̄ⲦⲌⲈ ⲀⲨⲈ̄Ⲓ ⲈⲬⲘ̄ ⲠⲒⲘⲞⲞⲨ) appearing at the conclusion to each of
the explanations in the list of kingdoms, is perhaps the most
enigmatic phrase in the entire section. The latter part of the
formula, ⲈⲬⲘ̄ ⲠⲒⲘⲞⲞⲨ, has been translated in two ways: "upon
the water" and "to the water." Böhlig in his *editio princeps*
translated "auf das Wasser," but later changed his translation
to "an das Wasser," under the influence of his understanding of
the background of the formula.[121]

For Böhlig, the issue seems to be the exact relationship
of the illuminator with respect to the water. Is he in direct
contact with the water, i.e., "auf das Wasser," or is he near
the water, i.e., "an das Wasser"? Kasser (apparently),[122]
Krause,[123] Beltz,[124] and Schottroff[125] translate the statement
in accordance with Böhlig's earlier translation. MacRae[126]
follows Böhlig's later translation. Rudolph[127] concludes, after
considering Böhlig's argument, that the exact translation must
remain undecided. The statement is ambiguous and on the basis
of grammar can be translated both ways. Therefore it appears
that Böhlig's method seems correct, and the formula should be
translated on the basis of its use in the context and how one
views its background.

On the basis of the statement of equivalency ("in this
way": Ⲛ̄ⲦⲌⲈ) in the concluding line to explanations 1-13 in the
list of kingdoms, it seems that the formula "he came to the
water": ⲀⲨⲈ̄Ⲓ ⲈⲬⲘ̄ ⲠⲒⲘⲞⲞⲨ is intended to summarize the total
statement made by each kingdom. Thus, "to come to the water"
is to perform the same action identified in the explanation.

There are in each explanation generally three phases in view:
physical birth (2-6,9-11,13),[128] rearing (1-4,6,8-9,11-12), and
the receiving of glory and power (1-10,12-13). Böhlig takes
these three phases as three separate events: birth, removal
into the wilderness (an act connected to watchcare and tutoring
by birds, angels, etc.), and the assumption of power.[129]

     This is not the only way that one can understand the ex-
planations, however. They can be conceived as collective parts
of a single whole, rather than as three separate and distinct
events. This is actually suggested in the text itself. There
is a close relationship in the concepts of birth and nourishing
(i.e., between the first and second phases of each explanation)
so that the latter can be viewed as a continuation of the former. This relationship is evident in the fourth explanation
where conception, birth and nourishing are all included as
parts of the first phase of the explanation. The nourishing
phase is then restated before the phase in which glory and
power are received. Thus:

> Phase 1: The virgin conceived; she gave birth to the
>   child in that place and nourished him.
> Phase 2: When he had been nourished,
> Phase 3: he received glory and power.

In most other explanations (6,8,9,12), while the conceptual
closeness of phases one and two is not emphasized, it is at
least not excluded by implying a separation between the phases
as is done in three of them (2,3,11). Explanations two, three
and eleven imply a separation between the birth phase and the
nourishing phase by having the child removed from the place of
birth before he is nourished. This is also true of explanation
four where the child is born "in that place," i.e., where the
virgin conceived; and nourished in a different place, i.e., "on
a border of the desert." In explanation four, however, the
immediate inclusion of a second statement of nourishing suggests that the author conceived the first nourishing statement
to be part of phase one and the second nourishing statement to
be phase two. If this is not the case, how else does one explain the second nourishing statement? Furthermore, there is a
break in tense immediately following the first nourishing

statement. The first nourishing statement is connected to what precedes by a string of perfect tenses. The second nourishing statement breaks with the string of perfect tenses by being cast in the *temporalis*. This is particularly striking since in every other explanation having a nourishing statement (3,6,8,9, 11,12) phase one and phase two are connected through a string of perfect tenses with no intervening conjunction except for explanation two that begins the nourishing statement with ⲁⲩⲱ ([78],12-13). And even in this instance, the perfect tense is used.

Finally, the fact that the second phase as a separate entity has been eliminated altogether from several of the explanations (5,7,10,13) suggests that the author did not maintain so sharp a separation between phase one and two as Böhlig wants to give it. Or put another way, one should not assume that the nourishing phase has been eliminated from these explanations because it is actually present by implication in the birth phase. The fourth explanation also implies a close relationship between nourishing and the receiving of glory and power. Here the receiving of glory and power occurs in the context of nourishing. In most of the other explanations, the nourishing and the receiving of glory and power occur in the same place (1,2,6,8,9).[130]

There is another structural argument for a close association among all three phases. Except for explanations two and nine,[131] the first major break in each explanation comes with the conjunction introducing the stereotyped concluding phase: "And in this way he came to the water." This effectively divides all but two explanations into two parts, thereby associating Bohlig's three phases as one unit in a quite obvious manner.

I would argue that when the author uses ⲛ̄ϯϩⲉ to explain the relationship of ⲁϥⲉⲓ ⲉϫⲙ̄ ⲡⲙⲟⲟⲩ to the rest of the narrative he intends that the reader understand the coming to the water as equal to the totality of these three phases. Thus "to come to the water" seems to describe some sort of epiphany in which the individual so described is born, prepared and commissioned. The emphasis is not that he was born at one moment in

a certain fashion, and then over a period of time reared, and
then finally after a number of years commissioned. Rather, the
emphasis is he *appeared* in a certain way.

It is not clear exactly what context provides the meaning
for the formula ("And in this way he came to the water": ⲁⲩⲱ
ⲛ̄ⲧⲍⲉ ⲁⲩⲉⲓ ⲉⲭⲙ̄ ⲡⲓⲙⲟⲟⲩ). A clarification of the meaning of the
formula and the identification of its background have given
rise to a divergence of scholarly opinion. H.-M. Schenke has
argued that the formula can be explained as an assimilation by
the Coptic word ⲙⲟⲟⲩ of a figurative use of the Egyptian word
mu. This assimilation allows one to understand the formula as
meaning: "and so he appeared."[132] However, his explanation
requires one to assume an original Coptic composition for the
list of kingdoms, and this is not possible if Nagel's explanation for the difficult reading at [81],17-20 is correct.[133]
Schenke's explanation has been rejected by Rudolph in favor of
Böhlig's explanation, an explanation which Schenke himself
acknowledges to be possible.[134] Beltz, on the other hand,
thinks that Schenke's explanation is more convincing than
Böhlig's, but prefers a more direct explanation in terms of
Jewish apocalyptic.[135]

Böhlig has drawn attention to a series of parallels to the
list of kingdoms from the Iranian tradition.[136] He argues that
one of these parallels, the legend of the great king of the
endtime, provides a striking parallel both to the structure of
the individual narratives in the list of kingdoms and to the
final formula ("And in this way he came to the water": ⲁⲩⲱ
ⲛ̄ⲧⲍⲉ ⲁⲩⲉⲓ ⲉⲭⲙ̄ ⲡⲓⲙⲟⲟⲩ).[137] According to Widengren, from
whose presentation of the legend Böhlig has drawn, three primary moments characterize the legend: birth, rearing and sei-
zure of power. This is a striking parallel to explanations
2-4,6,8-9,12, where each of these explanations is characterized
by three main events: birth, rearing and receiving glory and
power.[138]

He suggests two possible explanations for the final formula. He recalls that the seed of the Saošyants, the three
sons of Zarathustra (Hušetar, Hušetarmāh and Sōšyans), was preserved in the Kasaoya sea. In intervals of 1000 years, three

different virgins bathed in the sea, conceived and gave birth
to the three Saošyants. The third son to be born, Sōšyans, is
the Saošyant par excellence. The first two are only forerunners. At his appearing, evil is destroyed, the dead are
awakened and a kingdom of righteousness is established. In
hymns he is described as "coming forth out of the waters of the
Kasaoya sea."[139]

In a later article, Böhlig had questions about the applic-
ability of this parallel for the final formula, which he regards
as a reference to epiphany, the moment of intervention into
world afairs when youth is left behind. The parallel of the
Saošyants to which he had pointed, however, was to the moment
of birth only. If the parallel be admitted as appropriate with
regard to the formula, one must understand the appearance upon
the water as a fossilized vestige where Sōšyans arises from the
sea and then appears upon its surface. Böhlig, however, prefers to translate the formula differently and to consider
another parallel. Regarding the preposition $\in \overline{XN}$ as a Coptic
translation of the Greek ἐπί, he translates "an das Wasser" and
suggests that it could refer to an episode reported in the
Šāhnāmah where Rustam travels to the mountain Alburz in order
to pay tribute to Kaikōbad as the king of kings, and to take
him for his official coronation.[140] He finds the young king in
a palace on the mountain surrounded by trees and fountains.
The throne on which he was sitting was near the water. He argues that since the king is the reincarnated Mithra and possesses the character of a universal figure, he is justified in
taking the parallel seriously with reference to the illuminator
in the *Apoc. Adam*.[141]

Schenke has also briefly alluded to a third possible background for the formula. It may refer to the general representation in antiquity of the material world as originally consist-
ing of the waters of chaos.[142] However, Schenke rejects this
possibility as not completely satisfying because in his opinion
the mythological concepts throughout the list of kingdoms are
almost all non-gnostic.[143] This, of course, as Schenke himself
realized, is not sufficient basis on which to reject completely
this explanation. In gnostic texts, the description of the

material world as the waters of chaos is a common motif.[144]
It is specifically so identified in *Treat. Seth* (VII,*2*)50,13-18:

> I produced thought...about the
> descent upon the water, that is
> the regions below.[145]

In this passage, the "water" is specifically identified as the
regions below, i.e., the material world. A graphic description
is also set out in Right *Ginza* 3:

> He called Ptahil-Uthra...
> He gave him the name "Gabriel, the
> messenger," he called him, gave command,
> and spoke to him: "Arise, go, descend to
> the place where there are no skinas or
> worlds. Call forth and create a world for yourself....
> Ptahil-Uthra rose up, he went out and
> descended below the skinas, to the
> place where there is no world. He trod in the filthy
> mud, he entered the turbid water.[146]

The best description that I have found of water as a metaphor
for the material world is found in Hippolytus' (*Refutations*)
description of the Peratae.

> They call themselves Peratae, holding that nothing
> belonging to the world of becoming can escape the
> destiny laid down for things that come into being
> from their (moment of) coming into being. For he
> says, "Whatever comes into being is also completely
> destroyed," as the Sibyl has it. But we alone, he
> says, who have realized the necessity of coming-
> into-being and the routes by which man has entered
> the world, are exactly instructed and are the only
> ones who can pass through and cross over destruction.
> Now destruction he says, is water, and nothing else
> brings quicker destruction on the world than water.
> Now water is that which circles the Proastii,[147]
> they say, namely Cronos; for he says it is a power
> of the color of water; and this power namely Cronos
> cannot be escaped by anything belonging to the world
> of becoming for Cronos presides over the whole pro-
> cess of becoming so as to make it subject to
> destruction.[148]

> And departing from Egypt, he says, means departing
> from the body--for they consider the body a miniature
> Egypt--and crossing over the Red Sea, that is the
> water of destruction, namely Cronos, and crossing
> over beyond the Red Sea, that is, beyond the process
> of becoming, and arriving in the desert, that is,
> escaping from the process of becoming.[149]

> The power of the abysmal darkness, which supports the
> silt of the imperishable watery void, the whole power
> of the convulsion, coloured like water, which is
> ever-moving, bearing up what holds fast, consolidating
> what is unstable, resolving what is to come, lighten-
> ing what holds fast, cleansing what increases; the
> faithful treasurer of the path of the vapours, which
> enjoys what wells up from the twelve "eyes" of the law,
> showing the seal to the power that governs those un-
> seen waters that hover above, its name was Thalassa.
> To this power ignorance gave the name of Cronos,
> guarded with chains, since he bound together the
> complication of the dense and cloudy dim dark
> Tartarus.[150]

In these quotations from Hippolytus, Cronos, the power of
darkness, presides over the entire process of becoming, i.e.,
the world, or as it is referred to, the world-of-becoming,
and makes it subject to destruction (i.e., through change and
dissolution). "Destruction" is descriptive of the world condition. "The unseen waters that hover above" appear to be the
waters of chaos known from other sources.[151] These waters are
identified both with Cronos as the power that controls the
world-of-becoming and with destruction that is characteristic
of the world condition. The metaphor crystallizes in the concept of entering, and leaving the world. Man becomes (i.e.,
comes-into-being), that is, comes into the world, falls under
the power of Cronos and is subject to destruction. This is his
ultimate end, unless he can escape. Only those "exactly instructed" are the ones who can enter, pass through and cross
over destruction, that is, the world (or, as it is referred to,
water or Cronos). The Peratae used the imagery of the Exodus,
where crossing over the Red Sea is equivalent to crossing over
the water of destruction (i.e., Cronos or the world), and entering the desert is equivalent to escaping from the process of
becoming or destruction (or the world). Turning this figure
around, one could say that entering the world can be described
as coming to the water (of chaos, or destruction).

It is against this background that I would suggest the
concluding formula to the explanations in the list of kingdoms
should be understood. "Coming to the water" is a metaphor for
coming into the world. In the context, it is intended to describe the epiphany of the illuminator of knowledge.

A description of the provenance of each individual explanation and the kind of tradition it reflects is a difficult
problem that raises not only the natural issue of tradition
origins, but methodological ones as well. Beltz has assumed
that all the statements in the list are intended to explain the
birth of Jesus from the standpoint of a particular gnostic
group in antiquity.[152] Thus, he believes that the traditions
reflected in the individual statements have all been interpreted and transmitted through Christian Gnosticism and/or Manichaeism.[153] For example, explanation four reflects a gnostic
interpretation of the Jewish tradition of Solomon's control
over the demons and, according to Beltz, Solomon's desire to
take wisdom as his bride (Wis 8:2). Beltz understands the two
young women in the text to represent two Sophia figures, one
belonging to the Ogdoad above, and the other to the aeon of the
creator god. In the text, Solomon pursues the heavenly Sophia,
but only obtains the Sophia belonging to the lower aeon.[154]

Böhlig, on the other hand, because of his understanding of
certain of the explanations, argues that the document is a pre-
Christian text stemming from Jewish-Iranian Gnosticism. He
finds clear reference to the god Mithra in explanations seven,
eight, ten and eleven, and explanation two, he thinks, is the
result of a combination of Jewish and Iranian legends.[155] He
also argues that the Iranian legend of the great king of the
endtime, of which Mithra is the typical representative, is the
best parallel to explain the literary framework reflected in
the individual explanations, i.e., the threefold structure con-
sisting of birth, rearing and the assumption of power.[156] The
concluding refrain to each of the explanations, "and thus he
came to the water," is explained either by the birth of the
three Saošyants from the Kasaoya Sea or--a more recent position
by Böhlig--by a scene from the Šāhnamāh legends, the coronation
of Kaikōbad.[157]

The method used by both raises serious doubts about their
results. Beltz's approach to the narratives is not really objective. He *assumes* that all the stories are various (con-
testable) explanations about the birth of Jesus, but he fails
to demonstrate this fact conclusively in his discussion. His

accumulation of interesting similarities in motif is not
sufficient support for his sweeping assumption.

On the other hand, Böhlig's attempt to explain the provenance of the document as derived from an Iranian background by
identifying the origin of the individual stories, while more
objective than Beltz, fails to recognize that the derivation of
certain explanations should not be equated with the provenance
of the document. Even if he is persuasive about the derivation
of certain explanations, he has shown only that the author of
the list was familiar with those traditions he identified. The
operative explanation with respect to provenance is the statement of the kingless generation. This last explanation reflects
the position of the author of the list and, one would assume,
also that of the redactor. Böhlig's uncertainty as to the
parallel that best explains the refrain, of which the translations and meaning are uncertain, emphasizes the difficulty of
predicating provenance on the basis of obscure and uncertain
parallels.[158]

Further, we must at least consider the possibility that
these stories were created ad hoc as "strawmen" to be refuted
by the final correct explanation. In this sense, the author
would have drawn on traditions both contemporary and ancient,
but he considered none of them to be serious viable options.
His description of these traditions would either be biased
caricatures, or creations not intended to be taken seriously.

Several things speak in favor of this possibility. One is
our inability to identify with certainty convincing parallels
for any but a few of the explanations. A second is the fact
that where we can identify to everyone's satisfaction an
earlier parallel tradition, that feature lacking in the parallel
is precisely the one that would cause the earlier tradition to
"parallel" the given explanation. For example, in explanation
four, there is no record that Solomon sent his demons after a
"virgin" whom he impregnated when she was brought to him. And
in explanation nine, there is no known tradition that one of the
Muses drew apart to produce an offspring androgynously. One
might also argue that the reason explanation twelve is so abbreviated is that the author ran out of good ideas.[159] Arguing for

the thirteen explanations as reflecting viable ancient traditions is the fact that their literary structure is known elsewhere in antiquity, i.e., in the Gospel of Mark, Revelation,[160]
and, if Böhlig is correct, also in the Iranian tradition.

There needs to be discussion and general agreement among
specialists as to what constitutes a parallel. Böhlig's inability to determine with certainty which of his suggested
background traditions parallels and clarifies the refrain
points up the lack of criteria under which the enterprise of
parallel gathering labors. This is not to say that one should
not point out any and all similarities in motif, but there
needs to be clarity as to what constitutes a parallel and
parallels should be distinguished from incidental and general
similarities.

Further, there needs to be clarity about the function of a
parallel. Both Böhlig and Beltz have proceeded on the assumption that the identification and accumulation of parallels de-
cides provenance. Is this the case? Should a given provenance
for a text on the basis of parallels even be considered unless
there are extensive striking parallels in a given tradition to
the text with parallel clusters in motif? Even then it would
not seem that provenance can be assumed to be proven absolutely,
since what are cited as parallels may themselves be motifs derived from another milieu from which the text under consideration stems. This could easily be true of Beltz's Manichaean
argument, since the similarities cited by Beltz are neither extensive nor striking, but rather limited and general.

The problem may lie in the categories being used. Apparently any similarity to a given text, regardless of how vague
or general or limited, can be regarded as a "parallel." No
attempt is made to rank the "parallels" as to specificity of
analogue. All would agree that some "parallels" are more
appropriate and pertinent than others, but there is no provi-
sion to show this distinction in the terminology, as all analogues are considered to be "parallels." In the interests of
clarity, specialists should so refine terminology as to allow
for this distinction. For example, I and others have used
interchangeably the words "parallel" and "similarity." Actually,

they are not identical. A similarity suggests only *partial* and
general correspondence, while parallel suggests *close* and specific correspondence; that is, a given motif "matches" or
"equals" that to which it corresponds. One might also consider the use of the term "analogy" as used in biology. In
this life science, an analogy indicates similarity in function,
but dissimilarity in origin and structure. The term "resemblance," indicating vague or superficial correspondence, might
also be considered as a possible terminological tool.

The point is, if language were refined to accommodate the
nature of the correspondence between texts, then not every relationship between texts can or should be called a parallel,
although there might still be resemblances.[161] To some extent
this is already done. We do talk about "verbal parallels,"
"conceptual parallels," "language similarity," "formal parallels," and the like. However, there is sufficient lack of
clarity even in these expressions as to the value and meaning
of the analogue to lead to misunderstanding.

The parallel compiler should also be careful to show *how*
the "parallel" corresponds to the text under consideration. It
is not enough simply to list the extent of text thought to
correspond to another text or tradition; the analogue must also
be identified! If it is not identified, the reader is left to
determine it for himself, and this is not always a simple task.
While the parallel compiler may assume the analogue to be self-
evident, some are quite obscure. A description of how texts
relate should include a description of how the analogues function in *both* texts.[162] In some cases, "parallels" are cited
for a given text which, when carefully examined in their own
context, are found not to correspond at all.[163]

The use of parallels in the argument for provenance is a
difficult issue on which scholars can be expected to disagree.
The argument is too easily reduced to an accumulation of
appropriate "parallels" on both sides of an issue.[164] It
seems to me that a great deal of the confusion could be eliminated by a refinement in terminology and a careful description
of how the analogue functions.[165]

When one takes this stance toward the identification of
parallels and the use of parallels, neither Beltz nor Böhlig
can be said to have proven his thesis as regards the provenance
of the *Apoc. Adam*. With respect to the provenance of the list
of explanations, one should do two things: begin with those
motifs for which one can find clear specific and convincing
parallels, and then concentrate attention on the statement of
the kingless generation, since this is the explanation that one
would expect to reflect the attitudes of the redactor to whom
must be attributed the final form of the tractate.

There are only two of the explanations that have clear,
unambiguous and specific parallels in antiquity: four and nine.
In these two instances, the backgrounds are clear. Explanation
four is clearly derived from the Jewish tradition of Solomon's
control over demons.[166] But the tradition that Solomon fathered
a child with an unnamed virgin secured for him by his army of
demons is unknown elsewhere in antiquity. The only statement
that can be made with certainty is that the author of the explanation was familiar with the tradition about Solomon, although he may not have known it from Jewish circles.

Likewise, it is equally certain from explanation nine that
the author was familiar with the Greek tradition of the nine
Muses.[167] Yet there is no known tradition of one of the Muses
drawing apart and producing a child androgynously, i.e., without impregnation by a male partner. It is not even clear that
either of these explanations in their present form should be
called "gnostic." With respect to the other explanations,
there are no *clear* parallels that will allow us to associate
them with certainty to other known traditions in antiquity.

The one explanation that is decisive for the character of
the list as a whole is that of the kingless generation. This
generation says that the great illuminator was not born, but
was "chosen from all the aeons." This statement of his origin,
precisely in opposition to the preceding thirteen explanations
that indicate a birth of some sort, implies a negative view of
the material world. This observation is further strengthened
by the statement about receiving knowledge. It is indicated
that the illuminator possessed a knowledge of the "undefiled"

one. Presumably, had he entered the world in a way that associated him with materiality, he himself would have been "defiled" and would not therefore possess this knowledge (cf. the
devolution of Adam and Eve in source A above). However, he was
chosen from all the aeons[168] and came from a "foreign air,"[169]
i.e., in no way associated with the world of becoming and de-
generation. His origin had nothing to do with the process of
becoming, whether natural or miraculous.[170] Therefore, he
could be the bearer of the knowledge of the "undefiled" one.[171]
Unfortunately, all of these motifs--choosing, non-material
origin and possession of special knowledge--are found generally
in gnostic texts making a decisive argument for provenance
based on similarities difficult if not impossible.[172]

Beltz has argued that the statement of the kingless generation reflects a Manichaean provenance. At line [82],25 he
reads ⲠⲈϪⲀ[ⲥ],[173] and understands the subject of the verb to
be ⲅⲛⲱⲥⲓⲥ ([82],23). He argues that there are two speakers and
hence two statements. The first statement is made by the kingless generation ([82],20) regarding the figure previously mentioned in [77],16-18 who is, according to Beltz, Jesus. The
second statement is made by the (personified?) knowledge
([82],25) received by this figure (Jesus), and describes a
second different figure who is illuminator and savior. According to Beltz, the first figure, Jesus, is merely the prophet
and bearer of revelation who points to another who is illuminator par excellence. This second figure Beltz describes as
Mani.[174] The other possibility that the subject of ⲠⲈϪⲀ[ⲥ]
([82],25) is the same as Ϫⲱ ⲘⲘⲟⲥ ([82],20), i.e., the kingless generation, he rejects as not being the preferred
interpretation.[175]

His explanation of the text frankly hinges upon his restoration of ⲠⲈϪⲀ[ⲥ] at [82],25. However, this restoration
seems to be excluded by the vestiges of ink around the lacuna
that look more like ⲩ than ⲥ. On the basis of the present reading of the text (ⲠⲈϪⲀⲩ), the first speaker in the final explanation is the kingless generation, who describes God as saying that the illuminator came from a "foreign air."[176] Thus,
there are two statements about the illuminator, one made by the

kingless generation and one made by God, the undefiled one of
truth, as quoted by the kingless generation.

4. The Character of the Section

There are three motifs in this section that have been described as Christian:[177] the illuminator suffers in his flesh,[178]
his converts are called "fruitbearing trees,"[179] and the illuminator performs signs and wonders.[180] It is striking that they
appear here in a cluster, and this configuration raises the
possibility that they are indirect references to Jesus, although
the name of Jesus is not mentioned in the text. On this basis,
arguments have been made that the section should be characterized as Christian. I have avoided deciding provenance on the
basis of a simple accumulation of parallels. Using that method,
these motifs might be Christian, but they might equally as well
be non-Christian.[181] However, here we do have the added feature of clustering.[182] Perhaps the situation provides an excellent opportunity for pursuing the approach I suggested above;[183]
that is, to decide how these motifs function in the myth in the
Apoc. Adam.

Since the aim of such an examination of the *Apoc. Adam* is
to gain an understanding of its character, one should begin with
similar texts where there has already been general agreement
about how myth functions. By observing how motifs function in
these similar texts, it may be possible to establish guidelines
that will aid in the examination of the *Apoc. Adam*.

There are two such texts that possess a "redeemer myth"
similar to the section under consideration in the *Apoc. Adam*:
The Ascension of Isaiah and the *Concept of Our Great Power*
(VI,*4*). The Ascension of Isaiah (10-11) reflects a Christian
tradition that has been subjected to gnostic expansion and
elaboration.[184] On the other hand, the *Concept of Our Great
Power* (40,1-45,29) is a gnostic text that reflects Christian
influence.[185] The latter text is quite pertinent to the discussion since the elaboration of the myth, like the *Apoc. Adam*,
does not include any *specific* identification of the "redeemer"
as Jesus, while the Ascension of Isaiah does.

The fundamental Christian character of the myth in the
Ascension of Isaiah can hardly be contested.[186] The redeemer
is specifically identified as Jesus, the Lord Christ (10,7).
He enters the world as the son of the virgin Mary who was espoused to Joseph the carpenter, both of whom were descended
from the line of David (11,1-2). Joseph was espoused to Mary
and did not have sexual intercourse with her but "put her away"
until the child Jesus was born (11,3-11). The baby Jesus was
born in Bethlehem (11,12), and taken to Nazareth in Galilee
(11,15.17). When he matured, he worked signs and wonders in the
land of Israel and Jerusalem (11,18). Israel was roused
against him, he was delivered to the king and crucified (11,
21). On the third day following, he was raised (11,21), sent
out twelve apostles and ascended (11,22).

The gnostic elaboration and expansion is equally evident.
The appearance of the redeemer Christ is interpreted in gnostic
categories as a descent from the seventh heaven through the
"gate keepers" of the lower six heavens to the perceptible
world (10,8-13.17-31), and as an ascent to the right hand of
glory in the seventh heaven (10,14-16.24-32). The unrecognizability of the redeemer's true form (10,10-12.20-27; 11,24), a
motif that suits well the descent and ascent feature with its
gate keepers and antagonistic princes, angels and gods (10,12),
appears also as a secondary gnostic expansion of the New Testament tradition (11,14.16-17) where it really only makes sense
in relationship to the descent-ascent through the lower heavens
(cf. 11,16). However, this feature is also interpreted in the
myth in terms of recognizing the redeemer's true identity, and
not his true form (11,14).

The basic structure of the myth takes the form of a narrative relating the Christian tradition about Jesus, that is
elaborated and expanded in only three ways: descent,[187]
ascent[188] and unrecognizability.[189] These features are not
essential to the myth proper. In this case they are, so to
speak, gnostic features appended to a Christian trunk which,
when disregarded, affect the character of the narrative but do
not disturb its basic structure. Since these features are unnecessary to maintain the integrity and sense of the narrative,

they are to be described as secondary motifs; that is to say,
they serve a secondary function in the action of the narrative.
On the other hand, were we to disregard the characteristic
Christian elements, the structure of the narrative would be
radically altered. It would no longer be a redeemer myth.
There would only be left a narrative about descent (and ascent)
through the gate keepers of the six heavens to the perceptible
world. Further, the character of the narrative has also been
totally changed, since all Christian features have been removed. In this instance, these features are essential to the
sense and structure of the narrative and must therefore be described as primary motifs. Without them the narrative breaks
down. Their absence causes a gap in the action or logic of the
narrative; that is to say, they serve a primary function in the
narrative. Therefore, in this discussion it appears that we
have recognized a literary principle: when secondary features
are withdrawn from a narrative, the character may be changed,
but the basic structure of the story remains intact. On the
other hand, the removal of primary features alters *both* character and structure.

With respect to *Great Pow*. there can be little question
that it is primarily gnostic. There is likewise general agreement that it contains covert Christian motifs;[190] that is,
references to Jesus are present in the redeemer myth of *Great
Pow*., but without the use of Christian titles or a stated identification of the redeemer with Jesus. These Christian features appear to be secondary (with respect to function) to the
main structure of the myth.

The man (also called "logos" VI 43,28; VI 44,2; the
"living one" VI 36,29; "the life" VI 43,23) who knows the great
power came into being in the natural aeon (VI 40,24-27). He
proclaimed the aeon to come (VI 40,31) for 120 years (VI 43,
11-22). At his appearance, there was a disturbance and the
archons raised their wrath against him. They decided to deliver
him to the one who ruled over Hades (VI 41,13-17), so they
seized him and delivered him over (VI 41,23-30). However, the
ruler of Hades could not restrain him (VI 41,31-42,3), and he
was victorious over the command and rule of the archons

(VI 42,8-11). They recognized that he was from the logos of the power of life and that his word had abolished the law of the aeon (VI 42,4-8). His coming is the sign of the dissolution of the archons and the transition of the aeon (VI 42,11-15). Many who follow him will abandon his teaching (VI 42,31-43,3). The dissolution of the aeon will be accompanied by a great cosmic disturbance (VI 43,29-44,10) that will be preceded by a time of great wickedness (VI 44,10-29).

Those motifs that give the narrative a Christian character are actually blended into the story in such a loose way that their absence does not damage or alter the primary structure of the myth. Conversely, their presence gives an added dimension and meaning to the text. For example, the man who comes to proclaim the aeon to come will speak in parables (VI 40,30-31):

> Now concerning his words which he uttered, in all of them
> he spoke in seventy two tongues. And
> he opened the gates of the heavens with his words. And
> he put to shame the ruler of Hades;
> he raised the dead, and destroyed his dominion.
> (VI 41,3-12)[191]

The archons that wanted to hand him over to the ruler of Hades obtained his capture through his betrayal by one of his followers (VI 41,18-23).[192]

The main structure of the myth is non-Christian into which are incorporated Christian motifs.[193] When these are removed, the basic structure of the myth remains undisturbed, but the Christian character they suggest is lacking. On the other hand, were we to remove the non-Christian structure, there would be little left except an apparent Christian creedal confession. In effect, the Christian motifs function as an interpretative lever that inclines the reader to see the text in a particular slanted way. Therefore it appears that the same principle encountered in the discussion on the AscenIsa is applicable here also: when secondary features (with respect to function) are withdrawn from a narrative, the character may be changed, but the basic structure of the story remains intact. On the other hand, the removal of primary features alters *both* character and structure. In effect, we have identified a guide

that may be used for differentiating in a narrative those features that function in a primary and secondary manner.

It is on this basis that we need to consider the so-called
Christian motifs in the *Apoc. Adam*. The issue is how do they
function in the text? Are they to be considered, with respect
to how they function in the text, as primary or secondary literary features? The motif of "fruitbearing" trees ([76],14-15)
does not appear to be a primary motif.[194] The feature of something being left behind, however, does appear to be a primary
feature, since it is the ostensible reason for the illuminator's
appearance, but it is not required that what is left behind be
specifically "fruitbearing trees." The necessity for this specific term is not presupposed anywhere in the myth. In fact,
if one assumes that the term suggests followers who propagate
the γνῶσις of the illuminator, then the expression seems to be
in tension with the description that follows it ([76],15-27)
where those left behind are not described as "propagating the
faith" but as themselves being in need of salvation. Thus,
there is no gap in the primary structure of the myth without
the expression.

Nor does the motif of "signs and wonders" ([77],1-3) appear to be a primary feature. As a *terminus technicus*, it does
serve to authenticate the work of the illuminator, but it is
not an element essential to the primary structure of the myth.[195]
At no other point in the narrative is the illuminator assumed
to have performed signs and wonders, nor is the expression required in order to make sense of some other feature in the myth.
However, the fact that the illuminator scorned the powers and
their ruler is an essential feature since it explains why the
powers were disturbed and why great wrath was raised against
the illuminator. It is not necessary to the sense of the myth
that the illuminator perform signs and wonders in order to
achieve the scorning, but it is necessary to the structure of
the myth that he scorn the creator in order to explain the re-
action of the powers.

The motif of the illuminator suffering ([77],16-18) does
seem to be essential to the primary structure of the narrative
since it follows naturally upon the wrath of the powers. But

it does not seem to be essential to add that the "flesh" of the
redeemer was punished. It would have been sufficient merely to
have said, "then they will punish the man upon whom the holy
spirit has come." It would naturally be assumed that he would
suffer physically, or in his "flesh." The addition of the object "flesh" seems redundant and adds a different character to
the narrative. On the other hand, its absence does not actually
affect the structure of the narrative since one would naturally
assume that the man suffered physically.[196] Since he is described as a man ([77],4-7.16-18), the reader would assume that
his humanity is characterized by his body of flesh--the normal
state of all human beings. The text implies this state by describing the descent of the holy "spirit" upon him; that is, it
was upon man, the physical *creature*, that the *spirit* descended.
This contrast is particularly true if we are dealing with the
(docetic) "host" of the redeemer. One would certainly expect
the "host" of the redeemer to have been flesh and blood.
Therefore the inclusion of the object "flesh" at this point
seems to be a clumsy redundancy not required to make the point.

What is left after one disregards these three motifs is a
consistent narrative whose basic or primary structure not only
remains intact, but perhaps is somewhat improved by lessening
the clash between the redeemer's invisibility and the fact that
it is his "flesh" that suffers.[197] The only observable change
to the myth concerns its external character; that is, it no
longer contains features suggestive of Christian influence.
Therefore I would characterize these three motifs with respect
to function as secondary features[198] in the sense that they are
not part of the primary structure of the narrative. Their
presence is not essential to the integrity of the narrative.
In accordance with the literary principle worked out above, I
would judge any characterization attributed to the total narrative under the influence of these three motifs to be a description based upon secondary features, since they are not constitu-
tive of the narrative as a whole.[199] The narrative should be
characterized on the basis of its primary structure, and not on
attendant or secondary motifs that may or may not be in harmony
with the nature of the narrative as a whole. In other words,

if one judges these motifs to be evidence of Christian influence, a reasonable trajectory for the intention of the narrative should be gnostic → Christian, because the presence of
these motifs gives the narrative a character different from the
character of the narrative as a whole. Because of their presence the reader "sees" the text in a different light; that is,
he views the text through the total spectrum of the Christian
tradition, and is thereby misled as to its true or primary
character in that he attributes a character to the narrative
that is not evident from its primary motives. Therefore if one
insists on regarding these motifs as evidence of Christian influence, he should in all honesty describe the myth as non-
Christian with some possible Christian influence. A better
approach to the text is to interpret these motifs in harmony
with the nature of the text as a whole, since the use of these
motifs is not restricted to the Christian tradition only.[200]

C. The Position of the Text in the History of Religions

What I have described as source B has been preserved by
the redactor in two incomplete segments. That these two segments were originally part of one document is not completely
certain, although other possible explanations seem less
likely.[201] This uncertainty required that the two segments[202]
initially be treated separately. We are now in a position to
evaluate their relationship more closely. Aside from the general relationship noted above, it appears that there is greater
harmony between the two segments than was first apparent.[203]

Both segments reflect a similar threefold pattern describing man's condition and his world: man exists in a state of
ignorance in the world, a condition described as death;[204] each
man must anticipate his own individual day of physical death,
because he is part of a world described as dead;[205] just as all
men associated with this kind of world must die, so will the
cosmos itself be dissolved.[206]

As the first segment recognizes two states or conditions
for men in the world, ignorance and enlightenment,[207] so the
second segment recognizes two classes of people: the saved,
those who reflect on the knowledge of God, and the creatures of

the dead earth.[208]   In both segments there is a pronounced
dualism implied in the negative view of the world and the death
of the body.[209]

It is to be agreed that these are general gnostic concepts, but when contrasted to the A source, the basic harmony
of the two segments in the B source is more apparent and the
difference of the B source from the A source more apparent.   In
the A source, there is no evidence of the marked dualism that
we find in the B source.[210]   While the A source, like the B
source, recognizes two groups of people in the world, they are
characterized differently, and the organizing principle for
each group is different.   In the B source, there is a marked
emphasis upon the individual that does not appear in source
A.[211]   Individual men are described in source B as saved or
lost on the basis of whether or not they have received γνῶσις.
Those individuals who have received γνῶσις are called the
"chosen generation" ([82],28-[83],4).   Those who have not are
described as "creatures of the dead earth" ([76],17-20).

In the A source, two distinct communities are recognized
at the outset: the men of gnosis and the seed of Noah ([71],8-
[73],12).   The men of gnosis have a supernatural origin while
the seed of Noah have a natural origin.   It is possible for
some of the seed of Noah to unite themselves with the men of
gnosis if they share in their knowledge of and committment to
the true God ([73],13-[74],16).   On the other hand, the seed of
Noah are men who are corrupted by desire and who serve the
Παντοκρατωρ.[212]   In the A source, life is viewed as a cosmic
struggle between the creator and his community on the one hand,
and the community of the men of γνῶσις on the other.   In this
connection, salvation is not seen as a simple matter of an
isolated individual receiving special knowledge, but salvation
is determined on the basis of the community to which one belongs.
Thus, salvation is not depicted as an individual matter, but
primarily involves one in a community relationship.[213]

Further, the method of illumination is different.   In the
A source, the γνῶσις lost by Adam and Eve at their devolution
into the world was passed on in the primordial period to the
great generation (64,20-[65],3; [65],9-23; [66],12-[67],12),[214]

while in the B source, "illuminators" come into the world to bring enlightenment.[215] Source A also uses a different method of periodizing than does source B. In A, periodizing is done on the basis of idealized historical occurrences giving a linear concept of time to the events.[216] On the other hand, B is periodized as a threefold pattern of revelation of which the first two occurrences are lacking.[217]

In the contrast between sources A and B, the position of the text in the history of ideas becomes more clear. Source A draws heavily on Jewish traditions, and the narrative is constructed from these traditions.[218] On the other hand, in the B source, there are few specific references to the Jewish tradition and those that are present are modified.[219] Source B assumes a subtly different posture in that it presumes different "givens" from source A. The traditions and motifs from which its narrative is constructed are different and reflect a different "world" than source A. For example, source B does not draw upon the Old Testament as a sourcebook for its ideas and imagery, while source A does. To be sure, there are allusions to the Old Testament tradition in source B (for example, the use of the names Adam, Eve and Seth), but that tradition does not play a primary role in the narrative. Nor does source B draw upon the New Testament tradition as a sourcebook. There is no unequivocal reference made to the New Testament tradition, or motifs in source B. However, the text does draw upon material that is similar to known gnostic traditions.[220]

The two sources have been examined from the standpoint of their individual motifs in their isolation from one another. From this standpoint, it is possible, as has been seen,[221] to find conflicting parallels to different traditions. The true meaning of the text, however, derives from the configuration of its parts. The motives of the text break down the parameters of the isolated individual motifs, and the new configuration in the text gives them a different character. The key to understanding a text is to discover its motives. This is always difficult since the motives of a text are not usually written, but must be deduced from the general image conveyed by the text.

One must respect the integrity of the text. The general
impression it gives is as valid for determining its character
as its individual parts. Individual motifs are integrated by
the motives of the text. These inner drives, impulses or in-
tentions pull the motifs together into the whole we call the
text and impel them in a certain direction so as to give a
general impression which we describe as the character of a
text. This impression can be described as the overall effect
produced on the mind of the reader under the influence of the
text, or as an image of the author's world refracted through
the text. From this standpoint, source B should be described
as clearly gnostic, but as having no striking affinities to any
known gnostic group as reported in the reports of the Church
Fathers.[222]

NOTES

CHAPTER IV

[1]See above pp. 37-38 and 160-61. However, it is possible that the revelation story ([65],24-[66],12; [67],12-21) is the work of the redactor. See above, pp. 114-15.

[2]See above, pp. 23-25.

[3]For example, see above, p. 120, where a gnostic revelation story follows the model of an exorcism, and above, pp. 104-105, where the revelation story has become in actuality a dream vision. However, in this latter instance, the tension between metaphorical language about sleep and "real" language about sleep is evident. Compare also Poimandres 1.1-26 where the gnostic revelation story follows the model of a dream vision and Poimandres 1.27-29 where the gnostic revelation story has been modeled in a preaching context as a homily. In the former situation, the structure assumes the form of a dialog, while in the latter, the structure resembles most closely the gnostic revelation story in the *Apoc. Adam* (see above, pp. 99-101.

[4]This structure and language do not correspond closely to examples of visions that I have seen elsewhere. For the Old Testament material, see Moses Sister, "Die Typen der prophetischen Visionen in der Bibel," *Wissenschaft des Judentums* 78 (1934) 399-430. For the New Testament: Matt 17:1-9; Luke 24:13-27; Acts 10:1-17, 12:6-9, 16:9-10, 22:6-11.17-21, 26:12-19; Rev 1:9-12. For the Jewish apocalyptic literature: *2 Enoch* 1:1-38:3; *1 Enoch* 83:1-6, 85:1-91:42; *4 Ezra* 3:1-5:19, 5:20-6:34, 6:35-9:25, 9:26-10:57, 10:60-12:48, 13:1-53, 14:1-48; *3 Apoc. Bar.* 1:1-17:4; *2 Apoc. Bar.* 36:1-40:4, 53:1-12.

[5]Werner Foerster (ed.), *Gnosis* (2 vols.; trans. and ed. R. McL. Wilson; Oxford: Clarendon, 1972) 1.334. See also Nock and Festugière, *Corpus Hermeticum*, 1.16-17.

[6]See Hans Jonas, *Gnostic Religion*, 68, and George MacRae, "Sleep and Awakening in Gnostic Texts," *Le origini dello gnosticismo: Colloquio di Messina 13-18 Aprile 1966; Testi e discussioni* (*Numen* Supplement 12; Leiden: E. J. Brill, 1967) 496-507.

[7]A. F. J. Klijn, *The Acts of Thomas* (Leiden: E. J. Brill, 1962) 121-25.

[8]One might make a good argument that the Hymn of the Pearl is an expanded revelation story. The structure of the Hymn corresponds to the structure of the revelation story.
  I.   The lapse into ignorance, 108-109.
  II. The appearance of the revealer, 110.
  III. The revelation, 111a.
  IV. The enlightenment, 111b-113.

[9]A. V. Williams Jackson, *Researches in Manichaeism* (New York: Columbia University, 1932) 249-54.

[10]Cf. Martin Dibelius, *From Tradition to Gospel* (2nd ed. rev.; trans. B. L. Woolf; New York: Scribner's, n.d.) 86.

[11]See Jonas, *Gnostic Religion*, 81.

[12]Quotations from *Trim. Prot.* from the translation by John Turner in *The Nag Hammadi Library*, 461-470.

[13]The revelation (130,16-132,5) consists of a further series of injunctions the examination of which goes beyond the scope of this section. Translation by John Sieber in *The Nag Hammadi Library*, 393.

[14]Mark Lidzbarski, *Ginza: Der Schatz oder das grosse Buch der Mandäer* (Göttingen: Vandenhoeck & Ruprecht, 1925) 430-31.

[15]Jonas, *Gnostic Religion*, 87-88. Jonas discusses the unusual response of Adam to the revelation brought by the redeemer.

[16]Lidzbarski, *Ginza*, 387-88. Cf. idem, *Das Johannesbuch* (225-26) for an identical narrative.

[17]Lidzbarski, *Das Johannesbuch*, 56-57.

[18]Translation by Frederik Wisse in *The Nag Hammadi Library*, 115-16.

[19]As seen above, *Apoc. Adam* differs from the other revelation stories most radically at this point. In the *Apoc. Adam*, there are three revealers. Beltz has cited the parallels in the rabbinic and Mandaean traditions (57-58). He points out that triads are a favorite scheme in late antiquity. In Iranian thought, three archangels appear from heaven as witnesses from Ahura Mazda to the message of Zarathustra (see the footnote to the translation at [65],24-33). See also Michael Stone, "The Death of Adam--An Armenian Adam Book" (*HTR* 59 [1966] 283-91),where three revealers appear to Eve in a dream. See *2 Enoch* 1:6 (Charles, *APOT*, 2.431), where two messengers are sent from God to Enoch, and in this connection Gen 18:1ff. where three messengers appear to Abraham. See also the thrice-male Child in the *Gospel of the Egyptians* (Alexander Böhlig and Frederik Wisse, *The Gospel of the Egyptians: The Holy Book of the Great Invisible Spirit* [Leiden: E. J. Brill, 1975] 44-46).

[20]See above, p. 101.

[21]See above, Poimandres and Theodore bar Konai, pp. 99-101 and 102.

[22]See above, Left *Ginza* 1,2, pp. 104-105, and Jonas' comments in *Gnostic Religion* (87-88).

[23]This latter idea is clearly expressed in source A at
[67],10-12, and [84],1-3 also seems to assume the idea of
physical death when it contrasts souls that "shall surely die"
with those that will "live forever." However, compare [65],
14-16 and [73],30-[74],2, where the meaning of the word "dead"
is clearly metaphorical.

[24]See Beltz, 125.

[25]See above, 110-11.

[26]Charles (*APOT*, 2.139) reports that some manuscripts have
a preface explaining the reason Seth was chosen for the revelation. In both the *Apoc. Adam* and *Adam and Eve*, the revelation
to Seth comes through Adam. See also *Ap. John* (II,*1*)24,34-
25,2: Adam begat Seth according to the way of begetting in the
aeons, i.e., he "knew the likeness of his own foreknowledge."
Cf. Clem, *exc. Thdot.* 54,1-3 and Epiph. *Pan.* 40.7.1-4. For the
importance of Seth in the Samaritan tradition, see John Bowman,
*The Samaritan Problem: Studies in the Relationships of Samari-
tanism, Judaism, and Early Christianity* (trans. A. M. Johnson,
Jr.; Pittsburgh: Pickwick, 1975) 55, 100. See also the study
by A. F. J. Klijn, *Seth in Jewish, Christian and Gnostic Literature* (Leiden: E. J. Brill, 1977).

[27]See Beltz's discussion (47-50) for the significance of
Seth in antiquity.

[28]Other than the text under discussion, the name "Seth"
appears only five times in the *Apoc. Adam*: In source A: introduction 64,2-6 (two times), conclusion [85],19-22. In source
B: [67],14-21, and [76],28-[77],1. In the redactor's conclusion: [85],22-24. In every instance but one ([76],28-[77],1),
the use of the name Seth is part of the testament motif and
therefore unavoidable. Most of these references do nothing to
clarify the relationship of "that man," or "those men" to Seth.
[76],28-[77],1, on the other hand, does not seem to be part of
the testament motif, suggesting that it might be the one occurrence of the name Seth that clarifies such relationships. Unfortunately, it is near a lacuna. If the present reconstruction of this lacuna ([76],28-[77],1) is correct, it places
source B in contrast to source A with its use of the name Seth
in a mythological context apart from the testament motif.

[29]Compare the following references where one would have
expected a clear identification of Seth with the "great race"
or "that man": [65],3-9.25-32; [69],10-16; [72],5-9. Also see
above, p. 94 n. 52, where the great race is referred to only in
general terms and never by the name of their great ancestor
Seth (except, perhaps, for the allusion in the lacuna at
[76],28-[77],1).

[30]I assume that there is a concrete referrant intended
because the third statement ("who came from you and Eve") suggests a particular incident in the tradition of which we have
knowledge and because the purpose of these explanatory clauses
seems to be to identify Seth without actually naming him.

[31]Cf. also BG8502 65,1-6; *Ap. John* (II,*1*)25,23-24; 26,9-10.

[32]Translation by Foerster, *Gnosis*, 1.294. For the origin of Seth as the heavenly prototype of Adam's Son, see *Steles Seth* (VII,*5*)118,28 (brought forth without birth), and *Gos. Eg.* (III,*2*)51,5-14 (= [IV,*2*]62,30-63,17).

[33]I noted in the note to the text ([65],33-[66],8) that it is also possible to understand ⳁⳡⲧⲟⲣⲁ ⲙ̅ⲡⲣⲱⲙⲉ as indicating identity, i.e., the seed *is* that man: "the seed, namely, that man," taking the Ⲛ̄ to be the particle of identity (cf. in Codex V, [47],27; [54],8; [66],10; [76],26). This interpretation has the merit of support from [65],3-9, where "that man" is identified as "the seed of the great generations." So such an interpretation would not introduce a foreign idea into the text. Further, it would remove what I sense as an inappropriate dual emphasis in the statement of the three men. If one takes the Ⲛ̄ as a genitive, then the three men call on Adam to hear about the seed, the descendants of Seth, of whom they say nothing. Instead, they talk about "that man." Understanding the Ⲛ̄ as indicating identity gives the statement only one emphasis. On the other hand, understanding the Ⲛ̄ as a genitive ("the seed *of* that man") agrees with the statement in [69],10-17 where the seed is identified as those men who received life, i.e., the descendants of the heavenly Seth. Further, the predominant use of the term ⳡⲧⲟⲣⲁ in the tractate is to identify the descendants of Seth. However, see [85],24-32, where ⳡⲧⲟⲣⲁ clearly refers to Seth.

[34]Translation by Böhlig-Wisse, *Gospel of the Egyptians*, 98. See also the similar statement at 59,9-25.

[35]Ibid., 178-79.

[36]See [65],3-9; [69],10-17 and below, pp. 185-87.

[37]See above, pp. 37-38, and 160-63.

[38]See above, pp. 102-03 (Theodor bar Konai), where Adam "realized what he was" after the statement of revelation.

[39]See below, pp. 185-87.

[40]See above, pp. 53-54 n. 70. Only the kingless generation gives a specific identification for the subject of the stories as the illuminator of knowledge. In the statements of the thirteen kingdoms, the subject of the stories is not specifically identified. See above, pp. 117-18.

[41]Cf. MacRae, "Coptic Gnostic Apocalypse of Adam," 30-31. MacRae has also suggested (II,*5*)97,24-30 and (III,*3*)70,1-71,13 as examples for the contrasting of several wrong answers with a correct answer.

[42]It is true that the questions are not really clear. The nominal subject of the first question is indefinite, and its antecedent is open to question (see the note to the text at [77],23-27). ⲠⲖⲀⲚⲎ seems to be the most probable antecedent, for one reason because of its proximity to ⲀⲤⲰⲰⲦⲈ. It is the closest possible antecedent, and because of this nearness the scribe may have felt that it was unnecessary to clarify the subject through an Ⲛ6Ⲓ phrase following the verb. Another reason is that the two questions form a disjunctive parallelism and ⲠⲖⲀⲚⲎ makes a convenient parallel with ⲘⲚⲦⲚⲞⲨⲬ in the second question.

[43]This interpretation of the text as a whole was suggested by George MacRae as one way of making sense out of the text in its present form.

[44]The title ⲦⲘⲚⲦⲢⲢⲞ appears only three times in the tractate outside of the collection of explanations: [73],25-29 the twelve kingdoms formed by the sons of Noah; [74],12-16 the "dominion" of the creator; and [76],24-27 the "dominion" of the creator.

[45]Cf. *Orig. World* (II,*3*)101,31 where ⲦⲘⲚⲦⲢⲢⲞ is the feminine name of Adonaios.

[46]Also see below, pp. 200-201.

[47]See the note to [82],19-20 below.

[48]See above, pp. 39-40.

[49]See above, p. 94 n. 52.

[50]MacRae, "The Apocalypse of Adam Reconsidered," 574; Rudolph, "Gnosis und Gnostizismus," 43; Beltz, 140; Kasser, 317. Others call it an "excursus," thereby suggesting that in some way it is in tension with its present literary setting: Karl Troger (ed.), "Die Bedeutung der Texte von Nag Hammadi für die Moderne Gnosisforschung," *Gnosis und Neues Testament* (Berlin: Evangelische Verlagsanstalt, 1973) 46 (no author given--it is a joint work of the *Berliner Arbeitskreis für koptisch-gnostische Schriften*); Böhlig, 87; Krause, 2.14.

[51]Cf. MacRae, "Coptic Gnostic Apocalypse of Adam," 27-35. MacRae has assembled a number of parallels to this section from the Deutero-Isaiah tradition (p. 33) and argued that the "episode of the Illuminator-redeemer...can...be accounted for as a sort of gnostic midrash built on the Deutero-Isaiah Servant Songs." While MacRae was unable to develop his thesis in the short article, as he himself noted (p. 33), I agree with Schottroff ("Animae naturalitur salvandae," 83) that the parallels are not specific nor extensive enough in essential ideas to allow one to argue that the Servant Songs of Deutero-Isaiah provide a specific occasion for the illuminator-redeemer episode in the *Apoc. Adam*. The significance of his

article is that it flags a cluster of striking parallels to the
gnostic illuminator-redeemer episode in a Jewish text. His
cluster of parallels is more credible when regarded as an early
stage in the development of the tradition out of which the redeemer myth evolved. In a later article ("The Apocalypse of
Adam Reconsidered," 575), MacRae acknowledged that this was the
better explanation. In this sense, the parallels are a part of
the matrix that produced the myth, but not the direct cause of
the myth.

[52]The myth is alluded to at many points: *Gos. Eg.* (III,*2*)
51,5-14; 62,24-64,9; *Ap. John* (II,*1*)30,11-31,25; *Treat. Seth*
(VII,*2*)59,19-29; *Ep. Pet. Phil.* (VIII,*2*)136,16-28; 139,9-23;
Paraph. Shem (VII,*1*)15,28-34; 28,34-29,12; 32,5-18; 36,12-14;
Trim. Prot. (XIII,*1**)50,6-20; *Soph. Jes. Chr.* (III,*4*)96,19-21;
107,11-21; *Gos. Truth* (I,*2*)20,23-21,2; 31,4-8; 40,30-41,12;
cf. also the ascent of Zostrianos (VIII,*1*)4,20-31; 129,8-132,9.
For the New Testament, compare Phil 2:6-11, 1 Cor 2:6-9. See
also Hipp. *Ref.* 5.12.6; 8.10.3-8; Epiph. *Pan.* 39.3.5; 26.9.9;
10.4-6.

[53]*Treat. Seth* (VII,*2*)50,23-56,32; *Trim. Prot.* (XIII,*1**)
40,8-46,3; AscenIsa 10-11.

[54][76],17-27 is an exegetical statement that digresses
from the myth proper. See below, pp. 172-73 n. 77.

[55]Compare Rudolf Bultmann's mockup of the gnostic redeemer
myth from the Manichaean and Mandaean texts ("Die Bedeutung der
neuerschlossenen mandäischen und manichäischen Quellen für das
Verständnis des Johannesevangeliums," *ZNW* 24 [1925] 100-46):
1c = Bultmann's #25; 2b = Bultmann's #3; 3a = Bultmann's #26;
3c = Bultmann's #16; 4b = Bultmann's #14. See also the critique
by Carsten Colpe, *Die religionsgeschichtliche Schule: Darstellung
und Kritik ihres Bildes vom gnostischen Erlösermythes* (Göttingen:
Vandenhoeck & Ruprecht, 1961) 57-68, 171-93.

[56]Cf. *Gos. Eg.* (III,*2*)51,5-14.

[57][76],17-27.

[58]For example, the reference to the third pass of the
illuminator ([76],8-11) is inexplicable without mention of the
first two passes. The statement at [77],14-15 about the powers
not seeing the illuminator is likewise difficult to understand
since, immediately following, the text states that "his flesh
was punished." The statement becomes understandable only by
assuming a docetic motif similar to that in *Treat. Seth* (VII,*2*)
56,4-19. The text has also failed to record the coming of the
holy spirit upon the man whose "flesh was punished" ([77],
16-18). And finally, the statement about "using the name in
error" assumes a configuration of ideas not present in the text:
What is the name? How did they use it in error? What is the
relationship between punishing "the man on whom the holy spirit
has come," and the statement that immediately follows about
"using the name in error"? One of the most interesting features

of the myth in *Apoc. Adam* is what it does not say. The *Apoc. Adam* ends with the question of the perplexed powers and with the illuminator-redeemer still in the world. However, in the parallel texts, the illuminator has returned to the heavenly world: AscenIsa 11,22-32; *Treat. Seth* (VII,*2*)56,17-18; 57,7-16; *Trim. Prot.* (XIII,*1**)48,27-30; 49,11-15; 50,6-9.

[59]See Böhlig (87) who omits Codex XIII from the cluster of documents to be associated with the *Apoc. Adam.*

[60]The amount of text with which we are concerned here is quite brief. Thus, comments with reference to its characteristic religious ideas can for the most part be considered only as suggestive and not exhaustive.

[61]See above, pp. 30-31.

[62]Such an assertion does not reduce the received text to nonsense: One must consider the redactor's understanding of the text. The redaction of the text is an interpretation. The present form of the text would have some meaning to the redactor and his community.

[63]Böhlig-Wisse, *Gospel of the Egyptians*, 142-43.

[64]*Gos. Eg.* (III,*2*)60,25-61,23 = (IV,*2*)72,7-27. See Böhlig-Wisse, *Gospel of the Egyptians*, 191. The authors of the *editio princeps* state that "Seth passes through the three παρουσίαι experienced by his children: first the flood, secondly the conflagration, and thirdly the judgment of the archons." The difficulty is that at the place cited as proof, only two of the "three παρουσίαι" are mentioned: the flood and the conflagration ([IV,*2*]72,14-15 reads "conflagrations"). The "judgment of the archons" as such does not appear. However, the other visitations of wrath mentioned in the text at this point-- famines, plagues, temptations and falsehood of false prophets-- are interpreted by the text as the activity of the devil (= archon), his guises and schemes, and the persecutions by his powers and angels ([III,*2*]61,16-23). Since the text later refers to all three visitations as being mentioned previously ([III,*2*]63,4-8), it seems justifiable to understand the statement at (III,*2*)61,16-23 as the judgment of the archons, powers and authorities, assuming that the later reference has also interpreted it this way.

[65]No mention is made of the great Seth's redemptive activity during the visitations of wrath upon the seed of Seth. In fact, it is specifically stated that his race received "grace through the prophets and the guardians who guard the life of the race." It is only after the great Seth observes the "activity of the devil" that he asks for guards over his seed, and is commissioned to save his people.

[66]MacRae, "Sleep and Awakening," 496-507.

[67]Pheme Perkins, "Gnostic Periodization of Revelation and the Apocryphon of John," paper presented to the Nag Hammadi section of the Society of Biblical Literature (1970), mimeo.

[68]So Gesine Schenke, "Die dreigestaltige Protennoia," *TLZ*
99 (1974) cols. 731, 733, and so *Gnosis und Neues Testament*,
74.

[69]See pp. 48-49 n. 46.

[70]Böhlig-Wisse, *Gospel of the Egyptians*, 191.

[71]However, compare Böhlig's suggested parallel in the
Iranian tradition: the appearance of the third Saošyant,
Sōsyans. See below, pp. 144-45.

[72]See below, n. 73.

[73]The motif of "bearing fruit" as a demonstration of
religious dedication is too common in antiquity to allow one
to regard it as unique to any one religious movement. For the
OT, see Ps 1:3; Prov 11:30; Jer 11:19, 17:7-10, 21:14; Hos 10:1.
For the NT, see Matt 3:8-10, 7:15, 12:33, 21:43; Mark 4:19-20;
John 15; Rom 1:13, 7:4; Eph 5:9; Phil 1:11; Col 1:10; 2 Pet 1:8;
Jude 12; Rev 2:22.   See also Wis 4; *Apoc. Adam* [84],26-[85],3;
Ap. John (II,*1*)21,21-35; *Soph. Jes. Chr.* (III,*4*)97,1-11 (= BG
3,88,2-10); 107,16-20 (= BG*3*,104,14-18); BG*3*,122,5-123,1; *Thom.
Cont.* (II,*7*)39,1-2; 142,14-15; The Story of Ahikar 8:35 (Syr.)
in Charles, *APOT*, 2.775.   See also καρπός in *TDNT* 3 (1965) 614-
16.   C. R. C. Allberry, *A Manichaean Psalm Book* (Stuttgart:
Kohlhammer, 1938) 208 line 23. For the rabbinic tradition, see
H. L. Strack and Paul Billerbeck, *Kommentar zum Neuen Testament
aus Talmud und Midrasch* (5th ed.; 4 vols. in 5; München: C. H.
Beck, 1969) 1.466, 638-39.

[74]The situation is just reversed in Epiph. *Pan.* 39.3,1-3
where a remnant of the wicked seed of Ham is left behind in the
world.

[75]See above, pp. 110-11.

[76]See above, pp. 83-84.

[77]The exegetical statement has a homiletical character,
and is very clearly not a part of the structure of the myth.
It digresses from the main theme of the section--the events
surrounding the coming of the illuminator of knowledge.   It
does not describe any action by the characters in the episode,
but is formally a pause in that action that suggests a different context and a different group of actors.   It is an explanatory statement that clarifies why the illuminator must save the
souls of the gnostics and how he saves them.   Further, it is
the only exegetical-type statement in a section that is characterized by a highly abbreviated style.   In explaining the
statement at [76],15-17 ("and he will redeem their souls from
the day of death"), it would have been sufficient merely to
state why the illuminator must redeem the gnostics. A statement
to this effect would have not been inconsistent with the abbreviated style of the rest of the section, and would be understandable as a natural outgrowth of the statement being commented

upon. However, the second half of the statement indicating *how*
salvation was to be accomplished does not develop from the
statement ostensibly being explained. It is actually occa-
sioned by the lack of specificity in the myth about how salvation is accomplished. It attempts to fill out in the myth what
is only implied (or, perhaps, what had been clearly stated in
one of the two missing appearances of the illuminator). The
explanatory statement assumes a specific life situation and the
myth does not. The myth is concerned simply to narrate the
third appearance of the illuminator. There is no special
situation assumed by the narration. The narrative could be
directed to the gnostic community or to a group of potential
gnostics as a missionary tract. On the other hand, the explanatory statement has in view a homiletical situation in which
the audience is non-gnostic. They are warned of the dangers of
unenlightenment and advised of the means of salvation. The
most interesting thing about the explanatory statement is what
it implies about the myth as stated in the *Apoc. Adam*. It implies that it is a traditional unit that came to the author of
this section largely intact. The traditional character of the
unit resisted the author's attempts to rewrite the opening
lines of the section for the purpose of clarifying the role of
gnosis in the work of the illuminator, and forced him to clarify it in a parenthetical statement.

[78]Cf. the article σημεῖον in *TDNT* 7 (1971) 200-61. The
phrase σημεῖα καὶ τέρατα appears to be a technical expression
that authenticates an individual as an accredited envoy of God.
In the Jewish and Christian traditions, it is rooted in the
Exodus from Egypt in which God demonstrates himself to be God
of history and showed Israel to be his chosen nation. It also
appears to be a part of the Jewish messianic expectations as
the credentials by which the Messiah is accredited (cf. Deut
13:1-2 and John 1:21), but is rejected as a part of the expectations of the early Christian communities (Matt 24:24 = Mark
13:22). Paul picks it up as a traditional expression to show
that he is an accredited envoy of Christ (Rom 15:19, 2 Cor
12:12). In some cases, there is a close relationship between
"signs and wonders" and "power" (cf. Rom 5:19, 2 Cor 12:12,
2 Thess 9:9, Heb 2:4). In this case it is noticeable that
"power" also appears as a parallel manifestation of the illuminator ([77],4-7).

[79]In this context, these two motifs, as indicated above
(n. 58), are contradictory. However, they undoubtedly reflect
a docetic tradition in which the motifs were understandable,
as for example that found in *Treat. Seth* (VII,*2*)55,10-56,32.
In *Treat. Seth*, the redeemer figure is both unseen and yet
physically punished because the (spiritual) redeemer separated
himself from his (physical) host prior to the suffering. In
the *Apoc. Adam*, apparently in the interest of abbreviating the
myth, the docetic motif is lost and hence the resulting confusion and contradiction. The present form of the text consciously makes a distinction between the illuminator on the one
hand and "the man upon whom the holy spirit has come" on the
other.

[80]See the parallels listed above, pp. 119-22.

[81]See above, pp. 119-22.

[82]See above, pp. 122-24.

[83]See above, pp. 62-63.

[84]Beltz, 139.

[85]See the discussion above, pp. 111-15.

[86]See, for example, the parallels listed in the footnotes to the translation.

[87]Hipp. *Ref.* 5.6.4-5. Translation from Foerster, *Gnosis*, 1.263-64. Cf. Hipp. *Ref.* 8.12.5 and *Gos. Eg.* (III,*2*)66,8-24.

[88]The reference at [77],16-18 is not used in the same technical way. See the discussion above, nn. 58 and 79.

[89]Schottroff, "Animae naturalitur salvandae," 79.

[90]The soteriology of the text has already been discussed; see above, p. 125.

[91]The motif is so common in gnostic texts that it scarcely needs demonstration; cf. for example p. 170 n. 52 above.

[92]See above, n. 79.

[93]This assumes my argument above about the docetism, n. 58.

[94]See also the catalog of "forms" (pp. 195-97) through which Zostrianos passed: *Zost.* (VIII,*1*)5-7 and 53. The pertinent statements are as follows: 5,16; 6,17; 7,4.13.18-19.22; 53,18-19. See also Matt 5:21-45.

[95]Translation from Foerster, *Gnosis*, 1.264-65. I am indebted to Prof. H.-M. Schenke for pointing out this parallel to me.

[96]See above, pp. 54-55 n. 74 and pp. 117-19.

[97]James Rendel Harris, *The Commentaries of Isho'dad of Merv in Syriac and English* (5 vols.; Cambridge: University Press, 1911-1916) 1.22-23.

[98]See Böhlig (92-93), and idem, "Die Adamapokalypse," 48. But, see also his "Jüdisches und iranisches," 155, where he modifies his earlier statement and asserts that it must remain undecided whether or not we are dealing with an ascending scale or whether the thirteen kingdoms are to be contrasted with the kingless generation (to which he still refers as the fourteenth kingdom).

[99]Cf. also explanation eleven where the child came down to caves.

[100]Kasser thinks that explanations three and four may be doublets (317 n. 3).

[101]Explanations two and four have the word ⲁⲗⲟⲩ (child) in common with explanations seven and eleven.

[102]These two explanations, five and seven, may be doublets. In both, the origin of the illuminator is associated with a "heavenly drop," and in both he returns to heaven. The details of his physical birth are different, but could be accounted for as variants of the same tradition. Compare explanation ten where the word "drop" is also used. The origin of the illuminator is still associated with a "drop," presumably one may say "a drop of heaven," since he originates from the semen of a god, but he does not return to heaven.

[103]See Hipp. *Ref.* 6.30.6-31.2. See Schenke, col. 33; the citations by Beltz, 163; and *Ep. Pet. Phil.* (VIII,2)135,10-20.

[104]With the personification of λόγος, the thirteenth explanation is related to a widely used concept in antiquity. See H. Kuhn, R. Schnackenburg and C. Huber, "Logos," *Lexikon für Theologie und Kirche* (2nd ed. rev.; 10 vols.; eds. Josef Höfer and Karl Rahner; Freiberg: Herder, 1957-1965) 6.1119-1128; J. N. Sanders, "The Word," *Interpreters Dictionary of the Bible* (4 vols.; ed. George A. Buttrick, et al.; Nashville: Abingdon, 1962) 4.868-72.

[105]See the discussion above and pp. 38-39, 116-19.

[106]See above, pp. 54-55 n. 74.

[107]Böhlig, 91, 92, 94. In his *editio princeps*, Böhlig refers to them as fourteen kingdoms. He only later becomes aware of a distinction between the thirteen kingdoms and the kingless generation. See above, n. 98. Beltz (143) never discusses the issue of how one counts the explanations. However, he does call the kingless generation the fourteenth kingdom, thus implying that it was to be included with the first thirteen kingdoms (see particularly p. 178).

[108]The possibility that the list originally may have contained only twelve explanations has been suggested by Kasser (317) and in his "Textes gnostiques: Remarques" (92). He suggests twelve explanations by eliminating explanations four and fourteen on the basis of the "difference" of the explanation by the kingless generation from the first thirteen explanations, and the fact that the fourth explanation appears to him to be a doublet of the third. Note that explanations five and seven may also be doublets. See above n. 102.

[109]Schottroff, "Animae naturalitur salvandae," 73-79.
MacRae, "Coptic Gnostic Apocalypse of Adam," 30. R. Haardt,
"Böhlig, Alexander und Labib, Pahor, Koptisch-gnostische Apokalypsen aus Codex V von Nag Hammadi im Koptischen Museum zu Alt-
Kairo," *WZKM* 61 (1967) 155-59 (esp. 156-57). Rudolph ("Gnosis
und Gnostizismus," 43) thinks the author has listed those ideas
about the origin of the illuminator of which he was aware. In
the final explanation, he shows how they are surpassed.

[110]Böhlig, 91-92.

[111]Böhlig, "Jüdisches und iranisches," 158. See Carl
Schmidt, *Koptisch-gnostische Schriften; Erster Band: Die Pistis
Sophia. Die beiden Bücher des Jeû, Unbekanntes altgnostisches
Werk* (3rd ed.; ed. Walter Till; Berlin: Akademie, 1962) 322-27.
Schmidt's transcription has been translated into English by
Violet MacDermot, *The Books of Jeu and the Untitled Text in the
Bruce Codex* (Leiden: E. J. Brill, 1978) 183-201.

[112]*Gos. Eg.* (III,*2*)58,1-22 (Böhlig-Wisse, *Gospel of the
Egyptians*, 122-24, 183-84); Iren. *Haer.* 1.17.1 and 1.24.3-7
(Foerster, *Gnosis*, 1.213 and 59-62); *4 Ezra* 12:10-39 (Charles,
APOT, 2.613-15); *Ap. John* (II,*1*)10,19-11,10 and BG8502 38,14-42,15.
See also the twelve gods of chaos: *Orig. World* (II,*5*)104,25;
the twelve wicked angels of creation: Hipp. *Ref.* 5.26.3,11,27
(Foerster, *Gnosis*, 1.53, 54, 56); the twelve aeons in Allberry
(*A Manichaean Psalm Book*, 98 line 25). See the discussion by
H.-M. Schenke, *Die gnostischen Schriften des Koptischen Papy-
rus Berolinensis 8502* (Berlin: Academie-Verlag, 1972) 42-45.
Compare also the secret words that the initiate speaks as he
passes the seven archons that rule over the world (the other
five presumably rule over chaos): Or. *Cels.* 6.31-32 (Foerster,
Gnosis, 1.96-97). See also GL 1,4 (Foerster, *Gnosis*, 2.246-51)
for a similar tradition in Mandaean texts. See above, n. 45.

[113]Iren. *Haer.* 1.17.1 (Foerster, *Gnosis*, 1.212-13); Clem.
exc. Thdot. 1.25.1 (Foerster, *Gnosis*, 1.225); *Marsanes* X,44*,
1-7.

[114]See above, n. 108.

[115]This does not mean that in the literary history of the
list it could not have been first composed and compiled as a
total number of twelve explanations. It could have been (see
above pp. 137-38), but this should not influence our trying to
understand it *in its present context* as a total number of thirteen explanations.

[116]See above, pp. 135-37.

[117]See above, pp. 132-37.

[118]Cf. Col 2:8-15. See Böhlig-Wisse, *Gospel of the Egyptians*, 191-94.

[119]A certain identity for the kingdoms is a problem. Are
they idealized as the nations of the world in the sense of the
tradition that the world is divided into twelve kingdoms each

governed by a ruling angel (see above, pp. 137-38)? Or are
they to be conceived as evil powers associated with the archon
that was disturbed by the appearance of the illuminator? As
far as the meaning of the term in the original setting of the
list is concerned, it is difficult to say. However, in its
present setting, it seems unlikely that the list is intended to
reflect statements by the idealized nations of the world because of the sudden and inappropriate shift in scene (see
above, pp. 116-17). In its present setting, the list of thirteen kingdoms must be harmonized with the context if good sense
is to be made of it. That context requires that the thirteen
kingdoms be associated in some way with the heavenly realm of
the archon of the powers. The most reasonable explanation
seems to be as I have indicated above. The term "kingdom"
could identify the ruler of the dominion or the dominion itself, i.e., those over whom he rules. The latter alternative
makes a good contrast with the "kingless generation." See
Schottroff, "Animae naturalitur salvandae," 76 n. 26.

[120]The thirteenth aeon is called the aeon of righteousness
(Schmidt, *Koptisch-gnostische Schriften*, 31 lines 11-13, 60
lines 6-8, 65 lines 8-10), but its association with the twelve
aeons makes it clear that it is not the highest state to which
the soul will attain (ibid., 62 lines 16-20). Schmidt's text
has been translated into English by Violet MacDermot (*Pistis
Sophia* [Leiden: E. J. Brill, 1978]).

[121]Böhlig, 91-92, and idem, "Jüdisches und iranisches," 157.

[122]Kasser, "Textes gnostiques: Remarques," 92 n. 51. However, the French *sur* is ambiguous.

[123]Foerster, *Gnosis*, 2.27 et passim.

[124]Beltz, 143-44.

[125]Schottroff, "Animae naturalitur salvandae," 75 n. 23.

[126]MacRae, 179-87.

[127]Rudolph, "Gnosis und Gnostizismus," 41.

[128]The word "physical" might not be an accurate description of the situation in explanations five, six and ten since
these seem to be a more supernatural kind of occurrence. Yet
even here the text unquestionably refers to a birth of some
sort. With regard to statements one, seven, eight and twelve,
no specific birth language is used in the descriptive part of
the explanation, but there is language that can be so understood when read in the light of the majority of the explanations.

1. ⲁⲩϣⲱⲡⲉ [77],29, ⲁⲩⲕⲁⲛⲟⲩⲱ̄ⲱ̄ [78],1-2
7. ⲁⲩϣⲱⲡⲉ ⲛⲟⲩⲁⲗⲟⲩ [80],14-15
8. ⲁⲩϣⲱⲡⲉ ⲉⲃⲟⲗ ⲛ̄ⲍ̄ⲏ̄ⲧ̄ⲥ̄ ⲁⲩⲕⲁⲛⲟⲩⲱ̄ⲱ̄ [80],24-27
12. ⲁⲩϣⲱⲡⲉ ⲉⲃⲟⲗ ⲍ̄ⲙ̄ ⲫⲱⲥⲧⲏⲣ ⲥⲛⲁⲩ ⲁⲩⲕⲁⲛⲟⲩⲱ̄ⲱ̄ [82],6-8.

The kingless generation uses none of this kind of language, but is consciously in contrast to the first thirteen explanations precisely in the fact that the individual being described is chosen (ⲤⲰⲦⲠ) and not born; see above, pp. 136-37.

[129]Böhlig, "Jüdisches und iranisches," 157, and see above, pp. 53-54 n. 70.

[130]In explanation eleven, there is no statement about receiving glory and power. In explanation twelve, there is no indication of separation or relationship between the two phases. In explanation three, there seems to be a distance implied, assuming of course that ⲀⲨⲈⲒ [78],24-25 is not a scribal error. See the note to the text at [78],24-25.

[131]Explanation two begins phase two with a conjunction. Explanation nine begins phase three with a conjunction. Explanation ten concludes phase one with a conjunction as a summary statement but strings phases one and three together with perfect tenses. Phase two, the nourishing statement, is lacking in explanation ten.

[132]Schenke, col. 33, and idem, "Zum Gegenwärtigen Stand," 133-34.

[133]See below, the notes to the text at [81],17-20.

[134]Rudolph, "Gnosis und Gnostizismus," 44.

[135]Beltz, 144. In Jewish apocalyptic, Beltz argues, water and sea are virtual synonyms for world periods and the earth (142 n. 1). Thus, coming to the water is coming into the world.

[136]Böhlig, "Jüdisches und iranisches," 155-61.

[137]Ibid., 157.

[138]See above, pp. 53-54 n. 70.

[139]See Böhlig, 90-91; idem, "Jüdisches und iranisches," 157. See also his source material: H. S. Nyberg, *Die Religionen des Alten Iran* (Leipzig: J. C. Hinrichs, 1938) 28-30, and Geo Widengren, *Die Religionen Irans* (Stuttgart: Kohlhammer, 1965) 106-107. Compare to this the vision of the man arising from the sea in 2 Esdras 13.

[140]See James Atkinson, "The Sháh Námeh by Firdusi," *Persian and Japanese Literature* (rev. ed.; 2 vols.; New York: Colonial Press, 1900) 1.78-83. In the interest of consistency, I have adopted the spelling of Böhlig for the Persian names.

[141]Böhlig, "Jüdisches und iranisches," 157-58, and Widengren, *Religionen Irans*, 208. Rudolph ("Gnosis und Gnostizismus," 41) prefers the legend of the birth of the Saošyants.

[142]Schenke, "Zum Gegenwärtigen Stand," 133. The same suggestion is made by Schottroff ("Animae naturalitur

salvandae," 75 n. 23). She cites as parallels CH 1,14 and *Ap.*
John (BG8502)48,11 [*sic*! actually 48,9-11].

[143]This evaluation by Schenke of the contents of the list
of kingdoms is not carefully thought out. While the concepts
may not have originated in a gnostic milieu, they certainly
would not have been unacceptable for use by gnostics. The
syncretism of the gnostic movements of late antiquity is well
known. Compare, for example, the use of *Eugnostos the Blessed*
(III,*3*; V,*1*) by the gnostic author of *Sophia of Jesus Christ*
(III,*4*).

[144]For example: *Paraph. Shem* (VII,*1*)32,5-17; 36,11-29;
37,14-25 (cf. 2,15-3,11 and 15,5-34); Right *Ginza* 12 (Foerster,
Gnosis, 2.159, 162). Mandaean Liturgies Qolasta I (Foerster,
Gnosis, 2.168); Hipp. *Ref.* 5.8.15 (Foerster, *Gnosis*, 1.273).

[145]ⲁⲓⲧ ⲚⲚⲞⲨⲘⲈⲈⲨⲈ ... ⲈⲦⲂⲈ ⲠⲒⲈⲒ ⲈⲠⲈⲤⲎⲦ ⲈⳫⲘ ⲠⲒⲘⲞⲞⲨ Ⲛ̄ⲄⲒ
ⲚⲒⲘⲈⲢⲞⲤ ⲈⲦⲤⲀⲠⲈⲤⲎⲦ (cf. 52,5-14). Translation by Roger
Bullard in *The Nag Hammadi Library*, 330. See also *Testim.
Truth* (IX,*3*)30,18-23, where it is stated that the Son of Man
came into the world "by the Jordan river." See the discussion
below, p. 220 n. 50.

[146]Foerster, *Gnosis*, 2.171.

[147]οἱ προάστειοι, i.e., the outlying areas. Thus the
water is equated with the primordial waters.

[148]5.16.1-3. Translation by Foerster, *Gnosis*, 1.287.

[149]5.16.5. Translation by Foerster, *Gnosis*, 1.288.

[150]5.14.1. Translation by Foerster, *Gnosis*, 1.286.

[151]See Paul Heinisch, *Theology of the Old Testament*
(trans. William G. Heidt; St. Paul: North Central, 1955) 146-
47; B. W. Anderson, "Water," *Interpreters Dictionary of the
Bible* (4 vols.; ed. George A. Buttrick, et al.; Nashville:
Abingdon, 1962) 4.806-10.

[152]Beltz, 157, 178.

[153]Ibid.
#3--A Christian myth of Jesus' birth given a gnostic interpre-
    tation (p. 150).
#5--A story from the Sethian tradition (Hipp. *Ref.* 5.19.20)
    (p. 155).
#6--A story out of Christian Gnosticism that has affinities
    with the system from the Book of Baruch (p. 157).
#7--A story from Christian Gnosticism that has affinities with
    the Ophite system (p. 158).
#8--A myth of Mithra's birth given a gnostic interpretation
    (p. 162).
#9--A gnostic story of the savior's birth associated with the
    Greek Muse tradition (p. 163).
#10--Isis mythology adopted by Christianity and given a gnostic
    interpretation (pp. 166-67).

#11--A story from Christian Gnosticism that has affinities with
    Sethianism (p. 168).
#12--A story of Manichaean origin (p. 170).
#13--A story derived from the Hermetic tradition (p. 172).
The kingless generation--A story derived from the Manichaean
    tradition (p. 175).

[154]Beltz, 152. However, in the references cited by Beltz,
there seems to be only one Sophia figure (cf. *Hyp. Arch.* [II,4]
142,23-26 to *Orig. World* [II,5]103,15-32).

[155]Böhlig, "Jüdisches und iranisches," 155-56.

[156]Ibid., 156-57. Also see above, p. 144.

[157]Ibid. Also see above, p. 145.

[158]See above, pp. 144-45.

[159]See above, p. 136.

[160]See James M. Robinson, "On the *Gattung* of Mark (and
John)," *Jesus and Man's Hope* (2 vols.; ed. D. G. Buttrick;
Pittsburgh: Pittsburgh Theological Seminary, 1970) 1.99-129.

[161]See Samuel Sandmel, "Parallelomania," *JBL* 81 (1962)
1, 3, 7. Although he does not discuss it in detail, Sandmel
does see the problem. He uses such terms as "true parallels"
and "exact parallels." See also Claus Westermann, "Sinn und
Grenze religionsgeschichtlicher Parallelen," *TLZ* 90/7 (1965)
col. 491. He does not consider isolated individual motifs to
be "parallels."

[162]Westermann, "Sinn und Grenze," cols. 489-91.

[163]See Sandmel, "Parallelomania," 3 and 7.

[164]See Sandmel's warning about the dangers of parallelomania (ibid., 1).

[165]One must also consider parallel clusters in motif.
For example, if one could show that there were clusters of
motifs in the parallel that assume the same configuration as
those in the text under consideration, it would be an added
argument for provenance. The number of parallel motifs is
likewise important, especially if a given cluster of motifs
occurs *only* in a given parallel tradition.

[166]See below, the notes to the text. This motif appears
elsewhere in antiquity. In the Šāhnāmah, demons are used by
the king in the construction of palaces; see Atkinson, "The
Shâh Nâmeh," 1.11, 110.

[167]See the notes to the text below.

[168]Some aeons are regarded in a positive sense; see
[84],27-[85],6 and above, pp. 80-81.

[169]Cf. *Great Pow.* (VI,*4*)37,10-11: The "air" is the dwelling place of "the gods and the angels." See also Eph 2:2 and *Treat. Seth* (VII,*2*)52,8-10. See Kittel-Friedrich (eds.), *TDNT* 1 (1965) 163-64. The point is that the illuminator is not from the dwelling place of the demons, but rather from a "different" air.

[170]See Schottroff ("Animae naturalitur salvandae," 74-79), where she argues that the thrust of the slander of the thirteen kingdoms is that the child has a mixed origin and p. 79, where she notes that the kingless generation says that the child is not defiled, which one would understand to mean that he did not have a mixed origin.

[171]Cf. the discussion of Hipp. *Ref.* 5.12.1-4 and 16.1-10. See also above, pp. 146-47.

[172]Similar motifs do appear in other texts closely related to the *Apoc. Adam.* The choosing: Epiph. *Pan.* 39.2.7; 3.5; *Treat. Seth* (VII,*2*)50,1-24; *Gos. Eg.* (III,*2*)62,24-63,8; 64,1-8; *Steles Seth* (VII,*5*)126,20-21. Non-material origin: *Treat. Seth* (VII,*2*)56,4-32; *Ap. John* (II,*1*)30,11-21; *Steles Seth* (VII,*5*) 118,27-30; 119,22; 121,25-27.30-31; 124,25-26; *Trim. Prot.* (XIII,*1**)47,30-32; *Zost.* (VIII,*1*)20,4-15. Special knowledge: *Gos. Eg.* (III,*2*)64,6-9; *Treat. Seth* (VII,*2*)50,13-24; *Ap. John* (II,*1*)31,4-25; *Trim. Prot.* (XIII,*1**)41,21-42,2.

[173]Böhlig reads the text in the same way as Beltz. MacRae reads vestiges of ⲩ.

[174]His parallels for this interpretation are found in the Book of Baruch (Hipp. *Ref.* 5.26.29) and in Manichaeism, where Jesus is merely the prophet who points toward another that is the representative of God par excellence.

[175]Beltz, 175-78.

[176]This makes the subject of ⲁⲩⲧⲣⲉⲟⲩⲅⲛⲱⲥⲓⲥ ... ⲩ̄ⲱ̄ⲧⲉ ([82],24-25) and ⲧⲉⲭⲁⲩ ([82],25) to agree, i.e., both refer to ⲡⲛⲟⲩⲧⲉ.

[177]This does not include the motif of birth from a virgin in the list of explanations (explanation three and four) since it is not part of the cluster in that it does not appear in the statement of the kingless generation, or in the framework section, but only in the refuted explanations of the thirteen kingdoms, and because it is in direct opposition to the explanation of the kingless generation. Nor does it include the motif of the invisibility of the illuminator, a motif Robert Haardt incorrectly describes as "unrecognizability," and regards as a Christian motif (Haardt, "Böhlig, Alexander und Labib, Pahor," 158). Apparently Haardt associates this feature with the messianic secret in the Gospel of Mark, and assumes the motif to be understandable as a Christian trait on this basis. This is, of course, a debatable point since it is precisely this kind of feature that could have provided the early church and

the author of Mark with the interpretative principle for their understanding of the life of Jesus. See below, where this motif is found to be a secondary feature in the AscenIsa. Cf. the discussion of J. M. Robinson ("On the *Gattung*," 1.106-18).

[178]MacRae, "Coptic Gnostic Apocalypse of Adam," 32; Haardt, "Böhlig, Alexander und Labib, Pahor," 158-59; Orbe, "Alexander Böhlig und Pahor Labib," 170.

[179]MacRae, "Coptic Gnostic Apocalypse of Adam," 32.

[180]Ibid.

[181]See above, pp. 125-28.

[182]See above, n. 165.

[183]See above, pp. 150-52.

[184]See R. H. Charles, *Ascension of Isaiah* (London: Society for Promoting Christian Knowledge, 1917) x, xix-xxv; see also the review of the literature by Tisserant (*Ascension d'Isaie*, 42-61).

[185]See below, n. 190.

[186]In this connection, we consider only those motifs that are unambiguously Christian, and may be documented within the canonical New Testament. References cite the chapter and verse system of Charles, *Ascension of Isaiah*.

[187]Cf. Gal 4:4, John 3:13.

[188]Cf. Eph 4:9-10, Acts 1:9-11, John 6:62.

[189]See above, n. 79.

[190]Scholarly opinion is not as uniform as regards *Great Pow.* as it is in regards to AscenIsa. Jean Doresse (*The Secret Books of the Egyptian Gnostics: An Introduction to the Gnostic Coptic Manuscripts discovered at Chenoboskion* [trans. P. Mairet; New York: Viking, 1960] 187-88) first described the document as a gnostic apocalypse; see Martin Krause's discussion of Doresse's four descriptive categories for the Nag Hammadi texts ("Der Stand der Veröffentlichung der Nag Hammadi Texte," *Le origini dello gnosticismo* [ed. Ugo Bianchi; Leiden: Brill, 1967] 66-88). However, Krause showed that there was at least one section in *Great Pow.* that contained clandestine references to Jesus. This fact, Krause argued, demonstrates Christian influence. But whether it was to be identified as a Christian text, or a gnostic text that had been subjected to Christianizing influence, he did not say (72-73). On the basis of his argument for identifying texts as Christian or gnostic based upon the position awarded motifs in their association with one another (74-75), it would seem to fall in the second of these two categories, i.e., a gnostic text with Christian features. Frank Williams is undecided as to how the tractate should be

identified (*The Nag Hammadi Library*, 284). It is either a
"Christian-gnostic apocalypse, or else a Christian apocalypse
with gnosticizing features." (This latter description seems to
me to be unlikely.) In the description of the text by the
Berliner Arbeitskreis (Tröger, *Gnosis und Neues Testament*, 50-
52), it is called a gnostic apocalypse (50), although it is
also recognized to have been subjected to some Christian influence (51). See also Karl Martin Fischer, "Der Gedanke unserer
grossen Kraft (Noēma): Die vierte Schrift aus Nag Hammadi-Codex
VI," *TLZ* 98 (1973) cols. 169-70.

[191]Translation by Frederik Wisse in *The Nag Hammadi
Library*, 286. This little segment has all the earmarks of a
creedal confession. It is slightly out of order for the sense
of the narrative. For example, at the point where it occurs
in the narrative, the man had not yet "put to shame" the ruler
of Hades nor destroyed his dominion. This event does not actually occur until VI 41,30-42,11. Apparently the author (redactor?) included the statement at this point out of order on
the basis of the motif of "proclamation" with which the "confessional" section begins, and the preceding section ends:

> He will *speak* in parables; he will *proclaim* the aeon
> that is to come, just as he *spoke* to Noah in the
> first aeon... (VI 40,30-41,3; the italics are mine).

For a comparison with early Christian creedal formulations, see
Reginald Fuller, *The Foundations of New Testament Christology*
(New York: Scribners, 1965) 204-27; Oscar Cullmann, *The Earliest
Christian Confessions* (trans. J.K.S. Reid; London: Lutterworth,
1949); and Jack T. Sanders, *The New Testament Christological
Hymns: Their Historical Religious Background* (Cambridge: The
University Press, 1971) 9-25.

[192]I.e., Judas.

[193]The statement about performing "signs and wonders" is
made of the "imitator" (VI 45,1-15) and not of the man.

[194]See above, n. 73.

[195]See above, n. 78.

[196]As pointed out above (nn. 58 and 79), this feature
clashes with the motif of invisibility ([77],14-15). The question arises, "how could one be invisible and suffer in the
flesh at the same time?" The motif of invisibility itself
might be a secondary feature, although not on the basis of the
apparent clash. I accounted for this (n. 79) as one result of
so severely abbreviating the myth. The invisibility motif
seems to have been included almost as an afterthought under the
influence of the motif of the powers not seeing the glory of
the illuminator in the preceding sentence ([77],12-14).

[197]See the outline of the myth on p. 120 above. Consider
the outline with the alteration to 1b, 2c and 5c.

[198]Cf. Rudolph, "Gnosis und Gnostizismus," 40-41.

[199]See above, pp. 154-59.

[200]See the discussion above, pp. 125-28.

[201]See above, pp. 113-15.

[202]See above, pp. 115-19.

[203]See above, pp. 37-38.

[204]B-1, pp. 109-11; B-2, p. 128.

[205]B-1, p. 111; B-2, p. 128.

[206]B-1, p. 113; B-2, pp. 126-27 and the reconstruction at [76],28-[77],1.

[207]See above, pp. 109-11.

[208]See above, p. 128.

[209]B-1, pp. 109-11; B-2, pp. 128-29.

[210]See above, pp. 81-82. However, traces of the dualism do appear in the ascetic bias of source A. See above, pp. 84-85.

[211]See above, p. 125.

[212]See above, pp. 82-83.

[213]See above, pp. 83-84.

[214]See above, p. 61.

[215]Once to Adam ([65],24-[66],12; [67],12-21) and once by the great illuminator ([76],8-11.14-27).

[216]See above, pp. 66-79.

[217]See above, pp. 122-24.

[218]See above, pp. 85-87.

[219]For example, Solomon's army of demons, [78],27-[79],14.

[220]See above, pp. 122-24, 127-28, 145-47.

[221]For example, see above, pp. 141-47.

[222]However, there have been attempts to determine how the Sethian materials at Nag Hammadi are related. See Schenke's attempt to describe the Sethian system from the Nag Hammadi texts ("Das sethianische System," 165-73).

CHAPTER V

THE REDACTOR

Several statements have been identified as having been
added by a redactor at the time he combined sources A and B to
form the present document that is entitled the *Apocalypse of
Adam*. These statements serve as the key to the redactor's
theology and his understanding of the sources, and also as the
cohesive force that holds together the document in its present
structure. Thus, they allow the reader to make sense of the
text as a redacted whole. Since that whole originates with the
redactor, its distinctive features must therefore be sought in
the redactor's own statements and in his organization of the
sources.

There are two ways that the redactor's statements help to
convey the unity of the redacted text: the redactional statements can be considered apart from their context and the context can be considered under the light of the redactional
statements. Finally the redactor's organization of his material
can be considered with respect to the question: what does the
present structure of the tractate tell the reader about the
redactor's theology? Some of these issues were touched on
briefly in Chapter II, but now are to be discussed in detail.
The meaning of the tractate as a redacted whole, its date, and
provenance, if discoverable at all, can only be determined
through a more precise understanding of the redactor's theological position.

A. Statement One: [65],3-9[1]

Adam has called his son by the name of that man who is the
spore, or seed (CΠΟΡⲀ), from which the great generation, presumably bearing his name, has come. Although the name Seth is
not specifically used, it is clear that Seth, the son of Adam,
bears the name of a heavenly figure who must also be called
Seth. This heavenly figure is the primogenitor of a great race
that we might call the generation of Seth, or the Sethians, although they are not so called in *Apoc. Adam*. The reluctance of

185

the text to designate the heavenly figure as Seth, and his
descendants as Sethians, is puzzling,[2] but there can be little
question that this is the meaning of the redactor's statement.

Adam's reason for naming his son Seth after the heavenly
Seth is not really clear. Apparently, however, his statement
is intended to do two things. In the first place, it associates the origin of the Sethian community with the heavenly Seth
rather than Seth the son of Adam; that is, they do not have an
earthly origin, but a heavenly origin, because the heavenly
Seth from whom they are descended is himself descended from the
great aeons.[3] In the second place, it makes the Sethians privy
to the special knowledge that was originally possessed, then
lost, and finally regained by Adam, the primordial first man.
This knowledge originally was the exclusive possession of the
heavenly Seth, the seed produced by the great aeons, and then
it came to the generation of men who bear his name.[4] These two
motifs place the redactor within the purview of the Sethian-
Archontic tradition as is reported in Epiph. *Pan.* 39 and 40.[5]

This statement has been added by the redactor at this
point in the text to correct what he perceives to be an oversight in his *Vorlage*, i.e., the failure of the A source to show
where γνῶσις, lost by Adam and Eve, had gone. He uses this
opportunity both to "correct" his *Vorlage*, and to include the
statement on the origin of Seth's name.[6]

B.   Statement Two: [69],10-17[7]

The race of Seth is again called ⲤⲠⲞⲢⲀ, an expression
reserved almost exclusively for Seth and his descendants by the
redactor in the *Apoc. Adam*.[8] The same preference for the word
ⲤⲠⲞⲢⲀ to describe the race of Seth is not found in other tractates from Nag Hammadi,[9] although the idea of a special race as
"seed" is quite prominent.[10] As in statement one above, and in
the statement of the three men in the gnostic revelation story
in source B ([65],24-[66],12; [67],12-21), the content of
γνῶσις is not actually specified. However, the redactor leaves
his reader in no doubt as to what he means by γνῶσις. The
revelation that came from Adam and Eve ([69],12-16) and was

passed on to the seed of Seth ([69],10-17) is precisely the
information that Adam is revealing in the redacted tractate[11]
to his earthly son (64,2-4; [67],14-21) so that he in turn
might pass it on to his progeny ([85],19-22).[12]

The redactor includes statement two in order to show that
the flood came precisely for the purpose of destroying the
Sethians. Without the statement of the redactor, this interpretation of the flood is not clear in source A. That the
flood comes to destroy a special group of men is evident, but
the redactor clarifies that the special group is none other
than the ϹΠΟΡⲀ, who bear the name of the heavenly Seth. But
again, the redactor has been careless. Source A stated that
the flood came so that the creator might destroy "all flesh"
from the earth. If this statement be taken seriously, then the
special race would have already been included within the purview of the creator's intention, since "all flesh" would
naturally include the special group because they were also a
part of humanity.[13] Therefore, with respect to the sense of
source A, the statement that is attributed to the redactor is
both non-essential and excessive. It is only essential to the
redactor's intention to identify the "special race" of source A
as his own community, the seed of Seth.[14]

C.   Statement Three: [71],4-8

The redactor's third statement, included as a part of the
admonition of the creator to Noah, draws attention again to two
things the redactor stressed in statements one and two: the
special race of men cast forth from the knowledge of the great
aeons and angels ([71],8-14) is identified as the ϹΠΟΡⲀ of
Seth and the statement reaffirms the fact that the creator
brought the flood in an attempt to destroy particularly that
race. In source A, the creator assumes that his attack on the
special race had been successful and that they had been destroyed by the flood ([70],19-[71],4). The redactor includes
in the creator's command to Noah to repopulate the earth a sub-
sidiary injunction that Noah and his ϹΠⲈⲢⲘⲀ produce no ϹΠΟΡⲀ
of the Sethians, that group of men who possessed a glory unknown to him.

The "other" glory ([74],3-26) possessed by those men is an
affront to the creator's glory which pales in comparison to the
Sethians ([74],15-16) because their glory ([77],10-13) comes
from the eternal aeon (64,9-12; 64,24-32; [76],8-11). In the
refrain to the incorrect explanations of the illuminator's
origin, it is stated that he receives both power and glory.[15]
These qualities are not intended by the redactor in a negative
way, although the explanation of the kingless generation does
omit them. These attributes in themselves are not negative.
It is only the various means by which the illuminator is said
to acquire these qualities that are negative. In source B, the
illuminator himself is said to possess both power ([77],4-7)
and glory ([76],8-11; [77],9-12), and it is through these
qualities that he confuses the powers and their ruler. In
Gos. Eg. (III,*2*)51,1-4, glory and power are mentioned as qualities of the invisible Father of the holy men of the great light
who will come into the world. These qualities belong to the
invisible Father and his light, who will come into the world,[16]
that is, the illuminator of knowledge in the *Apoc. Adam*,[17] and
therefore also to his seed.[18]

D.   Statement Four: [76],6-7

The meaning of this statement by the redactor is not clear.
The contrast implied by ⲁⲗⲗⲁ suggests that those "men" (= the
imperishable ⲥⲡⲟⲣⲁ) at [76],3-6 are not strangers to the holy
angels since the holy angels work (in the world?) with them.
Three things seem to be affirmed by the redactor: "those men"
are identified as the ⲥⲡⲟⲣⲁ of Seth, they are part of a heavenly alliance with the holy angels, and the ⲥⲡⲟⲣⲁ is imperishable (ⲁⲧⲧⲁⲕⲟ). The first of these reflects the usual concern
of the redactor to identify the heroes of source A with the
Sethian community.[19] The second affirmation, that the Sethians
are part of a heavenly alliance in which the earthly work of
the Sethian community is shared by the holy angels, is met in
source A and in the redactor's later comments.

This liaison is also suggested of the special race in
source A where it is stated that the special race comes from
the knowledge of the aeons and angels ([71],10-14; [75],5-8),

and like Adam and Eve they resemble these angels (64,12-15;
[76],3-6). The angels of the great light dwell with them
([72],10-14), and are their protectors and helpers in the
world. They preserved the ⲤⲠⲞⲢⲀ from the flood caused by the
creator ([69],18-25), and from the fire ([75],22-27). The same
motif is evident in *Gos. Eg.* (III,*2*)62,12-14. Seth asks for
guards over his seed, and 400 ethereal angels come forth to
guard his race. Other angelic figures are also mentioned as
guardians of "the souls of the elect" (*Gos. Eg.* [III,*2*]65,6-9).
The redactor further tells the reader that these angels are the
means by which the words of imperishability are brought to the
Sethian community ([85],7-18).

As to their imperishability, both sources A and B agree
that the special race, subsequently identified by the redactor
as the ⲤⲠⲞⲢⲀ, will live forever ([83],7-19; [76],21-24). They
serve the imperishable aeons ([73],30-[74],2) and possess an
imperishable knowledge ([72],5-9; [85],12-18) that is communicated by the imperishable illuminators, Yesseus, Mazareus and
Yessedekeus ([85],22-31). Although they will be taken out of
the world, knowledge of them will last forever ([84],23-[85],3).

The fact that the seed of Seth is imperishable and will
therefore be removed from the world probably explains the redactor's arrangement of source B, the description of the appearance of the illuminator. After the preservation from the
fire, the Sethians have been taken out of the world ([75],17-
[76],6) and there is no longer a witness to the γνῶσις of Seth.
According to the redactor, the illuminator comes in order to
preserve such a witness in the world. His appearance is the
final prelude to the ultimate destruction of the evil creation
([76],28-[77],3).

This analysis explains a similar passage in *Gos. Eg.*
(III,*2*)62,13-64,9. The great Seth sends guards over his seed
to protect them until the consummation. At the consummation,
presumably, they are removed from the world into the third aeon,
Davithe.[20] At that time, the great Seth comes into the world
"to save the race that had gone astray" (*Gos. Eg.* [III,*2*]63,8).
This race that had gone astray is certainly *not* the Sethians,
as the editors of *Gos. Eg.* assume.[21] At least they are not

initially to be described as Sethians, although later some of
them do become Sethians. Such a designation as the "race who
had gone astray" would scarcely be used to describe the children of Seth. "The race that had gone astray" must correspond
to the "natural" seed, i.e., those who had not served the great
Seth. However, when they abandon dead knowledge for the aeons
of imperishability, they would be Sethians, just as the 400,000
sons of Ham and Japheth who followed the sons of Seth in re-
jecting the dominion of the creator ([73],13-[74],26). The
race that had gone astray is brought forth and armed with a
knowledge of the truth and with an unconquerable power of in-
corruptibility (*Gos. Eg.* [III,*2*]64,4-9). Those of this race,
when "saved," are called saints (*Gos. Eg.* [III,*2*]63,13-15) and,
like the sons of Seth, they too will live forever (*Gos. Eg.*
[III,*2*]65,26-66,8). According to H.-M. Schenke, this latter-
day group of Sethians (to be distinguished from those of the
previous generations), will have their final place of rest in
the 4th aeon Eleleth, as the sons of Seth have their eternal
abode in the 3rd aeon Davithe (*Gos. Eg.* [III,*2*]65,19-22).[22]

E.   Statement Five: [76],11-13

This is the redactor's first statement after he connects
his two sources. In the A source, the document had already
come to conclusion with the removal of the special race, who
were identified by the redactor with the seed of Seth ([75],17-
[76],6), and the condemnation of those who failed to recognize
the God of the Sethians ([83],7-[84],3). The B source, as we
have previously seen, was truncated by the redactor so that it
might be included at this point.[23] The subject matter and the
concerns of the B source are different, as the redactor apparently noticed. In order to smooth over the abrupt shift from A
to B and to ensure that B will be read from the perspective of
the A source, the redactor adds a statement that is intended to
bring the soteriological work of the illuminator in line with
the situation in source A. His statement identifies the people
in source B in need of salvation as the seed (ⲤⲠⲈⲢⲘⲀ) of Noah
and the sons of Ham and Japheth, a group that appears at no
other point in source B! He has also been careful to call them
ⲤⲠⲈⲢⲘⲀ rather than ⲤⲠⲞⲢⲀ.[24]

The theological motivation for the statement is provided
by the redactor's view of eschatology. After the seed of Seth
had been removed from the world ([75],17-[76],6), only the
"natural" seed of the creator remained, that is, the seed of
Noah and his sons Ham and Japheth ([76],11-13). The consummation of the aeon (cf. *Gos. Eg.* [III,*2*]62,13-25) in which this
world was to be destroyed ([76],28-[77],1) had not yet occurred,
and there was no witness left behind in the world for the God
of the Sethians during this interim period.[25] The purpose of
the illuminator's appearance[26] is to reintroduce the γνῶσις of
the God of the Sethians that had been lost to the world when
the Sethians were removed after the fire threat just as it had
been necessary to reintroduce it after Adam's loss of knowledge
in the garden ([66],31-[67],12), after the flood ([71],8-20),
and after the unknown threat ([73],13-24). In order to ensure
that there remained a witness in the world after this (final)
removal of the Sethians, the illuminator of knowledge was sent
into the world. But to whom would he come? All the Sethians
had been removed! It would have to be to those of the natural
seed (ⲤⲠⲈⲢⲘⲀ) of Noah who had not become followers of the
γνῶσις of Seth, as had some of their number previously ([73],
13-24), and among whom the γνῶσις of the Sethians might be expected to "bear fruit."

Why Shem is not included by the redactor at this point is
unclear. In fact, the general omission of Shem in the tractate
is a problem ([73],13-15; [73],25-29; [74],7-11; [76],11-13).
Shem is only mentioned once in the document. At the time God
divides the world among his three sons ([72],15-17), Shem is
included as receiving a division of the land. At one other
place in the text, I have assumed that it was Shem who was
pledging fidelity to the creator in a speech delivered to Noah
([72],30-[73],12). It may simply be an oversight on the part
of the text (and the redactor) that Shem is not included at each
place Ham and Japheth are mentioned, but it might also be in-
tentional. In the Sethian system, as reported by Epiphanius
(*Pan.* 39.3.2), it is reported that of all the seed of Noah *only*
Ham was preserved in the ark. This does not seem to have been
an *accidental* omission of Shem and Japheth. In the *Apoc. Adam*,

only *one* of the sons pledges fidelity to Noah and the creator!
If we assume that this was Shem, and that his seed did in fact
remain true to the creator, then Shem would have been omitted
at [76],11-13 because his seed was not the group from which the
"converts" to the γνῶσις would come. That one son did remain
true to the creator does seem to be indicated by the reference
to Noah and "his son" (sing.) that had done the creator's will
([74],17-26).

The depiction of Shem as the only son of Noah who remains
completely true to the evil creator (Sakla) is a reversal of
his role in the biblical tradition where faithfulness to the
creator is by definition a positive act. In the biblical tradition, Shem appears as "father of all the children of Eber"
(Gen 10:21-31); that is, he is the eponymous ancestor of the
Semites and of the Hebrews in particular. In a sense, he is
the original Israelite. Shem's negative image and low profile
in *Apoc. Adam* is probably to be traced to this reversal of
values. In its treatment of Shem, the text may be described
as anti-Jewish.

F.   Statement Eight: [84],4-[85],18; [85],22-31[27]

In Chapter II, I pointed out the difficulty of maintaining
a continuity between this section and its context because of
the apparent lack of identity between Micheu, Michar and
Mnesinous ([84],5-8) and the ill-defined group of people in
[83],10.[28] However, it appears that by his inclusion of this
section at just this point, the redactor does intend to imply a
relationship between these two groups; that is, the redactor
either assumes that the indefinite group of people in [83],10
and the three baptists are one and the same, or that they are
so closely associated that they are to be considered as part of
the same group.

This is clear from his similar characterization of the two
groups:

Source A: [83],7-[84],3   Redactor: [84],4-[85],6

Those people [83],8-9:   Micheu, Michar, Mnesinous
                                 [84],5-6:

have done the works of the   have drawn water in the will
  powers [83],23-25   of the powers [84],17-23
cried against God [83],28   cried against God [84],8-10
boasted in their trans-   with lawless voices and
  gression [83],26-27   tongues [84],10-12
are corrupted by desire   have obeyed their own desires
  [83],14-17[29] and   [84],26-28 and
shall surely die [84],1-3.   their fruit will wither
                                   [84],28-[85],1.[29]

The close association of these two groups ties together
the evil natural seed of the creator, those who serve the creator in servility and fear ([72],19-23) and who have done all
his will ([74],17-21), with the three baptists who are over the
holy baptism and the living water. The effect of the identification is to tie Micheu, Michar and Mnesinous into the whole
history of opposition to the seed of Seth from the primordial
time to the redactor's day. This is a striking shift in the
role of Micheu, Michar and Mnesinous. We encounter them elsewhere in related documents where a positive role is attributed
to them. They are the powers over the living water, or the
baptists who immerse in the spring of the water of life.[30]
However, as Françoise Morard has pointed out, there is a subtle
implication in some of the texts that Micheu, Michar, and
Mnesinous were at least at one time not entirely pure.[31] Codex
Bruce says that these figures "were purified" by Barpharanges.[32]
Also Zost. (VIII,2)6,7-12 says that, although he was baptized
by the powers over the living waters (Michar, Micheu), he was
"purified" through the great Barpharanges. The fact that puri-
fication was needed in these instances indicates that something
was lacking in the water baptism of the three baptists. In
Trim. Prot. (XIII,1*)48,15-32, the baptists immerse the gnostic
neophyte in the "spring of the water of life." This rite is
the second most basic, or primitive, step in a five-step series
that extends from a condition of ignorance to the moment when
the gnostic passes into the place of light of the Fatherhood.
Its position in the series gives it less importance than the
remaining four steps.

It seems that these subtle hints in the literature are
fully developed in the redactor's conclusion to the *Apoc. Adam*.
The three baptists, Micheu, Michar, Mnesinous, the living
water, are described in a highly negative way ([84],4-25). The
basic criticism of them is that they have "defiled the water of
life" and "drawn it according to the will of the powers" *whom
they now serve* ([84],17-23). In the light of the fact that
they are the powers who immerse in the spring of the water of
life, this appears to be a criticism of their role, and therefore of water baptism.

Deprecation of water baptism is also the purpose of the
redactor's comment seven ([83],4-7).[33] The descendants of Seth
"will fight against the power <of> those who receive his name
upon the water...." The relationship of this statement to the
context is not immediately clear. However, the intent of the
statement (as emended) is clear. The descendants of Seth not
only do not practice water baptism, but are openly opposed to
those who do.

The problem is that there is apparently nothing in the
context that alludes to baptism. Why did the redactor include
the statement at just this point? It comes exactly at the conclusion to the explanations on the illuminator's origin, which,
as we have seen above,[34] have no evident reference to baptism
when considered in their context. Yet this statement by the
redactor influences the reader to see the list of statements by
the kingdoms in a different light. Who are those "who receive
his name upon the water," and whose name is being received?
This seems to be a clear reference to baptism,[35] but there is
no group who baptize mentioned in the context, nor is there any
obvious allusion to baptism in the catalog of explanations.
This statement by the redactor ([83],4-7), coupled with his
comment six appended to the statement by the thirteenth kingdom
that the illuminator comes upon the water "in order that the
desire of these powers might be satisfied" ([82],18-19),[36] requires the reader to look at the thirteen statements by the
kingdoms with a baptism motif in mind.[37] Only if these explanations in the list related to baptism in the redactor's experience can sense be made of the redactor's statement at [83],4-7.

This suggests that the thirteen statements by the kingdoms
may have served at one time as a gnostic baptismal litany or
liturgy as, for example, was practiced by the Marcosians.[38]
Such an understanding would have to be a derived meaning for
the list of statements because, as we saw above, there is nothing in the statements themselves that suggests such an applica-
tion for them.[39]

A Sitz im Leben for the list as a baptismal liturgy is
suggested by the Marcosian baptismal liturgy where the setting
is the path through the heavenly spheres through which the gnostic passed at death. At each level, he was required to give the
proper response to the questions of the powers.[40] This is similar to the *Apoc. Adam* except that *Apoc. Adam* suggests a situation in which multiple baptisms were practised; perhaps each
statement in the list was accompanied by a baptism of some sort.

In the gnostic literature, reference is made elsewhere to
multiple baptisms through which the revealer figure passes. For
example, *Treat. Seth* (VII,2)58,16 speaks of Seth's third baptism
in a revealed image. And this is certainly the situation in
Zostrianos.

Zost. (VIII,1)5,11-7,22:[41]

Then I knew that the power within me was set over
the darkness because it contained the whole light.
I was baptized there and I received the image of the
glories there. I became like one of them. I left the
airy [earth] and passed by the copies of aeons, after
washing there seven times in a living [water], one for
each of the aeons. I did not cease until I saw all
the waters once.

I ascended to the Transmigration which [really]
exists. I was baptized and [...] world. I ascended
to the Repentance which [really] exists [and was]
baptized there four times. I passed by the sixth
[aeon...]. I ascended to the [...]. I stood there
having seen a light of the truth, which [really]
exists from its self-begotten root, and great messengers and glories [...] in measure.

I was baptized in the name of the Self-begotten
God by these powers which are upon living waters,
Michar and Mi[chea]. I was purified by [the] great
Barpharanges. Then [they revealed] themselves to me
and wrote me in the glory. I was sealed by those who
are on those powers, Michar <and> Mi[ch]eus and
Seldao and Ele[nos] and Zogenethlos. I became a
root-seeing messenger and stood upon the first aeon

which is the fourth. With the souls I blessed the
Self-begotten God and the forefather, Geradama(s)
[...] the self-begotten, the [first] perfect [man],
and Seth Emmach[a Seth], the son of [A]damas, the
[father of the immovable] race, and the [four lights
...], and Mirothea, the mother [...] and eminence
[...] of the lights and De[...].

I was [baptized] for the second time in the name
of the Self-begotten God by these same powers. I became a messenger of the perfect male race. I stood
upon the second aeon which is the third. With the
sons of [S]eth I blessed all these.

I was baptized for the third time in the name of
the Self-begotten God by these same powers. I became
a holy messenger. I stood upon the third aeon which
is the second. I [blessed] all these.

I was baptized for the fourth time by these same
powers. I became a perfect [messenger. I stood upon]
the fourth aeon [which is the first] and [blessed all
these].

Zost. (VIII,*1*)53,14-54,1:

> [I was] baptized the fifth [time] in the name of
> the Self-begotten by these very powers. I became
> divine. [I stood] upon the fifth inhabited aeon of
> all [these]. I saw all [those] who belong to the
> self-begotten ones who really exist, and I was bap-
> tized five [times...].

The idea of a path or a course of baptism through which the
neophyte must pass actually seems to be the meaning of *Zost.*
(VIII,*1*)25,2-20:[42]

> Concerning the path to the Self-begotten Ones,
> into whom you have now been baptized every time, a
> path which is worthy of seeing the [perfect] indi-
> viduals: Since it has come into being from the powers
> of the Self-begotten, it is knowledge [of] the All,
> knowledge which you acquire when you pass through the
> all-perfect aeons. And the third washing, if you
> should wash [...] you would hear [...].

This agrees with *Zost.* (VIII,*1*)15,1-16 where several kinds of
baptisms are suggested:

> Therefore, [...] waters are perfect. It is the
> [water] of Life which belongs to Vitality in which you
> now have been baptized in the Self-begotten One. It
> is the [water] of Blessedness which [belongs to] knowl-
> edge in which you will be baptized in the First-
> Appearing One. It is the water of Existence [which]
> belongs to Divinity and the Hidden One. The water of
> Life [is...] a power, the water belonging to Blessed-
> ness according to Essence, and the water belonging to
> Divinity according to [Existence].

The neophyte's confession after having passed through all
baptisms might correspond to the confession of Zostrianos in
the conclusion to the book (*Zost.* [VIII,*1*]129,4-22):

> Apophantes and Aphropais, the Virgin Light, came
> before me and brought me to the first-appearing, great,
> male, perfect Mind, and I saw how all these who were
> there dwell within one. I joined with all of them
> and blessed the Hidden Aeon and the Virgin Barbelo and
> the Invisible Spirit. I became all-perfect and received
> strength. I was written in glory and was sealed and
> received there a perfect crown.
> I came forth to the perfect individuals, and all
> of them were questioning me. They were listening to
> the greatness of the knowledge and rejoicing and re-
> ceiving strength.[43]

Compare this to the structure of the birth narratives in the
Apoc. Adam.[44]

Apoc. Adam [81],16-23	*Zost.* (VIII,*1*)129,12-17[45]
His god loved a cloud of desire.	
He begat it in his hand	
and cast onto the cloud near	
him (some) of the drop.	
And he was born	I became all-perfect.
He received glory and power	I received power, was written
	in glory and was sealed.
	I received a perfect crown
in that place	in that place,
And in this way he came to	and I came forth to the
the water.	perfect individuals.

The similarity in structure is striking.

The Marcosian liturgy also suggests a structure to which
the list of statements in the *Apoc. Adam* may be compared.

> The leader: I do not divide the spirit, the heart,
> and the super-celestial power which
> shows mercy. May I enjoy thy name,
> Savior of Truth.
>
> The initiate: I am established, I am redeemed, and I
> redeem my soul from this age and from
> all that comes from it, in the name of
> Iao, who redeemed his soul unto the
> redemption in Christ the living one.
>
> The Congregation: Peace be with all on whom this name
> rests.[46]

The liturgy is followed by the sacred baptism.

The arrangement of each statement in the catalog of explanations by the thirteen kingdoms easily lends itself for use
in a baptismal liturgy such as the Marcosians used. Perhaps
the leader would announce the individual kingdom units with an
appropriate phrase. Then the neophyte would respond with the
statement corresponding to the phases or "births" through which
the illuminator figure passed in his ascent to, or descent from,
the world of light,[47] and the congregation would respond with
the standardized refrain: "He received glory and power, and in
this way came to the water." Each baptism brought the neophyte
deeper into the inner mysteries of the cult.

The series of baptisms had a twofold symbolism. On the
one hand, the baptisms symbolized the redeemer's progressive
entry into the created world through the guardians of the heavenly spheres. On the other hand, they were a symbolical enact-
ment of and preparation for the passage out of the created
world upward through the heavenly spheres that the individual
gnostic would make at his own death. The statements spoken by
the kingdoms are conceived of as a repetition of the (deceiving)
words with which the redeemer responded (in the first person) to
the questions of the guardians as he entered the created world.
These deceptive and incorrect responses kept the redeemer's true
identity and origin concealed. The neophyte learns the same
deceptive responses that he also might deceive the guardians and
thereby ensure his own successful passage into the world of
light.

The antipathy of the redactor to water baptism is further
emphasized by the role that he assigns to the imperishable illuminators: Yesseus, Mazareus, Yessedekeus. These figures come
from the holy ⲤⲠⲞⲣⲁ, i.e., Seth himself, to bring secret
knowledge, the acquisition of which the redactor describes as
"the holy baptism" ([85],22-31). One should not understand
this statement in the sense of two correct baptisms, one of
which may be higher or better than the other, but both of which
have their value, as it appears, for example, in Clem. *exc*.
Thdot. 78. Rather, it should be understood as an outright rejection of water baptism.[48]

This phenomenon is found elsewhere in the Nag Hammadi Library (*Testim. Truth* [IX,*3*]69,7-24).[49]

> Some enter the faith [by receiving a] baptism, on the ground that they have [it] as a hope of salvation, which they call "the [seal]." They do not [know] that the [fathers of] the world are manifest to that [place, but] he himself [knows that] he is sealed. For [the Son] of [Man] did not baptize any of his disciples. But [...if those who] are baptized were headed for life, the world would become empty. And the fathers of baptism were defiled.
> But the baptism of truth is something else; it is by renunciation of [the] world that it is found.

Here it is clearly stated that true baptism is not by means of water. True baptism comes by a renunciation of the world. *Testim. Truth* goes on to compare the water of the Jordan with "the power of the body," i.e., the senses of pleasure. In fact, the "water of the Jordan is the desire for sexual intercourse" (*Testim. Truth* [IX,*3*]30,18-31,5).[50] The same attitude toward water baptism is expressed in the *Paraph. Shem*.[51]

Paraph. Shem (VII,*1*)30,21-27:

For at that time the demon will also appear upon the river to baptize with an imperfect baptism, and to trouble the world with a bondage of water.

Paraph. Shem (VII,*1*)36,25-29:

And many who wear erring flesh will go down to the harmful waters through the winds and the demons. And they are bound by the water.

Paraph. Shem (VII,*1*)37,10-38,9:

And it is blessedness if it is granted someone to contemplate the exalted one, and to know the exalted time and the bondage. For the water is an insignificant body. And men are not released, since they are bound in the water, just as from the beginning the light of the Spirit was bound.
O Shem, they are deceived by manifold demons, thinking that through baptism with the uncleanness of water, that which is dark, feeble, idle, (and) disturbing, he will take away the sins. And they do not know that from the water to the water there is bondage, and error and unchastity, envy, murder, adultery, false witness, heresies, robberies, lusts, babblings, wrath, bitterness, great [...]. Therefore there are many deaths which burden their minds. For I foretell it to those who have a heart. They will refrain from the impure baptism. And those who take heart from the light of the Spirit will not have dealings with the impure practice.

The redactor of the *Apoc. Adam* falls within the tradition
that rejected water baptism in favor of a metaphorical understanding of baptism. For the redactor, the reception of the
secret knowledge brought by the imperishable illuminators *was*
holy baptism with living water ([85],22-31).

Associated with this rejection of water baptism is the
implication that those who do practice water baptism are also
not leading ascetic lives. The three baptists are accused of
leading unbridled lives ([84],8-12) that are associated with
unspeakable deeds ([84],12-14), and their lifestyle is characterized as full of "pleasure and merriment" ([84],14-17).[52]

A final comment needs to be made about the redaction history of the catalog of explanations. In Chapter IV,[53] I argued
that the catalog of explanations had passed through at least a
three-phase redactional process. We are now in a better position to clarify that analysis. It appears that at first only
the thirteen kingdoms circulated together. At this initial
stage of the tradition, each statement described a birth. Exactly what the original context and meaning of the catalog was
is difficult to say. It appears to have been a collection of
various theological explanations as to the origin of some unknown individual. Possibly, the catalog was intended to be
used in a confessional statement. This possibility suggests
itself because there is nothing in them that is essentially
negative and because of the highly stylized structure of the
section. Later the catalog came to be associated with the
passage of the gnostic illuminator through the antagonistic
rulers of the heavenly spheres. The narratives came to be
associated with baptism and the catalog then came to function
as a baptismal liturgy.

The factor that brings together the motifs of baptism and
the passage of the illuminator through the heavens is not clear,
but that they were linked we know from their appearance together
in the passages cited above from *Zost.* (see above, pp. 195-97).
The imagery that was employed to explain the meaning of the
birth narratives may be the solution. One who left the heavenly world to come to the created world enters the "waters of
chaos" (see above, pp. 141-47). In this sense, the figures of

appearance and water do become associated. To come to appearance was equal to coming into the water, or to the water. The
Zost. passage is certainly a later development in this tradition and probably reflects a baptismal practice long established in the community. The waters through which Zostrianos
passes in the text are not the waters of chaos, but the baptismal waters of the community practice. In a sense, the *Zost.*
passage is a projection into the divine realm of an established
community practice. Thus, the neophyte was baptized thirteen
times (or twelve) to represent the passage through the thirteen
evil powers and cohorts of the creator god just as the illuminator before him had passed through them. That this kind of
practice actually occurred is shown by the Marcosian baptismal
practice.[54]

Then these thirteen statements along with the statement of
the kingless generation and the narrative framework of source B
were pulled together by a community that was opposed to water
baptism. At this point, the two features of birth and baptism
coalesce in the sense of the passage from *Zost.* cited above.[55]
This is evident from the statement of the kingless generation
which is clearly opposed to the first thirteen statements in
precisely these two points:[56] the illuminator was not *born* but
chosen; his appearance is not to be associated with water, a
feature that suggests desire.[57]

Finally, the redactor picks up source B and includes it in
the *Apoc. Adam* with the redactional statements that make it
clear that he sees in the kingdom statements a baptismal motif
to which he is radically opposed. This explanation allows for
the statement of the kingless generation to have been received
as *Vorlage* by the redactor, and is in agreement with the earlier analysis of the redactional history of the catalog of statements.[58] It also places early in the redactional process the
shift from understanding the catalog as a collection of birth
narratives to using it in a baptismal liturgy.

G.   The Redactor's Version of the *Apoc. Adam*

1.   Theological Implications of the Redacted Structure

The redactor betrays little sensitivity to literary form
in his arrangement of the tractate. His arrangement is purely
functional and theological. He received a document (source A)
that he knew as a revelation discourse by Adam to Seth. He
simply expanded it at certain points in the interest of promoting his own theological concerns. One of these expansions
by the redactor--the revelation of the three men ([65],24-
[66],12; [67],12-21)--has already been discussed.[59] The redactor inserted this gnostic revelation story into the narrative
of Adam's fall and loss of knowledge in source A as a dream
vision in order to provide Adam a means of regaining the knowledge he lost and thus to have a basis on which to have Adam
make a revelation to Seth.[60]

The problem faced by the redactor was: if Adam had lost
the knowledge of the eternal God in his fall and devolution
into an earthly condition prior to Seth's birth, how did he
regain that lost knowledge so as to pass it on to Seth before
his own death? Source A did not concern itself with this issue
since those men threatened by the creator were "cast forth from
the knowledge of the great aeons" ([71],10-13). Therefore, they
entered the world already possessing knowledge of the eternal
God, as well as the glory of the eternal aeon (64,28-[65],3).
Only the redactor, who was trying to establish a continuity of
revelation, was concerned that Adam regain his lost knowledge.

It was important to the redactor that he maintain an un-
broken special tradition of revelation from Adam to the Sethian
community of the redactor's own day. Adam, the *Urmensch*, had
personal intimate knowledge of the eternal God because he came
from his presence (64,5-15).[61] This knowledge is passed on to
Seth (64,2-4; [67],14-21), who in turn passes it on to his
progeny, the heroes of the faith ([85],19-22). When the great
men are removed from the world shortly before the *Eschaton*,
knowledge returns through the revelation of the great illuminator ([76],8-27),[62] and it is still available in the world in
the redactor's day through the imperishable illuminators:

Yesseus, Mazareus, Yessedekeus, the Living Water ([85],22-31),[63]
who know the eternal God in wisdom and teaching of eternal angels ([85],14-18). That revelation, "the words of imperishability and truth" ([85],12-14) is a special living tradition.
It has not been necessary to commit it to writing, since it is
communicated as a living tradition in every period of world
history: from Adam to Seth, through the holy seed of Seth,
through the great illuminator of the end-time, and in the redactor's day it is still communicated firsthand through angelic
beings that come from Seth himself ([85],3-9).[64]

The insistence of the redactor on a special living tradition that is not committed to writing may be understood as an
"anti-book motif," a feature that places the redactor in tension with both Judaism and the early Christian movement that
used the Old Testament as its holy scripture. It is an "anti-
book" motif in the sense that the redactor appeals to the special living tradition to authenticate his message while the
Jewish and Christian communities appealed to their written
traditions for authority.[65]

The redactor's second major expansion is the inclusion of
the narrative of the illuminator's appearance, and the list of
explanations on his origin (source B). It comes just before
the apocalyptic conclusion to the A source and immediately
following the removal of the great race from the world. This
position suggests two concerns of the redactor: the redactor
understands his own period to be a part of the end-time, and he
understands the means by which revelation comes in this period
to be through the great φωστήρ, as well as the imperishable
illuminators ([85],22-31).

With regard to the first of these concerns, it seems clear
that in the sequence of the A source, following the removal of
the great race, the *Eschaton* occurs. By the inclusion of B at
just this point, the redactor intends the reader to understand
an additional period prior to the end. That period before the
end begins with the revelation of the great illuminator, concludes with the *Eschaton*, and incorporates the redactor's own
time.[66]

The second concern of the redactor, revelation through the
great illuminator, is known in other related texts from Nag
Hammadi. *Gos. Eg.* (III,*2*)50,25-51,4 describes a "great light"
that will come into the world.[67]

> There may appear [   ] the glory and the power of
> the invisible Father of the holy men of the great light
> which will come into the world....[68]

To this quotation should be added a number of other references
from the *Gos. Eg.* that describe a "great light" in a personified sense[69] in distinction from the four great lights mentioned elsewhere: Harmozel, Oroiael, Davithe and Eleleth.[70]
The great light also appears to be in distinction from Adamas
(the heavenly prototype of the earthly first man) who is described as a "shining light" from the Father of light (*Gos. Eg.*
[III,*2*]49,8-9).

The metaphor of a personified light coming from the heavenly realm to earth also occurs in the *Paraph. Shem.*[71]

Paraph. Shem (VII,*1*)8,24-9,7:

Again I shall appear. I am Derdekeas, the son of the
incorruptible, infinite Light.
    The light of the infinite Spirit came down to a
feeble nature for a short time until all the impurity
of nature became void, and in order that the darkness
of Nature might be exposed. I put on my garment which
is the garment of the light of the Majesty--which I am.
I came in the appearance of the Spirit to consider the
whole light which was in the depths of the Darkness,
according to the will of the Majesty, in order that
the Spirit by means of the Word might be filled with
his light independently of the power of the infinite
Light.

Paraph. Shem (VII,*1*)28,11-34:

    Then Nature, which had been disturbed, wanted to
harm the seed which will be upon the earth after the
flood. Demons were sent to them, and a deviation of
the winds, and a burden of the angels, and a fear of
the prophet, a condemnation of speech, that I may
teach you, O Shem, from what blindness your race is
protected. When I have revealed to you all that has
been spoken, then the righteous one will shine upon
the world with my garment. And the night and the day
will be separated. For I shall hasten down to the
world to take the light of that place, the one which
Faith possesses. And I shall appear to those who will
acquire the mind of the light of the Spirit. For because of them my majesty appeared.

It also appears in the *Trimorphic Protennoia*.[72]

> *Trim. Prot.* (XIII,*1*)47,28-34:
>
> [I] am the Light that illumines the All. I am the
> Light that rejoices [in my] brethren, for I came down
> to the world [of] mortals on account of the Spirit that
> remains [in] that which descended (and) came forth
> [from the guileless] Sophia.

It appears in the *Apocryphon of John*.[73]

> *Ap. John* (II,*1*)30,32-31,22:
>
> Still for a third time I went--I am the light
> which exists in the light, I am the remembrance of
> the Pronoia--that I might enter into the middle of
> darkness and the inside of Hades. And I filled my
> face with the light of the completion of their aeon.
> And I entered into the middle of their prison which
> is the prison of the body. And I said, "He who hears,
> let him get up from the deep sleep." And he wept and
> shed tears. Bitter tears he wiped from himself and
> he said, "Who is it that calls my name, and from where
> has this hope come to me, while I am in the chains of
> the prison?" And I said, "I am the Pronoia of the
> pure light; I am the thinking of the virginal Spirit,
> he who raised you up to the honored place. Arise and
> remember that it is you who hearkened, and follow your
> root, which is I, the merciful one, and guard yourself
> against the angels of poverty and the demons of chaos
> and all those who ensnare you, and beware of the deep
> sleep and the enclosure of the inside of Hades."

It is picked up in the *Letter of Peter to Philip*[74] and applied
to Jesus.

> *Ep. Pet. Phil.* (VIII,*2*)133,17-134,18:
>
> Then, when the apostles had come together and
> thrown themselves upon their knees, they prayed,
> saying, "Father, Father, Father of the Light who
> possesses the incorruptions, hear us just as [...]
> in thy holy child Jesus Christ. For he became for
> us an illuminator (φωστήρ) in the [darkness]. Yea
> hear us."
> And they prayed again another time, saying, "Son
> of Life, Son of Immortality who is in the light, Son,
> Christ of Immortality, our Redeemer, give us power,
> for they seek to kill us."
> Then a great light appeared so that the mountain
> shone from the sight of him who had appeared. And a
> voice called out to them, saying, "Listen to my words
> that I may speak to you. Why are you asking me? I am
> Jesus Christ who is with you forever."

Ep. Pet. Phil. (VII,2)139,9-21:

And Peter opened his mouth, he said to his disciples,
"[Did] our Lord Jesus, when he was in the body, show
us everything? For he came down. My brothers, listen
to my voice." And he was filled with a holy spirit.
He spoke thus: "Our illuminator (φωστήρ), Jesus,
[came] down and was crucified. And he bore a crown
of thorns. And he put on a purple garment. And he
was [crucified] on a tree and he was buried in a tomb.
And he rose from the dead.

The followers of the illuminator take on his characteristics.
And just as he will "shine" at his coming, so they, the Sethians, will shine over the creation in the *Apoc. Adam* ([82],28-
[83],4) and so the followers of Christ in Christian gnostic
texts will become "illuminators" (*Ep. Pet. Phil.* [VII,2]137,
5-9).[75]

The motif of the light coming into the world is also known
in the hellenistic world,[76] the Old Testament tradition,[77] and
the Jewish apocalyptic literature.[78] In the apocalyptic literature, it appears as follows.

2 Enoch 46:1-3:[79]

Hear, my people, and take in the words of my lips.
If any one bring any gifts to an earthly ruler, and
have disloyal thoughts in his heart, and the ruler know
this, will he not be angry with him, and not refuse his
gifts, and not give him over to judgment? Or *if* one
man make himself appear good to another by deceit of
tongue, but *have* evil in his heart, then will not *the
other* understand the treachery of his heart, and himself be condemned, since his untruth was plain to all?
And when the Lord shall send a great light, then there
will be judgment for the just and the unjust, and there
no one shall escape notice.

2 Apoc. Bar. 71:2-72:6:[80]

This is the vision which thou hast seen, and this
is the interpretation. For I have come to tell thee
these things, because thy prayer has been heard with
the Most High.
Hear now also regarding the bright lightning which
is to come at the consummation after these black
(waters): this is the word. After the signs have come,
of which thou wast told before, when the nations become
turbulent, and the time of My Messiah is come, he shall
both summon all the nations, and some of them he shall
spare, and some of them he shall slay. These things
therefore shall come upon the nations which are to be

spared by Him. Every nation, which knows not Israel
and has not trodden down the seed of Jacob, shall
indeed be spared. And this because some out of every
nation shall be subjected to thy people. But all
those who have ruled over you, or have known you,
shall be given up to the sword.

T. 12 Patr.: *T. Levi* 18:2-14:[81]

Then shall the Lord raise up a new priest.
And to him all the words of the Lord shall be revealed;
And he shall execute a righteous judgement upon the earth
    for a multitude of days.
And his star shall arise in heaven as of a king.
Lighting up the light of knowledge as the sun the day.
And he shall be magnified in the world.
He shall shine forth as the sun on the earth,
And shall remove all darkness from under heaven,
And there shall be peace in all the earth.

T. 12 Patr.: *T. Jud.* 24:[82]

And after these things shall a star arise to you from
Jacob in peace, and a man shall arise [from my seed],
like the son of righteousness, walking with the sons of
men in meekness and righteousness; and no sin shall be
found in him. And the heavens shall be opened unto
him, to pour out the spirit, (even) the blessing of the
Holy Father; and he shall pour out the spirit of grace
upon you; and ye shall be unto Him sons in truth, and
ye shall walk in His commandments first and last.
[This Branch of God Most High, And this Fountain giving
life unto all.] Then shall the sceptre of my kingdom
shine forth; And from your root shall arise a stem;
And from it shall grow a rod of righteousness to the
Gentiles, to judge and to save all that call upon the
Lord.

The reference in Eusebius to Bar Kochba as a luminary ought
also to be incorporated at this point as part of the Jewish
apocalyptic expectations.

The Jews were at that time led by a certain Bar Choche-
bas, which means "star," a man who was murderous and a
bandit, but relied on his name, as if dealing with
slaves, and claimed to be a luminary who had come down
from heaven and was magically enlightening those who
were in misery.[83]

The motif is also picked up in the Christian tradition.[84]

John 1:9:[85]

The true light (φῶς--Jesus) that enlightens every man
was coming into the world. (RSV)

John 3:19-21:

And this is the judgment, that light (φῶς) has come
into the world, and men loved darkness rather than
light (φῶς) because their deeds were evil. For every
one who does evil hates the light (φῶς), and does not
come to the light (φῶς) lest his deeds should be exposed. But he who does what is true comes to the
light (φῶς) that it may be clearly seen that his
deeds have been wrought in God. (RSV)

John 8:12:

Again Jesus spoke to them, saying, "I am the light
(φῶς) of the world; he who follows me will not walk
in darkness, but will have the light (φῶς) of life.
(RSV)

Luke 1:76-79:

And you, child, will be called the prophet of the Most
High; for you will go before the Lord to prepare his
ways, to give knowledge of salvation to his people...
when the day (ἀνατολή) shall dawn upon us from on high
to give light (ἐπιφᾶναι) to those who sit in darkness.
... (RSV)

Acts of Philip 21:[86]

ἐλέησον ἡμᾶς ὦ φίλιππε, ἵνα σὲ ἴδωμεν καὶ διὰ σοῦ τὸν
φωστῆρα τῆς ζωῆς Ἰησοῦν.

Exactly who the redactor conceived the illuminator in the
Apoc. Adam to be is not certain. However, it is clear from his
placement of the section that the great illuminator comes at
the end of time. This eschatological figure is distinguished
from the imperishable illuminators, Yesseus, Mazareus, Yessedekeus, through whom the members of the redactor's community receive revelation, and is best understood in the sense of the
parallels collected above. In this sense, it is significant
that *Gos. Eg.* (III,*2*)68,10-69,5 indicates that the great Seth
is to return at the end of time.[87] This fact coupled with the
knowledge that Adamas, the heavenly prototype of the earthly
first man, was also described as a "shining light" from the
Father of light (*Gos. Eg.* [III,*2*]49,8-9) leads us naturally to
the conclusion that the great light in the *Gos. Eg.* and the
great illuminator in the *Apoc. Adam* are probably none other than
the great Seth.

2. Date and Provenance

The date and provenance of most of the Nag Hammadi tractates is largely a matter of conjecture based upon motif-
parallels with datable traditions.[88] The reason for this is
that the gnostic texts reflect little interest, if any at all,
in the mundane affairs of human history. The gnostic was in-
terested in the primordial history that explained how the world
got into such corrupt condition, and how he could get out of
it. As we have seen,[89] gnostic texts do refer to idealized
historical events, but these were in the context of a *Heils-
geschichte* that related to man's escape from the world. The
Apoc. Adam is no exception to this generalization. All that
may be said *with certainty* on the issue of provenance is that
the *Apoc. Adam* was composed in Greek, later translated into
Coptic and found in Egypt. On the issue of date, all that may
be said *with certainty* is that the document was written after
the appearance of the Septuagint (circa 200-250 B.C.),[90] and
before the date that the codices found in Egypt were manufac-
tured (i.e., before A.D. 350).[91]

Thus far, three different suggestions have been made for
the tractate's date of composition and provenance. Hans
Goedicke has noted the similarity of [75],9-21 to the description of the eruption of Vesuvius by Pliny the Younger in A.D.
79. On the basis of the similarity in reports, he argues in a
brief note that the *Apoc. Adam* could not be dated later than
the first decade of the second century A.D. (i.e., prior to
A.D. 110).[92]

On the basis of what I have called the redactor's conclusion (in particular [84],4-[85],31), Beltz suggests that a particular occasion for the document might be found in the persecution of the Manichaeans by the Church in the years following
Diocletian's edict against the Manichaeans in A.D. 297.[93] He
thinks that the document was written in Egypt, not only because
it was found there, but because the list of kingdoms suggests
what he considers to be an Egyptian provenance rather than an
Iranian provenance.[94] This allows approximately 70± years for
the document to have been written in Greek, translated into
Coptic, and transcribed in the codices later found at Nag Hammadi.

On the other hand, Françoise Morard, although acknowledging that the Manichaeans did not baptize, and to that extent a
Manichaean provenance would suit the situation reflected by the
Apoc. Adam, considers the possibility of a Manichaean provenance for the tractate improbable. Morard reasons, and I think
correctly, that it is doubtful that a later Manichaean author
would have insisted that the words of revelation be unwritten
and specifically not preserved in book form[95] ([85],3-18),
since Manichaeism is "essentially a book religion."[96] Morard
thinks that the gnostic sect of the Archontics described by
Epiphanius corresponds more closely with the community that
produced the *Apoc. Adam* than do the Manichaeans.[97] The
Archontics, probably a factional movement within the gnostic
sect known as Sethians,[98] still existed in Palestine in the
time of Epiphanius.[99] Morard suggests that the redactor of
Apoc. Adam, and hence the present form of the tractate, belongs
to a Sethian-Archontic milieu.[100] The lack of Christian allusions in the *Apoc. Adam* is attributed to the fact that the redactor, like the Archontic tradition to which he belongs, had
rejected the sacraments and attributed little significance to
the person of Jesus.

In discussing provenance, Morard considered primarily the
redactor's conclusion ([84],4-[85],31). As far as it goes, the
methodology is correct. Yet, Morard's discussion did not consider all the statements by the redactor, nor did it consider
the entire tractate from the redactor's perspective. As we
have seen above, the redactor has unified the entire tractate
by his comments and brought it within the purview of his theology. Therefore, one should examine more than just the redactor's conclusion when considering the provenance of the
document.

When the total document is considered from the redactor's
perspective, Morard's tentative identification of provenance on
the basis of the redactor's conclusion appears even more possible. There are a number of strong similarities between the
gnostics in the Sethian-Archontic tradition as reported in
Epiphanius, and the present form of the *Apoc. Adam*. The Sethians traced their descent from Seth, the son of Adam (*Pan.*

39.1.3), who was chosen to bear the seed of "power and purity" (*Pan*. 39.2.5,7).[101] This seed was an elect and special race (*Pan*. 39.2.6)[102] through whom destruction would come upon the powers of the angels who made the world (*Pan*. 39.2.5).[103] The Sethians believed this special seed would be taken up[104] from the world (*Pan*.39.2.6).[105] The Archontics also gave Seth a place of prominence. Seth had a special knowledge of the good God, having been caught up to the heavens (*Pan*. 40.7.1-3), and he acquired knowledge there that he many times revealed to his seed (*Pan*. 40.7.3). Both groups have composed books in the name of Seth (*Pan*. 39.5.1; 40.7.4). The Sethians,[106] like the *Apoc. Adam*, recognized only two classes of people in the world: the Sethians and the natural seed of Noah (*Pan*. 39.3.1-4).[107] The Archontic rejection of baptism (*Pan*. 40.2.6) and their non-Christian stance, as Morard clearly recognized,[108] are two of the major similarities with the *Apoc. Adam*.

While there is no mention of "the Mother," who plays such a prominent role in the Sethian-Archontic tradition as reported by Epiphanius (*Pan*. 39.2.3,7; 40.2.3), the *Apoc. Adam* does give a prominent role to Eve, in that she is the one who reveals to Adam the knowledge of their former life after Adam-Eve had come under the purview of the creator (64,5-15).[109] The flood also appears in the Sethian tradition, but it appears there as the means by which the good God attempts to destroy the evil seed of Ham (*Pan*. 39.3.2), while the redactor of the *Apoc. Adam* understands the flood as an attempt by the demiurge to destroy the Sethian race.[110] In this respect, the Sethian tradition in Epiphanius is much closer to the textual part of the Jewish midrash in source A, which preserves the Old Testament view that the flood is the means whereby a righteous God punishes a wicked world.[111]

The Archontic account of the ascension of Seth (*Pan*. 40.7.1-2) bears strong similarities to three of the rejected statements by the kingdoms, especially with respect to the ascension motif after birth.[112] Finally, in the Sethian-Archontic tradition, there is an emphasis upon a living special revelation. The γνῶσις came from Seth (and others, *Pan*. 40.7.6), and was preserved in books written in his name by his followers.

This parallels the situation in the *Apoc. Adam*. The redactor
rejected a *written* revelation for the special revelation from
Seth, although he himself could still write that revelation in
a book.

All of these similarities seem to argue in favor of
Morard's suggestion that the *Apoc. Adam* should be associated
with the Sethian-Archontic tradition. How, then, does one
account for the dissimilarities? Part of the answer may lie in
the nature of the sources. There is good reason to believe
that the heresiologists did not have independent knowledge of
most sects about which they wrote, and even when they do claim
to have such knowledge, they frequently disagree in their descriptions of the same sect.[113] One should also add to this
the fact that the reports are not objective historical reports,
but polemical attacks against heretics in defense of the
"orthodox" Christian faith. Certainly under these conditions
one should not approach the reports of the heresiologists with
an uncritical attitude, nor expect them to speak specifically
to modern issues, nor be surprised when there are dissimilarities between the reports of the heresiologists and the Nag
Hammadi texts. In fact, as Wisse has pointed out, dissimilarity is the rule rather than the exception.[114]

Epiphanius reports that in his day (end of the fourth century A.D.) the Archontics were still surviving, but only in
Palestine. At an earlier time, the group was apparently more
widespread because he reports that in the time of Constantine
(circa A.D. 306-337) they had spread as far as Armenia. This
suggests that Epiphanius is reporting on them in a period of
the movement's decline, and that the earlier time of Constantine represented a period of more vigorous activity and growth
on the part of the sect. This analysis suggests A.D. 200-400±
as possible dates during which the Archontic movement may be
identified as an independent group. These dates assume that
the time of Constantine represents the period of the Archontics'
greatest influence and allows approximately 100± years for them
to have reached their peak and 100± years for them to have
fallen into decline.

The other datable reports by the heresiologists give some support to this hypothesis. In none of the earlier reports from A.D. 100-200 are the Archontics mentioned. The Sethians,[115] however, are known by Josephus as early as circa A.D. 100[116] and circa A.D. 200 by Irenaeus,[117] and the anonymous author of *Adversus omnes haereses*,[118] and circa A.D. 220 by Hippolytus.[119]

One explanation for the omission of any reference to the Archontics in these early reports is that, during the period A.D. 100-200, the Archontics were probably indistinguishable from the general Sethian movement. Of course it is always possible that the heresiologists simply did not know of the Archontics, although at this early date they may already have existed as a separate group apart from the general Sethian movement, and indeed, as Bousset has suggested, they could have existed much earlier.[120] It is also possible that they were known by the heresiologists, but not as a Christian heresy; that is, they were known to the heresiologists as a non-Christian group. Therefore, since they were not Christian heretics, they could be omitted from any catalog of Christian heresies.

In the report of Epiphanius, there is also a suggestion of factionalism among the Archontics. At one time, some of the Archontics apparently practiced baptism (*Pan*. 40.2.6), but in the time of Epiphanius it is clearly stated that, as a group, the Archontics condemn baptism. In the Epiphanius report, we are apparently seeing the group when the theological controversy over baptism had been fought and won by that faction that rejected baptism. However, the group is still divided even in the time of Epiphanius by libertine and ascetic factions (*Pan*. 40.2.4). Some apparently lead "licentious" lives,[121] while others withdraw from the world as monks.

The evidence for identifying the place of redaction is quite meager, but what there is suggests that the *Apoc. Adam* may have been redacted in Palestine, possibly in Transjordan, before the second half of the second century A.D. (i.e., before A.D. 150). There are two reasons for locating it here. In the earliest report, in which the Archontics are mentioned as an independent group, they are located in Palestine, and the

indication by Epiphanius is that it was from here that they
spread out. The second reason is that the religious climate in
Transjordan at this time (i.e., A.D. 1-150) was well suited for
the kind of shift we see taking place in the *Apoc. Adam*. There
were a great number of Jewish baptist groups in the region of
Transjordan, some of which betray evidence of early gnostic
influence.[122]

The *Apoc. Adam* apparently was produced during an early
stage of the Sethian-Archontic tradition by a minority group
that argued for a spiritualized understanding of baptism and an
ascetic lifestyle. It is a part of that pluralism that develops in emerging religious movements before a stage of uniform-
ity is imposed by the ascendancy of one faction over all others.
This situation suits the ascetic anti-baptism stance of the
Apoc. Adam and the obvious similarities between *Apoc. Adam* and
what the heresiologists described as Sethian-Archontic gnostics.
The evident lack of Christian influence on the *Apoc. Adam* also
corresponds well with the lack of Christian influence on the
Archontics as described by Epiphanius. Therefore it would seem
that we must assume that the *Apoc. Adam* was redacted in a time
before the Sethian movement was Christianized, i.e., probably
before the first half of the second century A.D. (i.e., prior
to A.D. 100). Indeed, Christianization may well have been one
of the reasons for the ultimate separation of the Archontics
from the Sethians. In the Epiphanius report (*Pan.* 39.1.3; 3.5),
the Christian motifs look like secondary features. For example,
Christ is a secondary description of Seth, rather than the other
way around. This suggests that the Sethian tradition was already fully developed before it came under the influence of the
Christian movement. The Sethians maintained their original
mythology and simply incorporated Jesus into their existing
system. The Archontics, on the other hand, apparently rejected
efforts to Christianize them, and split away over that and other
issues. There is no evidence in the brief report by Josephus
(circa A.D. 100) that the Sethians by that time had fallen under
the influence of Christianity. However, by the time of Hippolytus (circa A.D. 200), there is ample evidence that the Sethian

movement had been influenced by Christianity.   This suggests
that Christianization took place A.D. 100-200±.   W. Bousset
thinks that the Archontics represent a very old gnostic sect
precisely because of the lack of even the slightest trace of
Christian influence.[123]

NOTES

CHAPTER V

[1] The simplest way to discuss the material is to take each redactional statement as it comes in sequence in the tractate.

[2] See above, p. 112.

[3] See above, p. 168 n. 32. For the heavenly origin of the seed of Seth, see *Gos. Eg.* (III,*2*)56,13-22; 59,9-25; 60,9-12.

[4] See *Zost.* (VIII,*1*)30,10-14 for γνῶσις coming from Seth.

[5] Note that similar ideas also appear in source B. See above, pp. 111-15.

[6] See the discussion above, pp. 26-27.

[7] See above, pp. 112-13.

[8] See the discussion above, pp. 38-40.

[9] In some cases, ⲤⲦⲞⲢⲀ is also used to describe the archon and his crowd: *Gos. Eg.* (III,*2*)59,21-22; *Treat. Seth* (VII,*2*)56,16. However, *Zost.* does use the term ⲤⲦⲞ ⲣⲀ only once, and that to refer to the "holy seed of Seth" (*Zost.* [VIII,*1*]130,16).

[10] For example, see: *Trim. Prot.* (XIII,*1**)36,16; 50,17-19 (ⲤⲦⲈⲣⲙⲀ); *Steles Seth* (VI,*5*)119,34; 120,10 (ⲤⲦⲞⲣⲀ); *Gos. Eg.* (III,*2*)54,7-11; 56,2-3; 59,25-60,2; 69,9-10 (ⲤⲦⲞⲣⲀ); *Ap. John* (II,*1*)9,15; 20,24; 25,10; 28,3; 30,13 (ⲤⲦⲈⲣⲙⲀ); *Zost.* (VIII,*1*) 47,10; 130,16 (ⲤⲦⲞⲣⲀ). See also Epiph. *Pan.* 39.2.5.

[11] See above, pp. 40, 202-203.

[12] The redactor's conclusion doesn't contain the statement about passing on revelation to his progeny. This might explain why the redactor incorporated the source A conclusion, since it does include such a statement. See above, p. 46 n. 33.

[13] See above, pp. 82-83.

[14] I have included [69],16-17: ⲚⲈⲨⲈ ⲄⲀⲣ Ⲛ̄ⲩⲘⲙⲟ Ⲙ̄Ⲙⲟⲩ ⲠⲈ as a part of the redactional statement assuming that it is part of the reason for the creator including the ⲤⲦⲞⲣⲀ in his wrathful designs. However, it could just as easily be part of the *Vorlage*, i.e., source A. If it were part of the *Vorlage* after [69],1-10, the text would read: "For rain-showers shall pour forth from God, the Almighty, in order that he might destroy all flesh [   ] the earth <...> by those (things) that they seek after, for they were strangers to him." In the latter case, the justification for the creator's act is the sinfulness of mankind. This is expressed by the statement that they were

217

strangers to him, i.e., strangers to his righteousness. I included it as a part of the redactor's statement because it
fitted in so well with the redactor's third statement.

[15]See above, p. 53 n. 70.

[16]See above, pp. 204-208.

[17]For the attribute of power as a quality of Seth, see
Epiph. *Pan.*39.2.4,7.

[18]For the positive quality of the power of the seed, see
[73],15-24 and [74],7-11.

[19]See above, pp. 185-88.

[20]Schenke, "Das sethianische System," 167-68. Schenke
argues that the Nag Hammadi Sethians viewed history as a division into periods or universal epochs. The four Sethian aeons,
Harmozel, Oroiael, Davithe, Eleleth, correspond to four different universal epochs in which the Sethians of each epoch have
their resting place.

[21]Böhlig-Wisse, *Gospel of the Egyptians*, 197.

[22]Ibid.

[23]See above, pp. 50-51 and 119-22.

[24]See the redactor's statements above, pp. 185-90.

[25]See above, pp. 48 (n. 46) and 362-63.

[26]See above, pp. 202-203.

[27]The redactor's statements six and seven reflect a major
concern of the redactor that is best considered in conjunction
with his conclusion. See above, pp. 194-95.

[28]See above, p. 33.

[29]This characterization is arrived at by contrast with the
other group mentioned in the context of the statement.

[30]See the note to the text as [84],5-6.

[31]Morard, "L'*Apocalypse de Adam* de Nag Hammadi," 36-38.

[32]See Charlotte Baynes, *A Coptic Gnostic Treatise contained in the Codex Brucianus* (Cambridge: The University Press,
1933) 180. In *Gos. Eg.* (IV,*2*)75,24-76,12, they are linked
with him "who presides over the baptism of the living," i.e.,
the purifier, Sesengen*barpharanges*. But compare (III,*2*)64,9-22
where a distinction is made between the "purifiers" and Sesengen*pharanges*.

[33]See the argument for emendation of the text in the note to the text at [83],4-7.

[34]See above, pp. 130-47.

[35]See the discussion by Wilhelm Bousset (*Hauptprobleme der Gnosis* [Göttingen: Vandenhoeck & Ruprecht, 1907] 278-96), who shows the close relationship that existed in gnostic sects between the ritual of baptism and the pronouncement of the "name" over the initiate.

[36]See also the statement made by the redactor concerning the three baptists: "Micheu, Michar, Mnesinous, you have defiled the water of life; you drew it according to the will of the powers whom you serve" ([84],17-23). Satisfying the desire of "these" powers seems to be submitting to the water baptism of the three baptists. See *Gos. Eg.* (III,*2*)67,22-26 and especially its parallel (IV,*2*)80,9-13 where it is stated that life is mixed with the baptismal waters *of all the archons*. In the Marcosian baptism, the neophyte is baptized into the communion of the powers, Iren. *Haer.* 1.21.3 (Foerster, *Gnosis*, 1.219).

[37]Note that the redactor's usual method is to include his redactional comment *following* the section to which he wishes it applied, and not before it. Observe the placement of his statements, pp. 284-87 below, and see pp. 37-40 above. Statement seven by the redactor also fits this pattern.

[38]Iren. *Haer.* 1.21.3-5 (Foerster, *Gnosis*, 1.219-21).

[39]See above, pp. 141-47.

[40]Iren. *Haer.* 1.21.5 (Foerster, *Gnosis*, 1.220-21).

[41]See also a fragmentary passage where the same motif is evident: *Zost.* (VIII,*1*)60,24-62,16. (The following series of quotations from *Zostrianos* are from the translation by John Sieber, as corrected by the ultraviolet collation of the text by Bentley Layton in September 1975 in *The Nag Hammadi Library*, pp. 368-93.) To this, compare the thirteen repentances of Sophia in PS where a similar passage through the heavens is suggested of Sophia (Schmidt, *Koptisch-gnostische Schriften*, 71, line 10 to 72, line 31).

[42]See also VIII 62,11-16: "The one who belongs to all [the glories], Yoel, said to me, 'You have [received] all the [washings] in which she is worthy to [give] baptism and you have become [perfect...].'"

[43]Protophanēs (the first appearing) and Kalyptos (the Hidden aeon) have their own baptismal waters; see VIII 18,6-10; VIII 22,8-14; VIII 23,5-20. Multiple baptisms appear also in PS (see Schmidt, *Koptisch-gnostische Schriften*, 188, lines 12-23; 192, lines 18-27; 216, lines 3-21).

[44]See above, p. 53 n. 70.

[45]Compare the translation by John Sieber in *The Nag Hammadi Library*, 392.

[46]Iren. *Haer.* 1.21.3; translation from Foerster, *Gnosis*, 1.219.

[47]That is, in the sense of the passages in *Zostrianos* quoted above (pp. 195-97). However, see Morard ("L'*Apocalypse d'Adam* de Nag Hammadi," 38), who believes that the water of the thirteen kingdoms equals *for the redactor* the waters of chaos. I agree that at its earliest stage the list referred to the waters of chaos (see above, pp. 141-47), but the redactor understood it as having a baptismal motif.

[48]Morard ("L'*Apocalypse d'Adam* de Nag Hammadi," 38-41) pulls together similar motifs in other gnostic texts that reflect a negative attitude towards water baptism:

> The Book of Justin: Hipp. *Ref.* 5.27.2-3 (Foerster, *Gnosis*, 1.57-58). *Gos. Eg.* (III,*2*)63,24; 65,24. *Orig. World* (II,*5*)122,14-16. *Trim. Prot.* (XIII,*1**) 45,15-20; 47,15-19; 48,15-22.

> To these may be added *Trim. Prot.* (XIII,*1**)46,14-25; see Schmidt, *Koptisch-gnostische Schriften*, 87, lines 34-36 and 245, lines 20-27; 308-12. *Zost.* (VIII,*1*) 17,4-15; 23,1-18; 24,20; 131,2-3; *Paraph. Shem* (VII,*1*)40,25-29.

Already in the New Testament there is the tendency toward a "higher" more spiritual form of baptism: Mark 1:8, Matt 3:11, Luke 3:16, Acts 1:5, 11:16, 19:1-6. See the discussion by Michel Tardieu, *Trois mythes gnostiques: Adam, Eros et les animaux d'Egypt dans un écrit de Nag Hammadi (II,5)* (Paris: Etudes Augustiniennes, 1974) 253-55.

[49]Translation by Birger Pearson in *The Nag Hammadi Library*, 414.

[50]This passage appears to be a Christian-gnostic allegory on Mark 1:9-10 in which the baptism of Jesus in the Jordan River represents the birth of the Son of Man, and coming to the Jordan River symbolizes coming to the world. The Jordan is the power of the body or the senses of pleasure. The water of the Jordan is the desire for sexual intercourse through which birth takes place. John, who baptizes, represents the archon of this world who enslaves men in bodies. The passage recalls the explanations of the kingdoms where the illuminator's entry into the world is expressed as "coming to the water."

[51]The following series of translations are by Frederik Wisse in *The Nag Hammadi Library*, 308-28. See also *Paraph. Shem* (VII,*1*)31,12-22.

[52]The ascetic stance of source A can also be incorporated as part of the redactor's position. See above, pp. 84-85.

[53]See above, pp. 118-19.

[54]Degrees of initiation into the mysteries is a motif known elsewhere in antiquity. See, for example: CH 13, *Disc.* *8-9* (VI,*6*), Apul. *Met.* 11.

[55]See above, pp. 195-97.

[56]See above, pp. 135-37.

[57]See above, pp. 194-95 and 199-200.

[58]See above, pp. 118-19.

[59]See above, pp. 97-115.

[60]See above, pp. 45 (n. 14) and 21-22.

[61]An interesting feature of the creation story in source A is that it is necessary for Eve to reinstruct Adam about the aeon from which they had come; see p. 44 n. 8, above.

[62]See above, pp. 191, 203-08.

[63]Whether these figures retain a mythological character at this point or are understood in a historical sense, or are understood both ways, is not clear.

[64]The insistence on living special revelation is a recognized feature of the gnostic traditions (see, for example, R.P.C. Hanson, *Tradition in the Early Church* [Philadelphia: Westminster, 1962] 22-35) and of the apocalyptic literature (see D. S. Russell], *The Method and Message of Jewish Apocalyptic* [Philadelphia: Westminster, 1964] 107-18, 158-73). It also appears in the earliest period of the Christian movement (i.e., from the apostolic age to circa A.D. 150) in the sense of a tradition that took its authority from the apostles who had both seen and heard Jesus. See J. N. D. Kelly, *Early Christian Doctrines* (2nd ed.; New York: Harper and Row, 1960) 31-35.

[65]See, for example, 1 Cor 10:11, 2 Tim 3:15-17, Heb 3:7-11.

[66]This is suggested by the redactor's conclusion, where he associates the three baptists with "those people" rejected at the *Eschaton.* See the discussion above, pp. 192-93.

[67]Translation by Böhlig-Wisse, *Gospel of the Egyptians*, 98.

[68]The operative expression in Coptic is: ⲚⲚⲢⲰⲘⲈ ⲈⲦⲞⲨⲀⲀⲂ ⲘⲠⲚⲞϬ ⲚⲞⲨⲞⲈⲒⲚ ⲠⲀⲒ̈ ⲈⲦⲚⲎⲞⲨ ⲈⲠⲔⲞⲤⲘⲞⲤ.

[69]*Gos. Eg.* (III,*2*)43,1-4.13-16; 49,1-4; 50,10-14; 51,14-16; 63,21-22; 68,24-26.

[70]*Gos. Eg.* (III,*2*)52,3-16; 56,13-57,11; 64,25.

[71]Translation by Frederik Wisse in *The Nag Hammadi Library*, 308-28.

[72]Translation by John Turner in *The Nag Hammadi Library*, 469.

[73]Translation by Frederik Wisse in *The Nag Hammadi Library*, 115-16.

[74]Translation by Frederik Wisse in *The Nag Hammadi Library*, 394-98.

[75]This metaphor of the righteous "shining" appears also in the Jewish apocalyptic literature: *2 Enoch* 66:7 and *Adam and Eve* 39:9; in the Old Testament: Exod 34:29-35, Job 11:17, Prov 4:18, Isa 60:1-3, Dan 12:3; in the New Testament: Matt 5:16, 13:43, 17:2, Luke 24:4, John 5:35, Acts 13:47, Phil 2:15, Rev 1:16; and elsewhere in the Nag Hammadi texts: *Trim. Prot.* (XIII,*1**)49,28-32.

[76]Wilhelm Bousset, *Kurios Christos* (trans. John Steely from German 5th ed.; Nashville: Abingdon, 1970) 232-37 and esp. 234 n. 91.

[77]Num 24:17; Isa 10:17; 14:12-13; 42:6; 49:6; 60:1-3, 19-20; Mic 7:8.

[78]The term "luminary" is generally used in the apocalyptic literature for the sun, moon and stars: *1 Enoch* 17:3; 20:4; 23:4; 72:1-2,4,35,36; 73:1; 79:6; 82:7; *Jub.* 1:29.

[79]Translation from Charles, *APOT*, 2.458.

[80]Translation from Charles, *APOT*, 2.518.

[81]Translation from Charles, *APOT*, 2.314.

[82]Translation from Charles, *APOT*, 2.323-24.

[83]Euseb. *Eccl. Hist.* 4.6.2; see also 5.24.2. Translation by Kirsopp Lake, *Eusebius: The Ecclesiastical History* (LCL; 2 vols.; London: William Heinemann, 1965) 1.311, 313. In this connection, see CD 9,4-9, where the same title "star" is used of the leader of the community.

[84]See also Luke 2:29-32, John 9:5, 12:46, Acts 9:1-5, 2 Cor 4:6, Jas 1:17, 1 John 1:5, Rev 22:5.

[85]See also John 5:35 where John the Baptist is described as a lamp that was burning and shining.

[86]Maximilianus Bonnet (ed.), *Acta Apostolorum Apocrypha* (2 vols. in 3; Hildesheim: Georg Olms, 1959) 2.2:11.

[87]"The great Seth wrote this book with letters in one hundred and thirty years. He placed it in the mountain that is called Charaxio, in order that at the end of the times and the eras, by the will of the divine Autogenes and the whole pleroma, through the gift of the untraceable, unthinkable, fatherly love, it may come forth and reveal this incorruptible, holy race of the great savior..." (Böhlig-Wisse, *Gospel of the Egyptians*, 162, 164). The text uses the feminine pronoun as object at III 68,10 (ⲁϥⲥⲁϩⲥ) and III 68,12 (ⲕⲱ ⲙ̄ⲙⲟⲥ) referring back to ⲧⲉⲉⲓⲃⲓⲃⲗⲟⲥ in III 68,10. The masculine pronoun is used as subject in these same two positions referring back to ⲡⲛⲟϭ ⲛ̄ⲥⲏⲑ . In III 68,19 (ⲉϥ<ⲉ>ⲡⲣⲟⲉⲗⲑⲉ ⲉⲃⲟⲗ) and III 68,20 (ⲛ̄ϥⲟⲩⲱⲛϩ), the masculine pronoun is used as subject. The editors of the text (Böhlig-Wisse, *Gospel of the Egyptians*, 205-206) argue that the Coptic scribe, in using the masculine pronoun at III 68,19 and III 68,20, intended the antecedent to be ⲧⲉⲉⲓⲃⲓⲃⲗⲟⲥ, which he conceived of as the Coptic masculine word ϫⲱⲱⲙⲉ rather than the Greek feminine word ⲃⲓⲃⲗⲟⲥ -- the word actually used by the text. Therefore, he used the masculine pronoun as subject rather than the feminine pronoun as subject because the *conceived* antecedent was masculine. This analysis is confirmed for the editors in the fact that ⲃⲓⲃⲗⲟⲥ makes better sense as the antecedent of ⲉϥ<ⲉ>ⲡⲣⲟⲉⲗⲑⲉ and ⲛ̄ϥⲟⲩⲱⲛϩ than does ⲡⲛⲟϭ ⲛ̄ⲥⲏⲑ. The sense of the text is: The great Seth wrote this book and placed it in the mountain Charaxio in order that at the end of time it (the book) might come forth and reveal this holy race. This explanation of the text would seem more likely if the verb at III 68,19 had read as a pseudo passive ⲉⲩⲉⲡⲣⲟⲉⲗⲑⲉ ⲙ̄ⲙⲟⲥ, i.e., that it might be brought forth. The use of the active rather than the passive at 68,19 is awkward. A book does not come forth, but is more properly brought forth. Another awkward feature is the revelation of the holy race. This statement is not at all clear.

I suggest that a simple emendation of the text might clear up its obscurities. This is not a radical suggestion since we know that the text in the context is elsewhere corrupt, i.e., III 68,13 and 19. I suggest that the text be emended at III 68,20 as follows: ⲛ̄ϥⲟⲩⲱⲛϩ <ⲙ̄ⲙⲟⲥ> ⲛ̄ⲧⲉⲉⲓⲅⲉⲛⲉⲁ . The sense of the text as emended would be:

> The great Seth wrote this book and placed it on a mountain in order that at the end of time he might come forth and reveal <it> to the holy race.

This suggestion removes the problem of the unclear statement about revealing the holy race. If one emends at III 68,19 ⲉϥ<ⲉ>ⲡⲣⲟⲉⲗⲑⲉ to read ⲉ<ⲩⲉ>ⲡⲣⲟⲉⲗⲑⲉ, one solves the problem of the awkward active voice but is still left with the problem of the obscure statement about revealing the holy race.

[88]Frederik Wisse thinks that there is a reference in *Great Pow.* (VI,*4*)40,7-9 to the Anomoean heresy, a controversy that arose in the early part of the second half of the fourth century A.D. See Wisse, "The Nag Hammadi Library and the Heresiologists," *VC* 25 (1971) 208 n. 16.

[89]See above, pp. 66-79.

[90] J. W. Wevers, "Septuagint," *Interpreters Dictionary of the Bible* (4 vols.; ed. G. A. Buttrick et al.; Nashville: Abingdon, 1962) 4.273-78.

[91] James M. Robinson, *Introduction to the Facsimile Edition of the Nag Hammadi Codices* (Leiden: E. J. Brill, 1972) 4.

[92] Goedicke, "An Unexpected Allusion," 340-41.

[93] Beltz, 191. However, Beltz gives the date for Diocletian's edict against the Manichaeans as A.D. 282. On the date of the edict, see W. Seston, "De l'authenticité et la date de l'édit de Dioclétien contre les Manichéens," *Mélanges de philologie, de littérature et d'histoire anciennes offerts à Alfred Ernout* (Paris: Klincksieck, 1940) 345-54. For the content of the edict, see A. Adam, *Texte zum Manichäismus* (Berlin: de Gruyter, 1954) 82-84. On p. 215, Beltz gives an approximate date for the document as around the middle of the third century A.D. (on the basis of his dates, this means A.D. 250-82). I have not found evidence of Manichaean influence in the tractate, and see no other reason for dating the document on the basis of the persecution of the Manichaeans.

[94] Beltz, 203.

[95] Morard, "L'*Apocalypse d'Adam* de Nag Hammadi," 40; see also idem, "L'*Apocalypse d'Adam* du Codex V," 225.

[96] Geo Widengren, *Mani and Manichaeism* (trans. Charles Kessler; New York/Chicago/San Francisco: Holt, Rinehart and Winston, 1965) 74-94.

[97] Morard, "L'*Apocalypse d'Adam* de Nag Hammadi," 40; see also idem, "L'*Apocalypse d'Adam* du Codex V," 226-33.

[98] Epiphanius treats the Sethians and Archontics as two separate groups. Of course, by the time Epiphanius knew them (end of the fourth century A.D.), they probably were two separate and distinct groups. However, it is worth noting that the third century author of *Adversus omnes haereses*, which Epiphanius used (Johannes Quasten, *Patrology* [2 vols.; Utrecht/Antwerp: Spectrum, 1953] 2.169-70 [*The Ante-Nicene Literature after Irenaeus*]), did not know the Archontics as a separate group, nor list them in his report. Yet, Epiphanius included them in his list immediately following his discussion of the Sethians. This seems to be a subtle indication that he recognized some similarity between the two groups. See H.-Ch. Puech ("Archontiker," *Reallexikon für Antike und Christentum* [8 vols.; ed. Theodore Klauser; Stuttgart: Hiersemann, 1950-] 1. col. 635), who thinks that the gnostic group in Palestine described as Archontics is a branch of the Egyptian group described as Sethians.

[99] Epiph. *Pan.* 40.1.1-3.

[100]Morard, "L'*Apocalypse d'Adam* de Nag Hammadi*,*" 41-42;
see also idem, "L'*Apocalypse d'Adam* du Codex V," 226-33.

[101]See above, pp. 111-13 and 185-88.

[102]See above, pp. 185-87.

[103]See above, p. 113.

[104]Καὶ τὸ γένος τοῦ Σήθ ἀφορισθὲν ἐντεῦθεν κατάγεται.
See Karl Holl (ed.), *Die Griechischen Schriftsteller der ersten
drei Jahrhunderte* (3 vols.; Leipzig: J. C. Hinrichs, 1915-33)
3.73 (*Epiphanius: Ancoratus und Panarion* [1922]).

[105]See above, pp. 189-90.

[106]Perhaps this is also true of the Archontics. They seem
to recognize two forerunners to the human race: Cain and Seth,
and a qualitative difference is made between the two groups
(*Pan.* 40.5.3-5; 7.1,5).

[107]This is identical to source A (see above, pp. 82-83)
where the conflict is between the seed of Noah and the great
men, whom the redactor understands to be the seed of Seth (see
above, pp. 185-87).

[108]Morard, "L'*Apocalypse d'Adam* de Nag Hammadi," 41-42.

[109]Other of the gnostic texts to which the *Apoc. Adam* is
closely related do refer to the "Mother." See, for example:
Zost. (VIII,*1*)29,17; *Trim. Prot.* (XIII,*1**)37,22 et passim;
Treat. Seth (VII,*2*)67,3.30 et passim; *Ap. John* (II,*1*)2,14 et
passim; *Gos. Eg.* (III,*2*)41,9.18 et passim; Codex Bruce Msf.
96v, 15 et passim.

[110]See above, pp. 187-88.

[111]See above, p. 89 n. 10.

[112]See the statements of kingdoms two, five and seven.

[113]Wisse, "Nag Hammadi Library," 205-23.

[114]Ibid., 207-208. Wisse argues that the explanation for
disagreement between the reports of the heresiologists and the
Nag Hammadi texts lies precisely in the incorrect categories
created by early heresiologists to describe the various gnostic
movements. These categories were then uncritically followed by
later heresiologists (218-19).

[115]Although the Sethian groups reported by the various
heresiologists are generally recognized to have been related
(see Puech, "Archontiker," 1. col. 636), the Sethians known by
Hippolytus and Irenaeus bear little resemblance to the Sethians
of Epiphanius.

[116]F. L. Cross and E. A. Livingston (eds.), *The Oxford Dictionary of the Christian Church* (2nd ed.; London: Oxford University, 1974) 759-60. Josephus' description of the Sethians has similarity to the Archontics and the *Apoc. Adam*. Josephus says that the Sethians had "discovered the science of the heavenly bodies and their orderly array" (*Ant.* 1.69-70: trans. H.St.J. Thackery, *Josephus* [LCL; 8 vols.; London: William Heineman, 1930] 4.32-33). This corresponds to the Archontic description of the several heavens in each of which there is a ruling archon. Josephus further reports that in order that their traditions might not be lost "they erected two pillars, one of brick and the other of stone, and inscribed these discoveries on both so that if the pillar of brick disappeared in the deluge, that of stone would remain to teach men what was graven thereon...." Compare this statement to the conclusion of the *Apoc. Adam* ([85],7-18).

[117]Berthold Altaner, *Patrology* (trans. Hilda Graef from the 5th German ed.; New York: Herder and Herder, 1960) 150.

[118]Quasten, *Patrology*, 2.169-170, 272. See also Adolf Harnack, *Geschichte der altchristlichen Literatur* (2 vols.; Leipzig: J. C. Hinrichs, 1904) 2.2:430-32.

[119]Quasten, *Patrology*, 2.168.

[120]W. Bousset, "Gnosis," *Real-Encyclopädie der classischen Altertumswissenschaft* (ed. A. Pauly, G. Wissova, and W. Kroll; 24 vols.; Stuttgart: Metzler, 1893-1972) 7.2 (1912) col. 1535.

[121]Compare the accusation made by the redactor against the three baptists: "your ways are full of pleasure and merriment" ([84],14-17).

[122]See Joseph Thomas, *Le mouvement baptiste en Palestine et Syrie* (Gembloux: J. Duclot, 1935) 431-32, 151-56, 169-83.

[123]Bousset, *Hauptprobleme der Gnosis*, 319-24.

PART II

TEXT, TRANSLATION AND NOTES

SOURCE A

ⲝ̅ⲇ̅ 1

ⲦⲀⲠⲞⲔⲀⲗⲨ⳽ⲓⲤ Ⲛ̅ⲀⲆⲀⲙ

ⲦⲀⲠⲞⲔⲀⲗⲨⲠⲓⲤ ⲈⲦⲀⲆⲆⲀ[ⲙ Ⲧ]ⲀⲙⲈ ⲠⲈϤϢⲎⲢⲈ

5 Ⲥ̅Ⲏ̅Ⲑ̅ ⲈⲢⲞ⳼ Ⲍ̅Ⲛ̅|ⲦⲙⲈⲌⲮ̅ Ⲛ̅ⲢⲞⲙⲠⲈ · Ⲉ⳨ϪⲰ Ⲙ̅/ⲙⲞⲤ

ϪⲈ ⲤⲰⲦⲙ̅ ⲈⲚⲀϢⲀϪⲈ ⲠⲀ|ϢⲎⲢⲈ Ⲥ̅Ⲏ̅Ⲑ̅ · ⲞⲦⲀⲚ

Ⲛ̅ⲦⲀⲢⲈ⳨ⲦⲀ|ⲙⲒⲞⲈⲒ Ⲛ̅ϬⲒ ⲠⲚⲞ⳨ⲦⲈ ⲈⲂⲞⲗ Ⲍ̅ⲙ̅|ⲠⲔⲀⲌ

ⲙ̅Ⲛ̅ Ⲉ⳨ⲌⲀ ⲦⲈⲔⲙⲀⲀ⳨·| ⲚⲈⲒⲙⲞⲞϢⲈ Ⲛ̅ⲙⲙⲀⲤ ⲠⲈ

10 Ⲍ̅Ⲛ̅ Ⲟ⳨Ⲉ/ⲞⲞ⳨ ⲈⲦⲀⲤⲚⲀ⳨ ⲈⲢⲞ⳨· ⲈⲂⲞⲗ Ⲍ̅ⲙ̅| ⲠⲒⲈⲰⲚ

ⲈⲚⲦⲀⲚϢⲰⲠⲈ ⲈⲂⲞⲗ| Ⲛ̅Ⲍ̅ⲎⲦ̅Ϥ · ⲀⲤⲦⲀⲙⲞⲒ̈ Ⲉ⳨ϢⲀϪⲈ|

Ⲛ̅ⲦⲈ Ⲟ⳨ⲄⲚⲰⲤⲒⲤ Ⲛ̅ⲦⲈ ⲠⲚⲞ⳨ⲦⲈ| ⲠⲒϢⲀⲈⲚⲈⲌ · Ⲁ⳨Ⲱ

15 ⲚⲈⲚⲈⲒⲚⲈ/ ⲠⲈ Ⲛ̅Ⲛ̅ⲚⲞϬ Ⲛ̅ⲀⲄⲄⲈⲗⲞⲤ Ⲛ̅ϢⲀ|ⲈⲚⲈⲌ ·

ⲚⲈⲚϪⲞⲤⲈ ⲄⲀⲢ ⲠⲈ Ⲉ|ⲠⲚⲞ⳨ⲦⲈ ⲈⲦⲀ⳨ⲦⲀⲙⲒⲞⲚ ⲙ̅Ⲛ̅|

ⲚⲒϬⲞⲙ ⲈⲦⲛ̅ⲙ̅ⲙⲀ⳨ · ⲚⲎ ⲈⲦⲈ| ⲚⲈⲚⲤⲞⲞ⳨Ⲛ ⲙ̅ⲙⲞⲞ⳨ ⲀⲚ/

20 ⲦⲞⲦⲈ Ⲁ⳨ⲦⲰϢ ⲚⲀⲚ Ⲛ̅ϬⲒ ⲠⲚⲞ⳨|ⲦⲈ ⲠⲀⲢⲭⲰⲚ

Ⲛ̅ⲦⲈ ⲚⲈⲰⲚ| ⲙ̅Ⲛ̅ ⲚⲒϬⲞⲙ Ⲍ̅Ⲛ̅ Ⲟ⳨ⲂⲰⲗ̅Ⲕ · ⲦⲞ|ⲦⲈ ⲀⲚϢⲰⲠⲈ

25 ⲈⲈⲰⲚ ⲤⲚⲀ⳨·| Ⲁ⳨Ⲱ Ⲁ⳨ⲔⲀⲀⲚ Ⲛ̅ⲤⲰ̅Ϣ Ⲛ̅ϬⲒ/ ⲠⲒⲈⲞⲞ⳨ ⲈⲦⲌ̅ⲙ̅

ⲠⲈⲚⲌ̅ⲎⲦ| ⲀⲚⲞⲔ ⲙ̅Ⲛ̅ ⲦⲈⲔⲙⲀⲀ⳨ Ⲉ⳨ⲌⲀ| ⲙ̅Ⲛ̅ ϯⲄⲚⲰⲤⲒⲤ

Ⲛ̅ϢⲞⲢⲠ̅ Ⲉ|[Ⲧ]Ⲉ ⲚⲈⲤⲚⲒϤⲈ Ⲛ̅Ⲍ̅ⲎⲦⲚ̅· Ⲁ⳨[Ⲱ]| Ⲁ⳨ⲠⲰⲦ

30 ⲈⲂⲞⲗ ⲙ̅ⲙⲞⲚ/[Ⲉ]⳨ⲂⲰⲔ ⲈⲌⲞ⳨Ⲛ [ⲈⲔ]ⲈⲚⲞϬ|[ⲙ̅ⲠⲒⲈⲰ]Ⲛ

[ⲝ̅ⲉ̅] 1

ⲙ̅Ⲛ̅ Ⲕ]ⲈⲚⲞ[ϭ| Ⲛ̅ⲦⲄⲈ]ⲚⲈⲀ[·] ⲦⲎ Ⲉ]ⲦⲀⲤϢ//[Ⲣ]Ⲱ [ⲈⲂⲟ]ⲗ Ⲍ̅ⲙ̅

ⲠⲈⲒ̈ⲀⲒⲰⲚ ⲀⲚ ⲈⲦ[ⲀⲚ]ϢⲰ[Ⲡ̅Ⲧ̅Ⲉ] ⲈⲂⲞⲗ Ⲛ̅Ⲍ̅ⲎⲦϤ ⲀⲚⲞⲔ|

ⲙ̅Ⲛ̅ Ⲉ⳨ⲌⲀ ⲦⲈⲔⲙⲀⲀ⳨· ⲯ/

9 ⲙ̅Ⲛ̅Ⲛ̅ⲤⲀ ⲚⲒⲌⲞ|Ⲟ⳨ ⲈⲦⲙ̅ⲙⲀ⳨ ⲀⲤⲞ⳨Ⲉ ⲈⲂⲞⲗ|

ⲙ̅ⲙⲞⲒ̈ ⲀⲚⲞⲔ ⲙ̅Ⲛ̅ ⲦⲈⲔⲙⲀⲀ⳨| Ⲉ⳨ⲌⲀ Ⲛ̅ϬⲒ ϯⲄⲚⲰⲤⲒⲤ

Ⲛ̅ϢⲀⲈ|ⲚⲈⲌ Ⲛ̅ⲦⲈ ⲠⲚⲞ⳨ⲦⲈ Ⲛ̅ⲦⲈ ⲦⲙⲈ| ϪⲒⲚ ⲠⲞ⳨ⲞⲈⲒϢ

15 ⲈⲦⲙ̅ⲙⲀ⳨ ⲀⲚ/ϪⲒ ⲤⲂⲰ ⲈⲌⲈⲚⲌ̅ⲂⲎⲦⲈ Ⲉ⳨ⲙⲞ|Ⲟ⳨Ⲧ̅ ⲌⲰⲤ

ⲌⲈⲚⲢⲰⲙⲈ · ⲦⲞⲦⲈ| ⲀⲚⲤⲞ⳨ⲰⲚ ⲠⲚⲞ⳨ⲦⲈ

ⲈⲦⲀ⳨|ⲦⲀⲙⲒⲞⲚ · Ⲛ̅ⲚⲈⲚⲞ̅ ⲄⲀⲢ ⲀⲚ ⲠⲈ| Ⲛ̅ϣ̅ⲙⲙⲞ

20 Ⲛ̅ⲚⲈ⳨ϬⲞⲙ · Ⲁ⳨Ⲱ/ ⲀⲚϢ̅ⲙϢⲈ ⲙ̅ⲙⲞ⳨ Ⲍ̅Ⲛ̅ Ⲟ⳨ⲌⲞ|ⲦⲈ

ⲙ̅Ⲛ̅ Ⲟ⳨ⲙⲛ̅Ⲧ̅ϩ̅ⲙϩⲀⲗ ·

64,1   The Revelation (ἀποκάλυψις) of Adam |

                The revelation (ἀποκάλυψις) that Adam taught |
            his son, Seth, in | the seven hundredth year: /
    5   "Listen to my words, my | son Seth. When (ὅταν)
            God created | me from | the earth along with Eve
            your (sg.) mother, | I walked with her in glory /
    10   that she had seen in | the eon (αἰών) from which
            we had come. | She taught me a word | of knowledge
            (γνῶσις) of the eternal | God, and we resembled /
    15   the great eternal angels (ἄγγελος), | for (γάρ) we
            were greater than | the God who had created us
            and | the powers that were with him, whom | we
            did not know. /
    20   Then (τότε) God, the ruler (ἄρχων) | of the
            eons (αἰών) and the powers, | divided us in anger.
            Then (τότε) | we became two eons (αἰών) | and the
    25   glory that was in our heart / abandoned us | --me
            and your (sg.) mother Eve-- | along with the first
            knowledge (γνῶσις) that | breathed in us. And |
    30   it (i.e., glory) fled from us / entering into
            [another] great | [eon (αἰών)] and [another great] |
            generation (γενεά), that was not [cast forth //
[65],1   from] this aeon (αἰών) from which [we] | had come--
            I | and Eve your (sg.) mother. ǂ /
    9   After those | days the eternal knowledge
            (γνῶσις) | of the God of truth | withdrew far
            from | me and your (sg.) mother Eve. | Since that
    15   time we / were taught dead things | as (ὡς) men.
            Then (τότε) | we knew the God who had | created us,
            for (γάρ) we were not | estranged from his powers,
    20   and / we served him in fear | and servility.

ⲙ̅ⲛ̅|ⲛ̅ⲥⲁ ⲛⲁⲓ̈ ⲇⲉ ⲁⲛϣⲱⲡⲉ| ⲉⲛⲉ ⲛ̅ⲛⲉⲃⲏ ⳓ̅ⲙ̅

[ⲝ̅ⲋ̅] 12 ⲡⲉⲛϩⲏⲧ·|‡// ⲧⲟⲧⲉ ⲁⲛϥⲓ ⲁ|ⳓⲟⲙ ⲁⲛⲟⲕ ⲙ̅ⲛ̅ ⲉⲩⳓⲁ

15 ⳓⲣⲁⲓ̈ ⳓ̅ⲙ̅| ⲡⲉⲛϩⲏⲧ· ⲁⲣⲱ ⲁⲡ ⲭⲟⲉⲓⲥ ⲡⲛⲟⲩ/ⲧⲉ

ⲉⲧⲁⲩⲧⲁⲙⲓⲟⲛ ⲁⲩⲁⳓⲉⲣⲁⲧ̄ϥ| ⲙ̅ⲡⲉⲛⲙ̅ⲧⲟ ⲉⲃⲟⲗ·

ⲡⲉⲭⲁϥ ⲛⲁⲛ| ⲭⲉ ⲁⲇⲁⲙ̅ ⲉⲧⲃⲉ ⲟⲩ ⲛⲉⲧⲉⲧⲛ̅|ϥⲓ

ⲁⳓⲟⲙ ⳓ̅ⲙ̅ ⲡⲉⲧⲛ̅ϩⲏⲧ· ϣⲓⲉ| ⲛ̅ⲧⲉⲧⲛ̅ⲥⲟⲟⲩⲛ ⲁⲛ ⲭⲉ

20 ⲁⲛⲟⲕ/ ⲡⲉ ⲡⲛⲟⲩⲧⲉ ⲉⲧⲁⲩⲧⲁⲙⲓⲉ| ⲧⲏⲩⲧⲛ̅· ⲁⲣⲱ

ⲁⲓ̈ⲛⲓϥⲉ ⲉⳓⲟⲩⲛ| ⲉⲣⲱⲧⲛ̅ ⲛ̅ⲟⲩⲡ̅ⲛ̅ⲁ ⲛ̅ⲧⲉ ⲡⲱⲛ̅ϩ|

ⲉⳓⲣⲁⲓ̈ ⲉⲩⲯⲩⲭⲏ ⲉⲥⲟⲛ̅ϩ· ⲧⲟ|ⲧⲉ ⲁⲩⲕⲁⲕⲉ

25 ϣⲱⲡⲉ ⳓⲓ ⲭ̅ⲛ̅ ⲛⲉⲛ/ⲃⲁⲗ

ⲧⲟⲧⲉ ⲁⲡⲛⲟⲩⲧⲉ ⲉⲧⲁⲩ|[ⲧ]ⲁⲙⲓⲟⲛ ⲁⲩⲧⲁⲙⲓⲟ

ⲛ̅ⲛⲟⲩ|ϣⲏⲣⲉ ⲉⲃⲟⲗ ⲛ̅ϩⲏⲧ̅ϥ ⲙ̅ⲛ̅ ⲉ[ⲧ]ⳓⲁ ⲧⲉ[ⲕ]ⲙⲁ[ⲁ]ⲩ

30 ⲉⲡⲉ[ⲓ̈]ⲃⲁ[ⲕⲉ][..]ⲕⲥ ⲁⲛ [ ]/[..]ⲉⲕⲉ.[..]. [ⲉⲃⲟ]ⲗ

[ⲝ̅ⲍ̅] 1 ⳓ̅ⲙ̅ ⲡⲉ[ⲧⲟⲧⲉ ⲁⲓ̈]//ⲧ[ⲱⲁⲙ ⳓ̅ⲙ̅] ⲡ̅ⲙⲉⲉⲩⲉ [ⲛ̅ⲧ]ⲉ|

ⲡⲁϣ[ⲉⲉ]ⲓ· ⲁⲓ̈ⲥⲟⲩⲱⲛ| ⲟⲩⲉⲡⲓⲑⲩⲙⲓⲁ ⲉⲥⳓⲟⲗ̅ϭ| ⲛ̅ⲧⲉ

5 ⲧⲉⲕⲙⲁⲁⲩ· ⲧⲟ|ⲧⲉ ⲁⲥⲧⲁⲕⲟ ⲉⲃⲟⲗ ⲛ̅ϩⲏ|ⲧⲛ̅ ⲛ̅ϭⲓ

ⲧⲁⲕⲙⲏ ⲛ̅ⲧⲉ| ⲡⲉⲛⲥⲟⲟⲩⲛ ⲛ̅ϣⲁⲉ|ⲛⲉϩ· ⲁⲩⲱ

10 ⲁⲩⲣ̅ⲇⲓⲱⲕⲉ| ⲛ̅ⲥⲱⲛ ⲛ̅ϭⲓ ⲟⲩⲙ̅ⲛ̅ⲧϭⲱⲃ/ ⲉⲧⲃⲉ ⲡⲁⲓ̈

ⲁⲩⲣ̅ ⲕⲟⲩⲉⲓ| ⲛ̅ϭⲓ ⲛⲉϩⲟⲟⲩ ⲛ̅ⲧⲉ ⲡⲉⲛ|ⲱⲛ̅ϩ· ‡/

22 ⲙ̅ⲛ̅ⲛ̅ⲥⲁ ⲧⲣⲁ ⲭⲱⲕ| ⲉⲃⲟⲗ ⲛ̅ⲛⲓⲟⲩⲟⲉⲓϣ| ⲛ̅ⲧⲉ

25 ⲧⲉⲓ̈ⲅⲉⲛⲉⲁ·/ ⲁⲩⲱ ⲛ̅ⲥⲉⲙⲟⲩⲛ̅ⲅ̅|[ⲛ̅ϭⲓ ⲛ̅]ⲣⲟⲙⲡⲉ

ⲛ̅ⲧⲉ|[ϯⲅⲉⲛⲉ]ⲁ· [ⲧⲟ]ⲧⲉ| [ⲛⲱⲣⲉ] ⲟ[ⲣⲉⲧ]ⳓ̅ⲁⲗ|

[ⲝ̅ⲑ̅] 1 [ⲙ̅ⲡⲛⲟⲩⲧⲉ ⲉ]ⲧⲁ[ ]**// ⲥⲉⲛⲁ[ⲟ]ⲩⲟⲧⲛⲟ[ⲩ

ⲉⲃⲟⲗ]| ⲅⲁⲣ ⲛ̅[ϭ]ⲓ ϩⲉⲛⲙⲟⲩ[ⲓ̈ⲉⲣⲉ]| ⲛ̅ϩⲱⲟⲩ ⲛ̅ⲧⲉ

5 ⲡ[ⲛⲟⲩⲧ]ⲉ ⲡ̅|ⲡⲁⲛⲧⲟⲕⲣⲁ[ⲧⲱⲣ· ⲭⲉ] ⲉϥⲉ/ⲧⲁⲕⲟ

8 ⲛ̅ⲥⲁⲣⲁⳓ [ⲛⲓⲙ]{ϩ}/ⲉⲃⲟⲗ[ ]ⲡⲕⲁϩ|<...> ⲉⲃⲟⲗ

ⳓ̅ⲧⲛ̅ ⲛⲏ [ⲉ]ⲧⲉⲩⲕⲱ|ⲧⲉ ⲛ̅ⲥⲱⲟⲩ· ‡/

18 ⲙ̅ⲛ̅ⲛ̅ⲥⲁ ⲛⲁⲓ̈ ⲥⲉⲛ̅ⲛⲏⲟⲩ ⲛ̅|ϭⲓ ϩⲉⲛⲛⲟϭ ⲛ̅ⲁⲅⲅⲉⲗⲟⲥ/

20 ⳓⲛ̅ ϩⲉⲛⲕⲗⲟⲟⳓⲉ ⲉⲩⲭⲟⲥⲉ| ⲉⲩⲛⲁⲭⲓ ⲛ̅ⲛⲓⲣⲱⲙⲉ

ⲉⲧⲙ̅|ⲙⲁⲩ ⲉⳓⲟⲩⲛ ⲉⲡⲧⲟⲡⲟⲥ ⲉⲧⲉϥϣⲟⲟⲡ

ⲛ̅ϩⲏⲧ[ϥ] ⲛ̅ϭⲓ ⲡⲉⲡ̅ⲛ̅ⲁ|ⲛ̅ⲧⲉ] ⲡⲱⲛ̅ϩ ⲛ̅[..]| * *

[ⲟ̅] 1 * * *//[ⲥⲉⲛⲁϯ ⲡⲉⲩϩ]ⲏⲧ ⲉ[ⲡ]ⲛ̅[ⲟϭ] ⲛ̅ⲉⲟ|[ⲟⲩ

ⲛ̅]ⲧⲉ [ⲡⲙ̅ⲧⲟ]ⲛ ⲉⲧⲙ̅ⲙⲁⲩ·|

And (δέ) | after these (things) we became |
[66],12   darkened in our heart. | ‡ // Then (τότε) we
sighed, | I and Eve in | our heart. And the Lord,
15   the God / who created us, stood | before us. He
said to us, | 'Adam, why were you (pl.) | sighing
in your (pl.) heart? | Do you (pl.) not know that
20   I / am the God who created | you (pl.) and breathed
into | you (pl.) a breath (πνεῦμα) of life | as a
living soul (ψυχή)?' Then (τότε) | darkness came
upon our eyes. /
25   Then (τότε) the God who | created us created
a | son from himself and Eve | your mother.
30   Because of [this conception] | */* from the [
[67],1   Then (τότε) I // was defiled in] thought [through] |
my [madness and] I knew | a sweet desire (ἐπιθυμία) |
5   for your (sg.) mother. Then (τότε) / the vigor
(ἀκμή) of | our eternal knowledge | perished in us |
10   and weakness | pursued (διώκειν) us. / Therefore
the days of | our life were | few. ‡ /
22   After I completed | the times | of this
25   generation (γενεά) / and [the] years of | [this
generation (γενεά)] | were brought to an end,
[then (τότε) | Noah], a servant | [of God   ] |
[69],1   ** // For (γάρ) rain-showers | shall pour forth |
from [God], the | Almighty (παντοκράτωρ), [in
5   order that] he might / destroy [all] flesh (σάρξ)
8   { } / [   ] the earth | <...> by those (things)
that they seek after. ‡ /
18   After these (events) great angels (ἄγγελος) |
20   shall come / on high clouds. | They will take
those men | into the place (τόπος) where | the
spirit (πνεῦμα) [of] life | dwells [   ] |
[70],1   ***** // [They will understand the great] glory |
of that [rest]. |

[ⲧⲟ]ⲧⲉ [ⲥⲉⲛⲁϣ]ⲱⲡⲉ ϫⲓⲛ ⲧⲡⲉ| ϣⲁ ⲡⲕ[ⲁϩ

5 ⲁⲩⲱ ⲉ]ⲩⲛⲁϣⲱⲝⲡ̄/ ⲛ̄ϭⲓ ⲡⲙ[ⲏⲏϣⲉ ⲧ]ⲏⲣ̄ϥ ⲛ̄ⲧⲉ
ⲧⲥⲁ|ⲣⲁⲝ ϩⲓ̄ ⲛ[ⲓⲙⲟⲟⲩ·] ⲧⲟⲧⲉ ⲡⲛⲟⲩ|ⲧⲉ
ⲛⲁⲙ̄[ⲧ]ⲟⲛ ⲙ̅ⲙⲟⲩ ⲉⲃⲟⲗ ⲙ̄|ⲡⲉⲩϭⲱ[ⲛ̄]ⲧ· [ⲁ]ⲣⲱ
ⲩⲛⲉⲛⲟⲩ|ⲭⲉ ⲛ̄ⲧⲉⲩ[ϭ]ⲟⲙ ⲉⲭⲛ̄ ⲛⲓⲙⲟⲟⲩ·/

10 ⲁⲩ̄ [ⲩⲛⲁ]†[ϭ]ⲟⲙ ⲛ̄ⲛⲉⲩϣⲏⲣⲉ| ⲙ̄ⲛ̄
ⲛⲉ[ⲣϩⲓ̄]ⲟ[ⲱ]ⲉ ⲉⲃⲟⲗ ϩⲛ̄ †ⲕⲓ|ⲃⲱⲧⲟⲥ· ⲙⲛ̄
[ⲛ̄]ⲧ̄ⲃ̄ⲛⲟⲟⲩⲉ ⲉ|ⲧⲁⲩ†ⲙⲉⲧⲉ ⲉϫⲱⲟⲩ· ⲙ̄ⲛ̄

15 ⲛ̄ϩⲁⲗⲁⲧⲉ ⲛ̄ⲧ[ⲉ] ⲧⲡⲉ ⲉⲧⲁⲩⲙⲟⲩ/ⲧⲉ ⲉⲣⲟⲟⲩ·
ⲁⲩⲕⲁⲁⲩ ϩⲓ|ⲭ̄ⲙ̄ ⲡⲕⲁ[ϩ·] ⲁⲣⲱ ⲡⲛⲟⲩ|ⲧⲉ
ⲛⲁⲭⲟⲟⲥ ⲛ̄ⲛⲱϩⲉ· ⲡⲏ ⲉ|ⲧⲉ ⲛⲓⲅⲉⲛⲉⲁ
ⲛⲁⲙⲟⲩⲧⲉ ⲉⲣⲟⲩ| ϫⲉ ⲇⲉⲩⲕ[ⲁ]ⲗⲓⲱⲛ· ϫⲉ ⲉⲓⲥ

20 ϩⲏ/ⲏⲧⲉ ⲁ̈ⲁⲣⲉϩ ⲉⲣⲟ<ⲕ> ϩⲛ̄ †ⲕⲓⲃⲱⲧⲟⲥ|
ⲙ̄ⲛ̄ ⲧⲉⲕⲥϩⲓ̄ⲙⲉ ⲙ̄ⲛ̄ ⲛⲉⲕϣⲏ|ⲣⲉ ⲙ̄ⲛ̄
ⲛⲉⲩϩⲓⲟⲙⲉ· ⲙ̄ⲛ̄ ⲛⲉⲩ|[ⲧ̄ⲃ̄]ⲛⲟⲟⲩⲉ ⲙ̄ⲛ̄
ⲛ̄ϩⲁⲗⲁⲧⲉ [ⲛ̄]ⲧ[ⲉ] ⲧⲡⲉ ⲛ̄ⲏ ⲉⲧⲁⲕⲙⲟⲩ[ⲧⲉ

25 ⲉⲣⲟ/ⲟⲩ ⲁⲕⲕⲁ]ⲁ[ⲩ] ϩⲓ̄[ⲭ̄ⲙ̄ ⲡⲕⲁϩ]| ✱✱✱✱//
[ⲟ̄ⲁ̄] 1 ⲉⲧⲃⲉ [ⲡ]ⲁ̈ⲓ †ⲛⲁ† ⲙ̄ⲡⲕ[ⲁϩ ⲛ]ⲁⲕ| ⲛ̄ⲧⲟⲕ ⲙ̄ⲛ̄
ⲛⲉⲕϣⲏⲣⲉ [ϩ]ⲛ̄ ⲟⲩ|ⲙ̄ⲛ̄ⲧ̄ⲣ̄ⲣⲟ ⲕⲛⲁⲣ̄ ⲣ̄ⲣⲟ
ⲉϫⲱϥ ⲛ̄ⲧⲟⲕ| ⲙ̄ⲛ̄ ⲛⲉⲕϣⲏⲣⲉ· ⸙/

8   ⲧⲟⲧⲉ ⲥⲉⲛⲁϣⲱ|ⲡⲉ ⲛ̄ⲑⲉ ⲛ̄†ⲕⲗⲟⲟⲗⲉ
10 ⲛ̄ⲧⲉ ⲡⲓ/ⲛⲟϭ ⲛ̄ⲟⲩⲟⲉⲓⲛ· ⲥⲉⲛ̄ⲛⲏⲩ ⲛ̄ϭⲓ|
ⲛ̄ⲣⲱⲙⲉ ⲉⲧⲙ̄ⲙⲁⲩ· ⲛⲏ ⲉⲧⲁⲩ|ⲛⲟⲭⲟⲩ ⲉⲃⲟⲗ ϩⲛ̄
†ⲅⲛⲱⲥⲓⲥ ⲛ̄|ⲧⲉ ⲛⲓⲛⲟϭ ⲛ̄ⲛⲉⲱⲛ ⲙ̄ⲛ̄

15 ⲛⲓⲁⲅ|ⲅⲉⲗⲟⲥ ⲥⲉⲛⲁⲁϩⲉⲣⲁⲧⲟⲩ ⲙ̄/ⲡⲉⲙⲧⲟ
ⲛ̄ⲛⲱϩⲉ ⲙ̄ⲛ̄ ⲛⲓⲉⲱⲛ·| ⲁⲩⲱ ⲡⲛⲟⲩⲧⲉ
ⲛⲁⲭⲟⲟⲥ ⲛ̄|ⲛⲱϩⲉ ϫⲉ ⲉⲧⲃⲉ ⲟⲩ ⲁⲕ̄ⲣ̄ ⲥⲁⲃⲟⲗ|
ⲛ̄ⲡⲉⲛⲧⲁ̈ⲓϫⲟⲟⲩ ⲛⲁⲕ ⲁⲕ|ⲧⲁⲙⲓⲟ ⲛ̄ⲅⲉⲛⲉⲁ

20 ϫⲉ ⲉⲕⲉ/† ⲥⲱϣ ⲛ̄ⲧⲁϭⲟⲙ ⲧⲟⲧⲉ ⲩⲛⲁ|ⲭⲟⲟⲥ
ⲛ̄ϭⲓ ⲛⲱϩⲉ ϫⲉ †ⲛⲁ|ⲣ̄ ⲙ̄ⲛ̄ⲧⲣⲉ ⲙ̄ⲡⲉⲙⲧⲟ
ⲙ̄ⲡⲉⲕ|ϫⲛⲁϩ· ϫⲉ ⲛ̄ⲧⲁⲧⲅⲉⲛⲉⲁ ⲛ̄ⲧ̣ⲉ̣ ⲛⲓⲣⲱⲙⲉ

25 ϣⲱⲡⲉ ⲉⲃⲟⲗ/ [ϩⲓⲧⲟⲟ]ⲧ̄ ⲁⲛ· ⲟⲩⲧⲉ ⲉⲃ[ⲟⲗ|
ϩⲙ̄ ⲡⲁ]ϣ[ⲏⲣ]ⲉ [ⲁ]ⲛ· [ⲁⲗⲗⲁ| ⲁⲥⲱ]ⲡ[ⲉ ⲉⲃⲟⲗ
[ⲟ̄ⲃ̄] 1 ϩ]ⲛ̣[   ]|✱ ✱ ✱// [ⲛ̄]ⲧⲉ †ⲅⲛⲱⲥⲓⲥ·

Then (τότε) [they will] come from the heaven |
to the [earth, and] the entire [multitude] of flesh

5   (σάρξ) / will be left behind | in the [waters].
Then (τότε) God | will rest from | his wrath. And

10   he will cast | his power upon the waters, / and
[will] strengthen his sons | and [their wives] by
means of the ark (κιβωτός), | [along with the]
animals, that | pleased him, and the | birds of

15   heaven, that he called / and released upon | the
earth. And God | will say to Noah--whom | the
generations (γενεά) will call, | Deucalion

20   (Δευχαλιῶν)--'Behold, / I have kept <you> (sg.)
safe in the ark (κιβωτός) | along with your (sg.)
wife, and your (sg.) sons | and their wives, and
their | animals and the birds [of | heaven], that

25   you (sg.) called / [and released upon the earth] |

[71],1   **** // Therefore, I shall give the [earth to]
you (sg.) | and your sons. In | regal fashion
will you (sg.) reign over it, you (sg.) | and
your (sg.) sons.' ‡ /

8   Then (τότε) they will become | as the cloud

10   of the / great light. Those men | will come--
those who were | cast forth from the knowledge
(γνῶσις) of | the great eons (αἰών) and the
angels (ἄγγελος). | They will stand before /

15   Noah and the eons (αἰών). | And God will say to |
Noah, 'Why have you departed from | what I told
you (sg.)? You (sg.) have | created another
generation (γενεά) so that you (sg.) might /

20   scorn my power.' Then (τότε) Noah will | say,
'I shall | testify before your (sg.) | might that
the generation (γενεά) of | those men has not come

25   from / me, nor (οὔτε) [from | my sons, but (ἀλλά) |

[72],1   it came from *** // of] knowledge (γνῶσις).

[ⲁ]ⲣⲱ ⲩ̣ⲛⲁ|[ⲕ]ⲱ [ⲉⲃⲟ]ⲗ ⲛ̄ⲛⲣⲱⲙⲉ
ⲉⲧⲙ̄ⲙⲁⲩ|[ⲛ̄]ⲧⲩ̣ⲛ̄ⲧⲟⲩ ⲉⲍⲟⲩⲛ ⲉⲡⲉⲩⲕⲁⲍ|
5 ⲉⲧⲙ̄ⲡⲩϣⲁ ⲛ̄ⲩⲕⲱⲧ ⲛⲁⲩ ⲛ̄ⲛⲟⲩ/ⲙⲁⲛ̄ϣⲱⲡⲉ
ⲉⲩⲟⲩⲁⲁⲃ· ⲁⲩⲱ| ⲥⲉⲛⲁⲙⲟⲩⲧⲉ ⲉⲣⲟⲟⲩ ⲍⲙ̄
ⲡⲓⲣⲁⲛ̣| ⲉⲧⲙ̄ⲙⲁⲩ ⲛ̄ⲥⲉϣⲱⲡⲉ ⲙ̄ⲙⲁⲩ|
ⲛ̄ⲥⲟⲟⲩ ⲛ̄ϣⲉ ⲛ̄ⲣⲟⲙⲡⲉ ⲍ̄ⲛ ⲟⲩ|ⲥⲟⲟⲩⲛ ⲛ̄ⲧⲉ
ⲧⲁⲫⲑⲁⲣⲥⲓⲁ·/ ⲁⲩⲱ ⲥⲉⲛⲁϣⲱⲡⲉ ⲛ̄ⲙ̄ⲙⲁⲩ
10 ⲛ̄ϭⲓ| ⲍⲉⲛⲁⲅⲅⲉⲗⲟⲥ ⲛ̄ⲧⲉ ⲡⲓⲛⲟϭ ⲛ̄ⲟⲩⲟ̣|ⲉⲓⲛ·
ⲛ̄ⲛⲉⲗⲁⲁⲩ ⲛ̄ⲍⲱⲃ ⲛ̄ⲃⲟⲧⲉ| ϣⲱⲡⲉ ⲍⲙ̄
ⲡⲉⲩⲍⲏⲧ· ⲉⲃⲟⲗ| ⲉⲧⲅⲛⲱⲥⲓⲥ ⲟⲩⲁⲁⲥ ⲛ̄ⲧⲉ
15 ⲡⲛⲟⲩ/ⲧⲉ·

        ⲧⲟⲧⲉ ⲛⲱⲍⲉ ⲛⲁⲡⲉⲩ ⲡⲕⲁⲍ|ⲧⲏⲣϥ̄
ⲉⲍⲣⲁⲩ ⲛ̄ⲛⲉⲩϣⲏⲣⲉ·| ⲭⲁⲙ· ⲙⲛ̄ ⲓ̈ⲁⲫⲉⲑ· ⲙⲛ̄
ⲥⲏⲙ·| ⲩⲛⲁⲭⲟⲟⲥ ⲛⲁⲩ ⲭⲉ ⲛⲁϣⲏⲣⲉ| ⲥⲱⲧⲙ̄
ⲉⲛⲁϣⲁⲭⲉ· ⲉⲓⲥ ⲡⲓⲕⲁⲍ/ ⲁ̇ⲓ̇ⲡⲟⲩ̣ϣ̣ϥ̄ ⲉⲝⲛ̄
20 ⲑⲏⲩⲧⲛ̄· ⲁⲗⲗⲁ| ϣ̣ⲙ̄ⲩϣ<ⲏ>ⲧϥ̄ ⲍⲛ̄ ⲟⲩⲍⲱⲧⲉ ⲙⲛ̄|
ⲟⲩⲙⲛ̄ⲧⲥ̄ⲙⲍⲁⲗ ⲛ̄ⲛ̄ⲍⲟⲟⲩ ⲧⲏⲣⲟⲩ ⲛ̄ⲧⲉ ⲡⲉⲧⲛ̄ⲱⲛ̄ⲍ·
ⲙ̄ⲡⲣ̄ⲧⲣⲉ|[ⲡ̄]ⲉⲧⲛ̄ⲥⲡⲉⲣⲙⲁ ⲣ̄ ⲥⲁⲃⲟⲗ ⲙ̄ⲡⲍⲟ/
[ⲙ̄ⲡ]ⲛ̄[ⲟ]ⲩⲧⲉ ⲡ̄ⲡⲁⲛⲧⲟⲕ[ⲣⲁⲧⲱⲣ|]ⲁⲛⲟⲕ ⲙⲛ̄
25 ⲡ[ⲉ]ⲧ̄ⲛ̄[ ]ⲙ̣[   ]ⲙ̄ⲛ̄[   ]✳✳|[ⲧⲟⲧⲉ

[ⲟ̄ⲓ̄] 1 ⲩⲛⲁⲭⲟⲟⲥ // ⲛ̄ϭⲓ ⲥⲏⲙ ⲡ̄]ϣⲏⲣⲉ ⲛ̄ⲛⲱ[ⲍ]ⲉ ⲭⲉ
[ⲡⲁ]|ϭⲣⲟϭ ⲛ[ⲁ]ϩ̄ ⲁⲛⲁⲩ ⲙ̄ⲡⲉⲕⲙ̄ⲧⲟ ⲉⲃ[ⲟⲗ·]|
ⲁⲩⲱ ⲙ̄ⲡⲉⲙ̄ⲧⲟ ⲛ̄ⲧⲉⲕϭⲟⲙ·| ⲁⲣⲓⲥⲫⲣⲁⲅⲓⲍⲉ
5 ⲙ̄ⲙⲟⲩ ⲍⲛ̄ ⲧⲉⲕ/ϭⲓⲭ ⲉⲧⲭⲟⲟⲣ ⲍⲛ̄ ⲟⲩⲍⲟⲧⲉ ⲙⲛ̄|
<ⲟⲩ>ⲟⲩⲁⲍ ⲥⲁⲍⲛⲉ· ⲭⲉ ⲡⲓϭⲣⲟϭ ⲧⲏ|ⲣϥ̄
ⲉⲧⲁⲩⲉⲓ̄ ⲉⲃⲟⲗ ⲛ̄ⲍⲏⲧ ⲛ̄ⲥⲉ|ⲛⲁⲣⲁⲕⲧⲟⲩ ⲛ̄ⲥⲁⲃⲟⲗ
10 ⲙ̄ⲙⲟⲕ| ⲁⲛ ⲙⲛ̄ ⲡⲛⲟⲩⲧⲉ ⲡⲓⲡⲁⲛⲧⲟ/ⲕⲣⲁⲧⲱⲣ·
ⲁⲗⲗⲁ ⲥⲉⲛⲁϣ̄ⲙ̄|ϣⲉ ⲍⲛ̄ ⲟⲩⲑⲃ̄ⲃⲓⲟ {ⲭⲟⲩ} ⲙⲛ̄|
ⲟⲩⲍⲟⲧⲉ ⲛ̄ⲧⲉ ⲡⲉⲩⲉⲓⲙⲉ·|

        ⲧⲟⲧⲉ ⲉⲣⲉⲍⲉⲛⲕⲟⲟⲩⲉ <ⲉⲓ> ⲉⲃⲟⲗ| ⲍⲙ̄
15 ⲡⲥⲡⲉⲣⲙⲁ ⲛ̄ⲧⲉ ⲭⲁⲙ ⲙⲛ̄/ⲓ̈ⲁ̣ⲫⲉⲑ· ⲉⲩⲉⲃⲱⲕ
ⲛ̄ϭⲓ ⲩⲧⲟⲟⲩ ⲛ̄ϣⲉ| ⲛ̄ⲩⲟ ⲛ̄ⲣⲱⲙⲉ· ⲛ̄ⲥⲉⲃⲱⲕ
ⲉ|ⲍⲟⲩⲛ ⲉⲕⲉⲕⲁⲍ ⲛ̄ⲥⲉϭⲟⲉⲓⲗⲉ| ⲉⲛⲣⲱⲙⲉ
ⲉⲧⲙ̄ⲙⲁⲩ· ⲛⲏ ⲉ|ⲧⲁⲩϣⲱⲡⲉ ⲉⲃⲟⲗ ⲍⲛ̄ ⲧⲛⲟϭ/
20 ⲛ̄ⲅⲛⲱⲥⲓⲥ ⲛ̄ϣⲁⲉⲛⲉⲍ· ⲭⲉ|ⲑⲁⲉⲓⲃⲉⲥ ⲛ̄ⲧⲉ
ⲧⲉⲩϭⲟⲙ ⲛⲁ|ⲁⲣⲉⲍ ⲉⲛⲉⲛⲧⲁⲩϭⲟⲉⲓⲗⲉ| ⲉⲣⲟⲟⲩ ⲉⲃⲟⲗ
ⲛ̄ⲍⲱⲃ ⲛⲓⲙ ⲉⲑⲟⲟⲩ| ⲙⲛ̄ ⲉⲡⲓⲑⲩⲙⲓⲁ ⲛⲓⲙ
ⲉⲧⲥⲟⲟⲩ·/

[And he] will | [release] those men, | [and]
bring them into their land, | (a land) that is
worthy (of them). And he will build for them a /
5   holy dwelling-place. And | they will be called by
that name | and dwell there | six hundred years
in a | knowledge of imperishability (ἀφθαρσία). /
10 And angels (ἄγγελος) of the great light | will
dwell with them. | Nothing loathsome shall |
dwell in their heart, but | only the knowledge
(γνῶσις) of God (will dwell therein). /
15   Then (τότε) Noah will divide the whole | earth
among his sons, | Ham and Japheth and Shem. | He
will say to them, 'My sons, | heed my words.
20 Behold, / I have divided the earth among you (pl.)
but (ἀλλά) | serve him (i.e., the creator) in fear
and | servility all the days | of your (pl.) life.
Do not let | your seed (σπέρμα) depart from the
25 face / [of] God, the Almighty (παντοκράτωρ), |
[   ] I and your (pl.) [|] and [   ] **
[73],1 [Then (τότε) Shem, // the] son of Noah [will
say, 'My] | seed [will be] pleasing before you
(sg.) | and before your (sg.) power. | Seal
5   (σφραγίζειν) it by your (sg.) / strong hand with
(godly) fear and | <a> mandate so that all the
seed | which has come from me may | not be inclined
away from you (sg.) | and God, the Almighty
10 (παντοκράτωρ), / but (ἀλλά) will serve | in
humility and | reverence for their knowledge.' |
Then (τότε) others will <come> forth | from
15 the seed (σπέρμα) of Ham and / Japheth. Four
hundred | thousand men will depart, and enter |
into another land and sojourn | with those men,
20 who | have come from the great / eternal knowledge
(γνῶσις), since | the shadow of their power will |
protect those who have sojourned | with them from
every evil thing | and every unclean desire
(ἐπιθυμία). /

25   ⲦⲞⲦⲈ ⲠⲤⲠⲈⲢⲘⲀ Ⲛ̄ⲬⲀⲘ ⲘⲚ̄|[ⲓ̈ⲁ]ⲫⲈⲐ ⲚⲀⲢ̄
ⲘⲚ̄ⲦⲤⲚⲞⲞⲨ[Ⲥ]| Ⲙ̄ⲘⲚ̄Ⲧ̄Ⲣ̄ⲢⲞ · ⲀⲨⲰ Ⲡ[Ⲉ]Ⲩ[ⲔⲈ|Ⲥ]ⲠⲈⲢⲘⲀ
30   ⲚⲀⲂⲰⲔ ⲈⲍⲞⲨ[Ⲛ]| ⲈⲦⲘ̄Ⲛ̄Ⲧ̄Ⲣ̄Ⲣ[Ⲟ] Ⲛ̄ⲔⲈⲖⲀⲞⲤ [·]/[ⲦⲞⲦ]Ⲉ
ⲤⲈⲚ[Ⲁ]ⲰⲞⲬⲚⲈ Ⲛ̄ϬⲒ [Ⲛ̄ⲀⲢ|Ⲭ]Ⲱ[Ⲛ] Ⲛ̄ⲦⲈ [Ⲛ̄]ⲈⲰⲚ ·
[ⲞⲆ] 1   ⲌⲀ ⲚⲈ[ⲦⲀⲔⲀ// ⲠⲈⲒ]ⲘⲈ ⲈⲦⲘⲞⲞⲨⲦ̄ [Ⲉ]Ⲧ[Ⲛ̄] Ⲛ̄ⲚⲞϬⲒ
[Ⲛ̄]ⲚⲈⲰⲚ Ⲛ̄ⲦⲈ ⲦⲀⲪⲐⲀⲢⲤⲒⲀ·|[Ⲁ]Ⲣⲱ ⲤⲈⲚⲀⲂⲰⲔ
ⲌⲀ Ⲥ̄ⲀⲔⲖⲀ| ⲠⲈⲨⲚⲞⲨⲦⲈ · ⲤⲈⲚⲀⲂⲰⲔ ⲈⲌⲞⲨⲚ/
5   ⲈⲚⲒϬⲞⲘ ⲈⲨⲢ̄ⲔⲀⲦⲎⲄⲞⲢⲒ Ⲛ̄ⲚⲒⲚⲞϬⲒ| Ⲛ̄ⲢⲰⲘⲈ ⲚⲎ
ⲈⲦⲰⲞⲞⲠ Ⲍ̄Ⲙ ⲠⲈⲨⲈ|ⲞⲞⲨ· ⲤⲈⲚⲀⲬⲞⲞⲤ Ⲛ̄Ⲥ̄ⲀⲔⲖⲀ
ⲬⲈ|ⲞⲨ ⲦⲈ ⲦϬⲞⲘ Ⲛ̄ⲚⲈⲒ̈ⲢⲰⲘⲈ ⲈⲦⲀⲨ|ⲀⲌⲈⲢⲀⲦⲞⲨ
10   Ⲙ̄ⲠⲈⲔⲘ̄ⲦⲞ ⲈⲂⲞⲖ/ ⲚⲀⲒ̈ ⲈⲦⲀⲨϤⲒⲦⲞⲨ ⲈⲂⲞⲖ Ⲍ̄Ⲙ
ⲠⲒ|ⲤⲠⲈⲢⲘⲀ Ⲛ̄ⲦⲈ ⲬⲀⲘ ⲘⲚ̄ ⲒⲀⲪⲈⲐ| ⲈⲨⲚⲀⲢ̄
ϤⲦⲞⲞⲨ Ⲛ̄ⲰⲈ <Ⲛ̄ⲰⲞ> Ⲛ̄ⲢⲰⲘⲈ| ⲀⲨϪⲒⲦⲞⲨ ⲈⲌⲞⲨⲚ
ⲈⲔⲈⲈⲰⲚ ⲠⲎ| ⲈⲦⲀⲨϢⲰⲠⲈ ⲈⲂⲞⲖ Ⲛ̄ⲌⲎⲦϤ̄ ⲀⲢⲰ/
15   ⲀⲨⲔⲦⲞ Ⲙ̄ⲠⲈⲞⲞⲨ ⲦⲎⲢϤ̄ Ⲛ̄ⲦⲈ ⲦⲈⲔ|ϬⲞⲘ Ⲙ̄Ⲛ̄
ⲦⲘ̄Ⲛ̄Ⲧ̄Ⲣ̄ⲢⲞ Ⲛ̄ⲦⲈ ⲦⲈⲔϬⲒⲬ| ⲬⲈ ⲀⲠⲈⲤⲠⲈⲢⲘⲀ Ⲛ̄ⲦⲈ
ⲚⲰⲌⲈ ⲈⲂⲞⲖ| Ⲍ̄Ⲙ ⲠⲈϤϢⲎⲢⲈ ⲀⲨⲈⲒⲢⲈ Ⲙ̄ⲠⲈⲔⲞⲨ|ⲰϢ
20   ⲦⲎⲢϤ̄ Ⲙ̄Ⲛ̄ ⲚⲒϬⲞⲘ ⲦⲎⲢⲞⲨ/ Ⲍ̄Ⲛ ⲚⲒⲈⲰⲚ
ⲈⲦⲀⲠⲈⲔⲀⲘⲀⲌⲦⲈ| Ⲣ̄ Ⲣ̄ⲢⲞ ⲈⲌⲢⲀⲒ̈ ⲈⲬⲰⲞⲨ· Ⲙ̄Ⲛ̄
ⲚⲒⲢⲰ|ⲘⲈ ⲈⲦⲘ̄ⲘⲀⲨ· Ⲙ̄Ⲛ̄ ⲚⲎ ⲈⲦⲈ Ⲛ̄|Ⲡ̄Ⲣ̄Ⲛ̄ϬⲀⲈⲒⲖⲈ Ⲍ̄Ⲙ
25   ⲠⲈⲨⲈⲞⲞⲨ·| [Ⲉ]Ⲙ̄ⲠⲞⲨⲈⲒⲢⲈ Ⲙ̄ⲠⲈⲦⲈⲌⲚⲀⲔ·/[ⲀⲖⲖ]Ⲁ
ⲀⲨⲠⲰⲰⲚⲈ Ⲙ̄ⲠⲈⲔ[ⲘⲎ]ⲚϢⲈ ⲦⲎⲢϤ̄·
ⲦⲞⲦⲈ ⲠⲚⲞⲨ|[ⲦⲈ] Ⲛ̄[Ⲧ]Ⲉ ⲚⲒⲈⲰⲚ ⲨⲚⲀϮ ⲚⲀⲨ|
[ⲈⲂⲞ]Ⲗ Ⲍ̄Ⲛ ⲚⲎ ⲈⲦⲰⲘ̄ϢⲈ Ⲙ̄ⲘⲞ[Ⲩ|...].Ⲁ̄Ⲧ Ⲛ̄ⲤⲀ
30   ϮⲂ[.]Ⲣ̄Ⲥ Ⲛ̄Ⲕ[   ]/ ⲤⲈ Ⲛ̄ⲚⲎⲨ ⲈⲬⲘ̄ Ⲡ[Ⲕ]ⲀⲌ
[ⲞⲈ] 1   Ⲉ[Ⲧ̄Ⲙ̄//Ⲙ̄]Ⲁ[Ⲩ Ⲙ̄]ⲠⲎ [Ⲉ]ⲦⲞⲨⲚⲀⳘⲰⲠⲈ Ⲛ̄[Ⲣ̄Ⲏ|]Ⲧϥ̄ Ⲛ̄ϬⲒ
ⲚⲒⲚⲞϬⲒ Ⲛ̄ⲢⲰⲘⲈ · ⲚⲎ ⲈⲦ[Ⲉ]| Ⲙ̄ⲠⲞⲨⲬⲰⲌⲘ̄· ⲞⲨⲦⲈ
5   Ⲛ̄ⲤⲈⲚⲀ|ϪⲰⲌⲘ̄ ⲀⲚ Ⲍ̄Ⲛ [Ⲛ̄]ϨⲈⲠⲒⲐⲨⲘⲒⲀ ⲚⲒⲘ/ ⲬⲈ
Ⲛ̄ⲦⲀⲦⲈⲨⲮⲨⲬⲎ ϢⲰⲠⲈ ⲀⲚ| Ⲍ̄Ⲛ ⲞⲨϬⲒϪ ⲈⲤϪⲀⲌⲘ̄
ⲀⲖⲖⲀ ⲀⲤϢⲰ|ⲠⲈ ⲈⲂⲞⲖ Ⲍ̄Ⲛ ⲞⲨⲚⲞϬ Ⲛ̄ⲞⲨⲀⲌ
ⲤⲀⲌⲚⲈ| Ⲛ̄ⲦⲈ ⲞⲨⲀⲄⲄⲈⲖⲞⲤ Ⲛ̄ϢⲀⲈⲚⲈⲌ·| ⲦⲞⲦⲈ
10   ⲤⲈⲚⲀⲚⲞⲨⲬⲈ Ⲛ̄ⲞⲨⲔⲰϨⲦ̄/ Ⲙ̄Ⲛ̄ ⲞⲨⲐⲎⲚ Ⲙ̄Ⲛ̄
ⲞⲨⲀⲘⲢⲎⲌⲈ ⲈⲬⲚ̄| ⲚⲒⲢⲰⲘⲈ ⲈⲦⲘ̄ⲘⲀⲨ· ⲀⲢⲰ
ⲈⲢⲈ|ⲞⲨⲔⲰϨⲦ̄ Ⲙ̄Ⲛ̄ ⲞⲨⲌⲖⲞⲤⲦ̄Ⲛ̄ ⲈⲒ ⲈⲬⲚ̄| ⲚⲒⲈⲰⲚ
ⲈⲦⲘ̄ⲘⲀⲨ Ⲛ̄ⲤⲈⲢ̄ⲔⲀⲔⲈ| Ⲛ̄ϬⲒ Ⲛ̄ⲂⲀⲖ Ⲛ̄ⲚⲒϬⲞⲘ Ⲛ̄ⲦⲈ
15   ⲚⲒⲪⲰⲤ/ⲦⲎⲢ Ⲛ̄ⲤⲈⲦⲘ̄ⲚⲀⲨ ⲈⲂⲞⲖ Ⲙ̄ⲘⲞⲞⲨ| Ⲛ̄ϬⲒ
ⲚⲒⲈⲰⲚ Ⲍ̄Ⲛ ⲚⲈⲌⲞⲞⲨ ⲈⲦⲘ̄ⲘⲀⲨ·|

25   Then (τότε) the seed (σπέρμα) of Ham and |
        Japheth will form twelve | kingdoms, and [their
        other] | seed (σπέρμα) will enter into | the king-
30   dom of another people (λαός). / [Then (τότε) the
        rulers (ἄρχων)] of [the] eons (αἰών) | will deliberate
[74],1 against those [who have abandoned] // dead [knowl-
        edge] for the great | eons (αἰών) of imperishability
        (ἀφθαρσία). | And they will go to Sakla, | their
5   God.--They will go in / to the powers accusing
        (κατηγορεῖν) the great | men who are in their
        glory.|--They will say to Sakla, | 'What is the
        power of these men who | stood before you (sg.), /
10   who have been taken from the | seed (σπέρμα) of Ham
        and Japheth? | When they were about to number four
        hundred <thousand> men, | they were received into
        another eon (αἰών) | from which they came, and /
15   they overturned all the glory of your (sg.) | power
        and the dominion of your (sg.) hand. | For the
        seed (σπέρμα) of Noah through | his son and all the
20   powers | in the eons (αἰών) over which / your (sg.)
        might reigns | have done all your (sg.) will, and
        those men, | and those who are | sojourners in their
25   glory, | have not done your (sg.) will, / [but (ἀλλά)]
        they have diverted your (sg.) | entire multitude.'
            Then (τότε) the God | of the eons (αἰών) will
        give them | (some) of those who serve [him |] |
[75],1 They will come upon that land // where those great
        men | who were not defiled | will dwell--nor (οὔτε)
        will they | be defiled by any desire (ἐπιθυμία), /
5   for their soul (ψυχή) has not come | from a defiled
        hand, but (ἀλλά) it has come | through a great
        command | of an eternal angel (ἄγγελος). | Then
10   (τότε) they will cast fire, / sulphur and asphalt
        upon | those men, and | fire and mist will come
        upon | those eons (αἰών) and the eyes | of the
        powers of the illuminators (φωστήρ) will be
15   blinded / so that the eons (αἰών) may not see
        through them | in those days. |

ⲁⲩⲱ ⲥⲉⲛ̄ⲛⲏⲩ ⲉⲍⲣⲁ̈ⲓ̈ ⲛ̄ϭⲓ ⲍⲉⲛ|ⲛⲟϭ ⲛ̄ⲕⲗⲟⲟⲗⲉ
ⲛ̄ⲟⲩⲟⲉⲓⲛ ⲛ̄ⲥⲉ|ⲉ̄ⲓ ⲉⲍⲣⲁ̈ⲓ̈ ⲉⲭⲱⲟⲩ ⲛ̄ϭⲓ
20   ⲍⲉⲛⲕⲉ/ⲕⲗⲟⲟⲗⲉ ⲛ̄ⲟⲩⲟⲉⲓⲛ ⲉⲃⲟⲗ ⲍ̄ⲛ̄| ⲛⲓⲛⲟϭ
     ⲛ̄ⲛⲉⲱⲛ· ⲥⲉⲛ̄ⲛⲏⲩ ⲉⲍⲣⲁ̈ⲓ̈| ⲛ̄ϭⲓ ⲁⲃⲣⲁⲥⲁⲝ ⲙ̄ⲛ
     ⲥⲁⲃⲗ̄ⲱ ⲙ̄ⲛ̄| ⲅⲁⲙⲁⲗⲓⲏⲗ· ⲛ̄ⲥⲉⲉⲓⲛⲉ ⲛ̄ⲛⲓ|ⲣⲱⲙⲉ
25   ⲉⲧⲙ̄ⲙⲁⲩ ⲉⲃⲟⲗ ⲍ̄ⲙ̄/ ⲡⲓⲕⲱϩ̄ⲧ̄ ⲙ̄ⲛ ⲡⲓϭⲱⲛ̄ⲧ̄
     ⲛ̄|ⲕⲉⲭⲓⲧⲟⲩ ⲛ̄ⲥⲁⲧⲡⲉ ⲛ̄ⲛⲓⲁⲓⲱ[ⲛ̄]| ⲙ̄ⲛ ⲛⲓⲁⲣⲭⲏ
     ⲛ̄ⲧⲉ ⲛⲓϭⲟⲙ ⲛ̄ⲥⲉ|[..]ⲧⲟⲩ· ⲉⲃⲟⲗ[|[.]ⲟⲩ ⲛ̄ⲱⲛ̄ϩ̄
30   ⲁ[/ ⲛ̄|ⲕⲉⲭⲓⲧⲟⲩ ⲉ[   ]| ⲛ̄ⲛⲉⲱⲛ̄· ⲡⲁ.[
[ⲟ̄ϩ̄] 1   ⲡⲙⲁ//ⲛ̄ⲩ̣|ⲱⲡⲉ ⲛ̄ⲧⲉ ⲛⲓⲛ[ⲟ]ϭ ⲙ̄ⲛ̄ ⲍ̣]ⲃⲁ̣| [ⲅⲁ]ⲣ
     ⲙ̄ⲙⲁⲩ ⲙ̄ⲛ ⲛⲓⲁⲅⲅⲉⲗⲟⲥ ⲉ|[ⲧ]ⲟⲩⲁⲁⲃ ⲙ̄ⲛ ⲛⲓⲉⲱⲛ·
5   ⲥⲉⲛⲁ|ⲩⲱⲡⲉ ⲛ̄ϭⲓ ⲛⲓⲣⲱⲙⲉ ⲉⲩⲉⲓⲛⲉ/ⲛ̄ⲛⲓⲁⲅⲅⲉⲗⲟⲥ
     ⲉⲧⲙ̄ⲙⲁⲩ ϫⲉ ⲍⲉⲛ|ⲩ̣ⲙ̄ⲙⲟ ⲙ̄ⲙⲟⲟⲩ ⲁⲛ ⲛⲉ· ‡ //
[ⲡ̄ⲅ̄] 7   ⲁⲩⲱ ⲟⲩⲛ̄ ⲟⲩⲕⲗⲟⲟⲗⲉ| ⲛ̄ⲕⲁⲕⲉ ⲛ̄ⲛⲏⲩ ⲉⲭⲱⲟⲩ·
10   ⲧⲟⲧⲉ| ⲥⲉⲛⲁⲱⲩ ⲉⲃ[ⲟ]ⲗ ⲍ̄ⲛ̄ ⲟⲩⲛⲟϭ ⲛ̄ⲥⲙⲏ/ ⲛ̄ϭⲓ
     ⲛⲓⲗⲁⲟⲥ ⲉⲩⲭⲱ ⲙ̄ⲙⲟⲥ ϫⲉ| ⲛⲁⲓ̈ⲁⲧ̄ⲥ̄ ⲛ̄ⲧⲯⲩⲭⲏ ⲛ̄ⲧⲉ
     ⲛⲓⲣⲱ|ⲙⲉ ⲉⲧⲙ̄ⲙⲁⲩ ϫⲉ ⲁⲩⲥⲟⲩⲱⲛ̄| ⲡⲛⲟⲩⲧⲉ ⲍ̄ⲛ
15   ⲟⲩⲅⲛⲱⲥⲓⲥ ⲛ̄|[ⲧ]ⲉ̣ ⲧⲙⲉ· ⲥⲉⲛⲁⲱⲛ̄ϩ̄ ⲩⲁ ⲛⲉ/ⲱⲛ
     ⲛ̄ⲧⲉ ⲛⲉⲱⲛ ϫⲉ ⲙ̄ⲡⲟⲩ|ⲧⲁⲕⲟ ⲍ̄ⲛ ⲧⲉⲩⲉⲡⲓⲑⲩⲙⲓⲁ|
     ⲙ̄ⲛ ⲛⲓⲁⲅⲅⲉⲗⲟⲥ· ⲟⲩⲧⲉ ⲙ̄|ⲡⲟⲩϫⲉⲕ ⲛⲓⲍⲃⲏⲩⲉ ⲛ̄ⲧⲉ
20   ⲛⲓ|ϭⲟⲙ ⲉⲃⲟⲗ· ⲁⲗⲗⲁ ⲁⲩⲁⲍⲉⲣⲁⲧⲟⲩ/ ⲙ̄ⲡⲉⲩⲙ̄ⲧⲟ
     ⲍ̄ⲛ ⲟⲩⲅⲛⲱⲥⲓⲥ| ⲛ̄ⲧⲉ ⲡⲛⲟⲩⲧⲉ ⲛ̄ⲑⲉ
     ⲛ̄ⲕⲟⲩⲣⲟⲩⲟ|ⲉⲓⲛ ⲉⲁⲩⲉ̄ⲓ ⲉⲃⲟⲗ ⲍ̄ⲛ ⲟⲩⲕⲱ|ϩ̄ⲧ̄ ⲙ̄ⲛ
     ⲟⲩⲥⲛⲟⲩ· ⲁⲛⲟⲛ ⲇⲉ| ⲁⲛⲣ̄ ϩⲱⲃ ⲛⲓⲙ ⲍ̄ⲛ
25   ⲟⲩⲙ̄ⲛ̄ⲧⲁⲧ/ϩⲏⲧ̄ ⲛ̄ⲧⲉ ⲛⲓϭⲟⲙ· ⲁⲛⲩⲟⲩ|ⲩⲟⲩ ⲙ̄ⲙⲟⲛ
     ⲍ̄ⲛ ⲧⲡⲁⲣⲁ|[ⲃⲁ]ⲥⲓⲥ ⲛ̄ⲧⲉ ⲛⲉⲛϩⲃⲏⲩⲉ|[ⲧⲏⲣ]ⲟⲩ
     ⲁⲛⲩⲟⲩ ⲟⲩⲃⲉ [ⲡⲛⲟⲩ|ⲧ]ⲉ ⲛ̄ⲧⲉⲛ[ⲟⲩ] ⲇⲉ
30   ⲛⲉⲩϩⲃⲏ[ⲣⲉ / ⲧ]ⲏⲣⲟ[ⲩ ⲛ̄ⲧⲁ]ⲣⲁⲙⲁ̣ⲣⲧⲉ̣ ϫⲉ]//
[ⲡ̄ⲇ̄] 1   ⲟⲩⲩⲁⲉⲛⲉϩ ⲡⲉ· ⲛⲉⲓ̈ϩⲁ ⲛⲉⲛ|ⲡ̄ⲛⲁ̄· ⲁⲛⲉⲓⲙⲉ ⲅⲁⲣ
     ϯⲛⲟⲩ ϫⲉ| ⲛⲉⲛⲯⲩⲭⲏ ⲛⲁⲙⲟⲩ ⲍ̄ⲛ ⲟⲩⲙⲟⲩ| ‡ //
[ⲡ̄ⲉ̄] 19   ⲛⲁⲓ̈ ⲛⲉ ⲛⲓⲁⲡⲟⲕⲁⲗⲩ ⲯⲓⲥ ⲉⲧⲁ|[ⲁ̄]ⲇⲁⲙ
     ϭⲁⲗⲡⲟⲩ ⲉⲃⲟⲗ ⲛ̄ⲥⲏⲑ ⲡⲉϥ|ⲩⲏⲣⲉ· ⲁⲩⲱ
     ⲁⲡⲉϥⲩⲏⲣⲉ ⲧⲁⲙⲉ| ⲧⲉϥⲥⲡ[ⲟ]ⲣⲁ ⲉⲣⲟⲟⲩ· ‡ /

32   {ⲧⲁⲡⲟ[ⲕⲁⲗⲩ]ⲯⲓⲥ ⲛ̄ⲁⲇ[ⲁⲙ]}

          And great clouds of light | will descend, |

20   and other clouds of light / from the great eons
(αἰών) | will come down upon them. | Abrasax,
Sablo, and | Gamaliel will descend and bring |

25   those men out of / the fire and wrath and | take
them above the aeons (αἰών) | and the rulers (ἀρχή)
of the powers. And they will | [|] of life

30   [ ] / and take them [ ] | of the eons (αἰών)

[76],1 [// the] dwelling [place] of the [great ones],
for (γάρ) | there is no distress with the holy |
angels (ἄγγελος) and the eons (αἰών). The men |

5   will become like / those angels (ἄγγελος) for |
they are not strangers to them. ‡ //

[83],7   And a cloud | of darkness will come upon them.

10   Then (τότε) | those people (λαός) / will cry out in
a loud voice, | 'Blessed is the soul (ψυχή) of those
men, | for they have known | God through a knowledge
(γνῶσις) of | the truth. They will live forever

15   (αἰών, αἰών), / for they have not been | corrupted
by their desire (ἐπιθυμία) | and the angels
(ἄγγελος), nor (οὔτε) have they | accomplished the
works of the | powers, but (ἀλλά) they have stood /

20   before him in a knowledge (γνῶσις) | of God as
light | that has come forth from fire | and blood.

25   But (δέ) we | have done every work / of the powers |
senselessly. We boasted in the transgression
(παράβασις) | of [all] our deeds, | and [cried]

30   against [God], | but (δέ) now all his deeds / have

[84],1 [prevailed, for] // he is eternal. These (deeds)
[are against] our | spirits (πνεῦμα), for (γάρ)
now we know that | our souls (ψυχή) will surely
die.'" | ‡ //

[85],19   These are the revelations (ἀποκάλυψις) that |
Adam made known to Seth, his | son, and his son
taught | his seed (σπορά) about them. ‡ /

32   The Revelation (ἀποκάλυψις) of Adam

SOURCE A

64,1-2

Böhlig (96), Krause (20) and MacRae "transliterate" the title as "Apocalypse" of Adam
and "interpret" the incipit as "revelation."
Beltz (6,1) and Kasser (318) transliterate
both title and incipit. In the former group,
there appears to be the tacit assumption that
the title was intended in some kind of technical sense; that is, that the ancient author
intended by the use of this word that the
document be associated with that body of
literature in antiquity that modern scholarship has defined by the term "apocalyptic
literature." On the other hand, the incipit
was used in a neutral sense and could therefore be translated into a modern word comparable to its meaning in antiquity. In the
latter group, the problem has gone unnoticed
or has been avoided by transliterating both
title and incipit. Since the document takes
the form of a "last testament" of Adam to
Seth (see above, pp. 63-65), it seems better
to assume that the title was not intended in
a technical literary sense and to translate
both title and incipit by the "less loaded"
(more neutral, at least to modern scholarship) expression "revelation." However, in
the interests of standardization, the usual
title "Apocalypse of Adam" has been retained
when referring to the document.

64,2-3

The tradition utilized by the author is that
of the LXX. In Gen 5:3-5 (LXX), Adam is 230
years of age when Seth is born and he lives
for another 700 years after the birth of Seth.
The total length of his life is 930 years (cf.
Joseph., *Ant.* 1.83). In the Hebrew text
(Gen 5:3-5), Adam is 130 years of age when
Seth is born and he lives for another 800
years after the birth of Seth. The total
length of his life is 930 years. The significance of the 700th year is that the revelation is given by Adam to his son Seth just
before the death of Adam. This suggests that
the document is to be read as Adam's "last
testament" and that it should be associated
with the genre of testamentary literature in
antiquity (so Pheme Perkins, "Apocalyptic
Schematization," 592). The dating of the
tractate in relationship to Seth's birth and
the fact that Seth is the one chosen to receive the special revelation of Adam are features that emphasize the "Sethian" character
of the text.

64,4-5   The expression ⲉⲩϫⲱ ⲙ̅ⲙⲟⲥ ϫⲉ serves as a
              quotation formula and in this case is equal
              to little more than quotation marks (cf.
              Till, §354).

64,6-8   The Coptic at this point is not clear. The
              implication seems to be that Adam was created
              from the earth, and Eve was also created, but
              how she was created is not specified. Pre-
              sumably, she was created from Adam's rib (Gen
              2:21-22) after the androgyne Adam-Eve had
              been created from the earth as is reported by
              the J account of creation. Böhlig, however,
              has translated: "Als Gott mich und deine
              Mutter Eva aus der Erde geschaffen hatte."

64,6-19   The precise meaning of these sentences is not
              clear. There is no explanation as to why
              only Eve had seen the glory in their previous
              "aeon." Nor is it clear why Adam must learn
              about the eternal God from Eve. There does
              appear to be a reversal of the biblical nar-
              rative of creation. Gen 3:1-7 reports that
              it was Eve who was responsible for man's
              "loss of glory," because she ate of the fruit
              first and then gave it to Adam. As a result
              of Eve's disobedience, they were driven from
              the garden. In *Apoc. Adam*, on the other hand,
              it is Eve who preserves the knowledge of glory
              and of the eternal God and reminds Adam about
              it. Apparently the previous "aeon" repre-
              sented a better situation than the situation
              reflected in the text. One can only conclude
              that if Adam had to be taught about the eter-
              nal God then the creation mentioned in 64,6-12
              represented a devolution in terms of quality
              and the "aeon" from which they had come was of
              a higher quality (see above, pp. 26-27; Adam's
              lapse into ignorance seems to provide a struc-
              ture for the narrative). However, they have
              not lost all the quality of that aeon since
              they walk in the "glory" of that previous aeon
              and are still aware of their origin. "God"
              in 64,7, therefore, must be the demiurge and
              what he does to Adam and Eve (creation) is not
              a good thing.

64,6-28   For the devolution of Adam-Eve, see Iren.
              Haer. 1.30.9. See also John Bowman, *The
              Samaritan Problem*, 55, 63, 99.

64,10   Compare Beltz's ingenious Boharic *temporalis*
              for ⲉⲧⲁⲥⲛⲁⲩ ⲉⲣⲟⲩ, which he translates, "after
              she had seen him" (i.e., the eternal God).

64,11 — Note that ἀιών in the Coptic text is spelled ⲈⲰⲚ. Twice in the tractate it appears as ⲀⲒⲰⲚ ([65],1 and [75],26).

64,16-17 — "We were greater than the God who had created us." It is difficult to be certain whether a cosmological difference or a difference in quality is intended. Translators are not agreed: MacRae (higher), Böhlig (höher), Kasser (plus élevé), Krause (erhabener), Beltz (über den Gott). Since the situation in the text suggests that Adam-Eve had passed from one aeon to that aeon controlled by the creator, the present translation suggests that the difference is in terms of quality (cf. Till, §152).

64,22-26 — Loss of glory: *Adam and Eve* 20:2-3, 21:6 (Charles, *APOT*, 2.144-45).

64,31 — "This aeon," i.e., the place from which Adam-Eve had come (64,6-12). Therefore, the great generation had an origin higher than that of Adam-Eve.

[65],3 — ‡ [65],3-9 = redactor's comment one. See below, pp. 284-85.

[65],9-11 — "Withdrew far"; cf. Schenke, col. 32: "war fern."

[65],14-16 — The meaning of the text is unclear. There appear to be two possibilities. One possibility is: we were taught dead things, as men (were taught). Another possibility is: as men (i.e., since we were men), we were taught dead things. Beltz (7,1) has added a verb to his translation (without emending the text) in an attempt to clarify the meaning of the passage: "Seit jener Zeit lernten wir wie (ὡς) Menschen tote Werke <zu tun>." Kasser (319) translates: "Nous fûmes enseignés dans des oeuvres mortes, comme <étant> des hommes." Krause (21) translates: "Seit jener Zeit erhielten wir über tote Dinge als Menschen Belehrung."

[65],22-23 — ⲀⲚⲨⲰⲠⲈ ⲈⲚⲈ ⲚⲚⲈⲂⲎ . This must be an attempt by the Coptic translator to translate the Greek passive. A possible reconstruction of his *Vorlage* is as follows: ἐσκοτίσθημεν ἐν καρδίᾳ ἡμῶν. What is interesting is that he opted to use the complicated structure that he did: the present circumstantial of the qualitative of ⲈⲒⲢⲈ after ⲨⲰⲠⲈ followed by the Ⲛ of identity (Crum says that ⲈⲂⲎ is *only* used with ⲈⲒⲢⲈ) when he could have used the simple pseudo passive: ⲀⲨⲢ ⲈⲂⲎ ⲘⲘⲞⲚ ⳉⲘ ⲠⲈⲚⳉⲎⲦ.

[65],23   ‡ See [65],24 in source B below, pp. 260-61.

[66],18-23   Adam's creation. Cf. Gen 2:7; *Ap. John* (II,*1*)
                   19,23-26 and parallels; *Hyp. Arch* (II,*4*)88,
                   3-15.

[66],21   ⲁⲩⲱ ⲁⲓ̈ⲛⲓⲩⲉ. See Walter Till (*Koptische Dia-
                   lektgrammatik* [München: C. H. Beck, 1961] §362)
                   for the continuation of the relative by the
                   perfect.

[66],22   Or, "spirit of life." Because of the context,
                   "breath" seems to be the best translation.

[66],22-23   The meaning of the text is not clear. Kasser
                   (320) has sensed this and translates: "et
                   <qui> ai souffle en vous un esprit de vie
                   pour <faire de vous> une âme vivante?" How-
                   ever, if one may reason that the thrust of
                   the preposition is purpose (Crum, 506), then
                   one may translate: "I have breathed into you
                   a breath of life for (as) a living soul" (so
                   Beltz, MacRae and Krause).

[66],25-28   For the creation of another son, see *Ap. John*
                   (II,*1*)24,8-36; *Orig. World* (II,*5*)117,15-18.

[66],25-31   There is no discussion of the lengthy recon-
                   structions of Beltz and Kasser ("Textes gnos-
                   tiques: Remarques," 71-98) once the present
                   collation of the text has excluded those re-
                   constructions as viable possibilities.

[66],31-[67],12   Cf. CH 1:18-19.

[67],2-3   Cf. *Ap. John* (BG8502)63,5-9 (ⲚⲞⲨⲈⲠⲒⲐⲨⲘⲓⲀ
                   Ⲛ̄ⲤⲠⲞⲣⲀ) and (III,*1*)31,23-32,1 (Ⲛ̄ⲞⲨⲤⲠⲞⲣⲀ
                   Ⲛ̄ⲈⲠⲒⲐⲨⲘⲓⲀ), (II,*1*)24,28-29, (IV,*1*)38,15-16.

[67],10-12   Shortness of life. See Gen 3:19, 24.

[67],12   ‡ See [67],12-21 in source B below, pp.
                   260-61.

[67],22   Text reads: ⲬⲈ Ⲙ̄ⲘⲚ̄Ⲛ̄ⲤⲀ ⲦⲣⲀⲬⲱⲔ. ⲬⲈ in
                   [67],21 appears to be a redactional device
                   intended to continue the speech of Adam in
                   source B by the inclusion of a segment from
                   source A.

[67],22-27   Adam seems to be talking about his own "gen-
                   eration" rather than projecting ahead to the
                   periods in his narrative. "Generation" (ⲅⲉⲛⲉⲁ)
                   appears to be used in the sense of "family"
                   or "race" rather than period of time, and is
                   similar to the divisions by "generation" in

Genesis 5-10 (cf. Gen 5:1, 6:9, 10:1). Beltz
(75) reports that the same use of "generation"
appears in Josephus and Philo. This section
completes the "generation" of Adam and begins
the "generation" of Noah.

[67],29-31   On the basis of profile correspondence between p. [65] and p. [67], one must allow for
at least thirty-one lines to p. [67].

[68]   Coptic page [68] was left uninscribed by the
Coptic scribe apparently because of a particularly high ridge resulting from a poor
kollesis that runs vertically through the
center of the page. See the discussion by
James M. Robinson (ed.), *The Facsimile Edition of the Nag Hammadi Codices: Codex V*
(Leiden: E. J. Brill, 1975) XI, XIII.

[69],1   Contrary to Böhlig (101), Beltz (10) and
MacRae, it is probable that no text is
lost in lacuna at the top of p. [69]. Their
assumption that something is lost is probably
to be attributed to profiling p. [69] with
pp. [65] or [67], on which the scribe began
writing slightly higher than he did on other
pages. But compare the profile of p. [69]
with pp. [71]/[72], [73]/[74], and [75]/[76].

[69],1-10   Joseph. *Ant.* 1.70 reported that Adam had
predicted the universe would be destroyed
once by flood and once by fire (cf. [75],9-
16). Compare also Gen 6:5-7.

[69],2-3   "Rain-showers"; or simply "rain." See Crum,
198a, 732a.

[69],5-6   The reconstructions in [69],5-6 are actually
too short to fill the lacunae. The lacuna in
[69],5 actually has room for at least five
letters and [69],6 actually has room for at
least four letters. The present reconstruction of these lines seems required on the
basis of the dittography ([69],3-8). The
reconstruction in [69],5 (ⲚⲒⳘ) is assured by
ⲚⲒⳘ in [69],8, and the reconstruction in
[69],6 (⟨ⲡ̅⟩ⲡⲁ[ⲚⲦⲟ]ⲕⲣⲁⲧⲱⲣ) is reinforced by
[69],4 (ⲡ̅ⲡⲁⲚⲦⲟⲕⲣⲁ[ⲧⲱⲣ]), assuming the probability of a similar spelling of the word in
both instances. If the reconstructions are
correct, one can only assume that at this
point the papyrus was defective requiring the
scribe to use a longer space between letters
at some point in the lacuna. Unfortunately
the present state of the papyrus is too poor
to allow any judgment as to its original
condition.

[69],5-8

{N̄TE|ⲠⲚⲞⲨⲦⲈ <Ⲡ>ⲠⲀ[ⲚⲦⲞ]ⲔⲣⲀ|ⲦⲰⲣ· ⲬⲈ ⲈⲨⲈⲦ[ⲀⲔ]Ⲉ ⲤⲀ|ⲣⲀⲍ̄
ⲚⲒⲘ}. The dittography is curious in that
there are two variations in what is assumed
to be two copies of identical text. The
article has been omitted before ⲠⲀⲚⲦⲞⲔⲣⲀⲦⲰⲣ
[69],6. In one instance ([69],7), the *status
nominalis* of the infinitive of ⲦⲀⲔⲞ is used
while in another instance ([69],5) the *status
absolutus* of the infinitive is used.

[69],8-10

MacRae transcribes: ⲈⲂⲞⲖ [Ⲍ̄Ⲱ]ⲠⲔⲀⲌ|ⲈⲂⲞⲖ Ⲍ̄ⲒⲦⲚ̄ ⲚⲎ
ⲈⲦⲈϤⲔⲰ|ⲦⲈ Ⲛ̄ⲤⲰⲞⲨ and translates: "so that he
(i.e., the Pantocrator) might destroy all
flesh from the earth on account of the things
that it (i.e., flesh) seeks after...." The
reading is suggested by Stephen Emmel, who
correctly in his analysis of the passage
eliminates the possibility of a reference to
the flood waters, as is suggested by Böhlig's
reading. The difficulty with this translation is that it attributes a causal sense to
ⲈⲂⲞⲖ Ⲍ̄ⲒⲦⲚ̄. In order to do this, one must assume
that the Greek *Vorlage* used διά with the genitive in a causal sense (see the relevant sections in Walter Bauer, *A Greek-English Lexicon
of the New Testament and Other Early Christian
Literature* [trans. W. F. Arndt and F. W. Gingrich; Chicago: University of Chicago, 1957]
and H. G. Liddell and R. A. Scott, *A Greek-
English Lexicon* [rev. and aug. by H. S. Jones
and R. McKenzie; Oxford: Clarendon, 1968])
rather than the more usual διά with the accu-
sative to express a causal meaning. The Coptic translator then literally translated the
Greek *Vorlage* with ⲈⲂⲞⲖ Ⲍ̄ⲒⲦⲚ̄, which in Coptic
seems to be used only for rendering the sense
of agent, rather than ⲈⲂⲞⲖ ⲬⲈ or ⲬⲈ, an expression that commonly renders a causal sense in
Coptic. This is certainly one possible solution. However, another possibility is equally
appealing. It is possible that haplography
has occurred following [69],9 and the scribe
has simply omitted a line, as earlier in the
immediate context he had duplicated material
in [69],4-9. Following Gen 6:13 (LXX 6:14),
the missing line probably read: ⲘⲞⲨⲌ ⲈⲂⲞⲖ
Ⲛ̄ⲀⲀⲒⲔⲒⲀ ("was filled with iniquity"). One
then does not need to force an unnatural
translation of ⲈⲂⲞⲖ Ⲍ̄ⲒⲦⲚ̄. [69],8-10 would then
be restored as follows: ⲈⲂⲞⲖ[ⲬⲈ Ⲁ]ⲠⲔⲀⲌ| <ⲘⲞⲨⲌ
ⲈⲂⲞⲖ Ⲛ̄ⲀⲀⲒⲔⲒⲀ> ⲈⲂⲞⲖ Ⲍ̄ⲒⲦⲚ̄ ⲚⲎ [Ⲉ]ⲦⲈϤⲔⲰ|ⲦⲈ Ⲛ̄ⲤⲰⲞⲨ,
"[because the] earth <was filled with iniquity
(ἀδικία)> by those (things) that they seek
after." Compare the reading of Gen 6:13 in
Augustini Ciasca, *Sacrorum bibliorum fragmenta
Copto-Sahidica Musei Borgiani* (2 vols.; Rome:
Typis eiusdem s. congregationis, 1885) 1.3.

[69],10

‡ [69],10-17 = redactor's comment two. See below, pp. 284-85.

[69],20

"High clouds." For the motif of "cloud" in the biblical tradition, see J. Luzarraga (*Las tradiciones de la nube en la biblia y en el judaismo* [Rome: Biblical Institute, 1973] and the review article by Leopold Sabourin ("The Biblical Cloud: Terminology and Traditions," *BTB* 4 [1974] 290-311) where he sets out Luzarraga's conclusions.

[69],21-22

"Those men," i.e., the "other great race" in 64,31-32. See also [71],8-20. I assume that the identity of "those men" was made more explicit in the text that followed their introduction into the narrative. This stylistic method of identifying something after its introduction into the narrative occurs elsewhere in the text (see [73],13-24 and [84],4-8).

[69],22-23

ⲉⲧⲉⲩϣⲟⲟⲡ. For ⲉⲧⲉ with the suffix pronoun, see Codex V, pp. [51],23 and [52],9.

[69],24-29

On the basis of profile correspondence between Coptic pp. [65] and [69], one must judge that there were at least twenty-nine lines to p. [69].

[70],1-2

Kasser's reconstruction is similar ("Textes gnostiques: Nouvelles remarques," 305: [ⲉⲩϣϣ]ⲧ ⲉ[ⲧ]ⲛ[ⲟ6] ⲛⲉⲟ[ⲟⲩ ⲉⲣ]ⲟ.ⲩ [ⲛⲧⲛ]ⲛⲉⲧⲙ̄ⲙⲁⲩ.

[70],3

"They," i.e., the rain-showers; see [69],2-3.

[70],10

"Strengthen his sons." Kasser (321) emends [70],10 and translates as follows: "et [il] épargne[ra] <Noé(?) et sa femme(?)>, et ses fils." Beltz (11) emends as follows: ⲁⲩⲱ [ⲩⲛⲁ]ϯ ⲥⲟ <ⲉⲛⲱ2ⲉ> ⲛⲛⲉⲩϣⲏⲣⲉ and translates: "Und <Noah> und seinen Söhnen wird er...Schonung [gewährt]...." MacRae transcribes the text as it appears. He reasons that if Noah is conceived as the actor in the sentence no emendation is necessary, but if God is conceived as the actor one might conceivably emend the text as Kasser has suggested. However, it would seem that if one understands "his sons" to include Noah along with his (i.e., Noah's) sons as the "children" of God (i.e., they are all conceived as "God's sons"), then an emendation is unnecessary.

[70],12-13

ⲉⲧⲁⲩ†ⲙⲉⲧⲉ ⲉ2ⲱⲟⲩ: literally, "which he was pleased over them."

[70],15-16   There is a blank space about the size of one-
                  two letters on the line [70],15 between
                  ЄϼΟΟΥ and ΔΥΚΔΔΥ and on the following line
                  ([70],16) between ΚΔϨ and ΔΥω. The corre-
                  sponding space in the lines above and below
                  these two locations has been utilized by the
                  scribe. There is no evident reason as to why
                  the scribe failed to write in the space be-
                  tween the words indicated above. The quality
                  of the papyrus at this point is not any worse
                  than the rest of the page.

[70],16-25   Gen 8:15-17.

[70],19   Deucalion: In Greek mythology, Deucalion was
                  the son of Prometheus who, with his wife
                  Pyrrha, escaped the catastrophic flood sent
                  over the world by Zeus. For nine days, Pyrrha
                  and Deucalion floated in a tiny boat that
                  Deucalion had built at the instructions of
                  his father, Prometheus. From his offspring,
                  the world was repopulated. See Apollod. *Bibl.*
                  1.7.2-3.

[70],20   Єϼο⟨κ⟩: Text reads Єϼοϥ.

[70],24-25   "That you called [and released upon the
                  earth"]: following MacRae's reconstruction.
                  The reconstruction of this sentence to re-
                  semble the similar sentence in [70],14-16
                  raises the issue of the identity of the actor
                  in both sentences. Since God is the speaker
                  in [70],16-[71],4, it is evident that the
                  actor here is Noah. However, in [70],8-16,
                  this clarity does not hold true. A cursory
                  reading of the passage suggests that it is
                  God who calls the birds and releases them
                  upon the earth, since it is God who rests
                  from his wrath and strengthens his sons.
                  However, it appears that there is a subtle
                  change in subject in [70],8-16 that is not
                  indicated in the text. It is actually Noah
                  that decides which animals accompany him in
                  the ark, calls the birds of heaven (into the
                  ark), and releases them on the earth.

[70],25-29   On the basis of profile correspondence be-
                  tween Coptic pp. [70] and [74] and between
                  pp. [70] and [66], one must allow for at
                  least twenty-nine lines to p. [70].

[71],4   ‡ [71],4-8 = redactor's comment three. See
                  below, pp. 284-85.

[71],8-10   Cloud of the great light: [72],10-11; [75],
                  17-21; *Gos. Eg.* (III,*2*)49,1-2 and (IV,*2*)61,
                  [1-2].

[71],26-30   On the basis of profile with Coptic p. [73],
                    it appears that one must allow for at least
                    thirty lines to p. [71].

[71],27-30   A possible restoration for the lines in
                    lacuna is as follows:

                    [71],27: [ⲁⲥⲱ]ⲱⲡⲉ ⲉⲃⲟⲗ ⳋ]ⲛ̄ [ⲍⲉⲛⲛⲟⲋ]
                         28:[ⲛ̄ⲉⲱⲛ · ⲧⲟⲧⲉ ⲡⲁⲣⲭⲱⲛ ·ⲛⲁⲧ]
                         29:[ⲟⲩⲃⲉ ⲛⲓⲣⲱⲙⲉ ⲉⲧⲙ̄ⲙⲁⲩ ⲁⲩⲱ]
                         30:[ⲥⲉⲛⲁⲙⲟⲩⲧⲉ ⲉⲭⲙ̄ ⲡⲛⲟⲩⲧⲉ]

                    [71],27: [It came from great]
                         28: [eons (αἰών). Then (τότε) the
                             archon (ἄρχων) will fight]
                         29: [against those men and]
                         30: [they will call upon the God]

[72],4   "Worthy." ⲙ̄ⲡϣⲁ in this context is a bit
                    vague. Kasser (322) senses this and emends
                    his translation to read: "leur terre, qui
                    <en est> digne." Krause (24) translates
                    with "angesehen ist," Böhlig (104) with
                    "angemessen ist" and Beltz (13,1) with "das
                    ihrer würdig ist." MacRae has made the rela-
                    tive clause into an adjective and translated
                    with "their proper land." The present trans-
                    lation assumes that the land is only suitable
                    or worthy in relationship to the great race
                    of men and has attempted to draw out what
                    seems to be implied.

[72],8   Above ⲛ̄ⲥⲟⲟⲩ the scribe has written the
                    number X̄.

[72],11-12   "Great light": cf. [71],10; [75],17.

[72],17   Literally: Cham, Japheth and Sēm. See Gen
                    9:18 (LXX).

[72],18-30   See Enoch's instructions to his children,
                    2 Enoch 2:1-4 (Charles, APOT, 2.432), and the
                    testament of Noah, Jub. 7:20-39 (Charles,
                    APOT, 2.24-25).

[72],19-30   The negative attitude of Apoc. Adam toward the
                    descendants of Noah is shared by the Qumran
                    community. See CD 4:1 (Charles, APOT, 2.805).

[72],21   ϣⲙ̄ⲩϣ<ⲏ>ⲧϥ̄ : text reads ϣⲙ̄ⲩϣⲙ̄ⲧϥ̄ . The text
                    leaves the reader in doubt as to the identity
                    of the object of ϣⲙ̄ϣⲉ. There are two pos-
                    sibilities. One might relate it to the clos-
                    est antecedent ([72],19) and translate
                    "minister to it" (i.e., the earth). MacRae
                    suggests this as a possibility with a meaning
                    of "to till the soil" (Gen 9:20). However,

the language of the passage would seem to
lessen this option as a strong possibility.
The expression has already been used with
reference to deference paid to the demiurge
([65],19-21; [73],5-12) and one would expect
"service" to the earth to be rendered "in
pain" and "in the sweat of the brow" (cf.
Gen 3:18-20 LXX).

The other, and more likely, possibility
is that it refers to the demiurge and all
translators have understood it in this way.
However, some (Böhlig, Beltz, Krause) are
bothered by the adversative ⲁⲗⲗⲁ and translate by "nun denn," a translation that sharply
reduces its adversative force and renders it
as an inferential conjunction. The two sentences in [72],19-23 do not contrast well,
and this is apparently their reason for regarding ⲁⲗⲗⲁ as an inferential conjunction.
The observation that the two sentences do not
contrast well and the fact that the indefinite object of ⲟⲩϫⲙ ⲩ̄ⲉ probably refers to the
demiurge, although it has no antecedent in
the context to clarify it, suggests that
something has been omitted by the scribe
before ⲁⲗⲗⲁ. The speech of Shem ([73],1-12)
suggests a possible emendation. If we may
assume that Shem is echoing Noah's command
in his affirmation of obedience, it may be
that the missing line before ⲁⲗⲗⲁ would read:
ⲙ̄ⲡⲣ̄ⲣⲓⲕⲉ ⲛ̄ⲥⲁⲃⲟⲗ ⲙ̄ⲡⲛⲟⲩⲧⲉ ⲡⲓⲡⲁⲛⲧⲟⲕⲣⲁⲧⲱⲣ (cf.
[73],7-12): "Do not be inclined away from
God, the Almighty."

[72],26-30	On the basis of profile with Coptic p. [74], one must allow at least thirty lines to p. [72].
[73],1	"Shem." For the reconstruction, see Schenke (col. 32).
[73],1-12	See Gen 9:25-27 where Shem is the preferred son of Noah.
[73],5	"(Godly) fear": understanding ⲍⲟⲧⲉ to be a translation of εὐλάβεια.
[73],7-8	ⲛ̄ⲥⲉⲛⲁⲣⲁⲇⲕⲧⲟⲩ. The scribe has marked out ⲉ before ⲛ̄ⲥⲉ.
[73],11	ⲑⲃ̄ⲃⲓⲟ ⲭⲱⲩ is a problem. ⲭⲱⲩ is unnecessary with ⲑⲃ̄ⲃⲓⲟ to get the meaning "humility." However, ⲭⲱⲩ is regularly used with ⲉ̄ⲛⲟⲛ (Crum, 821b), a construction for which ⲑⲃ̄ⲃⲓⲟ serves as a synonym. If ⲭⲱⲩ is to be used with ⲑⲃ̄ⲃⲓⲟ, one should emend as follows:

ⲑⲃⲃⲓⲟ <ⲛ̄>ϫⲱϥ. Kasser (323) recognizes this and translates: "dans l'humilité (de) leur tête." It is possible that ⲑⲃⲃⲓⲟ was originally written above the line as a synonym for ϭⲛⲉ ϫⲱϥ and later came to displace ϭⲛⲉ.

[73],12 "Reverence for their knowledge." Beltz (14,1) translates this line as "gewissensfürchtig." All other translators render the line as "fear of their (its) knowledge." For the present translation of ⲛ̄ⲧⲉ, cf. [67],3-4. For the translation of ϩⲟⲧⲉ, see above ([73],5).

[73],13 <ⲉⲓ> ⲉⲃⲟⲗ: emendation as Beltz (14), Böhlig (105), and Schenke (col. 32). MacRae does not emend the text but takes [73],13-15 (ⲧⲟⲧⲉ... [ⲙ]ⲁⲫⲉⲑ) as the subject of ⲉⲩⲉⲃⲱⲕ ([73],15).

[73],15 [ⲛ̄]ϣⲉ. See Böhlig's note on ϣⲉ (105). The ⲛ is present but written very small beneath the ⲩ of ϥⲧⲟⲟⲩ. ⲛ̄ϣⲉ is noticeably smaller than the rest of the letters in the line.

[73],15-16 "Four hundred thousand men." Böhlig (89) cites an interesting parallel from the Manichaean texts edited by H. J. Polotsky (*Manichäische Homilien* [Stuttgart: W. Kohlhammer, 1934] 68 line 18).

[73],26-27 "Twelve kingdoms." See Gen 10:2-6 (LXX). In the LXX, Ham and Japheth have twelve sons. In the Hebrew text, they have only eleven.

[73],27 ⲡ[ⲉ]ⲩ[ⲕⲉ]. Schenke (col. 32) reconstructs ⲡ[ⲕⲉϣⲱϫⲡ ⲙ], "the remainder." MacRae translates as "also."

[73],30-31 "Rulers of the aeons." *Gos. Eg.* (III,*2*)55,13 and *Steles Seth* (VII,*5*)124,8-9; Schmidt, *Koptisch-gnostische Schriften*, 7 lines 21, 29.

[74],3 "Sakla." Elsewhere Sakla (Saklas) is identified as Jaltabaoth or Jaldabaoth (*Ap. John* [III,*1*]18,10; [II,*1*]11,15-18 [IV,*1*]18,1; *Hyp. Arch.* [II,*4*]95,7-8; cf. *Ap. John* [III,*1*]17, 12-13). In *Gos. Eg.* (III,*2*)57 and 58 he is identified as the world ruler who in conjunction with the great demon Nebruel creates twelve angels and twelve aeons. In *Trim. Prot.* (XIII,*1**)39,26-29, he is identified as both Samael and Jaltabaoth. Beltz (109) points out that the church fathers describe Sakla as the evil demiurge of the Manichaeans who devours newly-born children (August. *De haer.* 46; Thdt. *Haer.* 1,26). In Epiph. (*Pan.* 1.26.1.10), he is described as the archon of

fornication. The *Apoc. Adam* does not clarify
the relationship between the "Almighty" and
Sakla. It simply assumes their identity.

[74],4-7   This sentence breaks the train of thought in
the passage. The sentence before it de-
scribes the rulers of the aeons going to
Sakla; the sentence following it describes
them speaking to Sakla. In this context, the
parenthetical statement has the character of
an exegetical comment.

[74],12   ⟨N̄ϣо⟩. The emendation brings the statement
into agreement with [73],15-16 on the assumption that the larger figure was intended to
reflect a large innumerable group. Multiples
of four and forty are quite commonly used to
reflect a large round number: viz., 400, 4000,
40,000, 400,000. See M. H. Pope ("Number,"
Interpreters Dictionary of the Bible [4 vols.,
ed. G. A. Buttrick et al.; Nashville: Abingdon, 1962] 3.564-66) for references and bibliography. The emendation has been made by
all translators.

[74],12   ЄYNАР̄. All other translators relate the
circumstantial clause to the sentence which
precedes. For example, see MacRae who translates: "who were taken from the seed of Ham
and Japheth, who will number four hundred
<thousand> men?"

[74],17-24   The string of three connectives (ⲙ̄N) in this
sentence has posed a problem to some translators. MacRae, Beltz, Böhlig and Krause
have understood the first connective ([74],
19-21; ⲙ̄N NI6ОⲨ...ЄⲬⲰОⲨ), to be part of the
sentence beginning at [74],17. They find
that a major break occurs after ЄⲬⲰОⲨ and
regard ⲙ̄N NIⲢⲰⲘЄ...ⲠЄⲨЄООⲨ as the subject of ЄⲘⲦОⲨЄIⲢЄ . Kasser (324), for some
unstated reason, wants to make all three
connectives (ⲙ̄N NI6ОⲨ ⲦНⲢОⲨ...ⲠЄⲨЄООⲨ) the
subject of ЄⲘⲦОⲨЄIⲢЄ.
     The relationship of the phrase ⲙ̄N
NI6ОⲨ...ЄⲬⲰОⲨ ([74],19-21) to the main
sentence beginning at [74],17 (ⲬЄ
АⲦЄⲤⲦЄⲢⲘА) seems to present another
problem. Böhlig does not attempt to clarify
the relationship but simply translates the
text with a prepositional phrase ("mit allen
Kräften..."). Schenke (col. 32; cf. Beltz
[15,1], who apparently adopts the solution
of his *Doktorvater* with no emendation of the
text and no reference to his article), argues
that the text ought to be emended at this

point to read: ⲘⲚ <ⲡⲀ> ⲚⲓⳒⲟⲨ..., "<den>
alle<r> Kräfte...." He understands the text
to be a literal translation of a Greek *Vorlage*: ἐποίησεν πᾶν τὸ θέλημά σου καὶ πάντων
τῶν δυνάμεων. The emendation would make good
sense ("the seed of Noah has done all your
will and <that> of all the powers...."), but
is it necessary? MacRae's understanding of
the phrase as part of the subject of Ⲁ𐅱ⲉⲓⲣⲉ
([74],18), seems the best solution to the
problem.

[74],18   "His son"; i.e., Shem.

[74],25   "Diverted." Translators are not agreed on
               the translation of Ⲁⲡⲉⲕⲙⲏⲛ𐅱ⲉ : Kasser
               (324), deplacer; MacRae (turn [aside]);
               Schenke (col. 32) and Krause (25), abwendig
               gemacht; Böhlig (106), haben verdreht; and
               Beltz (15,1), abspenstig gemacht. The diffi-
               culty lies in the ambiguity of the Coptic
               word and the wide range of Greek words that
               it can translate (see Crum, 263b). The im-
               plication seems to be that not only have
               these men and their "converts" failed to do
               the will of the creator, they have also di-
               verted "all" the subjects of the creator from
               following him (a slight exaggeration on the
               part of the narrator since he had just ad-
               mitted that some still do perform the will
               of the creator).

[74],28-29   Schenke (col. 32) followed by Beltz (15,1)
               reconstructs [ⲉⲧⲡⲱ]ⲧ ⲚⲤⲀ ┼ ⲃ[Ⲁⲟ]ⲣⲥ ⲚⲔ[ⲱⲍⲧ] ,
               "[indem sie] der F[euer]barke [folgen]"
               (except that Beltz reads ┼ⲃ[Ⲁⲣ]ⲓⲥ). Kasser
               ("Textes gnostiques: Nouvelles remarques,"
               305) reconstructs [ⲉⲧⲱ]ⲯⲧ ⲚⲤⲀ┼ⲃ[ⲟ]ⲣⲥ ⲚⲔ[ⲏⲙⲉ],
               "[pour être ahu]ris par la vache d'Egypt."
               Beltz objects to Kasser's reconstruction by
               noting that there is no evidence that ⲚⲤⲀ
               was ever used with Ⲧⲱⲯⲧ . Further, it should
               be observed that Kasser's reading strikes a
               discordant note in the text. At this point
               one does not expect to read of the "cow of
               Egypt!" On the other hand, Schenke's reading
               takes liberties with the text. The vestiges
               of the first letter in the line cannot be ⲱ
               since the ductus of the stroke is more like
               ⲗ, and there is room for only one letter be-
               tween ⲃ and ⲅ.

[75],3-8   ⲟⲩⲧⲉ... ⲚⲩⲀⲉⲚⲉⲍ . The sentence has the char-
               acter of an exegetical comment since it breaks
               the narrative and digresses into a theological
               reflection on the character of the "great men."

[75],4   ⲌⲚ ⲈⲦⲒⲐⲨⲘⲒⲀ; text reads ⲌⲚ ⲚⲈⲦⲒⲐⲨⲘⲒⲀ .
             The plural article with ⲚⲒⲘ is unattested.
             Crum (225b) cites examples of the singular
             article used with ⲚⲒⲘ but the usual con-
             struction would be without the article (Till,
             §231).

[75],9-16   See Gen 19:24-28.

[75],11-15   ⲀⲨⲰ ⲈⲢⲈⲞⲨⲔⲰⲌⲦ... ⲚⲒⲪⲰⲤⲦⲎⲢ. The sentence
             may be either 2nd pres. (Krause, 25) or 3rd
             future (MacRae; Kasser, 325; Beltz, 16,1;
             Böhlig, 107).

[75],11-16   Translators are not agreed on the meaning of
             these lines (see Böhlig, 107; Kasser, 325;
             Beltz, 16,1; Krause, 25 and MacRae). Appar-
             ently the fire and mist are intended to thwart
             the attacks of the aeons, who have cast fire,
             sulphur and asphalt against the great men, by
             blinding them that they may not be able to
             see in order to continue their attack. "The
             eyes of the powers of the illuminators" must
             be the sun, moon and stars through which the
             aeons have looked in order to mount their
             attack (see Beltz [116] for parallels).

[75],17-18   "Clouds of light" ([71],9-10; [72],10-12).

[75],18   There appears to be a tiny Ⲛ inscribed beneath
             Ⲛ in ⲚⲞⲨⲞⲈⲒⲚ .

[75],22-23   "Abrasax, Sablo and Gamaliel." In *Gos. Eg.*
             (III,2)52,16-53,12 the names are listed with
             Gabriel as "consorts" of the four great
             lights. In (IV,2)64,10-65,5 they are called
             "ministers of the great lights." The title
             "ministers of the great lights" appears in
             (III,2)64,22-65,1 (= [IV,2]75,12-19) where
             they have the additional description of "the
             receivers of the great race." The names also
             appear separately. Gamaliel is mentioned
             along with Strempsoukos and Agramas in the
             Bruce Codex (f. 110ᵛ, 31-112ᴿ,3) as one of
             three guardians who "gave aid to those who
             believed in the spark of light." In *Zost.*
             (VIII,1)47,1-4, Gamaliel, Strempsechos and
             Akramas are listed as keepers of the immortal
             soul. Abrasax appears at VIII 47,13 and
             Samblo is called "the inheritor" at VIII 47,24.
             In *Trim. Prot.* (XIII,2*)48,26-29, Kamaliel
             and Samblo are called "the servants of the
             great holy luminaries" who "transport." The
             names are known from the Jewish tradition
             (see Moïse Schwab, *Vocabulaire de l'angélolo-
             gie, d'après les manuscrits hébreux de la*

Bibliothèque nationale [Académie des inscriptions et belles-lettres 1:2; Paris: Klincksieck, 1897] 151, 209, 305). Cf. Lidzbarski
(*Ginza*, 250), where the three Uthras are sent
to aid the faithful. The evil planets attempt
to destroy them all by sword, fire and flood.

[75],26 ⲚⲤⲀⲦⲒⲦⲈ ; see Crum (313b).

[75],27-31 See Kasser ("Textes gnostiques: Remarques,"
95) and Beltz (16) for two (different)
possible reconstructions of the text.
Another possibility is as follows.

[75],27   ⲚⲤⲈ
28 [ⲤⲞ]ⲦⲞⲨ · ⲈⲂⲞⲗ [ⲬⲈ ⲀⲨⲬⲰⲌ̄Ⲙ Ⲙ̄ⲠⲘ]
29 [Ⲟ]ⲞⲨ Ⲛ̄ⲰⲚⲌ̄ Ⲁ[Ⲛ Ⲍ̄ⲚⲚ ⲞⲨⲞⲨⲰϢ]
30 [Ⲛ̄]ⲤⲈⲬⲒⲦⲞⲨ Ⲉ[Ⲡ̄Ⲣ̄Ⲁ̈Ⲓ ⲈⲚⲒⲚⲞϬ]
31 Ⲛ̄ⲚⲈⲰⲚ

[75],27   And they will
28 [rescue] them because [they have not
defiled the water]
29 of life [with desire].
30 [And] they will take them [up to the
great]
31 aeons (αἰών).

[75],28 Either [Ⲭ Ⲓ]ⲦⲞⲨ (Böhlig, Kasser and Beltz),
or [ⲤⲞ]ⲦⲞⲨ · is possible.

[76],6 ‡ [76],6-7 = redactor's comment four. See
below, pp. 284-85. And [76],8 in source B
below, pp. 260-61.

[83],7-[84],1 For the blessing-judgment formula, compare
Wis 5:1-16 and *Thom. Cont.* (II,*7*)143,8-
145,16.

[83],8 "Them"; synonymous with "those people"
([83],9). The group should be identified as
the followers of Ham and Japheth ([73],25-29;
[74],8-12) who, in conjunction with the
rulers of the aeons ([73],30), opposed the
race of great men.

[83],8 "Darkness." See Matt 24:29-30; *Sib. Or.*
5:344-350, 478-483; *Paraph. Shem* (VII,*1*)44,
2-5; 45,16ff.; *Dial. Sav.* (III,*5*)122,1-5;
2 Enoch 67:1-2 (Charles, *APOT*, 2.462); *Orig.
World* (II,*5*)126,10-15.

[83],10 "People." In Greek, λαός = "people" in
singular and plural. The Coptic article
here is plural.

[83],11-12 "Those men," i.e., the gnostic community.

[83],14-15   "Forever."   The Greek *Vorlage* must surely
                  read: εἰς τοὺς αἰῶνας τῶν αἰώνων.

[83],15-17   The translations vary: MacRae, "They have not
                  been corrupted by their desire along with the
                  angels" (so Kasser, 331?); Böhlig (115) and
                  Krause (29), "durch ihre und der Engel Be-
                  gierde."   Beltz (24,1) renders the text as
                  the present translation.

[83],22-23   "Fire and blood"; see *Sib. Or.* 3:337-338,
                  5:337-380.   The metaphor suggests that they
                  have successfully passed through a judgment.
                  See Joel 2:30-32.

[83],28-29   ⲀⲚⲰⲰⲩ ⲞⲨⲂⲈ [ⲠⲚⲞⲨⲦ]Ⲉ, following the recon-
                  struction of MacRae.   For "God of truth,"
                  see *Ap. John* (II,*1*)30,4.

[84],1-2   ⲚⲈⲒⲢⲀ ⲚⲈⲚⲦⲦⲚⲀ, following MacRae.   See Coptic
                  p. [54],11 for an example of the demonstra-
                  tive article used in an adverbial sentence.

[84],2   "Now."   To use the term "now" (expressing a
                  present contemporaneous concept) with the
                  perfect tense seems contradictory.   One would
                  expect it to be used with a present tense.
                  I have taken ⲀⲚⲈⲒⲘⲈ as a Boharic, Achmimic
                  or Fayumic second present (see Till, §248).

[84],3   "Surely"; literally "in death."   See Gen 3:5
                  (LXX); Beltz, 185 n. 2.

[84],3   ‡ [84],4-[85],18 = redactor's comment eight.
                  See below, pp. 286-87.

[85],22   ‡ [85],22-31 = redactor's conclusion.   See
                  below, pp. 286-87.

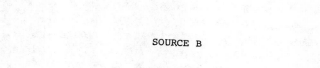

SOURCE B

[ⲝⲉ] 24   ⲀⲚⲞⲔ ⲆⲈ ⲚⲈⲒ̈ⲚⲔⲞⲦ ⲌⲘ̄ ⲠⲘⲈⲈⲦⲈ Ⲛ̄ⲦⲈ
           ⲠⲀⲌⲎⲦ· ⲚⲈⲒ̈ⲚⲀⲨ ⲄⲀⲢ ⲠⲈ ⲈⲨϢⲞⲘⲈⲦ Ⲛ̄ⲢⲰⲘⲈ
           Ⲙ̄ⲠⲀⲘ̄ⲦⲞ ⲈⲂⲞⲖ ⲚⲎ ⲈⲦⲈ Ⲙ̄ⲠⲒⲞ̄Ⲙ̄ϬⲞⲘ ⲈⲤⲞⲨ|ⲰⲚ
     30   ⲠⲈⲨⲈⲒⲚⲈ· ⲈⲠⲒⲆⲎ ⲚⲈ/ⲢⲈⲚⲈⲂⲞⲖ ⲀⲚ ⲚⲈ Ⲍ̄[N̄] ⲚⲒϬⲞⲘ
           Ⲛ̄ⲦⲈ ⲠⲚⲞⲨⲦⲈ ⲈⲦⲀⲨⲦ[Ⲁ̄ⲘⲒ]Ⲟ Ⲙ̄|ⲘⲞⲒ̈
           ⲈⲚ]ⲈⲨ[Ⲟ]ⲨⲞ̄ⲦⲂ Ⲉ[ⲚⲒϬⲞⲘ| Ⲍ̄Ⲙ ⲠⲈⲨ]ⲈⲞⲞⲨ· ⲀⲨ[ϢⲀⲬⲈ
[ⲝ̄ⲋ] 1   Ⲛ̄ϬⲒ ⲚⲒ]Ⲣ[Ⲱ]ⲘⲈ Ⲉ[Ⲧ̄Ⲙ̄ⲘⲀⲨ] // Ⲉ[Ⲩ]ⲬⲰ Ⲙ̄ⲘⲞⲤ ⲚⲀⲒ̈
           ⲬⲈ Ⲧ[ⲰⲰ]Ⲛ̄Ⲧ· Ⲙ̄ⲘⲀⲨ· ⲀⲆⲀⲘ ⲈⲂⲞⲖ Ⲍ̄Ⲙ̄ ⲠⲒⲚ̄ⲔⲞⲦ
           Ⲛ̄ⲦⲈ ⲠⲘⲞⲨ· ⲀⲨⲰ ⲤⲰⲦⲘ̄ ⲈⲦⲂⲈ ⲠⲒⲈⲰⲚ Ⲙ̄Ⲛ̄
     5   ⳁⲤⲠⲞⲢⲀ/ Ⲙ̄ⲠⲒⲢⲰⲘⲈ ⲈⲦⲘ̄ⲘⲀⲨ· ⲠⲎ ⲈⲦⲀⲠⲒⲰⲚ̄Ⲍ̄
           ⲠⲰⲌ ϢⲀⲢⲞϤ· ⲠⲎ ⲈⲦⲀⲨⲈⲒ̈ ⲈⲂⲞⲖ Ⲛ̄ⲌⲎⲦⲔ̄· ⲀⲨ|
           ⲈⲂⲞⲖ Ⲍ̄Ⲛ ⲈⲨⲌⲀ ⲦⲈⲔⲤⲨⲚⲌⲨⲄⲞⲤ| ⲦⲞⲦⲈ Ⲛ̄ⲦⲈⲢⲒⲤⲰⲦⲘ̄
     10   ⲈⲚⲈⲒ̈ϢⲀ/ⲬⲈ Ⲛ̄ⲦⲞⲞⲦⲞⲨ Ⲛ̄ⲚⲒⲚⲞϬ Ⲛ̄ⲢⲰⲘⲈ| ⲈⲦⲘ̄ⲘⲀⲨ·
[ⲝ̄ⲍ] 12   ⲚⲎ ⲈⲦⲈ ⲚⲈⲨⲀⲌⲈⲢⲀ|ⲦⲞⲨ Ⲛ̄ⲚⲀⲌⲢⲀⲒ̈‡ // ⲀⲒ̈ⲈⲒⲘⲈ ⲬⲈ
           ⲀⲒ̈ϢⲰⲠⲈ ⲌⲀ ⲦⲈⲌⲞⲨⲤⲒⲀ| Ⲛ̄ⲦⲈ ⲠⲘⲞⲨ·
     15   ⳁⲚⲞⲨ ϬⲈ/ ⲠⲀϢⲎⲢⲈ ⲤⲎⲐ ⳁⲚⲀ|ϬⲰⲖⲠ̄ ⲚⲀⲔ
           ⲈⲂⲞⲖ Ⲛ̄ⲚⲀⲒ̈| ⲈⲦⲀⲨϬⲞⲖⲠⲞⲨ ⲚⲀⲒ̈ Ⲉ|ⲂⲞⲖ· ⲬⲈ
     20   ⲚⲒⲢⲰⲘⲈ ⲈⲦⲘ̄|ⲘⲀⲨ ⲚⲎ ⲈⲦⲀⲒ̈ⲚⲀⲨ/ ⲈⲢⲞⲞⲨ
           Ⲙ̄|ⲠⲀⲘ̄ⲦⲞ ⲈⲂⲞⲖ· ‡ //
[Ⲟ̄ⳝ] 8   ⲠⲀⲖⲒⲚ ⲞⲚ ⲨⲚⲀⲤⲒⲚⲈ Ⲙ̄ⲠⲘⲈⲌ| ϢⲞⲘⲈⲦ
     10   Ⲛ̄ⲤⲞⲠ Ⲛ̄ϬⲒ ⲠⲒⳅⲰⲤ/ⲦⲎⲢ Ⲛ̄ⲦⲈ ⳁⲄⲚⲰⲤⲒⲤ Ⲍ̄Ⲛ ⲞⲨⲚⲞϬ
     14   Ⲛ̄ⲚⲈⲞⲞⲨ· ‡/ ⲬⲈ ⲈⲨⲈϢⲰ Ⲝ̄Ⲡ̄ ⲚⲀⲨ Ⲛ̄ⲌⲈⲚϢⲨⲎⲚ
     15   Ⲛ̄ⲢⲈⲨⳁ ⲞⲨⲦⲀⲌ· ⲀⲨⲰ ⲨⲚⲀⲤⲰ|ⲦⲈ Ⲛ̄ⲚⲈⲨⲮⲨⲬⲎ
           ⲈⲂⲞⲖ Ⲍ̄Ⲙ̄ ⲠⲈⲌⲞ|ⲞⲨ Ⲙ̄ⲠⲘⲞⲨ· ⲬⲈ ⲠⲒⲠⲖⲀⲤⲘⲀ|
           ⲦⲎⲢϤ̄ ⲈⲦⲀⲨϢⲰⲠⲈ ⲈⲂⲞⲖ Ⲍ̄Ⲙ̄| ⲠⲒⲔⲀⳌ ⲈⲦⲘⲞⲞⲨⲦ·
     20   ⲤⲈⲚⲀϢⲰ|ⲠⲈ ⲌⲀ ⲦⲈⲌⲞⲨⲤⲒⲀ Ⲙ̄ⲠⲘⲞⲨ·| ⲚⲎ ⲆⲈ
           ⲈⲦⲘⲈⲈⲨⲈ Ⲉⳁ ⲄⲚⲰⲤⲒⲤ| Ⲛ̄ⲦⲈ ⲠⲒϢⲀⲈⲚⲈⳌ ⲠⲚⲞⲨⲦⲈ|
           Ⲍ̄Ⲙ̄ ⲠⲈⲨⲌⲎⲦ Ⲛ̄ⲤⲈⲚⲀⲦⲀⲔⲞ| ⲀⲚ ⲬⲈ Ⲙ̄ⲠⲞⲨⲬⲒ
     25   Ⲡ̄ⲚⲀ/ ⲈⲂⲞⲖ Ⲍ̄Ⲛ ⲦⲈⲒ̈Ⲙ̄Ⲛ̄ⲦⲢ̄ⲢⲞ ⲚⲞⲨⲰⲦ| [Ⲁ]ⲖⲖⲀ
           Ⲛ̄ⲦⲀⲨⲬⲒ Ⲛ̄ⲦⲞⲞⲦϤ̄ ⲚⲞⲨ[ⲤⲀ|Ⲃ]Ⲉ Ⲛ̄ⲀⲄⲄⲈⲖⲞⲤ
           Ⲛ̄ϢⲀⲈⲚⲈⳌ·|
               [ⲦⲞⲦⲈ ⲠⲒⲚⲞϬ] Ⲙ̄ⳅⲰⲤⲦⲎ[Ⲣ] Ⲛ̄ⳁ ⲄⲚⲰⲤⲒⲤ
     30   ⲨⲚ̄Ⲛ]ⲎⲞⲨ Ⲉ Ⲝ̄Ⲛ̄/[ⳁ ⲔⲦⲒⲤⲒⲤ ⲈⲦⲘ̄]ⲞⲞⲨⲦ· ⲦⲎ|
[Ⲟ̄Ⲍ̄] 1   [ⲈⲦⲞⲨⲚⲀⲢⲀ]ⲫⲀⲚ]ⲒⲌⲈ Ⲙ̄ⲘⲞⲤ //[Ⲍ̄Ⲙ] Ⲡ[ⲬⲞ] Ⲛ̄ⲤⲎⲐ:
           Ⲛ̄ϤⲈⲒⲢⲈ Ⲛ̄ⲌⲈⲚ|ⲘⲀⲈⲒⲚ Ⲙ̄Ⲛ̄ ⳌⲈⲚϢⲠⲎⲢⲈ ⲬⲈ
           ⲈϤⲈⳁ ⲤⲰϢ Ⲛ̄Ⲛ̀Ⲓ̀[ⲈⲨ]ϬⲞⲘ Ⲙ̄Ⲛ̄ ⲠⲈⲨⲀⲢⲬⲰ[Ⲛ]|

[65],24   Now (δέ) I was sleeping in the thought | of
my heart, and (γάρ) I | saw three | men before me |
whose figure I was unable | to recognize since
30   (έπιδή) / they were not from the powers | of the
God who had [created | me]. They [were] superior
to [the powers | in their] glory. [Those men |
[66],1   spoke] // saying to me, | "Arise, Adam, from the
sleep | of death, and hear | about the eon (αἰών)
5   and the seed (σπορά) / of that man | to whom life
has come, he | who came from you (sg.) and | Eve,
your (sg.) wife (σύζυγος)." | Then (τότε), after
10   I had listened to these words / from those great
men | who were standing | before me, ‡ //
[67],12   I knew that I | had come under the authority
(έξουσία) | of death.

15   So now / my son, Seth, I shall | reveal to you
these (things) | that those men, | whom I | saw /
20   before me, | revealed to me. ‡ //
[76],8   Once again (πάλιν) for the | third time the
10   illuminator (φωστήρ) / of knowledge (γνῶσις) will
14   pass through in great | glory ‡ / in order to
15   leave behind for himself fruitbearing / trees.
And he will redeem | their souls (ψυχή) from the
day | of death--because every | product (πλάσμα)
20   that has come from | the dead earth will be / under
the authority (έξουσία) of ·death. | But (δέ) those
who reflect on the knowledge (γνῶσις) | of the
eternal God | in their heart will not perish, |
25   for they have not received spirit (πνεῦμα) / from
this same sovereign authority, | but (άλλά) it is
from a [wise] | eternal angel (ἄγγελος) that they
have received (spirit). |

[Then (τότε) the great] illuminator (φωστήρ) |
30   [of knowledge (γνῶσις) will come] upon / [the] dead
[creation (κτίσις), | that will be destroyed
[77],1   (άφανίζειν) // through] the [sowing] of Seth: And
he will perform | signs and wonders in order | to
scorn the powers and their ruler (ἄρχων). |

ⲦⲞⲦⲈ ⲨⲚⲀⲨⲦⲞⲢⲦⲢ̄ Ⲛ̄ϬⲒ ⲠⲚⲞⲨⲦⲈ/ Ⲛ̄ⲦⲈ̲
ⲚⲒϬⲞⲘ· ⲈⲨⲬⲰ Ⲙ̄ⲘⲞⲤ ⲬⲈ ⲀⲨⲒⲦⲈ Ⲧ̲ϬⲞⲘ Ⲛ̄ⲦⲈ
ⲠⲒⲢⲰⲘⲈ ⲈⲦ̲ⲬⲞⲤⲈ ⲈⲢⲞⲚ · ⲦⲞⲦⲈ ⲨⲚⲀⲦⲞⲨⲒⲚⲞⲤ
ⲞⲨⲚⲞϬ Ⲛ̄ϬⲰⲚⲦ̄ ⲈⲬ̲Ⲙ̄ ⲠⲒⲢⲰⲘⲈ ⲈⲦⲘ̄ⲘⲀⲨ· ⲀⲨⲰ
ⲈⲨⲈ/ⲞⲨⲰⲦ̄Ⲃ Ⲛ̄ϬⲒ ⲠⲒⲈⲞⲞⲨ Ⲛ̄ⲨⲨⲰⲠⲈ Ⲍ̄Ⲛ
ⲌⲈⲚⲎⲈⲒ ⲈⲨⲞⲨⲀⲀⲂ ⲚⲎ| ⲈⲦⲀⲨⲤⲞⲦⲠⲞⲨ ⲚⲀⲨ· ⲀⲨⲰ
Ⲛ̄|ⲤⲈⲚⲀⲚⲀⲨ ⲈⲢⲞⲨ ⲀⲚ Ⲛ̄ϬⲒ ⲚⲒϬⲞⲘ| Ⲍ̄Ⲛ ⲚⲈⲨⲂⲀⲖ·
ⲞⲨⲦⲈ Ⲛ̄ⲤⲈⲚⲀ/[Ⲛ]ⲀⲨ ⲀⲚ ⲈⲠⲒⲔⲈⲪⲰⲤⲦⲎⲢ·|ⲦⲞⲦⲈ
ⲤⲈⲚⲀⲢ̄ⲔⲞⲖⲀⲌⲈ Ⲛ̄ⲦⲤⲀ|ⲢⲀⲌ̄ Ⲙ̄ⲠⲒⲢⲰⲘⲈ
ⲈⲦⲀⲠⲒⲠ̄Ⲛ̄Ⲁ| ⲈⲦⲞⲨⲀⲀⲂ ⲈⲒ ⲈⲬⲰⲨ· ⲦⲞⲦⲈ|
ⲤⲈⲚⲀⲢ̄ⲬⲢⲀⲤⲐⲀⲒ Ⲙ̄ⲠⲒⲢⲀⲚ Ⲛ̄ϬⲒ/ ⲚⲒⲀ̄ⲄⲄⲈⲖⲞⲤ
Ⲙ̄Ⲛ ⲚⲒⲄⲈⲚⲈⲀ|ⲦⲎⲢⲞⲨ Ⲛ̄ⲦⲈ ⲚⲒϬⲞⲘ Ⲍ̄Ⲛ ⲞⲨ|ⲠⲖⲀⲚⲎ
ⲈⲨⲬⲰ Ⲙ̄ⲘⲞⲤ ⲬⲈ| ⲀⲤⲨⲰⲠⲈ ⲈⲂⲞⲖ ⲦⲰⲚ Ⲏ̄
Ⲛ̄|ⲦⲀⲨⲈⲒ ⲈⲂⲞⲖ ⲦⲰⲚ Ⲛ̄ϬⲒ ⲚⲒⲨⲀ/ⲬⲈ Ⲙ̄Ⲙ̄ⲚⲦⲚⲞⲨⲬ·
ⲚⲀⲒ̈ Ⲉ|ⲦⲈ Ⲙ̄ⲠⲞⲨϬⲚ̄ⲦⲞⲨ Ⲛ̄ϬⲒ ⲚⲒϢ[ⲞⲘ]|ⲦⲎⲢⲞⲨ·

ϮⲞⲨⲈⲒ̈ⲦⲈ ⲆⲈ| Ⲙ̄Ⲙ̄Ⲛ̄ⲦⲢ̄ⲢⲞ ⲬⲰ Ⲙ̄ⲘⲞⲤ ⲈⲢⲞⲨ|ⲬⲈ]
[Ⲁ]ⲨⲨⲰⲠ[Ⲉ ⲈⲂⲞⲖ Ⲍ̄Ⲛ   ]/[.....]Ⲛ̄Ⲧ[   ]|[.....]

Ⲥ̇Ⲁ̇.[   ]/ⲈⲦⲠⲈ Ⲛ̄ϬⲒ ⲞⲨⲠ̄Ⲛ̄Ⲁ
Ⲁ[ⲢϬ]ⲀⲚⲞⲨ|Ⲩ̄ Ⲍ̄Ⲛ Ⲙ̄ⲠⲎⲨⲈ
ⲀⲨⲬⲒ ⲠⲈⲞⲞⲨ| Ⲙ̄ⲠⲎ ⲈⲦⲘ̄ⲘⲀⲨ Ⲙ̄Ⲛ ϮϬⲞⲘ·
ⲀⲨⲈⲒ̄| ⲈⲬ̄Ⲛ ⲔⲞⲨⲚ̄ⲦⲤ̄ Ⲛ̄ⲦⲈⲨⲘⲀⲀⲨ·/
ⲀⲨⲰ Ⲛ̄ϮⲌⲈ ⲀⲨⲈⲒ̄ ⲈⲬ̄Ⲙ̄ ⲠⲒⲘⲞⲞⲨ·|

ϮⲘⲈⲌⲤⲚ̄ⲦⲈ ⲆⲈ Ⲙ̄Ⲙ̄Ⲛ̄ⲦⲢ̄ⲢⲞ ⲬⲰ|Ⲙ̄ⲘⲞⲤ
ⲈⲦⲂⲎⲎⲦⲨ̄ ⲬⲈ
ⲀⲨⲨⲰⲠⲈ|ⲈⲂⲞⲖ Ⲍ̄Ⲛ ⲞⲨⲚⲞϬ Ⲙ̄ⲠⲢⲞⲪⲎⲦⲎⲤ· |
ⲀⲨⲰ ⲀⲨⲈⲒ̄ Ⲛ̄ϬⲒ ⲞⲨⲌⲀⲖⲎⲦ ⲀⲨⲨⲒ/ ⲠⲒⲀⲖⲞⲨ
ⲈⲦⲀⲨⲬ̄ⲠⲞⲨ ⲀⲨⲬⲒⲦⲨ̄|ⲈⲌⲞⲨⲚ ⲈⲨⲦⲞⲞⲨ
ⲈⲨⲬⲞⲤⲈ·|
ⲀⲨⲰ ⲀⲨⲤⲀⲚⲞⲨⲨⲨ̄ ⲈⲂⲞⲖ Ⲍ̄Ⲙ̄| ⲠⲒⲌⲀⲖⲎⲦ Ⲛ̄ⲦⲈⲠⲈ·
ⲀⲨⲀⲄⲄⲈ|ⲖⲞⲤ ⲈⲒ ⲈⲂⲞⲖ Ⲙ̄ⲘⲀⲨ ⲠⲈⲬⲀⲨ ⲚⲀ[Ⲩ]/
ⲬⲈ ⲦⲰⲞⲨⲚ̄Ⲧ̄ ⲀⲠⲚⲞⲨⲦⲈ Ϯ ⲈⲞⲞⲨ| ⲚⲀⲔ·
ⲀⲨⲬⲒ Ⲛ̄ⲞⲨⲈⲞⲞⲨ Ⲙ̄Ⲛ ⲞⲨⲬⲢⲞ|
ⲀⲨⲰ Ⲛ̄ϮⲌⲈ ⲀⲨⲈⲒ̄ ⲈⲬ̄Ⲙ̄ ⲠⲒⲘⲞⲞⲨ·|

5   Then (τότε) the God of the powers / will be
disturbed, saying, "What sort of (power) | is the
power of this man, who | is loftier than we?"
Then (τότε) he will arouse | great wrath against |
10   that man, and the glory / will withdraw so that it
may dwell | in holy houses | that he has chosen
for it. And | the powers will not see it | with
15   their eyes, nor (οὔτε) will they / see the illumi-
nator (φωστήρ) either. | Then (τότε) they will
punish (κολάζειν) the flesh (σάρξ) | of the man
upon whom | the holy spirit (πνεῦμα) has come.
20   Then (τότε) | the angels (ἄγγελος) and all / the
generations (γενεά) of the powers | will use
(χρᾶσθαι) the name in | error (πλάνη) saying, |
"Where did it (i.e., error) come from or (ἤ) |
25   whence have come these deceiving / words that |
all the [powers] failed to discover?" |

And (δέ) the first | kingdom [says about him]: |
[78],1   "He came [from   ] ** // A spirit (πνεῦμα)
[   ] to heaven.
He was nourished | in the heavens.
He received the glory | and the power in
that place.
He came | to the bosom of his mother. /
5   And in this way he came to the water." |

And (δέ) the second kingdom says | about him:
"He came | from a great prophet (προφήτης). |
10   And a bird came and took the / child
who was born. He brought him | to a
high mountain. |
And he was nourished by | the bird of heaven.
An angel (ἄγγελος) | came forth there.
15   He said to [him]: / 'Arise! God has
glorified | you.'
He received glory and strength. |
And in this way he came to the water." |

ⲧⲙⲉⲍϣⲟⲙⲧⲉ ⟨ⲇⲉ⟩ ⲙ̄ⲙ̄ⲛ̄ⲧⲣ̄ⲣⲟ ⲭⲱ| ⲙ̄ⲙⲟⲥ
ⲉⲣⲟϥ ⲭⲉ
20 ⲁϥϣⲱⲡⲉ ⲉⲃⲟⲗ/ ⲍ̄ⲛ̄ ⲟⲩⲙⲏⲧⲣⲁ ⲙ̄ⲡⲁⲣⲑⲉⲛⲟⲥ|
ⲁⲩⲛⲟⲭ̄ϥ ⲉⲃⲟⲗ ⲍ̄ⲛ̄ ⲧⲉϥⲡⲟⲗⲓⲥ| ⲛ̄ⲧⲟϥ ⲙ̄ⲛ̄
ⲧⲉϥⲙⲁⲁⲩ ⲁⲩⲭⲓⲧ̄ϥ| ⲉⲧⲙⲁ ⲛ̄ⲉⲣⲏⲙⲟⲥ·
ⲁⲩⲥⲁⲛⲟⲩϣϥ ⲙ̄ⲙⲁⲩ·
ⲁⲩⲉ̄ⲓ
25 ⲁⲩⲭⲓ ⲛ̄ⲟⲩⲉ/[ⲟ]ⲟⲩ ⲙ̄ⲛ̄ ⲟⲩϭⲟⲙ·
ⲁⲩⲱ ⲛ̄ϯ|[ⲍⲉ] ⲁⲩⲉ̄ⲓ ⲉⲭ̄ⲙ̄ ⲡⲓⲙⲟⲟⲩ· |

[ϯ]ⲙⲉⲍ[ϥⲧⲟ]ⲉ ⟨ⲇⲉ⟩ ⲙ̄ⲙ̄ⲛ̄ⲧⲣ̄ⲣⲟ ⲭ[ⲱ|ⲙ̄ⲙⲟⲥ
ⲉⲣⲟϥ ⲭ]ⲉ
30 ⲁⲩϣⲱ[ⲡⲉ| ⲉⲃⲟⲗ ⲍ̄ⲛ̄ ⲟⲩⲡⲁⲣ]ⲑⲉ[ⲛⲟⲥ /]ⲧ
[ⲑ̄ⲑ̄] 1   ⲁⲥ[ ]// [ⲕ]ⲱⲧⲉ [ⲛ̄]ⲥⲱⲥ ⲛ̄ⲧⲟϥ ⲙ̄ⲛ̄
ⲫⲏⲣⲥⲁⲗⲱ| ⲙ̄ⲛ̄ ⲥⲁⲩⲏⲗ ⲙ̄ⲛ̄ ⲛⲉϥⲥⲧⲣⲁⲧⲓⲁ|
ⲉⲧⲁⲩⲧⲁⲟⲩⲟⲟⲩ· ⲁⲥⲟⲗⲟⲙⲱⲛ| ⲍⲱϣ ⲧⲁⲩⲟ
5   ⲛ̄ⲧⲉϥⲥⲧⲣⲁⲧⲓⲁ ⲛ̄/ⲧⲉ ⲛⲓⲇⲁⲓⲙⲱⲛ ⲉⲕⲱⲧⲉ
ⲛ̄ⲥⲁ ϯ|ⲡⲁⲣⲑⲉⲛⲟⲥ· ⲁⲩⲱ ⲙ̄ⲡⲟⲩϭⲙ̄|ⲧⲏ
ⲉⲧ⟨ⲁ⟩ⲩⲕⲱⲧⲉ ⲛ̄ⲥⲱⲥ· ⲁⲗⲗⲁ| ϯⲡⲁⲣⲑⲉⲛⲟⲥ
ⲉⲧⲁⲩⲧⲁⲁⲥ ⲛⲁⲩ| ⲛ̄ⲧⲟⲥ ⲡⲉⲛⲧⲁⲩⲛ̄ⲧⲥ̄·
ⲁⲩⲭⲓⲧ̄ϥ/ ⲛ̄ϭⲓ ⲥⲟⲗⲟⲙⲱⲛ` ⲁⲥⲉⲣ ⲃⲁⲕⲉ| ⲛ̄ϭⲓ
10   ϯⲡⲁⲣⲑⲉⲛⲟⲥ ⲁⲥⲙⲓⲥⲉ ⲙ̄|ⲡⲓⲁⲗⲟⲩ ⲙ̄ⲡⲙⲁ
ⲉⲧⲙ̄ⲙⲁⲩ·|ⲁⲥⲥⲁⲛⲟⲩϣϥ ⲍ̄ⲛ̄ ⲟⲩϣⲱⲗ̄ⲍ|ⲛ̄ⲧⲉ
ⲧⲉⲣⲏⲙⲟⲥ·
15 ⲛ̄ⲧⲉ/[ⲣ]ⲟⲩⲥⲁⲛⲟⲩϣϥ
ⲁⲩⲭⲓ ⲛ̄ⲟⲩⲉⲟ|ⲟⲩ ⲙ̄ⲛ̄ ⲟⲩϭⲟⲙ
ⲉⲃⲟⲗ ⲍ̄ⲛ̄ ϯⲥⲡⲟ|ⲣⲁ ⲉⲧⲁⲩⲭⲡⲟⲩ ⲉⲃⲟⲗ ⲛ̄ⲍⲏⲧⲥ̄|
ⲁⲩⲱ ⲛ̄ϯⲍⲉ ⲁⲩⲉ̄ⲓ ⲉⲭ̄ⲙ̄ ⲡⲓⲙⲟⲟⲩ·

20   ϯⲙⲉⲍϯ ⲇⲉ ⲙ̄ⲙ̄ⲛ̄/ⲧⲣ̄ⲣⲟ ⲭⲱ ⲙ̄ⲙⲟⲥ ⲉⲣⲟϥ ⲭⲉ|
ⲁⲩϣⲱⲡⲉ ⲉⲃⲟⲗ ⲍ̄ⲛ̄ ⲟⲩⲧⲗ̄|ϯⲗⲉ ⲛ̄ⲧⲉ ⲧⲡⲉ·
ⲁⲩⲥⲁⲧ̄ϥ| ⲉⲑⲁⲗⲁⲥⲥⲁ ⲁⲡⲛⲟⲩⲛ| ϣⲟⲡ̄ϥ ⲉⲣⲟϥ
25   ⲁⲩⲭⲡⲟⲩ/ⲁⲩⲟⲗ̄ϥ ⲉⲧⲡⲉ
ⲁⲩⲭⲓ ⲛ̄ⲟⲩⲉ|ⲟⲟⲩ ⲙ̄ⲛ̄ ⲟⲩϭⲟⲙ·
ⲁⲩⲱ| ⲛ̄ϯⲍⲉ ⲁⲩⲉ̄[ⲓ] ⲉⲭ̄ⲙ̄ [ⲡⲓⲙⲟⲟⲩ·]|

<And (δέ)> the third kingdom says | about him:
20   "He came from / a virgin (παρθένος) womb (μήτρα). |
He was cast out of his city (πόλις) |
--he and his mother--and was taken | to
a desolate (ἔρημος) place.
He <was> nourished | there.
He came (forth),
25   and received glory / and power.
And in this | [way] he came to the water." |

<And (δέ)> [the] fourth kingdom says |
[about him]:
30   "He came | [from a virgin (παρθένος)   ] / * //
[79],1   [sought] her, he and Phersalo | and Sauel and
his armies (στρατία), | that had been sent.
Solomon | also sent his army (στρατία)
5   of / demons (δαίμων) to seek the | virgin
(παρθένος). And they did not find | the
one whom they <sought>, | but (ἀλλά) the
virgin (παρθένος) who had been given to
them | was the one that they brought.
10   Solomon / took her, and the virgin
(παρθένος) | conceived. She gave birth
to | the child in that place, | and nourished
him on a border | of the desert (ἔρημος).
15   When / he had been nourished,
he received glory | and power
from the seed (σπορά) | from which he
was born. |
And in this way he came to the | water."

20   And (δέ) the fifth kingdom / says about him: |
"He came from a drop | of heaven.
He was cast | into the sea (θάλασσα).
The abyss | received him, gave birth to
25   him, / and brought him to heaven.
He received glory | and power.
And | in this way he came to [the water]." |

[ⲧ]ⲙⲉⲍⲥⲟ ⲇ[ⲉ] ⲙ̄ⲙ̄ⲛ̄ⲧⲣ̄ⲣⲟ | ⲭⲱ] ⲙ̄ⲙⲟⲥ
[<ⲉⲣⲟⲩ> ⲭⲉ
30   ⲟ]ⲣ ⲙⲛ̄ⲧ̄ⲣ̄ⲣⲟ /[ⲁⲥ+ ⲙ]ⲉⲧ[ⲉ ⲉ̄ⲓ ⲉⲍⲣ]ⲁ̈ⲓ

1   ⲉⲡⲓⲉ̄ⲱⲛ̄// ⲉⲧ·ⲥⲁⲍⲣⲁ̈ⲓ ⲭⲉ ⲉⲩⲉⲧ[ⲟⲩ]ⲧⲉ
ⲛ̄|ⲍⲉⲛⲍⲣⲏⲣⲉ· ⲁⲥⲱ̄ⲱ̄ ⲉⲃⲟⲗ ⲍ̄ⲛ|ⲧⲉⲡⲓⲑⲩⲙⲓⲁ
ⲛ̄ⲛⲓⲍⲣⲉⲣⲉ
ⲁⲥ|ⲙⲉⲥⲧⲩ̄ ⲙ̄ⲡⲧⲟⲡⲟⲥ ⲉⲧⲙ̄ⲙⲁⲩ/
5   ⲁⲛⲁⲅⲅⲉⲗⲟⲥ ⲥⲁⲛⲟⲩⲧⲩ̄ⲩ̄ ⲛ̄|ⲧⲉ ⲡⲓⲁⲛⲑⲉⲱⲛⲟⲥ
ⲁⲩⲭⲓ ⲛ̄|ⲟⲩⲉⲟⲟⲩ ⲙ̄ⲡⲙⲁ ⲉⲧⲙ̄ⲙⲁⲩ| ⲙ̄ⲛ ⲟⲩ6ⲟⲙ·
ⲁⲣⲱ ⲛ̄+ⲍⲉ ⲁⲩⲉ̄ⲓ| ⲉⲭ̄ⲙ ⲡⲓⲙⲟⲟⲩ·

10   ⲧⲙⲉⲍ ⲍ̄/ⲥⲁⲩⲩⲉ ⲇⲉ ⲙ̄ⲙ̄ⲛ̄[ⲧ]ⲣ̄ⲣⲟ ⲭⲱ
ⲙ̄|ⲙⲟⲥ ⲉⲣⲟⲩ ⲭⲉ
ⲟⲩⲧ̄ⲁ+ⲗⲉ ⲡⲉ|
ⲁⲥⲉ̄ⲓ ⲉⲃⲟⲗ ⲍ̄ⲛ ⲧⲡⲉ ⲉⲭ̄ⲙ ⲡⲕⲁⲍ|
ⲁⲩⲭⲓⲧⲩ̄ ⲉⲍⲣⲁ̈ⲓ ⲉⲍⲉⲛⲃⲏⲃ ⲛ̄6ⲓ| ⲍⲉⲛⲇⲣⲁⲕⲱⲛ
15   ⲁⲩⲩⲱⲡⲉ ⲛ̄ⲟⲩ/ⲁⲗⲟⲩ· ⲁⲩⲡ̄ⲛ̄ⲁ ⲉ̄ⲓ ⲉⲭⲱⲩ
ⲁⲩ|ⲭⲓⲧⲩ̄ ⲉⲡⲭⲓⲥⲉ ⲉⲡⲙⲁ ⲉⲧⲁ+| ⲧ̄ⲁ+ⲗⲉ
ⲩⲱⲡⲉ ⲉⲃⲟⲗ ⲙ̄ⲙⲁⲩ|
ⲁⲩ ⲭⲓ ⲛ̄ⲟⲩⲉⲟⲟⲩ ⲙ̄ⲛ ⲟⲩ6ⲟⲙ| ⲙ̄ⲡⲙⲁ ⲉⲧⲙ̄ⲙⲁⲩ·
20   ⲁⲣⲱ ⲛ̄+ⲍ[ⲉ]/ⲁⲩⲉ̄ⲓ ⲉⲭ̄ⲙ ⲡⲓⲙⲟⲟⲩ·

ⲧⲙⲉⲍ ⲏ̄|ⲩⲙⲟⲩⲛⲉ ⲇⲉ ⲙ̄ⲙ̄ⲛ̄ⲧⲣ̄ⲣⲟ ⲭⲱ
ⲙ̄|ⲙⲟⲥ ⲉⲣⲟⲩ ⲭⲉ
ⲁⲩⲕⲗⲟⲟⲗⲉ ⲉ̄ⲓ ⲉⲭ̄ⲙ ⲡⲓⲕⲁⲍ ⲁⲥⲕⲱⲧⲉ
ⲛ̄ⲟⲩ|ⲡⲉⲧⲣⲁ ⲉⲍⲟⲩⲛ
25   ⲁⲩⲩⲱⲡⲉ/ ⲉⲃⲟⲗ ⲛ̄ⲍⲏⲧⲥ·
ⲁⲧⲥⲁⲛⲟⲩ⳿ⲩⲩ̄| [ⲛ̄]6[ⲓ ⲛ̄ⲁⲅⲅ]ⲉⲗⲟⲥ ⲛⲏ ⲉⲧⲥ̄ⲓ[ⲭ̄ⲛ|
ⲧⲕ̄]ⲗⲟⲟⲗⲉ·]
ⲁⲩ[ⲭⲓ] ⲛ̄ⲟⲩⲉⲟ[ⲟⲩ]| ⲙ̄[ⲛ̄] ⲟⲩ6ⲟⲙ [ⲙ̄]ⲡⲙⲁ [ⲉⲧⲙ̄ⲙⲁⲩ·]|
ⲁⲣⲱ ⲛ̄+ⲍⲉ ⲁⲩ]ⲉ̄ⲓ ⲉ[ⲭ̄ⲙ ⲡⲓⲙⲟⲟⲩ·]//

And (δέ) [the] sixth kingdom | [says <about him>]:

"[A] kingdom / [consented to come down]
to this eon (αἰών) // below so that he
might [gather] | flowers (for her). She
conceived from | the desire (ἐπιθυμία) for
the flowers and |

5   gave birth to him in that place (τόπος). /
The angels (ἄγγελος) of the flower garden
(ανθεῶνος) | nourished him.
He received | glory and power | in that place.
And in this way he came | to the water."

10   And (δέ) the / seventh kingdom says | about him:
"He is a drop. |
It came from heaven to earth. |
Dragons (δράκων) brought him down to |

15   caves, and he became a / child. A
spirit (πνεῦμα) came upon him, and | took
him above to the place where the | drop had
come forth. |
He received glory and power | in that place.

20   And in this way / he came to the water."

And (δέ) the | eighth kingdom says | about him:
"A cloud came | to the earth, and enveloped
a | rock (πέτρα).

25   He came / from it.
The angels (ἄγγελος) | who were above the cloud |
nourished him.
He [received] glory | [and] power [in that] place. |
And in [this way he] came to [the water]." //

[ⲡ̄ⲁ̄] 1   [ⲧⲙ]ⲉϩⲯⲓⲧⲉ ⲇⲉ ⲙ̄ⲙ̄ⲛ̄ⲧⲣ̄ⲣⲟ ⲭⲱ ⲙ̄|ⲙⲟⲥ
     ⲉⲣⲟⲩ ϫⲉ
     ⲉⲃⲟⲗ ϩⲛ̄ ⲧⲯⲓⲧⲉ| ⲙ̄ⲡⲉⲣⲓⲇⲱⲛ ⲁⲟⲩⲉⲓ
     ⲡⲱⲣ̄ⲭ ⲉⲃⲟⲗ| ⲁⲥⲉ̄ⲓ ⲉϫ̄ⲛ̄ ⲟⲩⲧⲟⲟⲩ ⲉⲩϫⲟⲥⲉ
5   ⲁⲥⲣ̄/ ⲟⲩⲟⲉⲓϣ ⲉⲥϩⲙⲟⲟⲥ ⲙ̄ⲙⲁⲩ· ϩⲱⲥ|ⲧⲉ
     ⲛ̄ⲥⲉ}ⲣ̄ⲉⲡⲓⲑⲩⲙⲉⲓ ⲉⲣⲟⲥ ⲟⲩⲁⲁⲥ| ϫⲉ
     ⲉⲥⲉϣⲱⲡⲉ ⲛ̄ϩⲟⲟⲩⲧⲥϩⲓ̄ⲙⲉ| ⲁⲥϫⲱⲕ
     ⲛ̄ⲧⲉⲥⲉⲡⲓⲑⲩⲙⲓⲁ ⲉⲃⲟⲗ| ⲁⲥⲱ̄ ⲉⲃⲟⲗ ϩⲛ̄
     ⲧⲉⲥⲉⲡⲓⲑⲩⲙⲓⲁ/
10   ⲁⲩϫⲡⲟⲩ
     ⲁⲩⲥ[ⲁ]ⲛⲟⲩϣ̄ϣ̄ ⲛ̄ϭⲓ ⲛⲓ[ⲁ]ⲅⲅⲉⲗⲟⲥ ⲛⲏ ⲉⲧϩⲓϫⲛ̄
     ⲧⲉⲡⲓⲑⲩⲙⲓⲁ|
     ⲁⲣⲱ ⲁⲩϫⲓ ⲛ̄ⲟⲩⲉⲟⲟⲩ ⲙ̄ⲡⲙⲁ| [ⲉ]ⲧ̄ⲙ̄ⲙⲁⲩ ⲙ̄ⲛ̄
     ⲟⲩϭⲟⲙ'
     ⲁⲣⲱ ⲛ̄|[ⲧ̇ⲍⲉ ⲁⲩⲉⲓ ⲉϫ̄ⲙ̄ ⲡⲓⲙⲟⲟⲩ·
15   ⲧⲙⲉϩ ⲓ̄/[ⲙ]ⲏ̄ⲧⲉ ⲙ̄ⲙ̄ⲛ̄ⲧⲣ̄ⲣⲟ ⲭⲱ ⲙ̄ⲙⲟⲥ
     ⲉⲣⲟⲩ| ϫⲉ
     ⲁⲡⲉⲩⲛⲟⲩⲧⲉ ⲙⲉⲣⲉ ⲟⲩϭⲏⲡⲉ| ⲛ̄ⲧⲉ
     ⲧⲉⲡⲓⲑⲩⲙⲓⲁ ⲁⲩϫⲡⲟ ⲙ̄ⲙⲟⲩ| ⲉϩⲣⲁⲓ̈
     ⲉⲧⲉⲩϭⲓϫ' ⲁⲣⲱ ⲁⲩⲛⲟⲩϫⲉ| [ⲉ]ϫ̄ⲛ̄ ⲧⲕⲗⲟⲟⲗⲉ
20   ⲉϩⲟⲩⲉ ⲉⲣⲟⲩ/ⲉⲃⲟⲗ ϩⲛ̄ ⲧⲧ̄ⲗⲧⲗⲉ
     ⲁⲣⲱ ⲁⲣ| ϫⲡⲟⲩ·
     ⲁⲩϫⲓ ⲛ̄ⲟⲩⲉⲟⲟⲩ ⲙ̄ⲛ̄ ⲟⲩ|[ϭ]ⲟⲙ ⲙ̄ⲡⲙⲁ ⲉⲧⲙ̄ⲙⲁⲩ·
     ⲁⲣⲱ| ⲛ̄ⲧⲍⲉ ⲁⲩⲉⲓ ⲉϫ̄ⲙ̄ ⲡⲓⲙⲟⲟⲩ·|
25   ⲧⲙⲉϩⲙ̄ⲛ̄ⲧⲟⲩⲉ ⲇⲉ ⲙ̄ⲙ̄ⲛ̄/[ⲧ̄]ⲣ̄ⲣⲟ ⲭⲱ
     ⲙ̄ⲙⲟⲥ <ⲉⲣⲟⲩ> ϫⲉ
     ⲁⲡⲓⲱⲧ |[ⲣ̄ⲉⲡ]ⲓⲑⲩⲙⲓ ⲉ[ⲧ]ⲉⲩϣⲉⲉⲣⲉ
     [ⲟⲩ|ⲁⲁ]ⲧⲥ̄ ⲁⲥⲱ̄ϣ̄ ϩⲱⲱⲥ ⲉⲃⲟ[ⲗ| ⲙ̄ⲡⲉ]ⲥⲉⲓⲱⲧ
     ⲁⲥⲛⲟⲩϫⲉ ⲙ̄ⲙⲟⲩ| ⲙ̄ⲡⲁⲗⲟ[ⲩ ⲛ̄ⲟ̄]ⲩ̄ⲙ̄ϩⲉⲟⲩ
[ⲡ̄ⲃ̄] 1   [ⲛ̄ⲥⲁ]//ⲛ̄ⲃⲟⲗ ϩⲓ ⲧⲉⲣⲏⲙⲟⲥ
     ⲁⲡⲁⲅⲅⲉⲗⲟⲥ ⲥⲁⲛⲟⲩϣ̄ϣ̄ ⲙ̄ⲡⲙⲁ ⲉ|ⲧ̄ⲙ̄ⲙⲁⲩ·
     ⲁⲣⲱ ⲛ̄ⲧⲍⲉ ⲁⲩⲉⲓ ⲉ|ϫ̄ⲙ̄ ⲡⲓⲙⲟⲟⲩ:

[81],1   And (δέ) [the] ninth kingdom says | about him:
              "From the nine | Pierides (πιεριδῶν) one
              separated, | and came to a high mountain.
5   She spent / time seated there so that
              (ὥστε) | she desired (ἐπιθυμεῖν) her own
              self | in order to become androgynous. |
              She fulfilled her desire (ἐπιθυμία), | and
              conceived from her desire (ἐπιθυμία). /
10   He was born.
          The angels (ἄγγελος) | who were over the desire
              (ἐπιθυμία) nourished him, |
          and he received glory and power | in that place.
          And in | [this] way he came to the water."

15   And (δέ) / the tenth kingdom says about him: |
              "His God loved a cloud | of
              desire (ἐπιθυμία). He begat it |
              in his hand and cast | onto
20   the cloud near him / (some) of the drop.
          And | he was born.
          He received glory and | power in that place,
          and | in this way he came to the water." |

25   And (δέ) the eleventh kingdom / says <about
              him>:
              The father | desired (ἐπιθυμεῖν) his [own] |
              daughter, and she also conceived from | [her]
              father. She put | [the child in a] cavern
[82],1   out // in the desert (ἔρημος).
          The angel (ἄγγελος) | nourished him in that | place.
          And in this way he came to | the water."

5   ⲧⲙⲉϩ ⲓ̅ⲃ̅/ ⲙ̅ⲛ̅ⲧⲥⲛⲟⲟⲩⲥ ‹ⲇⲉ› ⲙ̅ⲙ̅ⲛ̅ⲧⲣ̅ⲣⲟ
     ϫⲱ| ⲙ̅ⲙⲟⲥ ⲉⲣⲟⲩ ϫⲉ
     ⲁⲩϣⲱⲡⲉ ⲉⲃⲟⲗ| ϩⲙ̅ ⲫⲱⲥⲧⲏⲣ ⲥⲛⲁⲩ·
     ⲁⲣⲥⲁ|ⲛⲟⲣⲱ̅ϣ ⲙ̅ⲙⲁⲩ
     [ⲁ]ⲩϫⲓ ⲛ̅ⲟⲩⲉⲟⲟⲩ| ⲙ̅ⲛ ⲟⲩϭⲟⲙ·
10   ⲁⲩ[ⲱ] ⲛ̅ⲧ̅ⲍⲉ ⲁⲩⲉ̅ⲓ/ ⲉϫ̅ⲙ̅ ⲡⲓⲙⲟⲟⲩ·

     ⲧⲙⲉϩ ⲓ̅ⲅ̅| ⲙ̅ⲛ̅ⲧϣⲟⲙⲧⲉ ⲇⲉ ⲙ̅ⲙ̅ⲛ̅ⲧⲣ̅ⲣⲟ
     ϫⲱ| ⲙ̅ⲙⲟⲥ ⲉⲣⲟⲩ ϫⲉ
     ϭⲓⲛⲙⲓⲥⲉ ⲛⲓⲙ| ⲛ̅ⲧⲉ ⲡⲉⲩⲁⲣⲭⲱⲛ ⲟⲩⲗⲟⲅⲟ[ⲥ ⲡⲉ·]|
15   ⲁⲩⲱ ⲁⲩϫⲓ ⲛ̅ⲟⲩⲧⲱϣ ⲙ̅ⲡⲙ̅[ⲁ]/ⲉⲧⲙ̅ⲙⲁⲩ
     ⲛ̅ϭⲓ ⲡⲉⲓ̈ⲗⲟⲅⲟⲥ·
     ⲁⲩ|ϫⲓ ⲛ̅ⲟⲩⲉⲟⲟⲩ ⲙ̅ⲛ ⲟⲩϭⲟⲙ·|
     ⲁⲩⲱ ⲛ̅ⲧ̅ⲍⲉ ⲁⲩⲉ̅ⲓ ⲉϫ̅ⲙ̅ ⲡⲓⲙⲟⲟⲩ|‡/

19   ⲧⲅⲉⲛⲉⲁ ⲇⲉ| ⲛ̅ⲛⲁⲧⲣ̅ ⲣ̅ⲣⲟ ⲉϩⲣⲁⲓ̈ ⲉϫⲱⲥ
     ϫⲱ| ⲙ̅ⲙⲟⲥ ϫⲉ
     ⲁⲡⲛⲟⲩⲧⲉ ⲥⲱⲧ̅ⲡ̅| ⲙ̅ⲙⲟⲩ ⲉⲃⲟⲗ ϩⲛ̅ ⲛⲓⲉⲱⲛ
     ⲧⲏⲣⲟⲩ| [ⲁ]ⲩⲧⲣⲉⲟⲩⲅⲛⲱⲥⲓⲥ ⲛ̅ⲧⲉ ⲡⲓⲁⲧ̣| [ϫ]ⲱϩ̅ⲙ̅
25   ⲛ̅ⲧⲉ ⲧⲙⲉ ϣⲱⲡⲉ ⲛ̅/[ϩⲏ̅ⲧ̅ⲩ̅]· ⲡⲉϫⲁⲩ ϫⲉ ⲁⲩⲉ̅ⲓ
     ⲉ[ⲃⲟⲗ| ⲛ̅]ⲟⲩⲁϩⲣ ⲛ̅ϣ̅ⲙ̅ⲙⲟ ⲉ[ⲃⲟⲗ| ϩⲛ̅ ⲛ̅]ⲛⲟϭ
     ⲛ̅ⲛⲉⲱⲛ ⲛ̅ϭⲓ [ⲡⲓ|ⲛⲟϭ] ⲙ̅ⲫⲱⲥⲧ[ⲏ]ⲣ· ⲁⲩⲱ
[ⲡ̅ⲡ̅] 1 ⲁⲩⲧⲣⲉ]//ⲧⲅⲉⲛⲉ[ⲁ] ⲛ̅ⲧⲉ ⲛⲓⲣⲱⲙⲉ ⲉⲧⲙ̅ⲙⲁⲩ|
     ⲣ̅ ⲟⲩⲟⲉⲓⲛ ⲛⲏ ⲉⲧⲁⲩⲥⲟⲧⲡⲟⲩ ⲛⲁⲩ| ϩⲱⲥⲧⲉ
     ⲛ̅ⲥⲉⲣ̅ ⲟⲩⲟⲉⲓⲛ ⲉϫ̅ⲙ̅ ⲡⲓ|ⲉⲱⲛ ⲧⲏⲣ̅ⲩ̅ ‡/

5   <And (δέ)> the twelfth / kingdom says | about
           him:
      "He came from | two illuminators (φωστήρ).
      He was nourished | there.
      He received glory | and power.
10   And in this way he came / to the water." |

           And (δέ) the thirteenth kingdom says | about
           him:
      "Every birth | of their ruler (ἄρχων) is a word
           (λόγος). | And this word (λόγος) received
15   a mandate / in that place.
      He | received glory and power. |
      And in this way he came to the water. | ‡ /

19   But (δέ) the | kingless generation (γενεά)
      says: |
      "God chose | him from all the eons (αἰών), | and
      caused a knowledge (γνῶσις) of the undefiled one |
25   of truth to come to be / [in him. He] said:
      '[from] | foreign air (ἀήρ) [out of] | the great
      eons (αἰών) has [the | great] illuminator (φωστήρ)
[83],1   come.' [And he caused] // the generation
      (γενεά) of those men | that he had chosen for
      himself to shine, | so that (ὥστε) they might
      shine over the | whole eon (αἰών)." ‡ /

SOURCE B

[65],24-33

See A. V. Williams Jackson, *Zoroaster: The Prophet of Ancient Iran* (New York: MacMillan, 1901) 65. Three archangels come from heaven as witnesses from Ahura Mazda to the message of Zarathustra.

[65],31-32

Böhlig (97), Beltz (7) and Kasser ("Textes gnostiques: Nouvelles remarques," 304) have all reconstructed the *status pronominalis* of TAΜΙΟ (ΔΥΤΑΜΙΟΝ, [65],18) under the influence of the many occurrences of the expression in source A. The first person pronoun seems required by the subject of ΜΠΙ6Μ6ΟΜ ([65],28) and the absence of Eve as an actor in this segment.

[65],32-34

An early photo taken by Jean Doresse has preserved parts of the first half of lines [65],32-34. Two letters on p. [65],32 (ЄΥ) were identified by the author in the fragments of Codex V. The rest of the fragment has been lost since Doresse took his picture.

[66],4-5

ⲦⲤⲠⲞⲣⲀ ⲘⲠⲒⲢⲱⲘⲉ; or, "the seed, namely, that man."

[66],12

‡ See [66],12-31 in source A above, pp. 232-33. Note that [65],24-[66],12 has been inserted by the redactor between [65],23 and [66],12.

[67],12

Text reads ⲀⲨⲈⲒⲘⲉ ⲅⲀⲣ Ⲭⲉ ⲀⲨⲱⲱⲠⲉ . ⲅⲀⲣ is attributed to the redactor, and hence does not appear in the B source.

[67],20

Text reads ⲈⲢⲞⲞⲨ Ⲛ̄ⲱⲞⲣⲡ̄ . Ⲛ̄ⲱⲟⲣⲡ̄ appears to be a redactional device intended to recall the revelation of the three men ([65],24-[66],12) that from the perspective of the redacted text had taken place earlier.

[67],21

‡ See [67],22 in source A above, pp. 232-33.

[76],8

See [76],6 in source A above, pp. 240-41, and [76],6-7 in the redactor's comments, below, pp. 284-85.

[76],8-9

"Third time." See *Gos. Eg.* (III,*2*)63,4ff. where the great Seth "passes through" three parousiai: the flood, the conflagration, and the judgment of the archons and powers. Cf.

273

Ap. John (II,*1*)30,11-31,31; *Treat. Seth*
(VII,*2*)58,13-59,11; *Trim. Prot.* (XIII,*1**)
47,1-35; *Gos. Eg.* (III,*2*)63,4-64,9; CH,
Asclepius 3.26a.

[76],9   "Illuminator." Cf. Euseb. *Eccl. Hist.* 4.6.2
              (where Bar Kochba claims to be a luminary
              [φωστήρ] from heaven enlightening those in
              misery) and 5.24.2.

[76],11   "Glory"; literally, "glories."

[76],11   ‡ [76],11-13 = redactor's comment five. See
              below, pp. 284-85.

[76],18   "Product." Translators are not agreed on the
              best way to translate πλάσμα: MacRae, "crea-
              tion"; Böhlig and Beltz, "Geschöpf"; and
              Krause, "Gebild." Kasser translates "toute
              la (substance) modelée." Compare *Ep. Pet.
              Phil.* (VIII,*2*)136,11-19 for a translation of
              πλαϲμα as product.

[76],25   "Same sovereign authority"; i.e., the same
              sovereign authority that produced from the
              dead earth "creatures" that came under the
              power of death.

[76],31   [ⲉⲧⲟⲩⲛⲁⲣⲁⲫⲁⲛ]ⲓⲍⲉ . The reconstruction of
              the Greek verb is not certain. There are
              many possibilities. The text that follows
              ([76],28-[77],27) suggests that the Greek
              verb should reflect the idea of struggle or
              combat with the dead creation, represented by
              the "powers and their ruler." See *Gos. Eg.*
              (III,*2*)51,5-14. MacRae suggests in a foot-
              note that one might reconstruct
              [ⲉⲧⲩⲛⲁⲣⲥⲫⲣⲁⲛ]ⲓⲍⲉ ⲙⲙⲟ⳹[ⲍⲱ]ⲧ[ⲣⲁⲛ] ⲛ̄ⲥⲏⲑ --
              "[which he will seal with] the [name] of
              Seth."

[77]1   [ⲍⲱ] ⲧ[ⲭⲟ] ⲛ̄ⲥⲏⲑ . Beltz (18) conjectures
              [ⲙ̄ⲧⲓⲣⲁⲛ]; Kasser ("Textes gnostiques:
              Nouvelles remarques," 305) conjectures
              [ⲍⲙ̄ ⲧⲓⲣⲁⲛ].

[77],2   "Signs and wonders." See *Great Pow.* (VI,*4*)
              45,4-15.

[77],5   ⲛ̄ⲛⲓϬⲟⲙ. Text reads ⲛ̄ⲛⲩ'{ⲉⳡ}Ϭⲟⲙ . The
              scribe dotted ⲉⲩ , thus indicating that the
              letters are to be removed, and has written
              iota above the line.

[77],7   "Loftier"; following a suggestion by MacRae
                    which captures both concepts of ϪІСЄ , that
                    of higher elevation in a spatial sense and
                    superiority in a qualitative sense.

[77],7-9   See F. Max Müller (ed.), *Sacred Books of the
                    East* (trans. James Darmesteter; 2nd ed.; 50
                    vols.; Oxford: Clarendon, 1879-1910) 4.224-
                    225. In the Zend-Avesta, the demons are dis-
                    turbed at the birth of Zarathustra.

[77],11   "Holy houses." See *Treat. Seth* (VII,*2*)51,
                    5-24; *Zost.* (VIII,*1*)130,5-7; *Ap. John* (I,*1*)
                    9,4-8; see Beltz (133).

[77],12   "Chosen for it," or, "that it has chosen for
                    itself."

[77],16   "Punish the flesh." See 1QpHab 9,1, commen-
                    tary on Hab 2:7-8a.

[77],21   "The name": CD 2:9,6:2 (Charles, *APOT*, 2.804,
                    808); Sir 23:10; Hipp. *Ref.* 5.6.5, 8.12.5;
                    Testim. Truth (IX,*3*)34,6; Rev 19:12.

[77],23   What appears to be writing at the end of line
                    23 is actually blotting from p. [76],24--the
                    first two letters in the line: ϪN . If one
                    looks closely, parts of the first eight let-
                    ters of p. [76],24 are visible as blotting
                    on p. [77].

[77],23   ϪСШШПЄ . MacRae, Böhlig (109) and Krause
                    (27) understand the antecedent of the 3rd
                    sing. fem. pronoun to be ПΛϪNH   (error) in
                    [76],22. Schenke (col. 39) and Beltz under-
                    stand it to be ТϬОЦ (power) at [77],6.

[77],27-[78],5   See Müller (*Sacred Books*, 23.231-38). In the
                    Zend-Avesta Verethraghna appears to Zara-
                    thustra in ten incarnations with the refrain:
                    "thus did he come bearing the good glory,
                    made by Mazda, the glory made by Mazda, that
                    is both health and strength."

[77],27   ✝ZOYЄІТЄ (see Kasser, "Textes gnostiques:
                    Nouvelles remarques," 305). This is the
                    logical reading on the basis of the form of
                    this section. However, it is based on the
                    assumption that the top stroke of Т is longer
                    than usual.

[77],28   "Kingdom." The identity of the kingdoms is
                    not certain. Beltz (141-43) has suggested
                    various possible parallels; see above, pp.
                    137-41.

[77],28   "About him," or, "to him."

[78],2-3   "The glory and the power." In the Sahidic
                   and Fayumic textual traditions, the familiar
                   doxology at the conclusion of Matt 6:13 at-
                   tests to "power and glory." Kingdom is
                   lacking.

[78],3   "In that place." Böhlig, Krause, Beltz and
                   MacRae translate, "of that one."

[78],5   The final ⲈⲬⲚ could also be translated
                   "over" or "upon." Translators are not agreed
                   as to how the expression should be trans-
                   lated: Beltz, Schottroff, and Krause, "auf
                   das Wasser"; Böhlig and MacRae, "to." How-
                   ever, see Kasser's ambiguous "sur." See the
                   discussion above, pp. 141-47. See also the
                   vision of the man arising from the sea in
                   2 Esdr 13:1-4,25,26,32.

[78],6   The number Ⲃ̄ is written above the line over
                   ϯⲙⲉⲣⲥⲚ̄ⲦⲈ. It appears to have been written
                   by the same scribe.

[78],6-17   See Epiph. *Pan.* 40.7.1-3.

[78],10   ⲔⲞⲨⲈⲒ is written above the line over ⲠⲒⲀⲖⲞⲨ.
                   It appears to have been written by the same
                   scribe.

[78],11   "To a high mountain." See *Gos. Heb.* in
                   Hennecke-Schneemelcher, 1.164.

[78],19   "About him," or, "to him."

[78],22   The scribe has drawn a line under ⲦⲞ in Ⲛ̄ⲦⲞⲨ.

[78],23-24   ⲀⲥⲨⲬⲀⲚⲞⲨⲱⲩ. Text reads ⲀⲩⲥⲀⲚⲞⲨⲱⲩ.
                   The 3rd masc. sing. is a problem since it in-
                   troduces another actor into the text. Who is
                   the indefinite "he" that nourishes the illu-
                   minator? Beltz simply regards it as a 3rd
                   plural and translates as passive--without
                   emending the text. This is basically what
                   MacRae has done. Krause translates as reflex-
                   ive although there are no such examples in
                   Crum. I have emended the text in the interest
                   of harmonizing the verb with the two preceding
                   passive constructions and this stanza with the
                   rest of the stories.

[78],24   Beltz (19) has emended the text by removing
                   ⲀⲩⲉⲒ which he regards as a "prolepsis."
                   MacRae also suggests that it may be a scribal
                   error because it breaks the pattern of the
                   refrain.

[78],25 — There is a stroke resembling a supralinear stroke clearly inscribed over the lacuna at the beginning of [78],25.

[79],2 — ⲤⲀⲨⲎⲗ; cf. ⲒⲤⲀⲞⲨⲎⲗ (*Gos. Eg.* [III,2]64,14).

[79],2-5 — Solomon's Army of Demons. The tradition of Solomon's control over demons is known elsewhere in antiquity: Joseph. *Ant.* 8.45-49; *Testim. Truth* (IX,3)70,5-8; *Testament of Solomon* (C. C. McCowan, *Testament of Solomon* [Chicago: University of Chicago, 1915]). See also Atkinson ("The Shâh Nâmeh by Firdusi," 11, 110) for a parallel motif in the Iranian tradition.

[79],6-9 — See *Orig. World* (II,5)116,25-117,15.

[79],7 — ⲈⲦⲤⲀⲨⲨⲔⲰⲦⲈ. The text reads ⲈⲦⲞⲨⲔⲰⲦⲈ. The emendation from present to perfect seems necessary to reconcile the time of this phrase with its context. There is no apparent reason for this verb to be present and the context to be perfect.

[79],10 — The scribe has written ⲱ̂ⲱ̂ above ⲈⲣⲂⲀⲔⲈ. These omegas are written slightly differently from the usual form and could reflect a different hand.

[79],13 — "Border." The word has posed a problem for translators: Krause (27) "an einer bestimmten Stelle"; Böhlig (111) "in einer Schlucht"; Kasser (327) "en un (camp) retranché" (see his note in "Textes gnostiques, Remarques," 95); Schenke (col. 33) and Beltz (20,1) "in einem Bezirk" and MacRae, "on a border."

[79],19-27 — Hipp. *Ref.* 5.19.17-22; *Orig. World* (II,5) 113,21-31.

[79],22 — The ink above [79],22 is blotting from the first ten letters of [78],22.

[79],24 — The ink above [79],24 is blotting from the first four letters of [78],24.

[79],28 — The number 3 has been written above ⳨ⲙⲉⳅⲟ .

[79],28-[80],6 — See *Orig. World* (II,5)111,8-20.

[79],28-30 — The difference from Böhlig's text is due to a new fragment having been placed at [79],28-30.

[80],1   ЄЧЄТ[ОҮ]ТЄ. The lacuna renders uncertain the
verb and what must be a synonym written over
it by the scribe. Schenke (col. 33) argued
against Böhlig's Т[ΔΔ]ТЄ for Т[ООҮ]ТЄ. MacRae
has conjectured the word to be ТООҮТЄ, rare
in Sahidic. Because of the lack of space in
the lacuna, he suggests that here the word is
written Т[ОҮ]ТЄ. He further suggests that
the synonym written above the word could be
ẒШ[Шλ]Є or ϾШ[ОҮ]ẓ. The dark area to the
right of the first Т may be discoloration in
the papyrus.

[80],2   "Flowers." See Siegfried Morenz and Johannes
Schubert, *Der Gott auf der Blume* (Ascona:
Artibus Asiae, 1954).

[80],4   The scribe has written the synonym ХПОЧ
(begat, bring forth) over МЄСТЧ (bear, bring
forth).

[80],5   "Flower garden." The Greek genitive (ἀνθεών,
ἀνθεῶνος) rarely occurs in Coptic. The word
has been translated differently. Krause (28)
transliterates, "Antheônos"; Böhlig (112),
"Pantheon"; Kasser (328), "Anthéon"; Beltz
(21,1), "Blume."

[80],11-20   See Epiph. *Pan.* 40.7.1. The Archontic narrative bears a close similarity to the state-
ments by kingdoms 2, 5 and 7.

[80],12   "From heaven." Cf. *Apoc. Pet.* 8:24 (Hennecke-
Schneemelcher, 2.307), where Jesus is said not
to have been born but to have come from a
heavenly place.

[80],12-15   Apollod. *Bibl.* 1.6 and Hes. *Theog.* 468-480
report that Zeus was born in a cave, and that
he received "nourishment" from the Curetes and
and the nymphs. See *Prot. Jas.* 19:2, where
Jesus is born in a cave and nourished at the
breast of his mother.

[80],16   "Above"; literally, "to the height."

[80],25   "It" could refer to the cloud or the rock
since both are feminine.

[80],27-29   The difference from Bohlig's text is due to a
new fragment having been placed at [80],27-29.
I have followed MacRae's reconstruction.

[81],1-14   Cf. Apollod. *Bibl.* 1.3.5. Hera is said to
have given birth to Hephaestus without intercourse. J. G. Frazier reports that belief in
the impregnation of women without the male

was a widespread phenomenon in antiquity
(J. G. Frazier, ed., *Apollodorus: The Library*
[LCL; 2 vols.; New York: G. P. Putnam, 1921]
1.21 n. 5). Cf. Hes. *Theog.* 925. See also
Hipp. *Ref.* 6.30.6-8; *Ap. John* (II,*1*)9,25-
10,1 and *Ep. Pet. Phil.* (VIII,*2*)135,10-136,10,
where Sophia produces offspring without a
partner.

[81],2   The number Θ has been written over ΨιΤε .

[81],3   ΠΕριᎠωΝ appears to be the Greek ablative
                of πιερίδες. It is not uncommon for the
                spelling of Greek words used in Coptic to
                differ from the customary Greek spelling.
                In this instance, the loss of iota in
                Pierides can probably be attributed to it
                having been assimilated into the sound of the
                initial π rather than pronounced as a dis-
                tinct sound. In Greek mythology, the
                "Pierides" are the nine muses, daughters of
                Mnemosyne and Zeus, who were born in Pieria
                (πιερία), a district in southwest Greece near
                Olympus. Hence, they were called αἱ πιερίδες.
                Originally they were the goddesses of music,
                song and dance. See Hes. *Theog.* 53-76. The
                text does not suggest which of the nine muses
                produced the child, and Beltz (164) could
                discover no Greek tradition about the muses
                that corresponds to *Apoc. Adam*.

[81],6   N̄C̄ρ̄ΕΠΙΘΥμει . Text reads N̄CΕρ̄ΕΠΙΘΥμει .
                The scribe has both dotted and crossed out Ε
                following N̄C. The use of Ε with the *status
                nominalis* of ΕιρΕ , i.e., ρ without supra-
                linear stroke, seems to be a variant for ρ̄.
                See [79],10. In this instance, the scribe
                did not need both Ε and the supralinear
                stroke.

[81],14-23   See Beltz (166) for the motif of divine
                masturbation in the Egyptian religion. Com-
                pare also *2 Enoch* 25:1-3.

[81],16   Above ϬΗΠΤΕ ([81],16), the scribe has written
                ΚλΟΟλΕ. This entry is somewhat different
                from the other instances. Both words are
                written in smaller letters. ϬΗΠΤΕ falls
                slightly below the line and ΚλΟΟλΕ is
                slightly above the line, as if the scribe
                wanted to give them equal weight.

[81],17   "It," i.e., the sperm.

[81],18   The scribe has written ϭ above Ⅹ in ΝΟΥⅩΕ
                ([81],18).

[81],19   Above Κλοολє has been written 6ΗΠє
                 ([81],19).

[81],19   "Near him." The text has posed a problem to
                 translators. Böhlig (113) and MacRae (in *The
                 Nag Hammadi Library*) have not emended the
                 text, but translated ЄΖΟΥЄ Є′ as "above him."
                 Beltz (22,1), following Schenke, has trans-
                 lated: "which was far from him." Schenke
                 ("Zum Gegenwärtigen Stand," 132) analyzes the
                 expression as a perfect relative of ΟΥЄ Є′.
                 The element ЄΖ′ he regards as an (unattested)
                 dialectal variant of the perfect relative
                 particle ΔΖ′. The analysis is apparently
                 accepted by Krause (28) who translates: "die
                 fern von ihm war," and gives Böhlig's trans-
                 lation as a possibility. He also suggests
                 that one might translate: "die grösser als er
                 war." The present translation follows the
                 analysis of Peter Nagel ("Marginalia Coptica,"
                 *Wissenschaftliche Zeitschrift der Martin-
                 Luther-Universität* 20 [1973] 111-15). Nagel
                 argues that the Greek *Vorlage* of ЄΖΟΥЄ Є′
                 read παρ′ αὐτόν (= near him) which the Coptic
                 translator incorrectly understood to have a
                 comparative meaning and translated it by a
                 Coptic expression of comparison, ЄΖΟΥЄ Є′.
                 However, it is also possible that ЄΖΟΥЄ Є′
                 is simply the result of a scribal error where
                 the copyist has incorrectly written ЄΖΟΥЄ Є′
                 for ЄΖΟΥ⟨Ν⟩ Є′, which translated the original
                 Greek *Vorlage* πρὸς αὐτῷ (= near him). In
                 either case, the translation is the same.
                 MacRae follows Nagel in *Nag Hammadi Codices
                 V 2-5 and VI*.

[81],24   The number ῙΔ has been written above
                 †μєζ ṂṆ̄ΤΟΥЄ.

[82],7   Above CΝΔΥ has been written the number B̄.

[82],12   Ⅹ is written above 6 in 6ΙΝṂΙCЄ.

[82],13   "Their ruler," i.e., the gnostic community.

[82],17   ‡ [82],18-19 = redactor's comment six. See
                 below, pp. 284-85.

[82],20-21   "Kingless generation." See *Jub.* 15:32; *Soph.
                 Jes. Chr.* (III,4)99,18-20; *Eugnostos* (V,1)
                 5,3-5; *Hyp. Arch.* (II,4)97,3-5; *Orig. World*
                 (II,5)127,13-14, and Kasser ("Textes gnos-
                 tiques: Remarques," 95).

[82],23-24   "Undefiled one of truth"; *Treat. Seth* (VII,2)
                 53,3-4.7; 54,6-8.

[83],3-4   "Shine over the aeon"; see *Paraph. Shem* (VII,*1*)28,24-25.

[83],4   ‡ [83],4-7 = redactor's comment seven. See below, pp. 284-85.

THE REDACTOR

1: [65],3-9. See above, p. 230.

[ⳄⲈ] 3 ⲁⲗⲗⲁ|ⲁⲥⲃⲱⲕ ⲉϩⲟⲩⲛ ⲉⲧⲥⲡⲟⲣⲁ ⲛ̄ⲧⲉ|ϩⲉⲛⲛⲟϭ
ⲛ̄ⲛⲉⲱⲛ· ⲉⲧⲃⲉ ⲡⲁⲓ̈|ϩⲱ ⲁⲛⲟⲕ ⲁⲉⲓⲙⲟⲩⲧⲉ
ⲉⲣⲟⲕ| ⲙ̄ⲡⲣⲁⲛ ⲙ̄ⲡⲣⲱⲙⲉ ⲉⲧⲙ̄ⲙⲁⲩ|ⲉⲧⲉ
ⲧⲥⲡⲟⲣⲁ ⲧⲉ ⲛ̄ⲧ̄ⲛⲟϭ ⲛ̄ⲅⲉⲛⲉⲁ|ⲏ̄ ⲉⲃⲟⲗ ⲛ̄ϩⲏⲧ̄ϥ̄·

2: [69],10-17. See above, p. 232.

[Ⳅⲑ] 10 ϩⲛ̄ [ⲛⲓⲉⲃ]ⲟⲗ| ϩⲛ̄ ⲧⲥⲡⲟⲣⲁ ⲛ̄[ϭⲓ] ⲛⲓⲣⲱ|ⲙⲉ· ⲛⲏ
ⲉⲧⲁ[ⲩⲟⲩ]ⲱⲧⲃ̄ ⲉ|ϩⲣⲁⲓ̈ ⲉⲣⲟⲟⲩ [ⲛ̄ϭⲓ ⲡ]ⲱⲛϩ̄
15 ⲛ̄|ⲧⲉ ⲧⲅⲛⲱⲥⲓⲥ [ⲡⲁ]ⲉⲓ ⲉⲧⲁⲩ/ⲉ̄ⲓ ⲉⲃⲟⲗ ⲛ̄ϩⲏⲧ̄
ⲙ̄[ⲛ̄] ⲉⲩϩⲁ|ⲧⲉⲕⲙⲁⲁⲩ· ⲛⲉⲩⲉ ⲅⲁⲣ| ⲛ̄ⲩϣ̄ⲙⲙⲟ
ⲙ̄ⲙⲟⲩ ⲡⲉ·

3: [71],4-8. See above, p. 234.

[Ⲟ̄ⲁ] 4 ⲁⲩⲱ ⲙ̄ⲙⲛ̄| ⲥⲡⲟⲣⲁ ⲛ̄ⲛⲏⲩ ⲉⲃⲟⲗ ⲛ̄ϩⲏⲧⲕ̄| ⲛ̄ⲧⲉ
ⲛⲓⲣⲱⲙⲉ ⲉⲧⲉ ⲛ̄ⲥⲉⲛⲁⲁϩⲉ|ⲣⲁⲧⲟⲩ ⲁⲛ ⲙ̄ⲡⲁⲙ̄ⲧⲟ
ⲉⲃⲟⲗ ϩⲛ̄| ⲕⲉⲉⲟⲟⲩ·

4: [76],6-7. See above, p. 240.

[Ⲟ̄ϥ] 6 ⲁⲗⲗⲁ|ⲉⲩⲣ̄ ϩⲱⲃ ϩⲛ̄ ⲧⲥⲡⲟⲣⲁ ⲛ̄ⲁⲧⲧⲁⲕⲟ·

5: [76],11-13. See above, p. 260.

[Ⲟ̄ϥ] 11 ϩⲓⲛⲁ ⲭⲉ ⲉⲩⲉϣⲱ̄ⲡ|<ⲛ̄ϩⲉⲛⲙ̄ⲛ̄ⲧⲣⲉ>ⲉⲃⲟⲗ ϩⲙ̄
ⲡⲓⲥⲡⲉⲣⲙⲁ ⲛ̄ⲧⲉ ⲛⲱϩⲉ| ⲙ̄ⲛ̄ ⲛⲓϣⲏⲣⲉ ⲛ̄ⲧⲉ
ⲭⲁⲙ ⲙ̄ⲛ̄ ⲓ̈ⲁⲫⲉⲑ|

6: [82],18-19. See above, p. 270.

[ⲡ̄ⲃ] 18 ϩⲓⲛⲁ ⲭⲉ ⲉⲩⲉⲧⲱⲧ̄ ⲛ̄ⲧⲉⲡⲓⲑⲩ|ⲙⲓⲁ ⲛ̄ⲧⲉ ⲛⲉⲓϭⲟⲙ·

7: [83],4-7. See above, p. 270

[ⲡ̄ⲅ̄] 4 ⲧⲟⲧⲉ ⲧⲥⲡⲟⲣⲁ ⲛⲁⲧ| ⲟⲩⲃⲉ ⲧϭⲟⲙ <ⲛ̄>ⲛⲏ
ⲉⲧⲛⲁϫⲓ ⲙ̄ⲡⲉⲩ|ⲣⲁⲛ ϩⲓϫⲙ̄ ⲡⲓⲙⲟⲟⲩ ⲁⲩⲱ<...>
ⲛ̄ⲧⲟⲧⲟⲩ| ⲧⲏⲣⲟⲩ·

1:    [65],3-9. See above, p. 231.

[65],3   But (ἀλλά) | it (i.e., knowledge) entered into the
5   seed (σπορά) of / great eons (αἰών). For this
           reason | I myself have called you (sg.) | by the
           name of that man | who is the seed (σπορά) of the
           great generation (γενεά), | which (ἥ) is from him.

2:    [69],10-17. See above, p. 233.

[69],10   (and) by [those] from | the seed (σπορά), [namely]
           those men | to whom passed | [the] life of | the
15   knowledge (γνῶσις) that / came from me [and] Eve |
           your mother, for (γάρ) they were | strangers to him.

3:    [71],4-8. See above, p. 235.

[71],4   And no | seed (σπορά) of those men | will come
           from you that they not stand | before me in |
           another glory.

4:    [76],6-7. See above, p. 241.

[76],6   But (ἀλλά) | they labor with the imperishable seed
           (σπορά).

5:    [76],11-13. See above, p. 261.

[76],11   in order to (ἵνα) leave behind <witnesses> | from
           the seed (σπέρμα) of Noah | and the sons of Ham
           and Japheth.

6:    [82],18-19. See above, p. 271.

[82],18   in order that (ἵνα) the desire (ἐπιθυμία) of these
           powers | might be satisfied.

7:    [83],4-7. See above, p. 271.

[83],4   Then (τότε) the seed (σπορά) will fight | against
           the power <of> those who will receive his | name
           upon the water and <...> with them | all.

8: [84],4-[85],18.22-31. See above, p. 240.

[ⲡ̅ⲇ̅] 4 ⲧⲟⲧⲉ ⲁⲩⲥⲙⲏ ϣⲱⲡⲉ ϣⲁⲣⲟⲟⲩ| ⲉⲥϫⲱ ⲙ̅ⲙⲟⲥ
ϫⲉ ⲙ̅ⲓⲭⲉⲩ ⲙ̅ⲛ̅| ⲙⲓⲭⲁⲣ ⲙ̅ⲛ̅ ⲙⲛⲏⲥⲓⲛⲟⲩⲥ· ⲛⲏ|
ⲉⲧϩ̅ⲓ ϫ̅ⲛ̅ ⲡⲓϫⲱⲕ̅ⲙ̅ ⲉⲧⲟⲩⲁⲁⲃ| ⲙ̅ⲛ̅ ⲡⲓⲙⲟⲟⲩ
ⲉⲧⲟⲛϩ̅ ϫⲉ ⲉⲧⲃⲉ| ⲟⲩ ⲛⲉⲧⲉⲧ̅ⲛ̅ϣϣ ⲟⲩⲃⲉ

10 ⲡⲛⲟⲩ/ⲧⲉ ⲉⲧⲟⲛϩ̅ ϩ̅ⲛ̅ ϩ[ⲉ]ⲛⲥⲙⲏ ⲛ̅ⲁⲛⲟ|ⲙⲟⲥ ⲙ̅ⲛ̅
ϩⲉⲛⲗⲁⲥ ⲉⲙ̅ⲛ̅ ⲛⲟⲙⲟ[ⲥ]|ⲧⲉ ⲉⲧⲟⲟⲧⲟⲩ ⲙ̅ⲛ̅
ϩⲉⲛ̅ⲯⲩⲭⲏ|ⲉⲩⲙⲉϩ ⲛ̅ⲥⲛⲟⲩ ⲙ̅ⲛ̅ ϩⲉⲛϩ[ⲃⲏⲩⲉ]|

15 ⲉⲩⲥⲟⲟⲩ· ⲉⲧⲉⲧ̅ⲛ̅ⲙⲉϩ ⲉ[ⲃⲟⲗ]/ϩ̅ⲛ̅ ϩⲉⲛϩⲃⲏⲩⲉ
<ⲁⲛ> ⲉⲛⲁ ⲧⲙⲉ {ⲁⲛ} ⲛⲉ| ⲁⲗⲗⲁ ⲛⲉⲧ̅ⲛ̅ϩ̅ⲓⲟⲟⲧⲉ
ⲙⲉϩ ⲛ̅ⲟⲩⲛⲟⲩ ⲙ̅ⲛ̅ ⲡ̅ⲧⲉⲗⲏⲗ· ⲉⲁⲧⲉ|ⲧ̅ⲛ̅ϫⲉϩ̅ⲙ̅
ⲡⲓⲙⲟⲟⲩ ⲛ̅ⲧⲉ ⲡ̅ⲱⲛ[ϩ̅]| ⲁⲧⲉⲧ̅ⲛ̅ⲥⲱ ⲕ ⲙ̅ⲙⲟⲩ

20 ⲉϩⲟⲩⲛ/ ⲉⲡⲟⲩⲱϣ ⲛ̅ⲧⲉ ⲛⲓϭⲟⲙ| ⲛⲏ ⲉⲧⲁⲩⲧ
ⲑⲏⲩⲧ̅ⲛ̅ ⲉⲧⲟⲟ|ⲧⲟⲩ ϫⲉ ⲉⲧⲉⲧ̅ⲛ̅ⲉⲩ̅ⲙ̅ϣⲉ| ⲙ̅ⲙⲟⲟⲩ·

25 ⲁⲩⲱ ⲙ̅ⲡⲉ{ⲡⲉ}|ⲧ̅ⲛ̅ⲙⲉⲉⲣⲉ ⲉⲓⲛⲉ ⲙ̅ⲡⲁ ⲛⲓ/[ⲣ]ⲱⲙⲉ
ⲉⲧⲙ̅ⲙⲁⲩ ⲁⲛ ⲛⲏ| [ⲉ]ⲧⲉⲧ̅ⲛ̅ⲡⲱⲧ ⲛ̅ⲥⲱⲟ[ⲩ| ϫⲉ
ⲙ̅]ⲡⲟⲩⲥ[ⲱⲧⲙ̅] ⲛ̅ⲥⲁ ⲛⲉ|[ⲧ̅ⲛ̅]ⲉⲡⲓⲑⲣⲙ[ⲓⲁ· ⲟ]ⲩⲧⲉ//

[ⲡ̅ⲉ̅] 1 ⲙ̅ⲁⲣⲉⲡⲉⲩⲟⲩⲧⲁϩ ⲗⲱⲱⲙ· ⲁⲗⲗⲁ| ⲥⲉⲛⲁϣⲱⲡⲉ
ⲉⲩⲥⲟⲟⲩⲛ ⲙ̅ⲙⲟⲟⲩ| ϣⲁ ⲛⲓⲛⲟϭ ⲛ̅ⲛⲉⲱⲛ· ϫⲉ
ⲛⲓϣⲁϫⲉ| ⲉⲧⲁⲩⲁⲣⲉϩ ⲉⲣⲟⲟⲩ ⲛ̅ⲧⲉ ⲡⲛⲟⲩⲧⲉ/

5 ⲛ̅ⲧⲉ ⲛⲉⲱⲛ ⲙ̅ⲡⲟⲩϩⲓⲧⲟⲩ ⲉ|ⲡϫⲱⲱⲙⲉ ⲟⲩⲧⲉ
ⲛ̅ⲥⲉⲥϩⲟⲩⲧ ⲁⲛ·|
ⲁⲗⲗⲁ ϩⲉⲛⲁⲅⲅⲉⲗⲓⲕⲟⲥ ⲉⲧⲛⲁⲛ̅ⲧⲟⲩ| ⲛⲁⲓ̈ ⲉⲧⲉ
ⲛ̅ⲥⲉⲛⲁⲙ̅ⲙⲉ ⲉⲣⲟⲟⲩ ⲁⲛ ⲛ̅ϭⲓ ⲛ̅ⲅⲉⲛⲉⲁ ⲧⲏ[ⲣⲟ]ⲩ

10 ⲛ̅ⲛ̅ⲣⲱⲙⲉ· ⲥⲉ/ⲛⲁϣⲱⲡⲉ ⲅⲁ[ⲣ ⲉ]ϫ̅ⲛ̅ ⲟⲩⲧⲟⲟⲩ ⲉⲩ|ϫⲟⲥⲉ
ϩⲓ ϫ̅ⲛ̅ ⲟⲩⲡⲉⲧⲣⲁ ⲛ̅ⲧⲉ ⲧⲙⲉ·| ⲉⲧⲃⲉ ⲡⲁⲓ̈ ⲥⲉⲛⲁϯ ⲣⲁⲛ
ⲉⲣⲟⲟⲩ| ϫⲉ ⲛⲓϣⲁϫⲉ ⲛ̅ⲧⲉ ϯⲁⲫⲑⲁⲣⲥⲓⲁ|[ⲙ̅ⲛ̅

15 ϯ|ⲙ̅ⲛ̅ⲧⲙⲉ ⲛ̅ⲛⲏ ⲉⲧⲥⲟⲟⲩⲛ/ [ⲙ̅]ⲡⲛⲟⲩⲧⲉ ⲛ̅ϣⲁⲉⲛⲉϩ
ϩ̅ⲛ̅ ⲟⲩ[ⲥ]ⲟⲫⲓⲁ ⲛ̅ⲧⲉ ⲟⲩⲅⲛⲱⲥⲓⲥ ⲙ̅ⲛ̅| ⲟⲩⲥⲃⲱ ⲛ̅ⲧⲉ
ϩⲉⲛⲁⲅⲅⲉⲗⲟⲥ <ⲛ̅>ϣⲁ|ⲉⲛⲉϩ ϫⲉ ⲩⲥⲟⲟⲩⲛ ⲛ̅ϩⲱⲃ ⲛⲓⲙ·|ϯ/

22 ⲧⲁⲓ̈ ⲧⲉ ϯⲅⲛⲱ|ⲥⲓⲥ ⲛ̅ⲛⲁⲡⲟⲕⲣⲩⲫⲟⲛ ⲛ̅ⲧⲉ ⲁⲇⲁⲙ|

25 ⲉⲧⲁⲩⲧⲁⲁⲥ ⲛ̅ⲥⲏⲑ· ⲉⲧⲉ ⲡⲓϫⲱ/ⲕ̅ⲙ̅ ⲉⲧⲟⲩⲁⲁⲃ ⲡⲉ
ⲛ̅ⲛⲏ ⲉⲧⲥⲟ|ⲟⲩⲛ ⲛ̅ϯⲅⲛⲱⲥⲓⲥ ⲛ̅ⲉⲛⲉϩ ⲉⲃⲟ[ⲗ]|
ϩ̅ⲓⲧⲟⲟⲧⲟⲩ ⲛ̅ⲛⲓⲗⲟⲅⲟⲅⲉⲛⲏⲥ ⲙ̅[ⲛ̅]| ⲛⲓⲫⲱⲥⲧⲏⲣ ·
ⲛ̅ⲁⲧⲧⲁⲕⲟ ⲛⲏ [ⲉⲧⲁⲩ]|ⲉⲓ ⲉⲃⲟⲗ ϩ̅ⲛ̅ ϯⲥⲡ[ⲟ]ⲣⲁ

30 ⲉⲧⲟⲩⲁ[ⲁⲃ]/ ⲓ̈ⲉⲥⲥⲉⲩⲥ ⲙ̅ⲁ[ⲍ]ⲁⲣⲉⲩⲥ [ⲓ̈ⲉⲥⲥⲉ]ⲇⲉⲕⲉⲩⲥ
[ⲡⲓ]ⲙⲟⲟⲩ ⲉⲧⲟ[ⲛ̅ϩ̅]

8: [84],4-[85],18.22-31. See above, p. 231.

[84],4   Then (τότε) a voice came to them | saying:
"Micheu, | Michar and Mnesinous"--those | who are
over the holy baptism | and the living water--"why |
10   did you (pl.) cry against the living / God with
lawless (ἄνομος) voices | and tongues that | have
no law (νόμος) given to them, and souls (ψυχή) |
full of blood and unclean | [works]? You (pl.)
15   are <not> full of / works that belong to the truth, |
but (ἀλλά) your (pl.) ways are full of | pleasure
and merriment. After you (pl.) had | defiled the
20   water of life, | you (pl.) drew it within / the
will of the powers | to whom you (pl.) have been
given | to serve. | And your (pl.) | thought is
25   not like that of / those men | whom you (pl.) per-
secute. | [For] they have not obeyed [your] (pl.) |
[85],1   desires (ἐπιθυμία), nor (οὔτε) // does their fruit
wither, but (ἀλλά) | they will be known | as long
as the great eons (αἰών) because the words | of the
5   God of the eons (αἰών) / which they have kept have
not been gathered into | the book, nor (οὔτε) have
they been written. |

But (ἀλλά) angelic (beings) (ἀγγελικός) will
bring | these (words) that all the generations
10   (γενεά) of men | will not know, for (γάρ) / they
will be upon a high | mountain upon a rock (πέτρα)
of truth. | Therefore, they shall be called: |
'The words of Imperishability (ἀφθαρσία) | [and]
15   Truth,' of those who know / [the] eternal God in |
wisdom (σοφία) of knowledge (γνῶσις) and | teaching
of eternal angels (ἄγγελος), | for he knows
everything." | ‡ /

22   This is the secret (ἀπόκρυφον) | knowledge
(γνῶσις) of Adam, | that he gave to Seth, which is
25   the holy / baptism of those who know | the eternal
knowledge (γνῶσις) through | those born of the word
(λογογενής) and | the imperishable illuminators
(φωστήρ), [who] | came from the holy seed (σπορά): /
30   Yesseus, Mazareus, Yessedekeus, | [The Living Water].

[65],4

"It." The feminine pronoun must refer back to γνῶσις (64,27) since it is the only feminine noun in the immediate context. The text of source A explains how the lost "glory" of Adam and Eve is preserved in the race of the great men, but fails to indicate that knowledge of the eternal God is also preserved, or where it is preserved. The redactor "corrects" this "oversight" in his *Vorlage* by indicating that it is preserved in the "seed" of great aeons. Since Adam "names" his son Seth after this "seed," the "seed" must also be named "Seth." This Seth (i.e., the seed) appears to be some sort of Ur-Seth, or semi-divine being, who does in the primordial drama what the "earthly" Seth does in the world when he preserves the knowledge of the eternal God by receiving such a revelation from Adam. The fact that Seth is chosen as bearer of a revelation from Adam is known from other sources (*Adam and Eve* 25-29; 38,4-5; Epiph. *Pan.* 39.1.3; 2,4-3,1.5; *Steles Seth* [VII,5]118,10-121,17). The preference for Seth apparently stems from the Old Testament tradition. After Cain killed Abel, he was banished from the presence of the Lord (Gen 4:16). His descendants were, therefore, a "rejected" race. Adam's final son, Seth, was born "in his own likeness, after his image" (Gen 5:4), that is, in the likeness and image of God (Gen 1:27).

[65],9

Ⲏ ⲈⲂⲞⲖ ⲚⲌⲎⲦⳒ . This awkward phrase ([65],9) has posed a problem for translators: Böhlig (97) translated "oder von dem (es stammt)"; Krause (21) "oder (stammt) aus ihm." Beltz (7,1) presumes the expression to be a gloss intended to show that the great race descends from the great Seth. MacRae also regards it as a gloss and translates "or from whom (it comes)." He understands it to be a reference to Seth from whom the great race descended.

It seems better to understand it as a quite literal translation of the Greek *Vorlage*: ὅς ἐστιν ἡ σπορὰ τῆς γενεᾶς μεγάλης ἢ ἐξ αὐτοῦ (see James Hadley and Frederic Allen, [*A Greek Grammar for Schools and Colleges* (rev. ed.; New York: D. Appleton, 1884) 205, 314] for the omission of the verb in the relative clause). Rather than supplying the understood verb in the second relative clause, the Coptic translator simply misunderstood the relative ἤ

to be the disjunctive particle ⲏ̄, and translated very literally, ⲏ̄ ⲈⲂⲞⲗ ⲚⲌ︤ⲎⲦⲨ︥, rather
than ⲦⲎ ⲈⲦⲈ ⲈⲂⲞⲗ ⲚⲌⲎⲦⲨ .

[69],11   ⲚⳲⳒ . MacRae, Böhlig (101), Kasser (321) and
Beltz (10) all reconstruct ⲚⲦⲈ .

[69],13   Böhlig (101) and Beltz (10) reconstruct
[ⲚⳒ︤Ⳓ︥ ⲦⲠⲒⲞⲨ]ⲕⲱⲚⲌ. However, the lacuna will not
accommodate more than four letters. The
present reconstruction follows MacRae ([65],
14).

[69],14   Beltz (10) and Böhlig (101) reconstruct ⲦⲀⲈⳲ .
However, because of the masculine pronoun in
the relative, it must be ⲦⲦⲀⲈⳲ .

[71],4-8   The meaning of the statement is difficult to
grasp. To begin with, it anticipates the
arrogance (from the perspective of the great
creator) of the great men and their refusal
to acknowledge the lordship of the creator.
This act actually follows at [71],8-20! The
great men are mentioned earlier in the text
(see below) in what are identified in this
paper as redactional comments and those redactional comments simply assume what is here
stated. From the perspective of the text, it
is confusing. Seth is named after the "man"
who is the "seed" from whom the great generation has come ([65],3-9). This great generation is attacked by the creator with the
flood ([69],10-17) although no reason is
given for the attack (also noted by Beltz
[78]). The reason for the attack is not
mentioned until later. From the perspective
of the redactor, however, there is no confusion since he already knows of the conflict
that surfaces later.
          The negative is also confusing. For the
text to say, "You will produce no seed of
those men who will not stand before me in
another glory," means that the seed produced
will be of those men who *will* stand before
him in another glory! In other words, Noah's
descendants will be those that oppose the
creator and that will be done by the creator's
order. Surely, this is not what one would
expect! The confusion is caused by the double
negative. To achieve the sense one expects,
only one of the clauses should be negated,
either the main clause or the relative clause.
Thus, for example, the creator would say: "No
seed will come from you of those men who dare
to stand before me in another glory"; that is,
you will not produce men who will disrespect

me or, conversely, you will produce those who will not disrespect me. But certainly it should not say: "You will not produce those who will not disrespect me." The latter is certainly a contradiction of the intent of the text. But this is precisely the meaning of the text when it says: "There shall not come from you (any) seed of those men who will not stand before me in another glory."

Beltz has apparently recognized this problem because he translates the relative clause as an affirmative without emending the text or explaining why he translates it as an affirmative (12,1).

I suggest that the Coptic scribe has translated his *Vorlage* literally and in so doing loses its meaning. The *Vorlage* used a Greek relative clause to express purpose (Hadley-Allen, *Greek Grammar*, 288). The Coptic scribe translated the relative faithfully but missed the use of the relative clause to express purpose. His *Vorlage* (τῶν ἀνθρώπων οἳ μὴ στήσουσιν ἔμπροσθέν μου ἐν ἑτερῇ δοξῇ) should have been translated with ϫⲉⲕⲁⲥ and the third future: ϫⲉⲕⲁⲁⲥ ⲛ̄ⲛⲉⲩⲁϩⲉⲣⲁⲧⲟⲩ ⲙ̄ⲡⲁⲙ̄ⲧⲟ ⲉⲃⲟⲗ ϩⲛ̄ ⲕⲉⲉⲟⲟⲩ. Hence, the present text ought to be translated: "That they not stand before me in another glory."

[76],6-7 The sentence is obscure in its context. For example, translators are divided on whether a new sentence begins with ⲁⲗⲗⲁ (so MacRae and Böhlig) or not (so Beltz, Krause and Kasser), and most translators have left open the identification of the subject of the sentence. Beltz, however, correctly suggests the subject is probably the angels (121), rather than the "great men," and connects the sentence with its context.

> The men will become like those angels for they (the angels) are not strangers to them (the men), but they (the angels) work with the imperishable seed (the men).

This identification of the men in the A narrative as "the seed" is a concern of the redactor ([65],3-9; [69],10-17) and the motif of the angels working with the seed is met again in the redactor's conclusion ([85],7-9; [85],14-18).

[76],11 "<Witnesses>." An object of the verb ϣⲱϫⲡ̄ appears to have been omitted through scribal error. This observation is suggested by the

translators: MacRae, leave (something) of the
seed; Böhlig (108), er (etwas) von dem Samen
Noahs übriglasse; and Kasser (325), afin
qu'il <fasse> subsister <quelque chose>. On
the other hand, Krause is not bothered by
what others have sensed as a problem and
translates (26) "damit er übriglasse vom
Samen Noahs," and Beltz translates (17,1),
rather freely, "damit er von dem Samen des
Noah...einen Rest erhalte." Krause's translation overlooks the problem and Beltz's
translation ignores the text. (Beltz appears
to be translating something like ⲍⲓⲛⲁ ⲭⲉ
ⲉⲩⲕⲱ ⲛ̄ⲥⲁ ⲡϣⲱ ⲭⲡ̄ ⲉⲃⲟⲗ ⲍⲙ̄ ⲡⲓⲥⲡⲉⲣⲙⲁ
rather than what actually appears in the
text.) Any emendation is, of course, open to
question, but by following what hints one can
observe in the text, the probability of a
given emendation might be increased. Observe
first that the redactor has modelled this
statement on that which immediately follows
in [76],14-15. With the exception of the object in the first statement, the form of the
statements reflect a remarkable similarity.

[76],11-13 ⲍⲓⲛⲁ ⲭⲉ ⲉⲩⲉϣⲱⲭⲡ̄ [   ]
[76],14-15   ⲭⲉ ⲉⲩⲉϣⲱⲭⲡ̄ ⲛⲁⲩ ⲛ̄ⲍⲉⲛϣⲏⲛ
ⲛ̄ⲣⲉⲩϯ ⲟⲩⲧⲁⲍ

Observe next the problem facing the redactor.
He had just indicated that the great men had
been removed by "divine" intervention and had
been taken to a place of safety "above the
aeons and the rulers of the powers" ([75],
23-27). Presumably by this act he has removed all "knowledge" of the eternal God from
the "world." This interpretation is in fact
suggested by the second statement ([76],14-
15) because the illuminator of knowledge
needs "fruitbearing trees" to continue his
work of illumination. It appears that the
redactor has clarified the source from which
those "disciples" will come: the seed of Noah.
The word omitted is probably something like
ⲍⲉⲛⲙ̄ⲛⲧⲣⲉ (cf. [71],22). There are naturally other possibilities that would render a
similar meaning.

[81],19   "Satisfied"; understanding ⲧⲱⲧ as a translation for κεραννύναι; the meaning is literally
"to temper" or "to cool."

[82],18-19   "The desire of these powers." See above p.
54 n. 74.

[83],4-7   The antecedent of the ΝΗ clause ([83],5) has posed a problem to translators. Böhlig (115) has not attempted to clarify the relationship of the clause to its two possible antecedents †ⲤⲠⲞⲢⲀ and †ⲂⲞⲨ. He simply translates the clause in the order that it appears in the text. However, he flags the problem of the antecedent by indicating that his *die* is plural and not the singular feminine. This only emphasizes the difficulty of it referring to either †ⲤⲠⲞⲢⲀ or †ⲂⲞⲨ, which are both singular. Krause (29) also leaves the antecedent of ΝΗ in doubt, translating it in the same order that it appears in the text, but solves the problem of the indefinite *die* by using the plural *diejenigen*. In both instances, one cannot be certain whether the positioning of the clause after ⲂⲞⲨ is intended to indicate that ⲂⲞⲨ is the antecedent or whether the translator is simply following the order of the Coptic text. The same uncertainty is true for Beltz's translation (24,1).

          Kasser (330) takes the antecedent of ΝΗ to be ⲤⲠⲞⲢⲀ, inferring a generic use of ⲤⲠⲞⲢⲀ with a translation *ensemencement* and understanding the ΝΗ clause as "les hommes faisant partie de cette semence (= ensemencement)." MacRae implies the same identification by breaking the Coptic word order and placing the ΝΗ clause after ⲤⲠⲞⲢⲀ, effectively setting it in apposition to "the seed." H.-M. Schenke (col. 33) takes the punctuation mark following †ⲂⲞⲨ seriously. Linking it with the obscure statement at [83],6-7 (ⲚⲦⲞⲦⲞⲨ ⲦⲎⲢⲞⲨ), he begins a new sentence with the ΝΗ clause and assumes that a line has been lost after ⲀⲨⲰ ([83],7) containing, among other things, the main verb that described the action of the ΝΗ clause.

          Diejenigen, die seinen Namen annehmen werden auf dem Wasser und <...werden gerettet werden (?)> vor ihnen allen.

Schenke is correct that it is possible to translate the passage as a two-part nominal sentence (Till, §247), and I agree that text has probably been lost following ⲀⲨⲰ. But his solution does not resolve the problem of the antecedent of ΝΗ. It could still be either ⲤⲠⲞⲢⲀ or ⲂⲞⲨ. It is more likely that the antecedent is ⲤⲠⲞⲢⲀ since ⲤⲠⲞⲢⲀ, although singular, can also be conceived generically. In [83],4, the redactor writes "the seed" in the singular but in the latter instance ([83],5) he conceives of "the seed"

as all those who make up the group identified
as "the seed" (cf. [85],22). Had 6Ο𝜦 been
intended as the antecedent, one would have
expected Ñ6Ο𝜦, since 6Ο𝜦 has not been used
generically in the text. 6Ο𝜦 is used as
another word for strength and to describe the
semi-divine associates of the demiurge, and
in the latter instance it is never used generically. Unfortunately, this does not resolve the problem. If CΠOPᴀ is to be identified as "those who receive his name upon
the water," one must explain this sudden pro-
baptism motif on the part of the redactor.
In other sections, the redactor has shown a
marked anti-baptism bias (cf. [82],18-19;
[84],4-8; [85],22-31).

The simplest solution that seems to fit
the situation is to assume that haplography
has occurred. Some scribe simply failed to
transcribe the genitival Ñ when he was writing ÑΝΗ . A later scribe, noting the confusion created by the loss of Ñ , could have
easily supplied the sentence divider.

[83],5   "The power <of> those." The text reads
                  †6Ο𝜦˙ ΝΗ .

[84],5-6   "Micheu, Michar, Mnesinous." In the Bruce
                  Codex (f. 136ᵛ, 18-21) and *Zost.* ([VIII,*1*]
                  6,8-17), Michar and Micheu are listed without
                  Mnesinous as "the powers who are over the
                  living water." In *Zost.* (VIII 47,4), Mnesi-
                  nous also appears, but as a "keeper of the
                  immortal soul." In *Gos. Eg.* (III,*2*)64,14-20
                  = (IV,*2*)76,2-10, the three names are found
                  together as "they who preside over the spring
                  of truth." At the same location, Micheu and
                  Michar are also called: "they who preside
                  over the gates of the waters." The Bruce
                  Codex seems to conflate both of these titles
                  given to Michar and Micheu in *Zost.* and *Gos.
                  Eg.* It reads (136ᵛ, 15-21):

                  > And in that place were powers
                  > appointed over the Source (πηγή) of
                  > the Living Waters (*sic*!) which
                  > straightway(?) were brought forth.
                  > These are the names of the Powers
                  > which are over the Living Water:
                  > Michar and Micheu. (Baynes, *A Cop-
                  > tic Gnostic Treatise*, 180)

                  In *Trim. Prot.* (XIII,*2**)48,18-21, they are
                  called "the baptists" who immerse in the
                  "spring of the water of life" (cf. XIII 45,
                  17-18).

[84],11

ЄⲘⲚ ⲚⲞⲘⲞⲤ] ([84],11). One wonders why the Coptic translator did not use ЄⲘⲚⲦⲞⲨ ⲚⲚⲞⲘⲞⲤ .

[84],11-12

H.-M. Schenke (col. 34) is correct in identifying ⲦЄ as an Achmimic qualitative of ϯ.

[84],14

"You are <not> full." All other translators leave ⲀⲚ as it appears in the text and understand the negative ⲀⲚ to negate the converted (circumstantial) nominal sentence: ЄⲚⲀ ⲦⲘЄ ⲀⲚ ⲚЄ ([84],15). However, the result is less than satisfactory when the adversative conjunction ⲀⲖⲖⲀ puts the following sentence in contrast to the statement: "You are full of works which do not belong to truth, but your ways are full of pleasure and merriment." What is the contrast? The first sentence asserts, "You are full of untruthful works," and the second sentence asserts, "Your ways are full of pleasure and merriment." The usual form of contrast is to oppose a negative statement with an affirmative, but here we have two unnegated statements. It is true that in a contrast the negative statement can be an unnegated statement, but it must be negative or critical in thrust; for example:

> You are a beautiful woman (affirmative), but today you look horrible (a negative [critical] statement although affirmative in form).

If one tries to understand the present text in that way, the first statement must be the negative assertation: "You are full of untruthful works." The second statement is forced into the role of positive assertion as follows:

> You are full of untruthful works (and that's bad), but your ways are full of pleasure and merriment (and that's good).

This makes a good contrast, but unfortunately seems to violate the intent of the text. It is not clear that the "voice" would be paying a compliment to Micheu, Michar and Mnesinous. However, if the ⲀⲚ could negate the entire first sentence, the problem is resolved. There is a good contrast between "not being full of truthful works, but being full of pleasure." Till reports (§403) that the negative ⲀⲚ floats rather freely with respect to its position in the sentence. Thus, it could come immediately after the verb or at the end of the sentence (cf. [84],23-25).

In this case, like [84],23-25, it comes at
the end of the sentence, but unlike [84],23-
25, the sentence ends with a converted (circumstantial) nominal sentence. In every example I have seen of a negated nominal sentence, when the ⲀⲚ comes at the end of the
sentence, it always comes before the demonstrative; cf. Till, §403; C. C. Walters, *An
Elementary Coptic Grammar of the Sahidic
Dialect* (Oxford: Blackwell, 1972) §47; cf.
2 Apoc. Jas. (V,*4*)[53],14; [55],15; 58,2;
61,10; and in the present tractate: [65],18;
[65],30; [76],6. What has apparently happened is that the scribe simply followed the
normal procedure of following the negative ⲀⲚ
by the demonstrative, although he intended it
to negate the entire sentence. Therefore I
have emended the text in the interest of
correcting what appears to be a scribal error.
However, I have not placed the negative ⲀⲚ
at the end of the sentence, since this position is excluded because of the demonstrative,
but I have placed it before the converted
circumstantial clause in order to negate the
main sentence. Another possibility for clear-
ing up the confusion is that the scribe has
incorrectly written ⲀⲗⲗⲀ ([84],16) for Ⲁⲩⲱ.
This correction would render a good sense to
the text.

> You are full of works which do not
> belong to truth <and> your ways are
> full of pleasure and merriment.

[84],19   "Within," i.e., "under the control of."

[84],23-24   ⲙ̄ⲡⲉⲧⲚⲘⲉⲉⲧⲉ . Text reads ⲙ̄ⲡⲉ{ⲡⲉ}ⲧⲚⲘⲉⲉⲧⲉ .
                   MacRae suggests that the error can be attrib-
                   uted to the negative ⲀⲚ being so far from
                   the verb that the scribe was led to think of
                   a 1st perfect negative.

[84],24   What appears to be writing above ⲙ̄ⲡⲀ ([84],
                   24) is blotting from ⳁ in ⳁⲅ̄Ⲛⲱⲥⲓⲥ ([85],26).

[84],27   Following the reconstruction of Beltz (25).

[84],28   Contrary to Beltz's assumption (25), [84],28
                   seems to be the last line of the page on the
                   basis of profile with p. [85].

[85],5   The scribe has changed ⲉⲓ̄ⲧⲟⲟⲧⲟⲩ to ⲉⲓ̄ⲧⲟⲩ
                   by marking out ⲧⲟⲟ with supralinear dots.
                   The translation "have not been gathered"
                   understands ⲉⲓ̄ⲧⲟⲩ to be a translation of
                   συνάγειν. MacRae understands the *Vorlage* to
                   read ἐπιβάλλειν. ⲙ̄ⲡⲟⲩⲉⲓ̄ⲧⲟⲟⲧⲟⲩ, the word

first written by the scribe, would be translated as: "They did not have hand laid to
them." The difference between "not gathered
into the book" and "not written" is not
clear. One would expect that "being gathered
into the book" would be an equivalent of
"being written."

[85],10-11

"Upon a mountain, upon a rock." Josephus
reports that the Sethians preserved their
traditions by inscribing them on two pillars:
one of brick and the other of stone. If the
brick pillar were destroyed in the great
flood predicted by Adam, the pillar of stone
would remain (*Ant.* 1.70-71). In *Adam and Eve*
50,1-2, Seth is instructed to make tables of
stone and others of clay containing the revelations of Adam and Eve. Should the earth
be destroyed by water, the tables of clay
would be dissolved, but those of stone would
be preserved. Should the earth be destroyed
by fire, the tables of stone would be broken
up, but the tables of clay would be baked
hard and thereby preserved (cf. Joseph. *Ant.*
1.115-116). The motif of preservation upon a
mountain is known elsewhere in the Nag Hammadi Library: *Gos. Eg.* (III,*2*)68,1-26;
Allogenes (XI,*2*)72,1-6. The title: "The
Three Steles of Seth" (VII,*5*) should also be
noted in this respect. See also *Jub.* 8:3 and
Zost. (VIII,*1*)130,1-4. Cf. W. Bousset, "Die
Beziehungen der ältesten jüdischen Sibylle
zur chaldäischen Sibylle und einige weitere
Beobachtungen über den synkretistischen
Charakter der spätjüdischen Literatur," *ZNW* 3
(1902) 23-49. See also the Greek *Life of*
Pachomius, §126.

[85],17-18

⟨Ⲛ̄⟩ⲩⲁ ⲈⲚⲈⲌ. MacRae suggests the emendation
in a footnote. Cf. [64],15-16; [75],8; [76],
27; [85],15. It is also possible to take
ⲩⲁ ⲈⲚⲈⲌ as an adverb, but it is somewhat
awkward since it is separated so far from the
verbal element (ⲤⲞⲞⲨⲚ, [85],14).

[85],18

"He knows everything," i.e., the eternal God.

[85],18

‡ See [85],19 in source A above, pp. 240-41.

[85],22-26

Knowledge as baptism: *Paraph. Shem* (VII,*1*)
30,21-27; 31,14-19; 37,19-35; *Testim. Truth*
(IX,*3*)69,15-28.

[85],30

"Yesseus, Mazareus, Yessedekeus." The names
appear in *Zost.* (VIII,*1*)47,5-6 as "the living
spirits." In *Gos. Eg.* (III,*2*)66,10-12 (=
[IV,*2*]78,10-16), they appear in an ecstatic
chant.

> Yesseus, Mazareus, Yessedekeus,
> O living water, O child of the
> child, O glorious name.

They are also called "the great attendant,
Yesseus, Mazareus, Yessedekeus, the living
water (sing.)"; cf. *Gos. Eg.* (III,*2*)64,9-12
(= [IV,*2*]75,24-27, where they are referred to
in the plural as "the great attendants"). The
name Mazareus appears at *Zost.* (VIII,*1*)57,5-6.

[85],13   "[The Living Water]." As reconstructed by
Beltz (26) and MacRae on the basis of *Gos.
Eg.* (III,*2*)64,10-11.

SELECTED BIBLIOGRAPHY

Adam, A. *Texte zum Manichäismus*. Berlin: de Gruyter, 1954.

Allberry, C. R. C. *A Manichaean Psalm Book*. Stuttgart: Kohlhammer, 1938.

Altaner, Berthold. *Patrology*. Trans. Hilda Graef from the 5th German ed. New York: Herder and Herder, 1960.

Anderson, B. W. "Water." Pp. 806-10 in *Interpreters Dictionary of the Bible*. Vol. 4. Ed. George A. Buttrick, et al. Nashville: Abingdon, 1962.

Atkinson, James. "The Shâh Nâmeh by Firdusi." Pp. 3-338 in *Persian and Japanese Literature*. Rev. ed. 2 vols. New York: Colonial Press, 1900.

Baltzer, Klaus. *The Covenant Formulary in Old Testament, Jewish and Early Christian Writings*. Trans. David Green. Philadelphia: Fortress, 1971.

Bauer, Walter. *A Greek-English Lexicon of the New Testament and Other Early Christian Literature*. Trans. William F. Arndt and F. William Gingrich. Chicago: University of Chicago, 1957.

Baynes, Charlotte. *A Coptic Gnostic Treatise contained in the Codex Brucianus*. Cambridge: University Press, 1933.

Beltz, Walter. "Die Adam-Apokalypse aus Codex V von Nag Hammadi: Jüdische Bausteine in gnostischen Systemen." Dr. Theol. dissertation; Berlin: Humboldt-Universität, 1970.

_____. "Bemerkungen zur Adamapokalypse aus Nag-Hammadi-Codex V." Pp. 159-63 in *Studia Coptica*. Ed. Peter Nagel. Berlin: Akademie, 1974.

_____ with P. L. Márton. "A gnósiz-Kutatás jelenlegi állása. Az Adám-Apokalipszis a Nag Hamadiban talált V. Codexben." *Theologiai Szemle* 12 (1969) 266-70.

_____. "NHC V, 5/p.64,1-85,32: Die Apokalypse des Adams (ApocAd)." Pp. 46-47 in *Gnosis und Neues Testament*. Ed. Karl-Wolfgang Tröger. Berlin: Evangelische Verlagsanstalt, 1973.

Bianchi, Ugo (ed.). *Le origini dello gnosticismo: Colloquio di Messina 13-18 Aprile 1966; Testi e discussioni*. Supplement to *Numen* 12. Leiden: E. J. Brill, 1967.

Böhlig, Alexander, and Labib, Pahor. *Koptisch-gnostische Apokalypsen aus Codex V von Nag Hammadi im Koptischen Museum zu Alt-Kairo*. Halle-Wittenberg: Wissenschaftliche Zeitschrift der Martin-Luther-Universität, 1963.

Böhlig, Alexander, and Wisse, Frederik. *The Gospel of the
    Egyptians: The Holy Book of the Great Invisible Spirit.*
    Leiden: E. J. Brill, 1975.

Böhlig, Alexander. "Die Adamapokalypse aus Codex V von Nag
    Hammadi als Zeugnis jüdisch-iranischer Gnosis." *OrChr* 48
    (1964) 44-49.

_____. "Jüdisches und iranisches in der Adamapokalypse des
    Codex V von Nag Hammadi." Pp. 149-61 in *Mysterion und
    Wahrheit: Gesammelte Beiträge zur spätantiken Religions-
    geschichte.* Leiden: E. J. Brill, 1968.

Bonnet, Maximilianus (ed.). *Acta Apostolorum Apocrypha.*
    2 vols. in 3. Hildesheim: Georg Olms, 1959.

Bousset, Wilhelm. *Hauptprobleme der Gnosis.* Göttingen:
    Vandenhoeck & Ruprecht, 1907.

_____. "Die Beziehungen der ältesten jüdischen Sibylle zur
    chaldäischen Sibylle und einige weitere Beobachtungen über
    den synkretistischen Charakter der spätjüdischen Litera-
    tur." *ZNW* 3 (1902) 23-49.

_____. "Gnosis." Col. 1535 in *Real-Encyclopädie der clas-
    sischen Altertumswissenschaft,* Vol. 7.2. Ed. A. F. Pauly,
    G. Wissova, and W. Kroll. 24 vols. Stuttgart: J. B.
    Metzler, 1893-1972.

_____. *Kurios Christos.* Trans. John Steely from the German
    5th ed. Nashville: Abingdon, 1970.

Bowman, John. *The Samaritan Problem: Studies in the Relation-
    ships of Samaritanism, Judaism, and Early Christianity.*
    Trans. A. M. Johnson, Jr. Pittsburgh: Pickwick, 1975.

Bultmann, Rudolf. "Die Bedeutung der neuerschlossenen
    mandäischen und manichäischen Quellen für das Verständnis
    der Johannesevangeliums." *ZNW* 24 (1925) 100-46.

Buttrick, George A. et al. (eds.). *Interpreters Dictionary of
    the Bible.* 4 vols. Nashville: Abingdon, 1962.

Charles, R. H. *Ascension of Isaiah.* London: Society for
    Promoting Christian Knowledge, 1917.

_____. *The Apocrypha and Pseudepigrapha of the Old
    Testament.* 2 vols. Oxford: Clarendon, 1913.

Ciasca, Augustini. *Sacrorum bibliorum fragmenta Copto-Sahidica
    Musei Borgiani.* 2 vols. Rome: Typis eiusdem s. congrega-
    tionis, 1885.

Colpe, Carsten. *Die religionsgeschichtliche Schule: Darstellung
    und Kritik ihres Bildes vom gnostischen Erlösermythes.*
    Göttingen: Vandenhoeck & Ruprecht, 1961.

Cross, F. L., and Livingston, E. A. (eds.). *The Oxford Dictionary of the Christian Church*. 2nd ed. London: Oxford University, 1974.

Crum, Walter. *A Coptic Dictionary*. Oxford: Clarendon, 1939.

Cullmann, Oscar. *The Earliest Christian Confessions*. Trans. J. K. S. Reid. London: Lutterworth, 1949.

Daniélou, Jean. "Histoire des Origines Chretiennes." *RSR* 54 (1966) 285-93.

Dibelius, Martin. *From Tradition to Gospel*. Trans. B. L. Woolf. 2nd ed. rev. New York: Scribner's, n.d.

Doresse, Jean. "'Le Livre sacré du grand Espirit invisible' ou 'L'Evangile des Egyptiens': Texte copte édité, traduit et commenté d'après la Codex I de Nag'a-Hammadi/ Khénoboskion: II. Commentaire." *JA* 256 (1968[1971]) 289-386.

_____. *The Secret Books of the Egyptian Gnostics: An Introduction to the Gnostic Coptic Manuscripts discovered at Chenoboskion*. Trans. P. Mairet. New York: Viking, 1960.

Eliade, Mircea. *Patterns in Comparative Religion*. New York: Sheed and Ward, 1958.

Fischer, Karl Martin. "Der Gedanke unserer grossen Kraft (Noema): Die vierte Schrift aus Nag Hammadi - Codex VI." *TLZ* 98 (1973) cols. 169-75.

Foerster, Werner (ed.). *Gnosis*. Trans. and ed. R. McL. Wilson. 2 vols. Oxford: Clarendon, 1972-1974.

_____. *Gnosis*. 2 vols. Zurich: Artemis, 1971.

Frazier, J. G. (ed.). *Apollodorus: The Library*. 2 vols. In the Loeb Classical Library. New York: Putnam's, 1921.

Fuller, Reginald. *The Foundations of New Testament Christology*. New York: Scribner's, 1965.

Goedicke, Hans. "An Unexpected Allusion to the Vesuvius Eruption in 79 A.D." *American Journal of Philology* 90 (1969) 340-41.

Haardt, R. "Böhlig, Alexander und Labib, Pahor, Koptisch-gnostische Apokalypsen aus Codex V von Nag Hammadi im Koptischen Museum zu Alt-Kairo." *WZKM* 61 (1967) 153-59.

Hadley, James and Allen, Frederic. *A Greek Grammar for Schools and Colleges*. Rev. ed. New York: Appleton, 1884.

Hammond, N. G. L. and Scullard, H. H. (eds.). *The Oxford Classical Dictionary*. 2nd ed. Oxford: Clarendon, 1970.

Hanson, R. P. C. *Tradition in the Early Church*. Philadelphia:
    Westminster, 1962.

Harnack, Adolf. *Geschichte der altchristlichen Literatur*.
    2 vols. Leipzig: Hinrichs, 1904.

Harris, James. *The Commentaries of Isho'dad of Merv in Syriac
    and English*. 5 vols. Cambridge: University Press, 1911-
    1916.

Hatch, Edwin and Redpath, Henry A. (eds.). *A Concordance to
    the Septuagint*. 2 vols. Graz: Akademischer Druck-V.,
    1954.

Hedrick, C. W. "The Apocalypse of Adam: A Literary and Source
    Analysis." Pp. 581-90 in *The Society of Biblical Litera-
    ture One Hundred Eighth Annual Meeting Book of Seminar
    Papers*. Vol. 2. Ed. Lane C. McGaughy. Missoula, MT:
    Society of Biblical Literature, 1972.

Heinisch, Paul. *Theology of the Old Testament*. Trans. William
    G. Heidt. St. Paul: North Central Publishing, 1955.

Hengel, Martin. *Judaism and Hellenism*. Trans. John Bowden.
    2 vols. Philadelphia: Fortress, 1974.

Hennecke, Edgar and Schneemelcher, Wilhelm (eds.). *New Testa-
    ment Apocrypha*. Trans. and ed. R. McL. Wilson et al.
    2 vols. Philadelphia: Westminster, 1959-1964.

Holl, Karl (ed.). *Die Griechischen Schriftsteller der ersten
    drei Jahrhunderte*. 3 vols. Leipzig: Hinrichs, 1915-1933.

"Instructions for Contributors." *JBL* 95 (1976) 330-46.

Jackson, A. V. Williams. *Researches in Manichaeism*. New York:
    Columbia University, 1932.

_____. *Zoroaster: The Prophet of Ancient Iran*. New York:
    MacMillan, 1901.

Jonas, Hans. *Gnosis und spätantiker Geist*. 2nd ed.
    Göttingen: Vandenhoeck & Ruprecht, 1955.

_____. *The Gnostic Religion*. 2nd ed. rev. Boston: Beacon
    Hill, 1963.

Kasser, Rodolphe. "Bibliothèque gnostique V: Apocalypse
    d'Adam." *RTP* 17 (1967) 316-33.

_____. "Böhlig, Alexander und Labib, Pahor, Koptisch-
    gnostische Apokalypsen aus Codex V von Nag Hammadi im
    Koptischen Museum zu Alt-Kairo." *BO* 22 (1965) 163-64.

_____. "Textes gnostiques: Nouvelles remarques à propos de
    Apocalypses de Paul, Jacques et Adam." *Le Muséon* 78
    (1965) 299-306.

Kasser, Rodolphe. "Textes gnostiques: Remarques à propos des éditions récentes du Livre secret de Jean et des Apocalypses de Paul, Jacques et Adam." *Le Muséon* 78 (1965) 71-98.

Kelly, J. N. D. *Early Christian Doctrines*. 2nd ed. New York: Harper and Row, 1960.

Kittel, G. and Friedrich, G. *Theological Dictionary of the New Testament*. Trans. and ed. G. W. Bromiley. 9 vols. Grand Rapids: Eerdmans, 1964-1974.

Klijn, A. F. J. *Seth in Jewish, Christian and Gnostic Literature*. Leiden: E. J. Brill, 1977.

_____. *The Acts of Thomas*. Leiden: E. J. Brill, 1962.

Krause, Martin. "The Apocalypse of Adam." Pp. 13-23 in *Gnosis*. Vol. 2. Ed. Werner Foerster. Oxford: Clarendon, 1974.

_____ (ed.). *Gnosis und Gnosticism*. Leiden: E. J. Brill, 1977.

_____. "Der Stand der Veröffentlichung der Nag Hammadi Texte." Pp. 66-88 in *Le origini dello gnosticismo*. Ed. Ugo Bianchi. Leiden: E. J. Brill, 1967.

_____, and Labib, Pahor (eds.). *Die drei Versionen des Apocryphon des Johannes im Koptischen Museum zu Alt-Kairo*. Abhandlungen des Deutschen Archäologischen Instituts Kairo, Koptische Reihe 1. Glückstadt: J. J. Augustin, 1962.

Kuhn, H.; Schnackenburg, R.; and Huber, C. "Logos." Cols. 1119-28 in *Lexikon für Theologie und Kirche*, vol. 6. Ed. Josef Höfer and Karl Rahner. 10 vols. 2nd ed. rev. Freiburg: Herder, 1957-1965.

Kümmel, Werner Georg. *Introduction to the New Testament*. Trans. Howard Clark Kee. Nashville/New York: Abingdon, 1975.

Lake, Kirsopp. *Eusebius: The Ecclesiastical History*. 2 vols. In the Loeb Classical Library. London: William Heinemann, 1965.

Lampe, G. W. H. (ed.). *A Patristic Greek Lexicon*. Oxford: Clarendon, 1961.

Liddell, H. G. and Scott, R. A. *A Greek-English Lexicon*. Rev. and aug. H. S. Jones and Roderick McKenzie. Oxford: Clarendon, 1968.

Lidzbarski, Mark. *Das Johannesbuch der Mandäer*. Giessen: A. Töpelmann, 1915.

_____. *Ginza: Der Schatz oder das grosse Buch der Mandäer*. Göttingen: Vandenhoeck & Ruprecht, 1925.

Luzarraga, J. *Las tradiciones de la nube en la biblia y en el judaismo*. Rome: Biblical Institute, 1973.

McCowan, C. C. *Testament of Solomon*. Chicago: University Press, 1915.

MacDermot, Violet. *The Books of Jeu and the Untitled Text in the Bruce Codex*. Leiden: E. J. Brill, 1978.

_____. *Pistis Sophia*. Leiden: E. J. Brill, 1978.

MacRae, George. "The Apocalypse of Adam." Pp. 256-64 in *The Nag Hammadi Library in English*. Ed. James M. Robinson. San Francisco: Harper and Row, 1977.

_____. "The Apocalypse of Adam." Pp. 151-95 in *Nag Hammadi Codices V,2-5 and VI with Papyrus Berolinensis 8502, 1 and 4*. Ed. Douglas M. Parrott. Leiden: E. J. Brill, 1978.

_____. "The Apocalypse of Adam Reconsidered." Pp. 573-77 in *The Society of Biblical Literature One Hundred Eighth Annual Meeting Book of Seminar Papers*. Vol. 2. Ed. Lane C. McGaughy. Missoula, MT: Society of Biblical Literature, 1972.

_____. "The Coptic Gnostic Apocalypse of Adam." *HeyJ* 6 (1965) 27-35.

_____. "Sleep and Awakening in Gnostic Texts." Pp. 496-507 in *Le origini dello gnosticismo*. Ed. Ugo Bianchi. Leiden: E. J. Brill, 1967.

Marxsen, Willi. *Introduction to the New Testament*. Trans. G. Buswell. Oxford: B. Blackwell, 1968.

Morard, Françoise. "L'*Apocalypse d'Adam* de Nag-Hammadi: un essai d'interpretation." Pp. 35-42 in *Gnosis und Gnosticism*. Ed. Martin Krause. Leiden: E. J. Brill, 1977.

_____. "L'*Apocalypse d'Adam* du Codex V de Nag Hammadi et sa polémique anti-baptismale." *RevScRel* 51 (1977) 214-33.

Morenz, Siegfried and Schubert, Johannes. *Der Gott auf der Blume*. Ascona: Artibus Asiae, 1954.

Müller, F. Max (ed.). *Sacred Books of the East*. Trans. James Darmesteter. 2nd ed. 50 vols. Oxford: Clarendon, 1879-1910.

Nagel, Peter. "Marginalia Coptica." *Wissenschaftliche Zeitschrift der Martin-Luther-Universität* 20 (1973) 111-15.

Nock, A. D. and Festugière, A.-J. *Corpus Hermeticum*. 4 vols. Paris: Société d'édition, Les Belles Lettres, 1945.

Nyberg, H. S. *Die Religion des Alten Iran*. Leipzig: Hinrichs, 1938.

Orbe, A. "Alexander Böhlig und Pahor Labib, Koptisch-gnostische Apokalypsen aus Codex V von Nag Hammadi im Koptischen Museum zu Alt-Kairo." *Greg* 46 (1965) 170-72.

Parrott, Douglas M. (ed.). *Nag Hammadi Codices V,2-5 and VI with Papyrus Berolinensis 8502, 1 and 4.* Leiden: E. J. Brill, 1978.

Pearson, Birger A. "Jewish Haggadic Traditions in *The Testimony of Truth* from Nag Hammadi (CG IX,3)." Pp. 452-70 in *Ex Orbe Religionum: Studia Geo Widengren.* Supplement to *Numen* 21. Leiden: E. J. Brill, 1972.

Perkins, Pheme. "Apocalypse of Adam: The Genre and Function of a Gnostic Apocalypse." *CBQ* 39 (1977) 382-95.

_____. "Apocalyptic Schematization in the Apocalypse of Adam and the Gospel of the Egyptians." Pp. 591-95 in *The Society of Biblical Literature One Hundred Eighth Annual Meeting Book of Seminar Papers.* Vol. 2. Ed. Lane C. McGaughy. Missoula, MT: Society of Biblical Literature, 1972.

_____. "Gnostic Periodization of Revelation and the Apocryphon of John." Paper presented to the Nag Hammadi section of the Society of Biblical Literature, 1970 (mimeo).

Polotsky, H. J. (ed.). *Manichäische Homilien.* Stuttgart: Kohlhammer, 1934.

Pope, M. H. "Number." Pp. 564-66 in *Interpreters Dictionary of the Bible,* vol. 3. Ed. G. A. Buttrick, et al. 4 vols. Nashville: Abingdon, 1962.

Puech, H.-Ch. "Archontiker." Cols. 634-43 in *Reallexikon für Antike und Christentum,* vol. 1. Ed. Theodore Klauser. 8 vols. Stuttgart: Hiersemann, 1950-.

Quasten, Johannes. *Patrology.* 2 vols. Utrecht/Antwerp: Spectrum, 1953.

Robinson, James M. *Introduction to the Facsimile Edition of the Nag Hammadi Codices.* Leiden: E. J. Brill, 1972.

_____. "Logoi Sophon." Pp. 71-113 in *Trajectories through Early Christianity* by James M. Robinson and Helmut Koester. Philadelphia: Fortress, 1971.

_____. "On the *Gattung* of Mark (and John)." Pp. 99-129 in *Jesus and Man's Hope,* vol. 1. Ed. D. G. Buttrick. 2 vols. Pittsburgh: Pittsburgh Theological Seminary, 1970.

[_____.] "The Coptic Gnostic Library." Pp. 81-85 in *Essays on the Coptic Gnostic Library.* Offprint Novum Testamentum 12.2. Leiden: E. J. Brill, 1970.

Robinson, James M.(ed.). *The Facsimile Edition of the Nag Hammadi Codices: Codex V.* Leiden: E. J. Brill, 1975.

_____ (gen. ed.). *The Nag Hammadi Library in English.* San Francisco: Harper and Row, 1977.

Robinson, Stephen E. "The Apocalypse of Adam." *Brigham Young University Studies* 17 (1977) 131-53.

Rohde, Joachim. *Rediscovering the Teaching of the Evangelists.* Trans. D. M. Barton. Philadelphia: Westminster, 1968.

Rudolph, Kurt. "Böhlig, Alexander und Pahor Labib: Koptisch-gnostische Apokalypsen aus Codex V von Nag Hammadi im Koptischen Museum zu Alt-Kairo." *TLZ* 90 (1965) cols. 361-62.

_____. "Gnosis und Gnostizismus, ein Forschungsbericht." *TRu* 34 (1969) 160-69.

Russell, D. S. *The Method and Message of Jewish Apocalyptic.* Philadelphia: Westminster, 1964.

Sabourin, Leopold. "The Biblical Cloud: Terminology and Traditions." *BTB* 4 (1974) 290-311.

Sanders, Jack T. *The New Testament Christological Hymns: Their Historical Religious Background.* Cambridge: University Press, 1971.

Sanders, J. N. "The Word." Pp. 868-72 in *Interpreters Dictionary of the Bible.* Vol. 4. Ed. George A. Buttrick, et al. Nashville: Abingdon, 1962.

Sandmel, Samuel. "Parallelomania." *JBL* 81 (1962) 1-13.

Schenke, Gesine. "Die dreigestaltige Protennoia." *TLZ* 99 (1974) cols. 731-46.

Schenke, Hans-Martin. "Alexander Böhlig und Pahor Labib, Koptisch-gnostische Apokalypsen aus Codex V von Nag Hammadi im Koptischen Museum zu Alt-Kairo." *OLZ* 61 (1966) cols. 23-34.

_____. "Das sethianische System nach Nag-Hammadi-Handschriften." Pp. 165-73 in *Studia Coptica.* Ed. Peter Nagel. Berlin: Akademie, 1974.

_____. *Die gnostischen Schriften des Koptischen Papyrus Berolinensis 8502.* Berlin: Akademie, 1972.

_____. "Zum Gegenwärtigen Stand der Erforschung der Nag-Hammadi-Handschriften." Pp. 124-35 in *Koptologische Studien in der DDR: Zusammengestellt und herausgegeben vom Institut für Byzantinistik der Martin-Luther-Universität Halle-Wittenberg.* Halle-Wittenberg: Martin-Luther-Universität, 1965.

Schmidt, Carl. *Koptisch-gnostische Schriften: Erster Band: Die Pistis Sophia. Die beiden Bücher des Jeû, Unbekanntes altgnostisches Werk.* 3rd ed. Ed. Walter Till. Berlin: Akademie, 1962.

Schottroff, Luise. "Animae naturalitur salvandae. Zum Problem der himmlischen Herkunft des Gnostikers." Pp. 68-83 in *Christentum und Gnosis.* BZNW 37. Ed. Walther Eltester. Berlin: A. Töpelmann, 1969.

Schwab, Moïse. *Vocabulaire de l'angelologie, d'après les manuscrits hebreux de la Bibliothèque nationale.* Académie des inscriptions et belles-lettres, 1:2. Paris: Klincksieck, 1897.

Scott, Walter. *Hermetica.* 4 vols. London: Dawsons, 1924-1936.

Seston, W. "De l'authenticité et la date de l'édit de Dioclétien contre des Manichéens." *Mélanges de philologie de littérature et d'histoire anciennes offerts à Alfred Ernout.* Paris: Klincksieck, 1940.

Sister, Moses. "Die Typen der prophetischen Visionen in der Bibel." *Wissenschaft des Judentums* 78 (1934) 399-430.

Stone, Michael. "The Death of Adam--An Armenian Adam Book." *HTR* 59 (1966) 283-91.

Strack, H. L. and Billerbeck, Paul. *Kommentar zum Neuen Testament aus Talmud und Midrasch.* 5th ed. 4 vols. in 5. München: C. H. Beck, 1969.

Tardieu, Michel. *Trois mythes gnostiques: Adam, Eros et les animaux d'Egypt dans un écrit de Nag Hammadi (II,5).* Paris: Etudes Augustiniennes, 1974.

Thackery, H. St. J. *Josephus.* 8 vols. In the Loeb Classical Library. London: William Heinemann, 1930.

Thomas, Joseph. *Le mouvement baptiste en Palestine et Syrie.* Gembloux: J. Duclot, 1935.

Till, Walter. *Koptische Dialektgrammatik.* München: C. H. Beck, 1961.

_____. *Koptische Grammatik: Sahidic Dialect.* 3rd ed. rev. Leipzig: VEB Verlag, 1966.

Tisserant, Eugene. *Ascension d'Isaie.* Paris: Letouzey et Ané, 1909.

Tröger, Karl-Wolfgang (ed.). *Gnosis und Neues Testament.* Berlin: Evangelische Verlagsanstalt, 1973.

Vermes, Geza. *Scripture and Tradition in Judaism.* Leiden: E. J. Brill, 1961.

Walters, C. C. *An Elementary Coptic Grammar of the Sahidic Dialect*. Oxford: Blackwell, 1972.

Westermann, Claus. "Sinn und Grenze religionsgeschichtlicher Parallelen." *TLZ* 90 (1965) cols. 489-96.

Wevers, J. W. "Septuagint." Pp. 273-78 in *Interpreters Dictionary of the Bible*. Vol. 4. Ed. George A. Buttrick et al. Nashville: Abingdon, 1962.

Widengren, Geo. *Die Religionen Irans*. Stuttgart: Kohlhammer, 1965.

_____. *Mani and Manichaeism*. Trans. Charles Kessler. New York/Chicago/San Francisco: Holt Rinehart and Winston, 1965.

Wisse, Frederik. "The Nag Hammadi Library and the Heresiologists." *VC* 25 (1971) 205-23.

Wright, A. G. *The Literary Genre: Midrash*. New York: Alba House, 1967.